A Theory of Subjective Wellbeing

PHILOSOPHY, POLITICS, AND ECONOMICS

Ryan Muldoon, Carmen Pavel,
Geoff Sayre-McCord, Eric Schliesser, Itai Sher

Series Editors

Published in the Series

The Open Society and Its Complexities
Gerald Gaus

A Theory of Subjective Wellbeing
Mark Fabian

A Theory of Subjective Wellbeing

MARK FABIAN

OXFORD
UNIVERSITY PRESS

OXFORD
UNIVERSITY PRESS

Oxford University Press is a department of the University of Oxford. It furthers
the University's objective of excellence in research, scholarship, and education
by publishing worldwide. Oxford is a registered trade mark of Oxford University
Press in the UK and certain other countries.

Published in the United States of America by Oxford University Press
198 Madison Avenue, New York, NY 10016, United States of America.

Library of Congress Control Number: 2022930046
ISBN 978–0–19–763526–1

DOI: 10.1093/oso/9780197635261.001.0001

1 3 5 7 9 8 6 4 2

Printed by Integrated Books International, United States of America

To Nora, who helped me start, and Maddy, who helped me finish

Contents

Contents

Acknowledgments

This book was the product of my doctoral candidacy, completed in antipodean isolation at the Australian National University. Given that, I have few people to thank for creative input. Instead, I have many people to thank for morale support. The self-esteem of junior researchers is notoriously fragile, and mine was especially tenuous until quite recently owing to my bull-headed insistence on being interdisciplinary. Robert Breunig did an admirable job as a PhD supervisor, especially given that he is a tax and econometrics specialist, neither of which features in this volume. I must also thank Geoffrey Brennan and Carol Graham, both of whom agreed to join my dissertation panel very late in the piece. My supervisors gave me the main thing I needed: open-ended chats over coffee and beer. Speaking of which, Richard Ryan gave me an enormous confidence boost simply by hearing out my ideas over a few beers one glorious Sydney afternoon. I must also thank my thesis examiners Marc Fleurbaey and Matthew Adler, who were very positive while also offering constructive comments on the philosophy and economics sections in particular. My next round of thanks goes to my friends, especially those who came to my dinner parties. There were many times when I managed to get back on the horse by reminding myself that people I think are brilliant seem to enjoy my opinions, so I'm probably not a fool. Finally, I have to thank Luke Hurst and Emeritus Professor Peter "APEC Daddy" Drysdale for bringing me into the East Asia Forum and rebuilding my intellectual confidence after the academic dumpster fire of my undergraduate years.

While this book is my own brainchild, in the long interim between tendering it to publishers and submitting final copy for publication I had the great privilege to interact with many first-rate scholars whose comments helped me to substantially polish the end product. I particularly want to thank Malte Dold, for helping me better understand preference satisfaction accounts of well-being; Richard Ryan, Kennon Sheldon, and Frank Martela, who helped me scrub up the self-determination theory content; Anna Alexandrova, Valerie Tiberius, Michael Bishop, Kate Kirkpatrick, Michael Prinzing, and an anonymous reviewer at OUP, who tightened the philosophical sections (which are probably still a bit loose); Caspar Kaiser,

Eileen Tipoe, Alberto Prati, Michael Plant, and participants at the workshop we organized on measurement issues in life satisfaction research, especially Katya Oparina; Joel McGuire for alerting me to a huge and shameful error in chapter 10; participants and organizers of the Human Development and Capabilities Association seminar series who helped me grasp some important shortcomings in my account of capabilities; and finally, Jessica Pykett and my wonderfully stimulating and supportive colleagues at the Bennett Institute for Public Policy in the University of Cambridge, who have helped me enhance my thinking around well-being public policy (still very much a work in progress). A tip of the hat must also be given to Peter Ohlin, my editor at Oxford University Press, and the members of the Philosophy, Politics, and Economics Society editorial board, who organized an enjoyable peer review (fancy that!) and editing process, as well as to anonymous reviewers 1 and 2, who had only good things to say—a blessing I received with deep gratitude.

Introduction

The Science of Wellbeing

Man does not strive for happiness; only the Englishman does that.
—Friedrich Nietzsche, *Twilight of the Idols*

There has been a tremendous upwelling of interest in subjective well-being (SW-B) in the past four decades or so, driven in large part by hedonic psychology (Kahneman et al. 1999) and happiness economics (Frey and Stutzer 2002; Bruni and Porta 2005; Weimann et al. 2015). Until quite recently, this research has been mostly atheoretical (Argyle 2001, p. 227) and has relied on an approach that might be described as exploratory data analysis. Researchers began with simple metrics for measuring SW-B, notably life satisfaction scales and experience sampling tools for studying mood. They delved into the data collected using these metrics with mostly correlational statistical techniques to derive insights into the nature of SW-B. The concept itself was defined operationally by how it was measured: as experienced affect, measured using day reconstruction methods in particular, and as evaluated life satisfaction. Early findings by researchers in the field were built on using richer data sets, and insights were steadily if slowly refined.

This line of inquiry has opened important new vistas. Most significantly, it has convinced many people that SW-B can in fact be studied empirically, something that economists have been skeptical of since an influential publication by Robbins (1934). It has identified a vast landscape of empirical phenomena to be explained, which is critical for establishing a scientific field (Eronen and Bringmann 2021). Many of these phenomena concern the character of hedonic experiences, such as why our memory of pleasure depends heavily on the highest level of pleasure we experienced during an event. Others concern the cognitive evaluation of wellbeing, including the

A Theory of Subjective Wellbeing. Mark Fabian, Oxford University Press. © Oxford University Press 2022.
DOI: 10.1093/oso/9780197635261.003.0001

possibility of adaptation to new circumstances and the impact of changing reference points on life satisfaction judgments. Finally, SW-B scholarship has freed wellbeing scholarship from the arguably stagnant debates of philosophers and allowed it to be discussed independently from the tricky normative issue of prudential value—what is "good for" someone or makes their life "go well." In the process, SW-B scholarship has even revitalized philosophical inquiry into wellbeing (Fletcher 2015a).

Encouraged by these successes, SW-B research has started to press into the public policy and welfare economics discourses, notably as part of the movement to go "beyond GDP" (Diener and Seligman 2004; Diener et al. 2009; Clark et al. 2018). In this, SW-B scholarship seems to have overstepped its limits. As calls to more thoroughly integrate perspectives from SW-B research into public policy have increased in volume, critiques of such actions have also increased in quantity and prominence. Long-standing arguments pertaining to the difficulty of measuring SW-B with the precision required for public policy (Adler 2013; Benjamin et al. 2020; Fleurbaey and Blanchet 2013), the potential for perverse outcomes from "affective governance" (Jupp et al. 2016; Davies 2015), and the ethical dubiousness of making SW-B the target of policy have come once again to the fore (Haybron and Tiberius 2015; Singh and Alexandrova 2020).

To date, SW-B scholarship has not responded to these criticisms in detail (Fabian and Pykett 2021). This is understandable given the historical context of the field. SW-B had to push past many of these critiques to establish itself. Its limited purview sheltered it from most critiques and allowed SW-B to mature into a credible science. If it wants to venture beyond that limited purview it will have to overcome its critics by increasing the sophistication of its theories and the precision of its metrics. Now is an excellent time for this critical reflection, as the field's efforts in recent decades have granted it the requisite credibility and respect. There is a growing appreciation for the research questions of the field, interest in its findings, and patience with its shortcomings. This is indicated by the growing frequency of publications associated with SW-B appearing in top journals across economics, psychology, and philosophy. SW-B has attained the latitude required to engage in a period of more speculative, potentially messy research that may undermine the field in the short term but will ultimately strengthen its foundations.

The present volume is an attempt to accelerate this new wave of scholarship. It provides the holistic theory of subjective wellbeing that SW-B scholarship arguably lacks. It also articulates the measurement problems SW-B faces in a policy context, and presents novel solutions. Finally, it explains the normative issues that confront SW-B as it seeks to venture into public policy. This will hopefully guide SW-B policy advocates toward applications of their knowledge that will be welcomed rather than met with suspicion.

A secondary aim of this book is to clarify terms and debates and to *translate* them across disciplines. Wellbeing is a complex topic discussed in different ways across multiple fields. There is consequently substantial and pernicious confusion in interdisciplinary wellbeing studies. I attempt to alleviate this. One consequence is that some sections of the book will appear elementary to specialist scholars in one field or the other. Meanwhile, other sections drawing on fields outside their expertise may be perplexing because they use unfamiliar terms or familiar terms in an unconventional way. I ask that readers please be patient at such times and not assume that my writing is at fault for their boredom or confusion. We must learn to speak the same language. A final consequence is that I might occasionally get things a bit wrong. Integrating work from so many different disciplines is hard. I welcome clarifications and corrections and hope that specialists can value the ambitious scope of the book rather than dismissing it for imprecision in their area of expertise.

The integrated theory of subjective wellbeing (SWB, *unhyphenated*) at the heart of this book draws on ideas in clinical, developmental, moral, and behavioral psychology, analytical and continental philosophy, and economics. *Subjective* wellbeing here refers broadly to how well individuals believe themselves to be. This is distinct from *objective* wellbeing, which refers to how well individuals are according to criteria that are independent of their own assessment or perception. SWB is also distinct from, or rather broader than, SW-B, which I use to refer only and specifically to affect, life satisfaction, and (to a lesser extent) meaning and purpose, and to the literatures in hedonic psychology and happiness economics (and occasionally other disciplines) that have studied these items. In a sense, the theory developed here merges the field of "subjective well-being" (hyphenated) with the broader literature on "subjective wellbeing" (unhyphenated), such as that which prevails in philosophy. I apologize for the confusion this might cause (and to anyone listening by audiobook), but I must be able to talk about SW-B as a *body of scholarship* independently of SWB as a concept. A summary of these different terms and their meanings as used in this book is provided in table 0.1.

For the sake of brevity, I will use the acronyms "SW-B" and "SWB" for subjective well-being and subjective wellbeing, respectively. I will use the

Table 0.1 Wellbeing Terms and Their Meanings

Concept	Definition	Example
The prudential good	What is "good for" someone	
Wellbeing	The prudential good	
Subjective wellbeing (SWB)	Individual's own judgment and perceptions of their wellbeing	"I would say my life is going badly" "I felt sad yesterday"
Objective wellbeing	Things that are supposedly "good for" people independently of their attitudes toward those things	The birth weight of a baby
Subjective well-being (SW-B)	A school of thought regarding what wellbeing and subjective wellbeing are	SWB is affect, life satisfaction, and meaning and purpose
Welfare	The standard of living	Income, health, education (the Human Development Index)

term "wellbeing" to describe *all* research concerned with the topic and all conceptualizations of it, including SW-B and those lines of inquiry concerned with objective wellbeing. Critically, I will use "wellbeing" synonymously with "the prudential good," as is customary in philosophy and welfare economics. The prudential good is what is "good for" somebody. In welfare economics and related fields where the notion of a "social planner" is instantiated, the prudential good is the thing the planner is trying to maximize across society. SWB might not be the prudential good. Indeed, few philosophers have considered it such in recent decades. Subjective well-being might also not be life satisfaction and affect. To tease these issues apart, I need different terms for all these concepts. Further complicating matters, I use the term "welfare" to refer specifically to matters concerning objective standards of living. This may be jarring to welfare economists and some analytical philosophers who use "wellbeing" and "welfare" synonymously. This strikes me as a waste of word variety. The standard of living has an important role to play independently of wellbeing when thinking about the proper role of government in promoting wellbeing. "Welfare" is a useful term to this end.

The broad theory of SWB presented in this book has two parts. The first is a description of SWB as an *outcome*. This aspect of the theory is called the *subjective wellbeing production function* (SWBPF), depicted graphically in figure 0.1. SWB is here modeled as a dependent variable that is a function

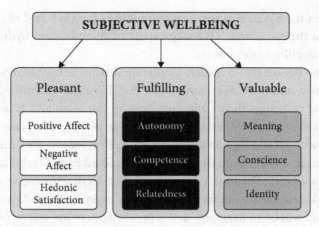

Figure 0.1 The subjective wellbeing production function

of three "dimensions" that serve as independent variables. These are hedonia, eudaimonia, and conscience. These three dimensions roughly correspond to whether life is pleasant, fulfilling, and valuable, respectively. Each dimension is made up of further subvariables. Hedonia is a function of positive affect, negative affect, and hedonic satisfaction. Eudaimonia is a function of the three basic psychological needs of autonomy, relatedness, and competence. And conscience is a function of the three themes of existentialism: meaning and purpose, identity, and virtue.

The dimensions of the SWBPF are *necessary conditions* for the emergence of SWB. This aligns with Bishop's (2015) "network theory of well-being." Bishop argues (p. 8) that "to have wellbeing is to be stuck in a self-perpetuating cycle of positive emotions, positive attitudes, positive traits, and successful engagement with world the world." He refers to this self-perpetuating cycle as a "positive causal network" or PCN. He further argues that PCN "fragments" come together to form a PCN of increasing complexity, power, and robustness. My elaboration of the items of the items in the SWBPF populates Bishop's PCN and explains how many of its pieces fit together. There is a sense then that the variables of the SWBPF are constituents of SWB in that they are fragments that come together to form a PCN. There is also a sense in which they cause SWB in that their networking results in a "self-perpetuating cycle." However, my contention is that when a PCN is fully "networked" it *activates* in a sense and brings about a particular state of being that is the left-hand-side variable of the SWBPF, namely SWB. Thus I think it is more accurate to think of the variables in the SWBPF as necessary conditions for SWB and of their net-working as the cause, much the way a spark of energy causes hydrogen and oxygen molecules to form water.

The state of SWB that is the left-hand-side variable of the SWBPF is a *generalized* form of flow (Csikszentmihaly 1992). Flow is commonly described as a feeling of being "in the zone" or "lost in the moment." It is typically studied as it emerges in certain activities, like playing the piano (Bakker 2005). However, I stress *generalized* because by flow I mean something much more expansive than the construct typically studied by flow scholars, which seems to be a kind of hedonic experience. I am referring instead to a grander vision Csikszentmihaly put forward, which he expressed as follows: "actions and feelings will be in harmony, and separate parts of life will fit together—and each activity will 'make sense' in the present, as well as in view of the past and of the future." This is a mode of being, rather than an experience. I cannot explain this generalized flow state properly without first introducing many other ideas, especially from existentialism, so I will have to pass over it for now. Suffice to say that it is misleading to think of the individual items of the SWBPF as causes of the state of SWB because it is rather their *being networked* that is the cause. Someone asked about their wellbeing will inevitably say that they are well if they score highly on the three dimensions of the SWBPF. However, neither these dimensions nor the subjective report they empirically predict are SWB. Instead, SWB, when fully realized at least, is the flow state.

The second part of the theory is a model of the *process* by which the items of the SWBPF are networked and SWB is attained. This aspect of the theory is called *the coalescence of being*. It is a model of self-actualization in the eudaimonic tradition (Besser-Jones 2015), blending insights from psychology and philosophy. Coalescence involves the individual harmonizing their actual self with their ideal and ought selves through goal setting and achievement. This process is guided by affective signals that accompany goal pursuit and social self-verification. Introspection upon these signals helps the individual to comport toward an identity that is self-concordant and wellbeing-promoting. Coalescence has substantial complementarities with Tiberius' (2018) theory of well-being as value fulfillment. She argues (p. 13) that well-being "consists in the fulfillment of an appropriate set of values over a lifetime." She defines "appropriate values" as those that (p. 41) "are (1) suited to our desires and emotions, (2) reflectively endorsed, and (3) capable of being fulfilled together over time . . . appropriate values are objects of relatively sustained and integrated emotions, desires, and judgments." Coalescence is the process through which "appropriate" values are identified, refined, harmonized, and ultimately fulfilled.

This two-part theory is arguably a hybrid theory of wellbeing. In recent accounts from analytical philosophy, hybrids are characterized as theories of wellbeing that blend two or more of the traditional schools of thought regarding the nature of wellbeing, namely mental state, objective list, desire fulfillment, subjectivist, and eudaimonic accounts (Woodard 2015). I ultimately argue that wellbeing is a state, namely SWB. I do not describe it as a *mental state*, as it is thoroughly embodied and better described as a *mode of being*, but it has close parallels with mental state accounts. However, the SWBPF is an objective list of criteria that determine someone's subjective well-being in a causal way. I also argue that the SWBPF predicts subjective assessments of SWB. Moreover, individuals pursue coalescence in heterogenous ways. As such, the model posits *objective ends with subjective means*. Coalescence is also a prudential *process* of value fulfillment. This integrates eudaimonic and desire fulfillment perspectives on wellbeing into the theory of SWB. Finally, affective signals play a critical role in steering self-actualization. This means that hedonism, a classic mental state account of well-being, is central to the model. So it seems that all the classic schools of thought regarding well-being are present somewhere in my account.

Some philosophers might nonetheless dispute that this is a hybrid theory given that I ultimately locate SWB within a specific state. I will argue in chapter 3 that this kind of debate over what is "intrinsic" to well-being and what is merely "instrumental" is counterproductive. Mental states, preference satisfaction, nature fulfillment, and process are all integral to the model. So it is largely meaningless to say that one is intrinsic while others are merely instrumental, for they are all *necessary*. A holistic and *practical* account of well-being will need to involve each school of thought. Philosophers will doubtless push back on my claims here, and I welcome their improvements to my thinking. Nonetheless, I want to make the case that we would get more value out of scholars turning relatively more attention to how different elements of well-being fit together, rather than further debating where prudential value ultimately obtains. As I hope to demonstrate herein, key insights into well-being only reveal themselves when such an integrationist perspective is adopted.

The theory of SWB presented herein is innovative in that it is integrative, interdisciplinary, and describes SWB in terms of its causal structure. It complements existing statistical studies of SWB as an outcome variable (Ryff 1989b; Van Dierendonck 2004; Springer et al. 2006; Springer and Hauser 2006; Diener et al. 2010; Huppert and So 2013) with a sophisticated theoretical account of how different aspects of SWB interact in the process by which SWB is achieved. In so doing, it clarifies (i) why certain variables overlap in correlational analysis while others do not, (ii) the nature of apparent two-way causal relationships between SWB variables, and (iii) how the many seemingly divergent conceptions of wellbeing in philosophy, psychology, and economics can be harmonized in a manner that brings clarity rather than merely added complexity.

My arguments raise various normative issues for public policy to promote SWB. Psychological accounts of the prudential good have been unpopular in recent decades in large part because of their seeming incompatibility with ethical constraints facing governments and policymakers in liberal democracies. I am sympathetic to many of the associated arguments. My view is that even if SWB is the prudential good, governments should not promote it, at least not *directly*. The goal of government should be the improvement of welfare. I discuss these political issues throughout the book, but especially in the final chapter.

This volume is structured as follows. It begins in chapter 1 with an account of SW-B, including its history and positive contributions to wellbeing scholarship. The history of the field is important because it explains why SW-B proceeded with its peculiar methodology and why it was helpful and appropriate that it did so. I present most of the findings of SW-B in chapter 6, on hedonia. Chapter 1 discusses the merits of the field in a more abstract way.

Chapter 2 reviews weaknesses in the paradigm of SW-B. Foremost among these is that SW-B's operationalist epistemology gives rise to circularity. Construct validation exercises are pushed into service to resolve this issue. However, construct validation requires theorizing at step one, and this theorizing is lacking in SW-B, at least for the new lines of inquiry it now wishes to explore. SW-B's operationalist epistemology is particularly problematic in the context of studying SWB because it gives rise to what Alexandrova (2017) calls "evidential subjectivism," which is where both the definition of the construct of interest and the way it is measured are subjectively defined. It is logically impossible to ensure that you are analyzing a consistent construct when utilizing an evidential subjectivism paradigm. These epistemic issues point to the need for deeper theorizing to bridge SW-B and SWB. This deeper theory is elaborated over the next seven chapters.

Chapter 3 commences this theoretical elaboration with analytical philosophy's perspectives on wellbeing. These are concerned with wellbeing as the prudential good, meaning what is "good for" an individual. The presence of the word "good" alerts us to the value judgments inherent to defining wellbeing. It is this normative element that has preoccupied the analytic philosophy of wellbeing, which is typically published in ethics journals. There are five traditional theories of wellbeing in analytical philosophy: mental state, preference satisfaction, objective list, eudaimonic, and subjectivist. I argue that analytical philosophy's tendency toward differentiation and classification has predisposed it to overlook important complementarities between these different theories. These complementarities are manifesting in greater overlap between the theories in recent cycles of debate. Focusing on the overlaps reveals that the theories are more interdependent than their advocates might presume. This motivates the production function model of subjective wellbeing, which tries to integrate rather than differentiate various theories of wellbeing. Chapter 3 also argues that analytical philosophy has tended to emphasize wellbeing as an outcome and thereby miss important prudential issues associated with how wellbeing is pursued. There is a right way of achieving wellbeing regardless of which philosophical definition of it is used. Understanding this process requires integrating perspectives from the eudaimonic branch of wellbeing theories.

I outline my theory of SWB as a response to these shortcomings in SW-B and philosophy from chapter 4 onward. Some readers might wonder why I don't present my theory in chapter 1. There are two reasons for this. The first is to make it easier for SW-B scholars and analytical philosophers of wellbeing to absorb my theory by grounding it in their own literatures. In my experience, discipline-specific scholars tend to become confused, dismissive, and hostile, in that order, if you use language in a manner that they are not accustomed to. I recall one philosopher asking me, "What could psychologists possibly tell us about wellbeing?" Given that using language in such a way is inevitable in interdisciplinary work, my solution is to contextualize my theory in the status quo of both SW-B and philosophy before presenting it. The second reason is that it is appropriate to explain what problems you are trying to solve before you present your solution.

Chapter 4 sketches the subjective wellbeing production function (SWBPF) in full, providing a preliminary description of its components. Chapters 5 through 8 then explain these components in more detail and justify their inclusion in the model. The SWBPF extends the consumer's problem in economics from one where an individual maximizes their utility from consumption subject to a budget constraint to a broader problem where the individual tries to improve[1] their SWB subject to a capabilities constraint and a lack of wisdom and information. Capabilities define what an individual can be and do. There is a vast universe of capabilities that determine what options or "possible lives" are open to a person. I focus on five major headings for the sake of a concise exposition, namely income, health, education, political enfranchisement, and environmental quality. These variables are justified in chapter 5 with reference to the development studies literature, particularly the work of Sen (1999a, 1999b). The information constraint is a learning problem—individuals need to figure out what life suits them. These are the "appropriate values" Tiberius (2018) emphasizes. The coalescence of being, outlined in chapter 9, describes how to navigate this learning process.

The nature and content of hedonia is elaborated in chapter 6, drawing especially on the work of hedonic psychologists and happiness economists. This chapter explains hedonia and how to get it. This explanation covers a range of techniques for mood management developed in recent decades, including gratitude, savoring, positive activity interventions, mindfulness, and prosociality.

Chapter 7 continues work started in chapter 6 differentiating hedonia and eudaimonia. It also goes into more detail on the nature of the three eudaimonic variables: autonomy, competence, and relatedness. These are the basic psychological needs postulated by self-determination theory (SDT), the most prominent school of eudaimonic psychology. SDT has much wisdom to contribute to our understanding of wellbeing-as-process. This wisdom is foregrounded at some length in this chapter. It includes insights into the nature of human motivation, how values can be internalized over time, and what goals nurture well-being and why.

Chapter 8 analyzes the conscience dimension, which concerns meaning, identity, and virtue. Succinctly and crudely, meaning refers to the need for life to feel purposeful—like it is creating value and perhaps contributing to something beyond the individual. Identity refers to the need to have a sense of self, something developmental psychologists emphasize but which has yet to meaningfully penetrate the SWB discourse. Virtue refers to our need to

---

[1] I say "improve" rather than "maximize" because maximization is a behavioral claim and it is unclear that individuals *maximize* their wellbeing rather than merely trying to make it more than it is presently.

feel like we are a good person and be regarded as such by our peers. The body of scholarship most committed to these themes is existential philosophy, so much of this chapter is given over to an accessible elaboration of its ideas. I also present complementary ideas and empirical evidence in support of these three SWB variables from various branches of psychology, especially logotherapy, terror management theory, and the evolutionary psychology of moral cognition.

Chapter 9 presents a relatively complete account of the coalescence of being, building on ideas from SDT presented in chapter 7 and ideas from existentialism presented in chapter 8. The coalescence of being models how agents come to gain the wisdom, information, and especially self-knowledge required to leverage their capabilities to attain wellbeing. The coalescence of being is a model of self-actualization—the process by which we discover, create, affirm, and become our identity. Coalescence involves goal setting with the intention of becoming one's ideal self. As the individual goes about achieving these goals they will be met with successes and failures that are accompanied by affective signals like depression, anxiety, exhilaration, and joy. These signals help the individual to navigate away from goals that are not self-concordant and toward an ideal self that is inspiring and feasible. Steady progress toward becoming this ideal self in reality brings with it a preponderance of positive affect and gradually reduces negative affect, nourishes the basic needs for autonomy, competence, and relatedness, generates a sense of meaning through intrinsic motivation, promotes virtue through the need for integrity and fealty toward the desired self, and fosters identity by building an internally consistent, palpable, and rationally accessible sense of self. Coalescence thereby carries us to wellbeing.

Chapter 10 uses the model of wellbeing developed in chapters 3 to 9 to reflect on how wellbeing is measured. It argues that each dimension of the SWBPF, besides maybe virtue, can be measured with existing tools. It then explains why many applications, especially cost-benefit analysis and other mainstays of public policy, would benefit from a single-item measure of wellbeing. I argue that the dominant SW-B metric—life satisfaction scales—are unfortunately unfit for many of these applications. The reason for this is scale-norming. This is where respondents recalibrate their scales over time such that the numbers on their scales correspond to different levels of latent satisfaction from one survey to the next. The existence of scale-norming undermines the precision of interpersonal and intertemporal comparisons of responses.

Chapter 11 closes with a discussion of normative issues that arise when applying wellbeing science in a policy context. I argue that there are ethical challenges associated with government promotion of SWB, which is meaningfully distinct from individual pursuit of SWB. Owing to these normative concerns around SWB policy, governments should not, in general, promote SWB. They should instead focus on welfare—improving the objective standard of living of their citizens and ensuring that the social and economic conditions for SWB are met. This indirectly promotes SWB by relaxing citizens' capabilities constraint. I discuss ways that SWB research could be applied in public policy that do not transgress various red lines. An important opportunity is ensuring that citizens have the practical wisdom needed to prosecute the coalescence of being.

1

Subjective Well-Being

> They say that to know oneself is to know all there is that is human.
> But of course no one can ever know himself. Nothing human is cal-
> culable; even to ourselves we are strange.
>
> —Gore Vidal, *Julian*

Introduction

The purpose of this chapter is to review the paradigmatic approach to understanding wellbeing adopted by the subjective well-being (SW-B) literature. This paradigm dominates contemporary policy thinking on wellbeing
among hedonic psychologists and happiness economists. The chapter begins
with a brief history of the study of wellbeing in general to explain why SW-B
adopted its unique paradigm in the first place. SW-B scholarship emerged
at the end of the 1960s against a backdrop of logical positivism and skepticism toward anything that wasn't objectively measurable. Economics had
just about completely done away with the mind in its theories. The cognitive revolution was well underway in psychology, but neither this new paradigm nor the old behaviorist one could effectively accommodate research
into the kinds of questions SW-B scholars were interested in. Meanwhile, the
philosophy of wellbeing was hundreds of years old and mired in a swamp of
theoretical conjectures. These were so dense as to be difficult to apply in the
context of scientific practice. To survive in this hostile environment, SW-B
scholarship had to adopt a radically empirical methodology with a princi-
pled aversion to theorizing. Early work in happiness economics developed
alongside this literature and was then increasingly folded into it until today
happiness economics is basically a subfield of SW-B scholarship.

The second part of the chapter explores the definition of wellbeing used
in SW-B scholarship. This definition emphasizes *experienced* and *evaluative*

A Theory of Subjective Wellbeing. Mark Fabian, Oxford University Press. © Oxford University Press 2022.
DOI: 10.1093/oso/9780197635261.003.0002

wellbeing, typically operationalized if not explicitly defined in terms of affect and life satisfaction, respectively. The merits of this definition are discussed in the third part of the chapter, which highlights three main strengths: generality, the insights that emerge from the innovative delineation between experienced and evaluative wellbeing, and liberalism. The focus on very general outcomes in the definition of SW-B leaves it free of theoretical priors regarding the ingredients and causal structure of wellbeing. This allowed SW-B scholarship to break away from the weighty history of wellbeing theory and focus on empirically validating claims, something philosophy was unable or disinclined to do. The emphasis on experienced wellbeing contrasted with philosophical views, which often regarded experienced wellbeing as of marginal significance or a function of evaluative wellbeing. Neither of these claims appears true today. The subjectivity of the definition allows people to decide whether they are well and what exactly this means. This liberal quality inoculates SW-B from some forms of political abuse. These strengths have allowed SW-B to prosecute its empirical inquiry into SWB, and the many fruits of its research are discussed at length in chapter 6, on hedonia.

A Brief History of Wellbeing Research

Scholarship of SWB in general but especially among economists is presently dominated by the frameworks developed in the SW-B literature. Succinctly, SW-B defines SWB and the prudential good as a preponderance of positive over negative affect and a high level of life satisfaction (Angner 2009). Increasingly, SW-B scholars are adding a sense of meaning and purpose to this list (Stone and Mackie 2013; OECD 2013; Clark et al. 2018).

It is important to distinguish this literature from the broader literature on SWB and wellbeing more generally. One contention of this book is that scholars of SWB but especially those interested in welfare economics and policy applications should be interested in SWB and wellbeing more broadly than the relatively narrow SW-B paradigm. The SW-B literature is and will continue to be valuable to furthering our understanding of wellbeing, but it has shortcomings, especially when it comes to public policy. To effectively distinguish SW-B from SWB and wellbeing more broadly we must spend some time discussing the history of wellbeing research and the various schools of thought within it. That is the purpose of this section. I will return to some of these themes in more detail in chapter 3.

It is important to understand that wellbeing is not an ateleological concept. It must be defined *before* it can be measured, and it is quite nebulous (Alexandrova 2017). Furthermore, because wellbeing is a value-laden concept, what definition is ultimately settled on has normative implications in any applied context. For example, if you decide that wellbeing is pleasant or "happy" mental states (Clark et al. 2018), then it would seem to behoove benevolent governments to make citizens happier even if that is not citizens' preference. The implications of this exact example are eloquently explored in Huxley's *Brave New World*. It is because of this value-laden nature that philosophers in the analytic tradition treat wellbeing as synonymous with the *prudential good*—that is, what is "good for" individuals. This makes the normative associations of the concept apparent.

Since Parfit (1984), philosophers have distinguished at least three different categories of wellbeing theory: mental state accounts, desire fulfillment accounts, and objective list accounts. While they sometimes overlap with these three categories, it is helpful to also separate out subjectivist and eudaimonic accounts. This five-theory taxonomy is summarized graphically in figure 1.1. Mental state accounts argue that the prudential good is something in the brain (Haybron 2008). The most famous mental state account is hedonism— that the prudential good is pleasure. SW-B is a mental state account, as affect, satisfaction, and a *sense* of meaning are all mental states (Diener et al. 2009). Desire fulfillment accounts argue that the prudential good is having one's objectives met, preferences satisfied, or values fulfilled, regardless of whether they produce a positive mental state (Adler 2019). Objective list accounts specify some set of criteria that determines someone's wellbeing (Fletcher 2015b). A simple example is the healthcare conception of wellbeing. The prudential good of a baby, for example, might be reasonably conceived in terms of body weight and brain development. Speaking of a baby's preferences or subjective assessment is vacuous. Eudaimonic accounts come in various guises. In Besser-Jones' (2014) and Norton's (1976) analyses, there is a *way of living* that constitutes wellbeing—it is a *process* rather than a *state*. For example, eudaimonic accounts in the Aristotelian tradition argue that individuals are well if they live in accordance with reason and virtue (Kraut 1989). Other varieties of eudaimonism (see Haybron 2008) seem instead to have a *state* in mind. For example, "nature fulfillment" varieties argue that wellbeing consists in fully realizing one's type, personality, or "true self." Perfectionist accounts are similar but focus on fully realizing one's potential. These varieties of eudaimonic theories specify some criteria of what a good life is and so

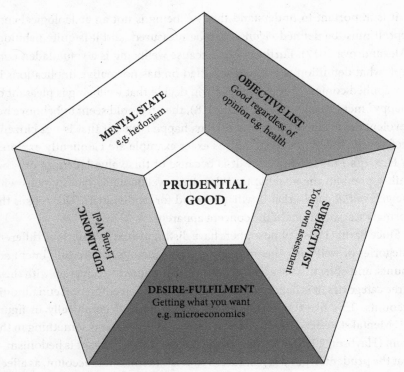

Figure 1.1 A taxonomy of wellbeing theories

are often grouped within objective list accounts. Finally, subjectivist theories emphasize that someone is well if they say so, but often with a range of caveats around things like self-deception (Sumner 1996). SW-B thus contains elements of both subjectivist and mental state accounts because it emphasizes hedonic states like joy and satisfaction, but defines SW-B in terms of people's self-reports of those states. It is somewhat unclear whether SW-B scholars think that the underlying mental state or the subjective report is constitutive of wellbeing (Angner 2009).

Objective list theories were common in classical philosophical perspectives on wellbeing, particularly among scholastics. They are also prominent in contemporary welfare economics and quality-of-life studies. The capabilities approach, which is ascendant in welfare economics, draws heavily on Aristotelian thinking and, in some of its stronger formulations, lays claim to universal values that underpin intersubjective comparisons of welfare (Nussbaum 2000). Even its weakest formulations tend to argue that certain objectively observable factors, such as health and human rights, constitute wellbeing or at least welfare (Robeyns 2017).

The prominence of objective list theories in classical literature owes substantially to Aristotle's dismissal of mental state accounts, specifically hedonism, in the earliest days of Western philosophy. He said that pleasure was the concern of swine, not men. Hedonism enjoyed a substantial revival during the Enlightenment under the influence of the early utilitarians. It was, perhaps consequentially, integral to postulates in early economics, which held that people make consumption decisions based on expected outcomes in terms of pleasure or at least positive sensations (Bruni and Sugden 2007). However, hedonism was largely ejected from economics following, first, Mill's revival of Aristotle's swine argument and subsequent delimitation of higher and lower pleasures, and then especially after Robbins' (1934) influential argument that "utility" was unmeasurable and so economics should focus on observed behavior and simply infer utility from that. Thereafter, utility in economics went from being thought of as something like pleasure to being seen instead as anything to which one could affix a positive (+) sign.

Curiously, this would seem to return to a conception of utility that is found in Bentham (1780). He is often considered a sensory hedonist because of his famous claim that "nature has placed mankind under the governance of two sovereign masters, *pain* and *pleasure.*" But almost immediately after this statement he makes comments that suggest that he uses pain and pleasure as shorthand for the more general categories of value and disvalue:

> The *principle of utility* recognises this subjection, and assumes it for the foundation of that system, the object of which is to rear the fabric of felicity by the hands of reason and law. . . . By utility is meant that property in any object whereby it tends to produce benefit, advantage, *pleasure*, good or happiness, (all this in the present case comes to the *same thing*) or (what comes again to the same thing), to prevent the happening of mischief, *pain*, evil or unhappiness to the party whose interest is considered: if that party be the community in general, then the happiness of the community: if a particular individual, then the happiness of that individual. (Bentham 1780, p. 2, emphasis added)

Bentham here seems to be suggesting that utility means anything that is "good" and disutility anything that is "bad." This approach of treating utility as anything positive was revived and prosecuted to its logical extreme by

Samuelson (1938, 1948) in his revealed preferences approach, wherein utility became only a representation of a preference ordering and utility as some state of mind was completely removed from economics. Economics consequently became associated with a preference satisfaction account of wellbeing. This grounded it in liberal values of treating individuals as sovereign over themselves and paved the way for interpersonal welfare comparisons based on income and prices. I return to some of these issues in the final chapter.

The history of *happiness economics* is substantially a history of bringing utility *as a state of mind* back into economics. Easterlin (1974) first used measures of life satisfaction from Gallup polling as a proxy for utility to examine the effect of income. Van Praag and his Leiden School (Van Praag and Frijters 1999) then used similar assumptions about synonymy to estimate utility functions.

While early work in happiness economics like that of Easterlin and Van Praag developed independently of the SW-B literature, in recent years the two have basically moved in parallel. Indeed, it may be fair to say that SW-B scholarship consists of the work of hedonic psychologists and happiness economists, with only a smattering of work from adherents in other fields, notably sociologists and geographers. Indeed, Ruut Veenhoven, a key figure in the early decades of SW-B research, is sometimes described as a "maverick sociologist" for breaking with disciplinary orthodoxy and engaging with SW-B (Okulicz-Kozaryn 2019, p. 14). Both happiness economists and hedonic psychologists almost exclusively use the SW-B definition of SWB and wellbeing.

The arguments of Robbins (1934) and the approach of Samuelson (1938) mirror in some ways the behavioral turn in anglophone psychology. Metaphysical questions pertaining to the nature of mind were thought to be impeding progress on understanding human psychology (Davies 2015). To remedy this, an emphasis was placed on observable behavior and its explanations. An individual's subjective reports were irrelevant. This attitude persisted to some extent through the cognitive revolution. As Kahneman et al. (1999) note, even the relatively simple or narrow model of wellbeing advocated by hedonism could not be accommodated within the strictures of these paradigms of psychological science.

It was against this backdrop of widespread skepticism toward subjective or otherwise unobservable phenomena in economics and psychology that the study of subjective well-being had to emerge. As Diener et al. (2009, p. 15) outline:

> In psychology, several researchers were developing and testing affective theories of well-being in the first decades of the 20th century (Beebe-Center, 1932). Behaviourism ended this program of research, and the scientific study of feelings in psychology reemerged only gradually in the 1960s (Bradburn 1969, Schacter and Singer 1962, Nowlis 1965). It was only after the *affective revolution* in the 1980s that psychologists rediscovered feelings as an important research topic (Bower 1981, Frijda 1986, Schwarz and Clore 1983).

SW-B seems to have gone about establishing itself in this context by strongly prioritizing empirics. It began its research program by developing instruments for measuring the cluster of phenomena it was interested in, notably emotions, affect, and subjective judgments of life quality. A theory of SWB was only developed later and only on the basis of what could be observed in data that had been collected. Kahneman, Diener, and Schwartz's 1999 volume, *Wellbeing: The Foundations of Hedonic Psychology*, was the first substantial statement of theory in SW-B scholarship. Even that volume is arguably light on conjecture. Early SW-B research tended to progress from measurement to theory rather than in the more conventional direction of theory to empirical test. By utilizing this data-driven approach, SW-B scholarship was able to fend off critics who disliked the study of subjective phenomena due to their empirical inaccessibility, and progress without getting bogged down in the reams of theory that dominated philosophical and psychoanalytic perspectives on wellbeing.

Definitions of Subjective Well-Being

It is understandable given this historical background that SW-B scholarship employs a very general definition of what SW-B is. In what follows, I survey several prominent examples of this definition while trying to clarify some confusions. I then discuss the strengths of the definition and the SW-B paradigm more broadly.

One of the most recent and comprehensive engagements with the SW-B literature is the Organisation for Economic Cooperation and Development's 2013 report *Guidelines for Measuring Subjective Well-Being*. It defines wellbeing as

> good mental states, including all of the various evaluations, positive and negative, that people make of their lives and the affective reactions of people to their experiences. (OECD 2013, p. 10)

This is one of the most general definitions of SW-B in its emphasis on "good mental states" broadly defined and "all the various evaluations" that people make of their lives. The definition apparently draws on Diener et al. (2006), "Beyond the Hedonic Treadmill: Revisiting the Adaptation Theory of Wellbeing." That article uses a more circumspect definition of wellbeing (note that happiness is here used synonymously with wellbeing and SW-B):

> The idea of happiness set points implies that well-being is a single entity with a single baseline. However, work by Lucas, Diener and Suh (1996) indicates that the global category of happiness is composed of separable well-being variables. . . . Thus, the idea of a unitary set point is not tenable, because *positive and negative emotions* might both decline in tandem or *life satisfaction* might move upward while positive emotions decrease. (p. 307, emphasis added)

This definition of subjective well-being as a combination of positive affect, negative affect, and life satisfaction is standard in the field. Its principal evangelist was Ed Diener, and its preeminence is perhaps due in large part to his leadership of SW-B scholarship from the beginning.

A similar definition appears in the Stiglitz-Sen-Fitoussi Commission Report (2009, p. 16). This definition is notable because it comes from three mainstream economists:

> Subjective well-being encompasses different aspects (cognitive evaluations of one's life, happiness, satisfaction, positive emotions such as joy and pride, and negative emotions such as pain and worry): each of them should be measured separately to derive a more comprehensive appreciation of people's lives.

We see again an emphasis on affect and cognitive evaluations. This is why SW-B is classified as a mental state and/or subjectivist account of wellbeing. Recent articulations of SW-B maintain this focus but add feelings of meaning and purpose to the list of mental states that constitute SW-B. Consider the following from Clark et al. (2018, p. 3):

> In our view, we should evaluate people's happiness as they themselves evaluate it. People are often asked, "Overall, how satisfied are you with your life these days?" They answer on a scale of 0–10, where 0 means "not at all satisfied" and 10 means "extremely satisfied." . . . When people answer this question, they are evaluating their own overall well-being. That is why we like this question. But well-being is often measured in other ways. One approach is to try to catch people's mood—their current hedonic feelings of enjoyment or discomfort. . . . A third approach is to ask people how worthwhile they consider the things they do in their life—the measure of so-called eudaimonia. These measures are interesting, but we prefer life satisfaction as our measure of well-being for a number of reasons.

This definition demonstrates SW-B scholars' tendency to think of wellbeing, life satisfaction, and happiness as basically the same thing. It is also notable in that it doesn't so much define wellbeing as argue for a particular measure of it, namely, life satisfaction as opposed to eudaimonic or affect-based measures. This is a central feature of the SW-B literature in general: the construct of interest is defined in terms of the measurement instruments used. There is very little distinction made between the construct of SWB and empirical indicators of it. A final noteworthy feature of Clark et al.'s definition is that what they call "eudaimonic" aspects of wellbeing are considered alongside the more traditional affect and satisfaction aspects. This reflects the growing awareness among SW-B researchers of the importance of meaning and purpose to wellbeing. The OECD's 2013 guidelines provided an almost identical definition:

> The guidelines also provide advice on measuring people's experiences and evaluations of particular domains of life, such as satisfaction with their financial status or satisfaction with their health status, as well as measures of "meaningfulness" or "purpose" in life (often described as "eudaimonic" aspects of subjective well-being). This definition of subjective well-being hence encompasses three elements:

- Life evaluation—a reflective assessment of a person's life or some specific aspect of it
- Affect—a person's feelings or emotional states, typically measured with reference to a particular point in time
- Eudaimonia—a sense of meaning or purpose in life

Before proceeding, it is worth noting that the association of eudaimonia with meaning and purpose is erroneous. Neither of the progenitor literatures for eudaimonia in clinical psychology (Ryan et al. 2008; Waterman 2013) and Aristotelian philosophy (Annas 2004) gives a central role to meaning and purpose. Indeed, self-determination theory, perhaps the most well-known eudaimonic account of wellbeing in psychology, has explicitly argued that meaning is not a basic psychological need (Weinstein et al. 2010). The defining feature of most eudaimonic accounts of wellbeing is an emphasis on how one lives rather than how one is (well-living rather than wellbeing). By extension, talking about "feelings" or "a sense of" meaning and purpose does not jibe with eudaimonic perspectives because they don't think of wellbeing as a mental state. The growing acknowledgment of meaning and purpose in SW-B scholarship is certainly appropriate and welcome. There is a substantial literature attesting to its importance for wellbeing (King and Hicks 2012; Steger 2010). But this body of work is distinct from eudaimonic theories. Thus, rather than referring to the "eudaimonic" dimension of SW-B, scholars in that literature should just refer to meaning and purpose.

SW-B scholars sometimes argue that we must be cautious with incorporating meaning into our definition of SWB because its literature is underdeveloped (OECD 2013; Clark et al. 2018). This puzzles me because the study of meaning and wellbeing predates the study of SW-B by decades, going back at least to Frankl ([1946] 2008) if not the Jungian tradition (Peterson 1999). These early works are not quantitative or experimental, but more recent writings in the logotherapy tradition (Wong 2010) and elsewhere (Baumeister 1992) certainly are.

The confusion between meaning and eudaimonia perhaps reflects a rush by SW-B scholars to incorporate eudaimonia and meaning into their thinking following criticisms by associated scholars (see the discussions in the following articles: Waterman 2008; Kashdan et al. 2008; Biswas-Diener et al. 2009; Ryan and Huta 2009). This rush should be applauded even if it is a little muddled. It hopefully reflects a growing convergence of these literatures. I elaborate on the differences between eudaimonia and meaning in chapters 7 and 8.

Similar confusions arise when SW-B scholars move to policy discussions and must contend with whether SW-B is the prudential good (Angner 2009). For example, consider the following definition of wellbeing from Diener et al.'s (2009, p. 20) volume *Wellbeing and Public Policy*:

> In short, we have defined well-being as a life that matches an individual's own ideals. We think of income, affect, and well-being judgements as alternative indicators of well-being. These indicators reflect well-being for different reasons and they have their own biases and measurement problems. By integrating the information across different indicators, it is possible to obtain a better impression of individuals' and societies' well-being.

This definition has a few noteworthy features. First, it appears to be a definition of wellbeing, that is, the prudential good, not just SW-B. This is understandable given the context—a book about policy. Second, the authors appear to endorse a preference satisfaction account of wellbeing when they say that wellbeing is "a life that matches an individual's own ideals." The variables typically associated with SW-B, namely, affect and life satisfaction judgments, are presented only as indicators of preference satisfaction. Clark et al. (2018) make a similar point shortly after introducing their definition. They say that they prefer to focus on life satisfaction because "it allows individuals to assess their lives on the basis of whatever *they* consider important to themselves" (p. 4). This is very different from regarding mental states themselves as the prudential good and thus the objective of policy.

Yet such a mental state view—that wellbeing is the state of being happy or satisfied with your life—seems implicit in recent calls by SW-B scholars, including Clark et al. (2018) to conduct cost-effectiveness analysis on the basis of life satisfaction rather than income and price data, which are the traditional measures of preference satisfaction used by economists (Frijters et al. 2019).[1] To appreciate the difference, consider results from an experiment conducted by Benjamin et al. (2012). They presented respondents with a series of choices between two outcomes. They first asked: "Which one do you

---

[1] While sometimes less clear cut than choice data, income and prices provide a unidimensional, interpersonal cardinal means of measuring preference satisfaction. The architecture of how this is done was the central project of twentieth-century welfare economics, culminating in the methodology of cost-benefit analysis. See Adler 2019 for a review.

think would make you happier?" They then asked: "Which one would you choose?" They found that happiness and choice only coincided on average in 83 percent of cases. On some questions, coincidence was below 50 percent. These results make clear that happiness and preference satisfaction are distinct ends for public policy to pursue. Confusion among SW-B scholars regarding what they consider the prudential good to be is understandable: these are questions for philosophers. However, this confusion needs to be clarified if SW-B scholarship wants to penetrate into the policy domain effectively and legitimately. There are substantial ethical differences in promoting wellbeing as preference satisfaction as compared to wellbeing as happiness or some other mental state.

The next section reviews the strengths of the contemporary methodological approach of SW-B scholarship. I then review important findings from the SW-B literature in chapter 6. Before proceeding, it is worth summarizing the themes that definitions of SW-B share. First, SW-B is commonly and classically defined as a combination of how people *experience* and *evaluate* their own lives. Experienced and evaluative wellbeing are then defined in terms of *affect* and *life satisfaction*, respectively. A sense of *meaning and purpose* is gaining traction as an additional element. All of these are mental states. Second, SW-B uses measures of these mental states that leverage an individual's own self-assessments. SW-B is thus a subjectivist doctrine.

The Strengths of the Subjective Well-Being Approach

There is a lot to commend in the last four decades or so of SW-B scholarship and its open definition of the outcome variable of interest. First, the methodological approach of SW-B scholarship to matters of definition and its sidestepping of prudential issues avoided the presupposition of a specific theory of the prudential good. This allowed the first generation of SW-B research to place a strong and overdue emphasis on empirical approaches to improving our understanding of wellbeing. Second, the delineation between experienced and evaluative wellbeing was novel and important for understanding a range of findings in behavioral and hedonic psychology. Historical definitions, especially in philosophy, rarely made this distinction, or else were somewhat dismissive of experienced wellbeing as compared to evaluative wellbeing. This cynicism toward affective issues is implicit in Aristotle's disdain for hedonia, and in continental (Nietzsche [1889] 1990) and analytical philosophy's (Haybron 2001) skepticism about the importance of hedonism in accounts of the good life (though, of course, hedonism remains a popular theory among some philosophers). Finally, the disinclination to engage with prudential issues in definition allowed SW-B scholarship to investigate *subjective* wellbeing in a sustained way. Philosophers of wellbeing had spent relatively little time exploring the concept because of concerns around the prudential implications of a subjective account of wellbeing. They were only interested in the prudential good, but subjective wellbeing is interesting to psychologists and other scholars for reasons that don't necessarily pertain to prudential matters.

The definition of subjective well-being as affect and satisfaction arguably only posits *indicators* of wellbeing and is thus an open definition of the concept. As Sheldon (2013, p. 132) explains, it does not strongly imply particular ingredients for wellbeing or propose how these ingredients translate into wellbeing, at least in a research context:

> Tiberius also calls for a general definition of well-being that does not presuppose a particular theory, just as I do (which is one reason I use the subjective well-being measure). However, in my view she may make a mistake in saying that eudaimonic measures describe ingredients "that go beyond positive affect and life-satisfaction." If she means that eudaimonic theories (e.g. the self-concordance model) specify ingredients for happiness that go beyond hedonic theories, I agree. However, if she means that positive affect and life satisfaction (and low negative affect) are insufficient as indicators of well-being, then I disagree, for reasons already discussed. These three variables, combined, provide an admirable criterion for studying what produces happiness, in part because they are content free and do not presuppose a particular theory and in part because they really do discriminate between hedonic and eudaimonic activities. In a similar vein, Tiberius states that "psychologists who study subjective well-being . . . take the ingredients of well-being to be subjective, psychological states such as life satisfaction or positive affect." Again, I disagree; I am a psychologist who studies subjective well-being, but I take states of satisfaction and positive affect as the outcome to be predicted by the proper ingredients, not the proper ingredients themselves.[2]

---

[2] My sense is that Tiberius' (a philosopher) reference to "psychologists" was to those in the hedonic tradition who initiated the study of SW-B—people like Diener, Kahneman, and Schwarz. These psychologists do seem to consider mental states as definitive of wellbeing. They also captured a lot of

An important benefit of SW-B's approach is that it discourages empirical work from becoming biased (in the partisan rather than statistical sense of the word) by theoretical priors. This is arguably a double-edged sword, as we shall see in chapter 2, but it makes sense in the historical context of SW-B scholarship. The definition puts to one side the long history of theorizing about wellbeing and effectively hits reset, restarting inquiry from a more empirical foundation. Previously, inquiry into wellbeing tended to get rapidly derailed by arguments emerging out of theoretical priors. For example, non-hedonists were liable to be dismissive of inquiry into pleasure-based models of wellbeing on the grounds that, among other things, affective states are merely the phenomenal surface of deeper constructs like virtue and self-actualization (Haybron 2001; Annas 2004). A critical and underappreciated corollary outcome of this empirical turn is that it has opened the study of SWB independent of the prudential good. There is now a rich body of work about people's experiences and assessments of their life that are valuable even if these experiences and assessments turn out to be distinct from the prudential good. It seems unlikely to me that philosophy would ever have engaged in this research.

Differentiating between experienced and evaluative wellbeing is important to make sense of a range of empirical observations in behavioral and hedonic psychology. A prominent example is the peak-end rule, where people tend to judge how pleasant or unpleasant an experience was based on its most intense point and/or how the experience felt at its conclusion (Kahneman 1999). For example, mildly painful colonoscopies with very painful conclusions are remembered as more painful than colonoscopies where pain was high throughout but mild near the end of the procedure. Such phenomena are important for understanding SWB over time. Take the context of goal setting and achievement. Many goals are mostly arduous but come with a substantial, albeit brief, final hedonic payoff. The *experience* of running a marathon is typically negative. While some people genuinely enjoy running, marathons are typically justified from an *evaluative* point of view. They have benefits for your health and your identity.

---

the wellbeing spotlight in psychology through the 2000s, at least from the perspective of other disciplines. Sheldon is representative of the eudaimonic tradition in self-determination theory, which sees life satisfaction and affect as only *indicators* of wellbeing rather than constitutive of it. In my estimation, self-determination theorists have only recently (since the late 2000s or thereabouts) come to be associated with SW-B through the merging of various schools of psychology in the "positive psychology" movement. All this goes to explain the disagreement here between Sheldon and Tiberius. From my perspective, they are both right.

Running a marathon constitutes a lasting achievement that provides a floor to self-esteem.

Historically, wellbeing theory was arguably dismissive of experienced wellbeing, or at least argued that experienced wellbeing was substantially a function of evaluated wellbeing. For example, Nozick's (1974) famous "experience machine" thought experiment was frequently used (perhaps inaccurately) to debunk the idea that experienced wellbeing was of primary importance. The experience machine is a fictional device that you can plug into and be transported to some simulated reality, like in the movie *The Matrix*, wherein you have only positive experiences. In some other iterations of the thought experiment it is even implied that you can live out all your dreams, including the experience of achieving your goals. Would you plug in?

Philosophers generally assume that people would not plug in because they would rather lead a life that is in contact with reality. This implies that hedonic experiences aren't preeminent in people's SWB, or at least that there are other "goods" that they care about. There is a common argument in philosophical discussions of wellbeing that an illusory life or one in which the individual is deceived is somehow worse than a life lived with perfect knowledge (for examples, see Kagan 1984; Adams 1999, p. 84). However, in empirical studies of the experience machine thought experiment, people seem to be more comfortable with the idea of living in *The Matrix* than philosophers typically suppose (De Brigard 2010). In work by Weijers (2014), 16 percent of respondents chose to plug in, while in a study by Hindriks and Douven (2018), it was 29 percent.

A different critique of experienced wellbeing is that it is merely a function of evaluated wellbeing, or at least inseparable from it. This sort of argument is implied in, for example, self-discrepancy theory, which will be discussed in greater detail in chapter 9. Self-discrepancy theory argues that people try to harmonize who they are with who they want to be. If they achieve this, they experience positive affect like a sense of achievement, whereas failure brings depression. On the one hand, these affective signals provoke conscious reflection and evaluation, so they seem distinct from evaluative wellbeing. On the other hand, the affective signals are themselves a function of subconscious evaluations. The signals merely communicate this subconscious evaluation to consciousness. It becomes hard to distinguish the experienced and evaluated aspects of SWB here.

The problem with this sort of reductive, "root cause" analysis is that there are undeniably ways for experienced wellbeing to change, at least temporarily, independently of changes in evaluative wellbeing. Many of the techniques of mood management discussed in chapter 6, like savoring, rely on this, and are used in interventions with depressed patients to help them improve their mood, while other, longer-term techniques are used to heal the evaluative sources of their depression. Focusing on evaluative wellbeing, even if it accounts for the lion's share of the causes of experienced wellbeing, obfuscates the existence of these independent sources of experienced wellbeing.

A final, arguably commendable feature of the SW-B definition is that it gives sovereignty to the individual to decide their state of being. This is attractive to anybody who subscribes to liberal norms, which can come into conflict with some theories of wellbeing. Some objective list theories, for example, are open to abuse by authoritarian states that desire to dictate to their citizens. In theocracies or any of the totalitarian regimes of the twentieth century, citizens' wellbeing was defined in terms of how well society conformed to a utopian vision or religious text. The negative impacts of China's Cultural Revolution on SWB were justified on the grounds of accelerating and deepening revolutionary communism.

The indicators developed by SW-B scholars can be used for sanity checks on government policy. Imagine a government that delivers economic growth but does not ensure that this growth reaches all citizens. Looking at the GDP figures will provide a misleading assessment of societal trends in wellbeing, whereas SW-B indicators could provide a clearer picture (see Graham 2017 for an extended example). Now, of course it is possible to get this clearer picture using more nuanced objective metrics, like GDP growth rates at the local area level. However, subjective wellbeing metrics might end up being cheaper and provide richer insights because they capture a range of social trends.

Summary

At its genesis, the field of SW-B research had to define itself against a backdrop of skepticism toward anything subjective and a centuries-old body of wellbeing theory. To do this effectively, it opted for a fundamentally empirical approach that emphasized a general, outcomes-based definition of wellbeing derived in no small part from the instruments used to measure that conception of wellbeing. This definition initially emphasized affective states (derived from experience sampling methods) and life satisfaction (derived from scale questionnaires). More recently, SW-B scholars have come to suspect a role for meaning and purpose in SW-B but have stopped short of a full-blown engagement owing to what they perceive as a lack of effective measurement tools (OECD 2013, pp. 32–33).

In this chapter I discussed three merits of the SW-B definition of wellbeing. First, the loose definition obviates the possibility of research being biased by theoretical priors. It places a strong and overdue emphasis on the empirical as opposed to theoretical investigation of wellbeing—on what the data says rather than what our intuitions tell us (Bishop 2015). Second, the discrimination between experienced and evaluative wellbeing makes clear the important distinction between these two aspects of SW-B and allows their natures and interrelationships to be more accurately understood. Finally, centering the respondent in both the definition of subjective well-being and its assessment ensures a degree of commitment to liberal norms that is arguably important in the context of wellbeing policy. In chapter 2, I turn to consider shortcomings of the SW-B paradigm, motivating a deeper engagement with the wider wellbeing literature.

2

Problems with Subjective Well-Being

> But I don't want comfort. I want God, I want poetry, I want real
> danger, I want freedom, I want goodness. I want sin.
> —Aldous Huxley, *Brave New World*

Introduction

As discussed in chapter 1, the paradigm of SW-B certainly has merits. But it also has weaknesses. These are the subject of this chapter. I argue that while the definition and methodology of SW-B were acceptable within the field's original remit, they are inappropriate to the new value-laden domains it seeks to explore, notably therapy, normative economics, and public policy. Once you move beyond the realm of scholarly SW-B research with its relatively narrow questions and peculiar disciplinary and historical background you need to integrate prudential philosophy in a sophisticated manner and develop metrics more precise than life satisfaction scales. This requires engaging with all the interdisciplinary theory that SW-B scholarship has largely and deliberately avoided. It then requires subjecting a fit-for-purpose theory of SWB to empirical tests designed to unearth the causal structure of that SWB.

This contrasts with the exploratory data analysis approach of SW-B scholarship to date. As Alexandrova (2017) has argued, the definition and methods of SW-B are suitable for a "field" science. Such research gathers data on novel items and explores that data predominantly with descriptive methods. It establishes a landscape of empirical phenomena to be theorized and explained. SW-B is only just exiting the field science stage (Kashdan et al. 2008; Biswas-Diener et al. 2009), but already claims enough causal understanding of a value-laden concept (wellbeing) to make policy recommendations (Diener et al. 2009; Clark et al. 2018). Its field science tools are not up to this task. SW-B must mature into a "theory-led" science, testing

A Theory of Subjective Wellbeing. Mark Fabian, Oxford University Press. © Oxford University Press 2022.
DOI: 10.1093/oso/9780197635261.003.0003

thoroughly articulated hypotheses with precise instruments. This will lay further foundations for the long-run objective of becoming a "laboratory" science that relies principally (though by no means exclusively) on experimental and quasi-experimental methods. These allow for strong causal identification, which lends *epistemic* legitimacy to policy advocacy. Developing the *normative* legitimacy for public policy requires a more thorough engagement with prudential philosophy. Philosophers have historically been somewhat disinterested in helping psychologists with this task, seeing wellbeing as something that philosophers must define before psychologists can measure and study it (Bishop 2015). However, some philosophers have recently broken ranks and advocated collaboration with psychologists, perhaps in a process of "conceptual engineering," to develop a prudentially sensitive account of SWB (Tiberius and Hall 2010; Prinzing 2021). The takeaway message is that deeper theorizing about what SWB is and how it can be measured is required. Given that the field has achieved increasing academic credibility in recent years, now is a perfect time to engage in this critical reflection.

This chapter focuses on the epistemic shortcomings of SW-B scholarship. These find their roots in SW-B's shallow theoretical base. They give rise to measurement problems, which I discuss in detail in chapter 10. Under the heading of epistemic shortcomings, I discuss issues of circularity, the application of construct validation techniques in SW-B scholarship, and evidential subjectivism. SW-B is defined in terms of the instruments used to measure it. These are then justified on the grounds that they do indeed measure SW-B. This is circular. "Construct validation" exercises are required to exit this circularity. However, construct validation is only epistemologically sound if it begins with thorough theorizing about its construct of interest. Owing to the field's history, SW-B scholarship has arguably neglected this initial theorizing. SWB scholarship's approach is further undermined epistemologically by its adherence to evidential subjectivism. This is where both the measurement of a construct and the construct itself are subjectively determined.

Epistemic Concerns

Circularity

In conventional scientific method of the Popperian variety, research proceeds from hypothesis to test (Popper [1934] 1959). You begin with a theory and you attempt to find evidence refuting that theory. If it stands up to the scrutiny of tests designed to prove it false, you treat the theory as factually accurate until falsifying evidence comes along. The purpose of this approach is to overcome the problem of induction. This concerns the difficulty of making inferences about a population from a sample of that population. An intuitive statement of this problem is that if you observe swans a million times and every time they are white, you still can't be certain that somewhere in the world (like Australia) there isn't a swan that is black. All empirical knowledge is based on sampling and it may be the case that you simply haven't seen enough of the distribution. Falsification is a kind of solution to the problem of induction because you are not trying to prove something but rather to disprove it. You are not trying to demonstrate the *truth* of the statement that "all swans are white" but rather to find an exception. Until such an exception is discovered, we can treat the statement "all swans are white" as *fact* (not truth) based on our existing sample of observations. We can build a paradigm based on our existing facts.

In important ways, the science of SW-B does not adhere to this approach (at least not yet). One of these ways is that SW-B scholarship did not first develop a clear theory of what SW-B is, then metrics that could test aspects of this theory. Instead, it began by developing measurement instruments and collecting data. Only then did it begin to make theoretical conjectures about the nature of wellbeing, or in this case, SW-B. SW-B is arguably defined in terms of the instruments that are used to measure it. Experience sampling tools were developed for measuring affect, and affect then became a component of SW-B. Life satisfaction scale questions were developed for measuring evaluative well-being, and then life satisfaction came to be part of the definition of SW-B. SW-B scholars are now considering incorporating meaning and purpose into SW-B but are holding off until they develop a measure of the concept (Stone and Mackie 2013; OECD 2013; Clark et al. 2018). Again, the measure of the construct is preceding theory about what the construct is.

Circularity ensues when data collected using these instruments is then used to justify the instruments as accessing the construct that researchers are interested in. A positive result is inevitable. There is virtually no way that a question about life satisfaction could fail to capture life satisfaction. *That doesn't mean that life satisfaction is (subjective) wellbeing.* What (subjective) wellbeing is was never defined in the first place. The definition of the phenomenon of interest comes after something has been measured, and the phenomenon is then defined as whatever it is that is measured.

Another example might make this clearer. After SW-B was defined as some function of affect and life satisfaction, SW-B scholars noted that the two were not closely correlated statistically (Diener et al. 2006). From there, they posited that wellbeing is both experienced (affect) and evaluated (life satisfaction). However, there was never any theoretical justification of why affect and life satisfaction are both part of wellbeing. As noted in chapter 1 (in praise), this definition does not map neatly onto any definition in the philosophical, economic, or health traditions. Even hedonistic mental state conceptions, which are perhaps the closest analogy, typically emphasize experience *or* evaluation (Feldman 2002). Sumner's (1996) "authentic happiness" theory of well-being, which gives a central role to subjective life satisfaction, is sometimes used by SW-B scholars (e.g., Diener et al. 2009) to underpin their arguments. Yet as we will see in chapter 3, Sumner explicitly stresses that such subjective assessments are not well-being if they are ill-informed or not autonomous. His theorizing goes beyond the empirical approach of SW-B scholar to construct definition.

The harmful consequence of this circularity is that SW-B never actually posits a hypothesis about reality that is then subjected to tests. Theory comes after the empirical test. It is logically impossible to arrive at a fact about *reality* using this method. Instead, one develops theories about *constructs* or statistical regularities. This is a common challenge in such research, and psychologists have developed the tools of "construct validation" to exit circularity. Unfortunately, SW-B scholarship runs into epistemic problems in how it executes construct validation.

Construct Validity

The primary means by which SW-B scholars justify their definition of wellbeing is by appeal to psychometric evidence, especially construct validation exercises (Cohen Kaminitz 2018, p. 433). "Constructs" in this context are "literally something that scientists 'construct' (put together in their own imagination) and which does not exist as an observable dimension of behaviour" (Nunnally and Bernstein 1994, p. 85). There are many things in psychology that cannot be observed objectively and thus require the development of a construct to be operationalized. Intelligence is a famous example. Construct validity refers to the degree to which a test measures what it claims, or purports, to be measuring (Cronbach and Meehl 1955). More specifically, construct validity refers to whether a "measure performs in the way theory would suggest with respect to the construct being measured" (OECD 2013, p. 49). In the case of SW-B, scholars claim that life satisfaction scale questions measure SWB.

Alexandrova (2017, p. 131) describes the "implicit logic" of construct validation as follows:

A measure (M) of a construct (C) is validated to the extent that M behaves in a way that respects three sources of evidence:
1. M is inspired by a plausible theory of C
2. Subjects reveal M to track C through their questionnaire answering behavior
3. Other knowledge about C is consistent with variations in values of M across contexts

Hedonic psychologists have certainly produced a great many studies that employ the logic just outlined to demonstrate the construct validity of SW-B. The OECD Guidelines on Measuring Subjective Wellbeing (2013) provide a good summary of the construct validity evidence that exists for life satisfaction and affect as measures of wellbeing. To wit:

Among individuals, higher incomes are associated with higher levels of life satisfaction and affect, and wealthier countries have higher average levels of both types of SW-B than poor countries (Sacks, Stevenson and Wolfers 2010). At the individual level, health status, social contact, education and being in a stable relationship with a partner are all associated with higher levels of life satisfaction (Dolan, Peasgood and White 2008), while unemployment has a large negative effect on life satisfaction (Winkelmann and Winkelmann, 1998). Kahneman and Krueger (2006) report that intimate relations, socialising, relaxing, eating and praying are associated with high levels of net positive affect; conversely, commuting, working, childcare and housework are associated with low levels of net positive affect. Boarini et al. (2012) find that affect measures have the same broad sets of drivers as measures of life satisfaction, although the relative importance of some factors changes.

Further, it is clear that changes in SW-B—particularly life evaluations—that result from life events are neither trivial in magnitude, nor transient. Studies have shown that changes in income, becoming unemployed, and becoming disabled have a long-lasting impact on life satisfaction (e.g., Lucas 2007; Lucas et al. 2003; Diener et al. 2006). Although there can also be substantial individual differences in the extent to which people show resilience, or are able to adapt to, adversity over time. In the case of negative life experiences, Cummins et al. (2002) note that extreme adversity is expected to result in "homeostatic defeat"—thus, life experiences such as chronic pain of arthritis or the stress of caring for a severely disabled family member at home can lead to stably low levels of SW-B. Similarly, Diener et al. (2006) describe evidence of partial recovery from the impacts of widowhood, divorce and unemployment in the five years following these events, but SW-B still fails to return to the levels observed in the five years prior to these events. Thus, although there is evidence of partial adaptation to changes in life circumstances, adaptation is not complete, and the impact of these life events on evaluations is long-lasting. (pp. 49–50)

It is worth noting that these studies typically draw on panel data and do not use sources of exogenous variation or quasi-experimental methods to establish the causal claims they make. However, the weight of evidence points to SW-B measures moving broadly in the directions we would expect following events commonly associated with positive and negative effects on wellbeing, such as divorce, unemployment, and disability.

Despite this evidence, the OECD Guidelines are ultimately measured in their conclusions as to the validity of SW-B metrics. They argue that "an extensive body of evidence" accumulated over the last two decades "strongly supports the view that measures of both life evaluation and affect capture valid information." However, they note that this does not mean "that measures of SW-B are universally valid or devoid of limitations." They emphasize that SW-B measures should only be regarded as "fit for purpose" if "used with appropriate caveats" (p. 50).

The OECD's reasons for hesitation all concern statistical matters. They note that SW-B measures have a relatively high noise-to-signal ratio of around 20:80–40:60. Things like the day of the week, the season, and the weather can all influence certain SW-B metrics. SW-B measures are also sensitive to survey content. For example, questions about the political state of the nation result in lower responses to subsequent life satisfaction questions (Deaton and Stone 2016). Husser and Fernandez (2018) found that simply adding "in your life" to the end of life satisfaction questions resulted in respondents giving higher scores. This implies that the words made people think more of the state of their own life rather than society in general.[1] The OECD also notes that respondents vary in their response styles and how they interpret questions.

The OECD does not discuss more abstract theoretical concerns with SW-B construct validation. Of note in this regard is Alexandrova's (2017) argument that construct validation in the context of SW-B does not use enough theory to support its implicit logic:

> None of the conditions as they are currently implemented are strong enough to ensure validity. . . . Indeed the philosophical heart of condition 1 [M is inspired by a plausible theory of C] is often enough replaced by an informal report of folk views or an unsystematic literature review. Instead of examining the nature of wellbeing of the relevant kind by building at least in outline a mid-level theory of it, the temptation is to canvass how this concept is understood by the relevant population and be done. (p.131)

The list of validations referred to by the OECD makes this charge of "folk theorizing" clear. Only the most straightforward postulates about well-being are used to validate the instrument—things like income effects and unemployment. Deeper issues like goal attainment, self-concordance, autonomy, and prudential matters are overlooked, in part because of data limitations. This is a shallow engagement with what SWB is. There is little reference to the rich history of philosophical or psychological literature on the topic.

This approach is especially problematic when the validation of measures using such simple theory is then taken to make the measures valid for more nuanced work, like cost-benefit analysis (Diener et al. 2013). That a metric correlates well with a very general well-being item like suicide doesn't mean that the metric is precise or measures without systematic error.

To appreciate this, consider the problem of scale-norming, which I discuss at length in chapter 10. Scale-norming is where respondents use qualitatively different scales to respond to life satisfaction scale questions at different times. For example, prior to graduating, a college student might say that they are 8/10. After all, they are healthy, educated, and set for a good life. Anything less than 8 might seem ungrateful. Imagine that they

---

[1] A curious corollary of this observation is that it suggests people think society is worse than it actually is. If on average people are more satisfied with their life than with society in general, then presumably they think others are more miserable than they actually are.

then graduate into precisely the job they wanted. We could reasonably assume that their life satisfaction rises. However, their new circumstances radically change the way that they make sense of their life, and so the scale they use to report their satisfaction also changes. They might perceive further possible improvements, so they say 8/10 again despite their life satisfaction being higher. Researchers do not observe this scale change, and so erroneously conclude that the individual's satisfaction has not increased. They put their static satisfaction down to changing reference points. This conclusion is partly correct—reference points have changed—but so has life satisfaction. Teasing the two forces apart is impossible with the scale instrument alone. Yet such teasing apart is precisely what we need to be able to do if we want to measure the causal effect of various structural changes on people's life satisfaction. In a large enough sample, a positive correlation between graduating and life satisfaction will emerge even if its full effect is often swamped by scale norming. This will provide statistical validity to life satisfaction scales, but it obfuscates their impression. This example hopefully makes clear that the standard of "validity" depends heavily on *context*. What was fine for the exploratory phase of SW-B research may not be good enough for new applications.

This is what Alexandrova is getting at when she refers to the "wellbeing of the relevant kind." Wellbeing is a rich concept with a great deal of political and sociological baggage. How we understand it can vary from context to context. For example, orthodox economists tend to think of it in terms of the distribution of material goods (Angner 2015), while midwives think of it in terms of baby body weight (Waldfogel et al. 2010). Even if we avoid the perhaps impossible task of building an "all things considered" theory of wellbeing, it is necessary to develop at least a rich *midlevel* theory of well-being—that is, a context-appropriate theory—before embarking on construct validation. SW-B arguably did this for its context of exploring subjective assessments of experience and life satisfaction. However, SW-B is now moving into the policy discourse, among other domains, which requires a different midlevel theory or a broadening of the theory that suited the original context of SW-B science. Crucially, because policy is a highly normative domain, construct validation must confront prudential theory and consider whether its measures are sufficiently precise for new tasks like policy analysis (Borsboom et al. 2021).

The understandable tendency of SW-B scholars to assume *conceptual* validity and *legitimacy* from *statistical* validation also poses a technocratic risk. Validating a construct using the broadest possible theoretical postulates makes sense if you are trying to carve out a niche amidst logical positivism, but it is inappropriate when you are engaging in a broader sociopolitical exercise. In the context of such an exercise, outsourcing theory to statistics inadvertently robs normative issues of their significance by turning them into technical questions. Alexandrova (2017) explains well the dangers of this tendency in SW-B scholarship:

> But it is less modest once we see its political context. Historians of psychological sciences have long noted the convenience of the methods of these sciences to the political order in which they arose and endure . . . psychologists, psychometricians, psychotherapists, and even psychoanalysts, have long played a crucial role in the management of individuals in liberal democracies. Their authority as advisors depends on their adoption of technical methods for handling questions that were not previously within the domain of science—what it means to be normal, intelligent, well-adjusted and so on. As Rose argues, this is how moral or prudential questions are turned into psychological ones. Similarly in our case, in undertaking the validation of measures of well-being, psychometrics puts itself forward as the arbiter of questions that are properly moral and political. . . . Appeals to subjects' behaviour or their reports is a standard move. It makes validation procedures seemingly democratic and grounded in facts—and evidence-based too, so very convenient. Far from being modest and safe, this avoidance of philosophy and its replacement with a technical exercise in construct validation is epistemically wrong and morally dangerous. (p. 147)

Such arguments are echoed by Davies (2015), who focuses specifically on the sociopolitical implications of happiness studies and their potentially insidious consequences. It is important to underline, as Alexandrova (2017, p. 147) does, that "these questions cannot be resolved by checking more correlations." In the context of public policy advocacy, there needs to be "explicit deliberation of what counts as wellbeing to a given community." SW-B scholars have engaged in some minimal deliberation regarding what counts as SW-B *for themselves*. But now they are attempting to foist their context-specific definition onto other actors in a different context. Worse, they are insensitive to how the value judgments inherent in defining a value-laden term like "well-being" might differ across these contexts.

Evidential Subjectivism

There is an additional epistemic problem for SW-B associated with the circularity of its definition: evidential subjectivism. Unlike other applications of operationalism, such as the measurement of intelligence, SW-B scholarship not only uses subjective *measures* of its construct of interest, but also uses a subjective *definition* of that construct (Alexandrova 2017, p. 130). The principal epistemic problem with evidential subjectivism is that responses to SW-B questions across individuals do not necessarily elicit a measure of the same construct. We don't know how respondents are defining the construct when they answer SW-B questions. This makes developing a clear and unified definition of wellbeing using such questions difficult if not impossible. We may think we are developing a theory of a single construct that we observe in data when we are actually looking at many different constructs. In this context, it is worrying that construct validation in social psychology typically eschews cognitive interviewing. This is where respondents "think out loud" while answering psychometric surveys to give researchers a sense for how they interpret the questions. Aside from revealing whether respondents understand concepts the way researchers do, cognitive interviewing can reveal whether the surface-level statistical validity of a psychometric instrument belies conceptual variety in its target construct, important cognitive or linguistic complexity in answering the question, or imprecision in the instrument.

Evidential subjectivism also undermines our ability to develop better theory by admitting any and all conceptions of, among other things, life satisfaction. This limits the beneficial role of theorists in refining the concepts under investigation and gives too much credence to bad theories. While there is merit to empowering citizens to tell researchers what they think life satisfaction, happiness, or SWB is, it is common sense that there are better and worse theories of these concepts. Experts are helpful in making such judgments.

Now seems a good juncture to take stock and develop a coherent and precise definition of SWB to take our research further. This is what I do over the following seven chapters. Before commencing that project, I spend a bit more time exploring the history of SW-B's operationalist methodology. This makes it possible to pinpoint where SW-B crosses over from a domain where operationalism is appropriate to where it is not. This is important for properly understanding the complex challenges facing scientists who want to work with value-laden concepts.

Operationalism in SWB and Psychology More Generally

The methodology of SWB research is grounded in the field's historical context. As discussed in chapter 1, when SW-B scholarship emerged, psychology was dominated by logical positivism. SW-B scholarship could only carve itself a niche by focusing resolutely on empirics rather than theory. In a recent article, Cohen Kaminitz (2018) uncovers the history of the SW-B approach in psychology more generally, especially with regard to interpersonal comparisons of utility and satisfaction. She notes that where difficulties associated with interpersonal comparisons of utility and satisfaction led economists to focus on the objectively observable metrics of real choices and money, psychologists instead opted for a different epistemic approach (Cohen Kaminitz 2018, p. 432):

> An interesting starting point is the reaction of psychologists to logical positivism in the 1930s and 1940s, the period of intellectual history that saw economists embracing the sceptical approach to the question of scientific comparisons of utility between individuals. Significantly, positivistic influence led psychology along a completely different path. In particular, the work of S. S. Stevens . . . actually opened the door to quantified scientific comparisons between individuals' inner worlds. The key to unlocking this door was Stevens' (1946) seminal definition of measurement: "measurement, in the broadest sense, is defined as the assignment of numbers to objects or events according to rules." This is what philosophers of science would call a *nominalist* definition of measurement. For Stevens, methods of measurement are definitive of concepts; a view that stands in opposition to *realism*, which takes measurements to be methods of finding out about objective quantities that we can identify independently of measurement. Indeed, Stevens' nominalism took the radical form of *operationalism*: the view that the meaning of a concept is fully specified by its method of measurement, implying that each measurement operation *defines* its own concept. The relevancy of this stance to our concerns is straightforward: scientists who hold to nominalism do not commit to measuring *real* entities—real life-satisfaction/happiness included; so from this perspective the impossibility of inter-personal comparisons of *real quantities* of satisfaction is obvious, but irrelevant.

Cohen Kaminitz's observations reveal the roots of the SW-B approach and why it is problematic when used outside the disciplinary boundaries of SW-B scholarship. SW-B scholarship uses an *operationalist* epistemology rather than a *realist* one: SW-B is defined by its measurement, as we have seen. This contrasts with the other traditions investigating wellbeing. They require a concept of interest to be pinpointed in reality before metrics are developed to measure it. It was precisely the quagmire of theory these traditions had developed that SW-B wanted to avoid at its genesis. Cohen Kaminitz notes (pp. 432–433), as I did in chapter 1, that psychology in general, and SW-B scholarship in particular, was able to make a great deal of progress by side-lining such complex theoretical issues.

Where this approach becomes problematic is when SW-B scholars move into other wellbeing domains and inadvertently ride roughshod over definitions of wellbeing therein. The argument used in favor of the SW-B approach to wellbeing in such cases is that it is grounded in evidence and value-neutral. But this is misleading. Due to their operationalist approach, what SW-B scholars have is an empirical understanding of *SW-B*, not "wellbeing." Specifically, they have an empirical understanding of affect and life satisfaction. It does not follow that this way of understanding wellbeing is appropriate for contexts other than SW-B scholarship. In other domains people are interested in a particular conception of wellbeing and justify this conception with reference, typically, to a range of political, ethical, and contextual issues. Another way of thinking about this is that early SW-B scholarship defined its construct of interest as a purely technical term—subjective well-being is how people say they feel about their life. Whether these reports or feelings are "valuable" can be put to one side while data is collected and empirical phenomena explored. But when you cross over into policy, therapy, or other value-laden domains you must justify why and how these things are valuable, with reference to competing points of view. SW-B scholarship has largely *assumed* the value of these things instead, and in a very simplistic way.

The importation of an operationally defined concept of wellbeing into value-laden domains amounts to sneaking in a variety of ethical and political assumptions regarding the nature of wellbeing under the guise of what appears to be a sterilized concept. The SW-B definition of wellbeing is in such cases presented as admirably theory-free, but it should instead be criticized for theory *avoidance*. As Alexandrova (2017, p. 93) explains:

When eminent economists including Nobel Prize winners advocate a measure of national well-being that takes into account only the average ratio of positive over negative emotions of the populace (Kahneman et al. 2004b), the citizens can legitimately object if they take well-being to consist in more than that. Perhaps they believe that national well-being should also encompass compassion, kindness, and mutual trust of their community, the sustainability of their lifestyle, not to mention justice.

The items Alexandrova lists at the end of that quote—compassion, kindness, trust, sustainability, and justice—are all features of the long history of philosophical engagement with wellbeing. As already discussed, SW-B scholarship had to put such considerations to one side to make progress in its domain, which is fair enough. But it is now bringing its view to other domains and failing to acknowledge, let alone engage with, the greater complexity of wellbeing in the context of those domains. To attain legitimacy, SW-B scholarship must provide theoretical argument as to why its conceptualization of wellbeing is superior to others.

The Way Forward

Alexandrova neatly sums up the weaknesses of contemporary SW-B research in the following passage:

> By sticking to a resolutely anti-realist metaphysics the psychometric approach wrongly outsources to statistics what is essentially a theoretical problem: What must well-being be like, as a causal system, for questionnaires to detect it? (2017, p. 148)

These weaknesses can be traced back to the implicit logic of construct validation. In the concluding passages of her book *A Philosophy for the Science of Wellbeing*, Alexandrova (2017, p. 150) advocates for a "Better Implicit Logic" to inform construct validity in wellbeing research (emphasis added to differentiate from the basic implicit logic quoted previously):

> A measure M of construct C can be considered validated to the extent that M behaves in a way that respects three sources of evidence:

1. M is inspired by a plausible theory of C. *This theory should be articulated as fully as possible and defended against alternatives.*
2. M is shown to track C *as C is understood and endorsed by the subjects to whom C is applied.*
3. Other knowledge about C is consistent with variations in values of M across contexts. *This knowledge should encompass the normative significance of C, including moral and political contexts of the use of C.*

Over the next seven chapters, I attempt to fulfill condition (1). I elucidate a plausible theory of SWB that is appropriate to a range of domains. In the penultimate chapter, I consider whether contemporary SW-B metrics track this SWB with enough accuracy for the purposes of wellbeing researchers and other stakeholders, thereby making a start on (2). While generally positive and optimistic about measurement, I argue that life satisfaction scales are limited in their usefulness, and consequently I propose extensions as a step toward better measures of SWB. In the final chapter, I consider the conception of SWB I develop against other accounts of wellbeing that are salient in public policy specifically. This makes a start on (3).

I hope that this extensive theoretical analysis will have three additional benefits. First, it will synthesize the many existing perspectives on SWB and wellbeing into a clear and coherent model. This will clarify how these different perspectives complement one another and how different aspects of SWB fit together. Second, this integrated model will be a source of tightly articulated causal hypotheses. The instruments we have for measuring SWB leave much to be desired, and we may never have especially accurate ones. Our progress therefore depends on having precise *hypotheses* that can be tested with imprecise *instruments.* Third, integration should go some way toward curing SWB studies of what Antonakis (2017) calls "disjunctivitis." When researchers work in disciplinary silos and are disinclined to theorize they are prone to produce internally inconsistent bodies of knowledge. Periodic handbooks and edited volumes go some way to redressing this, but often lack enough unifying chapters that stitch everything together. My contention is that a unifying project is overdue in the field of SWB and I humbly present this book an attempt at it.

3

The Analytical Philosophy of Wellbeing

> My principal work now lies in tracing out the exact nature and conditions of utility. It seems strange indeed that economists have not bestowed more minute attention on a subject which doubtless furnishes the true key to the problem of economics.
> —William Stanley Jevons, *The Theory of Political Economy*

I begin the development of the subjective well-being production function from the analytical philosophy literature. There are two reasons for this. The first is that analytical philosophy is very attentive to issues of categorization and delineation. Discussing the analytical literature allows the question "What is wellbeing?" to be made quickly tractable by outlining schools of thought. Explaining these schools and their strengths and weaknesses provides a picture of the landscape of wellbeing theory. The details can then be filled in. The second is that the analytical philosophy of wellbeing takes as its object of inquiry the prudential good. A key motivation for this volume is that SW-B's recent forays into public policy pay insufficient regard to normative issues pertaining to the prudential good, so it is appropriate to lead with them here.

This chapter makes two principal claims. First, that recent cycles of debate between the most prominent classes of wellbeing theories in analytical philosophy—hedonistic or mental state accounts, subjectivist, preference satisfaction, eudaimonic, and objective list—have resulted in a great deal of convergence between those different theories. Increasingly, advocates of one or another theory are only able to respond to critiques of their position by, in a sense, subsuming their interlocutor's perspective. This trend suggests that there might be value in giving greater thought and consideration to the similarities between wellbeing theories rather than focusing almost exclusively on their differences. This brings us to the second claim, which is

A Theory of Subjective Wellbeing. Mark Fabian, Oxford University Press. © Oxford University Press 2022. DOI: 10.1093/oso/9780197635261.003.0004

that considering both what well-being is *and how it is obtained* reveals that these theories are more interdependent than their advocates might presume. Notably, self-actualization seems critical to the acquisition of sustained wellbeing regardless of which theory of wellbeing you are employing, with only a few exceptions. Furthermore, themes from all accounts of wellbeing are required to understand how self-actualization works to promote wellbeing. Philosophers distinguish between things that are intrinsic to wellbeing and those that are merely instrumental. They focus on the former because prudential value is in the intrinsic goods. But if very many things are *necessary* for achieving wellbeing, then this distinction between intrinsic and instrumental is, *practically speaking*, largely inconsequential. Certainly there seems to be enormous merit in understanding how all the instrumental items fit together—a project philosophy has largely neglected.

This focus on the practicalities of obtaining wellbeing, wherever it might ultimately lie intrinsically, leads me to adopt Bishop's (2015) "inclusive approach" to wellbeing scholarship. He begins his analysis with the question "What do we need a theory of wellbeing to do?" This question typically leads to three criteria, well articulated by Tiberius (2018): descriptive, normative, and empirical adequacy. Philosophers tend to emphasize descriptive adequacy, which requires that a theory of wellbeing accord with our common sense or intuitive judgments. It would be hard to argue that a depressed person is well, for example. Philosophers also place a strong emphasis on normative adequacy, which refers to whether a theory of wellbeing has appealing ethical consequences. For example, a crude sensory hedonist account of wellbeing might define it as being in a good mood. A good Samaritan seeking to maximize the wellbeing of others might then spike the communal water supply with antidepressants. This seems creepy and thus speaks against the normative adequacy of the theory. Philosophers give much less attention to empirical adequacy, which refers to whether a theory accords with scientific evidence. Bishop explains (2015, p. 24) that philosophers often consider themselves insulated from this requirement. As wellbeing is a value-laden concept, it must be defined before it can be studied. Bishop argues that this attitude is erroneous because empirical facts have historically upended our intuitions, even regarding normative matters, on multiple occasions. He builds from this to a deeper attack on the dominance of descriptive adequacy in philosophy. He argues that theories of wellbeing should be judged not by their resilience to the at times highly contrived counterexamples that are the stock in trade of analytical philosophy, but instead according to their *explanatory power*.

This leads to Bishop's "inclusive approach" to wellbeing theorizing, which looks across the interdisciplinary gamut of wellbeing scholarship and asks, "All this is the study of wellbeing, so what is wellbeing?" An accurate theory of wellbeing should explain as much of this conceptual landscape as possible. Argument by counterexample isn't particularly useful here, as that methodology is oriented toward demarcating what is and is not wellbeing. Rather than trying to explain the complex, multifaceted construct many different scholarly groups claim is wellbeing, it is instead inclined to dismiss some of those lines of inquiry as not being about wellbeing. For example, philosophers inclined toward an Aristotelian account of wellbeing might say that SW-B scholarship does not study wellbeing *simpliciter* because it does not account for virtue, which is intrinsic to wellbeing. The inclusive approach still gives weight to descriptive adequacy—wellbeing cannot be a banana—but it gives much less credence to intuitive judgments than the traditional philosophical approach. In turn, it puts much more emphasis on normative adequacy than empiricists typically do, recognizing that defining wellbeing requires a value judgment.

I propose that the theory I elaborate over the course of this book is a good theory because it has a lot of explanatory power and is sensitive to the prudential aspects of subjective wellbeing. As mentioned in the introduction, I populate Bishop's "positive causal network," which is a theory of wellbeing designed from the vantage point of the inclusive approach. Furthermore, because I attend to prudential matters quite thoroughly, I am able to explain what is "positive" about the "positive causal network." I hope that this theory is useful both to SWB scientists and to people applying SWB science to more value-laden domains, notably policy. However, while I endeavor to be sensitive to prudential matters, I do not defend the claim that the SWB theory I outline is the prudential good, at least not head-on. I leave that debate to the philosophers.

Theories of Wellbeing

Parfit (1984) influentially partitioned wellbeing theories into three classes: hedonistic, desire satisfaction, and objective list. My impression is that this tripartite classification has since evolved into a larger nebula of accounts (Fletcher 2015a). Hedonism as a class has been replaced by the broader class of mental state theories. Hedonism now refers to theories that define wellbeing as *pleasant* mental states specifically (Gregory 2015). Desire fulfillment accounts continue to dominate economics, but there the language is usually preference satisfaction rather than desire fulfillment (Heathwood 2015). Individuals are thought to act to satisfy their preferences, and it is from attaining things that they prefer that they derive utility. Contemporary preference satisfaction theories recognize that some preferences can be dumb, irrational, or ill-considered, and thus emphasize "well-laundered" preferences (Hausman 2015). Objective list accounts, which define well-being according to some set of observable criteria, are common. For example, the capabilities framework and its associated indicators, like the Human Development Index (a composite of income, years of schooling, and life expectancy), occupies a preeminent position in development policy. Eudaimonic accounts were traditionally housed within the objective list class of well-being theories but are increasingly parsed out into their own category. Besser-Jones (2015) argues that eudaimonic theories conceive the prudential good in terms of how one lives rather than how one is. Other theorists might take a slightly different tact. Some instead emphasize the "nature fulfillment" or "perfectionist" aspect of eudaimonic wellbeing (Haybron 2008). For example, in most Aristotelian and scholastic accounts, eudaimonia involves living so as to make full use of humans' supposedly unique capacities for reason and morality. Finally, subjectivist accounts that emphasize an individual's own judgment of their well-being have grown in prominence alongside SW-B. These have been particularly influential in the philosophy of happiness (Vitrano 2013). Note that philosophers are careful to distinguish between happiness and wellbeing. They do not use the terms interchangeably and are often quite vehement that happiness does not constitute well-being (Sumner 1996).

It is arguably possible to break out even more classes, and some theorists are consequently moving away from Parfit's tripartite classification to a more fine-grained taxonomy (see, for example, Woodard 2012). I want to take the opposite approach herein. Analyzing the similarities between wellbeing theories rather than their distinctions provides a range of important insights. The rest of this section explores recent articulations of the five classes I identified earlier with an eye to complementarities and overlaps between them. I argue that recent iterations of the debate between these different perspectives have seen their distinctions reduced. The theories are now increasingly borrowing from each other. This motivates a deliberately integrative account of well-being, which I then present over several chapters.

Hedonism

Prominent hedonistic theories in history are those of the Epicureans and the classical utilitarians, especially Mill. A more recent entry into this class of theories is Feldman's (2002) attitudinal hedonism. Attitudinal hedonism is distinct from sensual hedonism, which concerns only feelings, specifically pleasure and pain.[1] In contrast, attitudinal hedonism is concerned with attitudes, especially enjoyment, which Feldman argues is phenomenologically not a feeling. He argues that attitudinal hedonism "is a mode of consciousness" and considers it robust to many classical critiques of hedonism. For example, attitudinal hedonism can explain why the stoic and ascetic are well in a way that sensual hedonism cannot. Stoics want peace of mind and ascetics want to cleave tightly to religious practices. They do not seek sensory pleasure. On a sensory hedonist account, they cannot possibly be well. Intuitively, though, we feel that the stoic's positive disposition toward her life brings her wellbeing, so this account seems flawed. Attitudinal hedonism is robust to this critique, because while the stoic does not feel pleasure, she has a pleasant attitude toward it, and thus her life goes well under a hedonistic account (Feldman 2002, p. 7).

Feldman also claims that attitudinal hedonism can withstand normative critiques. However, to do so, Feldman's attitudinal hedonism must subsume tropes from other accounts of well-being. There are three critiques that Feldman takes up. The first is that someone living a pleasant but deceived life is considered to have just as valuable a life according to hedonism as someone who experiences as much pleasure but is not deceived, and this seems wrong. The second is that hedonism does not differentiate between worthless and worthwhile pleasures—what Crisp (2006) calls the "worthless swine" criticism in reference to Aristotle and Mill. The final critique is that while hedonism might give us an account of what sort of life is worth living, it does not give us an account of what sort of world is worth creating.

In each case, Feldman responds by expanding his theory. First, he suggests that pleasure could be accorded more weight when it is drawn from a true state of affairs. Second, he suggests that pleasures from certain sources could

---

[1] A high-profile philosopher of happiness once remarked to me that "not one contemporary philosopher even holds" the sensual hedonist view. That may be the case, but it seems alive and well among happiness economists, so I think I should at least mention it. For example, in a letter to the *Financial Times* in June 2019, Andrew Oswald, a prominent happiness economist, wrote: "Human feelings are the only things that matter." Bramble (2016) also appears to defend a "felt quality" (as distinct from "attitude-based") hedonistic account of wellbeing.

be weighted to take into consideration the worthiness of those sources of pleasure. He calls this "desert-adjusted intrinsic attitudinal hedonism." Finally, he suggests that we also weight pleasure to capture the worthiness of the subject receiving the pleasure. In this way, hedonism can answer the third critique by saying that the value of a world is the sum of the *double* desert-adjusted values of the intrinsic attitudinal pleasures enjoyed and pains suffered in that world.

While Feldman's theory maintains an emphasis on a "mode of consciousness" as well-being, his three extensions to attitudinal hedonism seem to subsume the core themes from objective list and eudaimonic theories of wellbeing. He says (p. 17):

> Such things as excessive or deficient prior receipt, legal or moral "rights" to pleasure, hard work, virtue and vice etc. probably influence the extent to which someone deserves some pleasure.

Aristotelian accounts of well-being argue that these sorts of questions— "What is vice?," "Who is virtuous?," and so on—cannot be meaningfully answered with a hedonistic conception of wellbeing (Annas 2004). Feldman's hedonism escapes these critiques only by, in a sense, admitting them. He augments his hedonistic emphasis on pleasure with objective criteria about what *sort* of pleasure is good for an individual. Note that these criteria are not merely instrumental. The sort of pleasure that is intrinsically good for a person cannot be understood without recourse to these items.

An arguably more telling critique of hedonism comes from Haybron (2001). He directs his critique to hedonistic theories of happiness, but his logic applies to hedonistic theories of wellbeing as well. He argues that hedonism "does little more than skim the phenomenal surface off our emotional states" while missing the deeper character of wellbeing.[2] This deeper character includes the fact that wellbeing is dispositional. A well person might be suffering right now, but we would still say that they are "well in general." We would also predict them to be well in the future. These are clearly not matters of present mental state, nor can they be adequately described by the notion of a positive attitude.

---

[2] This critique seems particularly powerful when aimed at some of the early hedonic psychology conceptualizations of SWB, notably Kahneman's (1999) "objective happiness." This involved adding up someone's pleasure score over (moment-by-moment) time by taking an integral.

Despite these shortcomings, it is important to rescue from the hedonistic tradition the idea that pleasure has a role to play in wellbeing. Philosophers can be too categorical in this regard. It is possible for pleasure and pain to causally contribute to other conceptions of wellbeing, which makes teasing them apart from hedonism tricky. For example, sciatic pain might make someone irritable and impatient, undermining their mental state. Being unusually irritable and impatient in turn could affect their sense of self, which undermines their self-actualization and eudaimonic wellbeing. During episodes of sciatic pain, this individual might say that they are unwell (subjectivism), and one of their primary goals in life might be to rid themselves of sciatic pain (preference satisfaction). Even if the prudential good is not the sciatic pain itself, the pain is so entangled with wellbeing however you might want to conceive it that one is left with an unnecessarily impoverished understanding of well-being if one does not incorporate the pain somewhere. Haybron's (2001) point that happiness and wellbeing are *more than* the phenomenal surface of our emotional states is a good one, but it doesn't mean that the phenomenal surface isn't nonetheless an important aspect of wellbeing.

Subjectivist Theories

One of the most prominent subjectivist theories of wellbeing is Sumner's (1996) life satisfaction or "authentic happiness" theory. He provides a summary statement in the following passage (p. 172):

> [Happiness], we have found, can be equated with life satisfaction, which has both an affective component (experiencing the conditions of your life as fulfilling or rewarding) and a cognitive component (judging that your life is going well for you, by your standards for it). The best way of determining people's happiness levels is to ask them. . . . However, an individual's report will accurately reflect his perceived happiness only if it is relevant (focused on the prudential dimension of the value of his life), sincere (uninfluenced by the desire to maintain a particular social image), and considered (uncoloured by transitory feelings of elation or depression). The question then is whether happiness, as so measured, is identical to wellbeing. We have found two reasons for thinking that it is not: a person's self-evaluation may not be informed and may not be autonomous. In either case

it is inauthentic, in that it does not accurately reflect the subject's own point of view. Welfare therefore consists in authentic happiness, the happiness of an informed and autonomous subject. This theory of welfare as authentic happiness is clearly subjective.

The first thing to note in passing is that Sumner distinguishes between happiness and well-being. His definition of happiness is very close to the definition of SW-B: "*experiencing* the conditions of your life as fulfilling or rewarding" and "*judging* that your life is going well for you, by your standards for it." However, he is unequivocal that this happiness does not constitute well-being unless other criteria are met, namely "an informed and autonomous subject." Unlike SW-B scholars, subjectivist philosophers tend not to see happiness, wellbeing, and life satisfaction as interchangeable.

The second thing to note is that Sumner, like Feldman, subsumes other theories of wellbeing into his subjectivist account. The "affective component" of Sumner's theory is a form of sensory hedonism. The cognitive component is, as he says, clearly subjectivist. He then seems to incorporate objective list items. He is aware of this synthesis, saying (p. 175):

> The happiness theory resembles hedonism . . . in its endorsement of an experience requirement . . . [but because] it also incorporates an information requirement (as part of its condition of authenticity], it is a state-of-the-world theory.

The requirements of relevance, sincerity, consideration, information, and autonomy are all objective criteria; hence Sumner's theory is partially about states of the world (specifically of the person whose wellbeing is in question). I would note further that these concepts are difficult to understand deeply without engaging the eudaimonic tradition. One *becomes* informed via a process of learning that is described in eudaimonic accounts of self-actualization. Authenticity is also impossible unless one has integrated the various dimensions of one's personality. Clinical and developmental psychologists emphasize that most humans are compartmentalized, with internally inconsistent value systems (Harter 2012). Such individuals are not of one mind and so cannot be described as a unified "subject." Unsurprisingly, therapists tend to be among the most prominent advocates of eudaimonic accounts of wellbeing (Waterman 2013; Ryan and Deci 2017). Their perspective is informed by the *process* of therapy, wherein an authentic subject emerges after integration and learning eliminate compartmentalization. Fleshing out Sumner's account requires borrowing such eudaimonic ideas to explain how someone becomes authentic and informed.

Preference Satisfaction

The existence of compartmentalization and multiple selves undermines not just subjectivist theories like Sumner's but also preference satisfaction accounts. To understand why, we need to outline preference satisfaction accounts in a bit more detail. Such accounts have long recognized that the satisfaction of "bad" or "dumb" preferences is not wellbeing. For example, Harsanyi (1981, p. 311 n. 7) noted that consumers' "notorious irrationality" makes their "actual" preferences a poor guide to their wellbeing. He consequently argued that economics should instead consider their "true" preferences, which he defined as "the preferences that they *would* manifest under 'ideal conditions,' in possession of perfect information, and acting with perfect logic and care." The notion of "true" preferences has become controversial of late, as research in behavioral economics has demonstrated that preferences are highly sensitive to contextual factors like framing, priming, social cues, and seemingly trivial environmental adjustments like the size of cafeteria plates (Kahneman 2011). Experimental results suggest that what someone's "true" preferences are, as opposed to those created by various cognitive and behavioral "biases," is nigh on impossible to determine (Sugden 2018). Hausman (2015, sec. 10.4) consequently opts for the notion of "well-laundered" preferences instead. These are defined as those held by individuals who are "(i) self-interested, (ii) well-informed, (iii) evaluatively competent, (iv) free of deliberative defects, and (v) have complete and transitive preferences among all alternatives."

This is a highly idealized, almost mathematical definition. As such, it might be useful for thinking about prudential value, but it is impractical for individual people to apply to themselves or people they care about in their daily lives. Furthermore, despite being about individual preferences, it has little relevance to *subjective* wellbeing because the criteria for "good" or "choiceworthy" preferences are mostly objective—rational, self-interested, perfectly informed, et cetera. The definition is also highly unrealistic. People are not perfectly informed nor perfectly rational, and they are not a single unified "self" with well-ordered preferences that are more or less satisfied. Instead, humans comprise multiple, often incompatible selves that are sometimes harmonized over the life course through the process of self-actualization (described in chapter 9). Through self-actualization, individuals learn what preferences are "right" for them. These preferences become what might be called "agentic" preferences, ones that are *meaningfully* informed and reasonable. Fabian and Dold (2021) argue that the satisfaction of such preferences is an appropriate criterion for wellbeing in some policy settings. However, unless self-actualization is in a late stage, preferences are unlikely to be agentic and so it is questionable to assume that their satisfaction will in fact improve someone's wellbeing.

Tiberius (2018) provides a psychologically realistic notion of preferences that is compatible with these issues of multiple selves and highly relevant to SWB. She posits (p. 13) that "well-being consists in the fulfilment of an appropriate set of values over a lifetime." She goes on (p. 41) to define "appropriate" values as "(1) suited to our desires and emotions, (2) reflectively endorsed, and (3) capable of being fulfilled together over time . . . appropriate values are objects of relatively sustained and integrated emotions, desires, and judgements." I am highly sympathetic to Tiberius' account. Indeed, it is my preferred theory of prudential value. However, it is underexplicated in the sense that the *process* by which "appropriate" values are identified, affirmed, refined, and harmonized such that they integrate emotions, motivations, and judgments is lacking from her analysis. I try to provide it in my model of coalescence, but that model draws heavily on ideas and themes from hedonistic and eudaimonistic accounts of wellbeing. Among other things, I argue that appropriate values are substantially determined by nature fulfillment in the form of what psychologists call "self-concordance" of goals, and, further, that nature fulfillment is guided by affected signals. Tiberius seems to concur when she argues (p. 52) that "appropriate" values integrate emotions and motivations and are meaningfully circumscribed by "personality." As such, a person living a value-fulfilled life will also have eudaimonia, positive feelings, and a pleasant attitude toward that life. So it seems that the preference satisfaction account of SWB needs to fold in other theories of wellbeing as at least instrumentally *necessary* to wellbeing.

But if these things are *necessary*, then how meaningful is the intrinsic/instrumental distinction in this case? If positive emotions and nature fulfillment must be present in order for appropriate value fulfillment to occur, then how meaningful is it to locate prudential value in one of these rather than another, or all of them simultaneously? Think of it from a diagnostic point of view. A therapist or friend helping someone to achieve wellbeing would need to examine not just their values but also their "nature" or personality and emotions, because otherwise the "appropriateness" of those values is obfuscated. They could not give a holistic assessment of someone's wellbeing without reference to values, emotions, and nature. So in *practical terms* it seems that these things are *all* intrinsic to wellbeing. Why is one of them the "ultimate" object of concern if they are all interdependent? This diagnostic perspective seems especially relevant to Tiberius' theory because she is one of the blessed few philosophers who is explicitly interested in helping people to achieve wellbeing. If we are interested in giving practical advice with regard to wellbeing then we should rebalance our philosophical efforts toward the puzzle of how the necessary components of wellbeing fit together, instead of focusing almost exclusively on which of them is intrinsic rather than merely instrumental.

Objective List

Sumner's (1996, p. 175) principal criticism of objective list accounts is that they do not describe "what it means for a life to be going well not just in itself or from some other standpoint but *for its subject.*" While this is a strong critique of some objective list approaches like the Millennium Development Goals, other accounts are robust to it. This is because they borrow from mental state and subjectivist accounts to develop rich descriptions of what wellbeing feels like. For example, self-determination theory notes that integrated, authentic individuals report their behavior as largely intrinsically motivated and thus easy and fulfilling (Deci and Ryan 2000). Such individuals also have high levels of positive affect and vitality (see chapter 7 for a longer discussion). Self-discrepancy theory provides empirical evidence that self-concordant individuals report experiencing anxiety and depression infrequently while experiencing positive affective states like exhilaration, confidence, and satisfaction relatively more frequently (Silvia and Eddington 2012). The eudaimonic individual will also experience flow more frequently (Csikszentmihalyi 1992). This is the feeling of being "in the zone" or "lost in the moment." Now, it is important to note that these theories do not locate wellbeing within these feelings. For self-determination theory, for example, wellbeing consists in living in a way that nourishes our basic psychological needs for autonomy, competence, and relatedness. Affect, satisfaction, and vitality are symptoms or indicators of this wellbeing but not constitutive of it.

Along with some description of how wellbeing feels for a subject, recent objective list and eudaimonic accounts also tend to borrow subjectivist theories of ethics. This is to respond to long-standing critiques of eudaimonic wellbeing in the Aristotelian tradition. In his conception of eudaimonic wellbeing, Aristotle argued that wellbeing can only be achieved by living in accordance with certain values. Specifically, individuals must be reasonable, virtuous, and perfect their nature (Annas 1998). These claims have come in for heavy criticism owing to the seeming arbitrariness of singling out these particular values. Invoking Hursthouse (1999) and Kraut (2009), DeYoung and Tiberius (2021) observe that "Aristotelians have accepted that the conception of human nature at the heart of their theories must rest on value judgements." Additionally, Haybron (2008), among others, has noted that perfection in the form of fulfilling one's nature is an aesthetic quality rather than a moral one, and certainly has nothing phenomenologically in common with wellbeing. For example, Floyd Mayweather is very close to a perfect boxer, but he is also a wife beater and hardly a moral paragon.

Some non-classical eudaimonic accounts of wellbeing dispense with this notion of objective values. Examples include existentialism (Sartre and Beauvoir 1946) and Norton's neo-Aristotelianism (Norton 1976). They take as one of their foundational assumptions the idea that *norms are inherently and inescapably subjective.* Indeed, they argue that creating and affirming one's *subjective* values is the only way to achieve eudaimonia. External normative standards are a threat to this process (Nietzsche [1886] 1990). In so doing, these theories become hybrid theories combining elements from eudaimonic and subjectivist accounts. They establish objective *ends* that must be met for an individual to achieve the *experience* of wellbeing, but the *means* by which these ends are acquired are subjective.

The emphasis on subjective values in this philosophical literature is also present in psychology schools that advocate a eudaimonistic perspective. Self-determination theory, for example, posits objective psychological needs that define wellbeing but also emphasizes the role of autonomy and being guided by one's intrinsic motivations in the achievement of wellbeing (Deci and Ryan 2000). It argues that objective normative standards could in many cases only be adhered to non-autonomously by way of extrinsic motivation and self-regulation. Far from producing wellbeing, this could lead to weariness, self-discrepancy, and neurosis.

By extension, these modern eudaimonisms argue that the individual must fulfill their unique, *individual nature*. "Human nature" is here understood not as belonging to the category "human" and perfecting the qualities of that category, such as reason. Instead, human nature is defined by something like the two existentialist maxims—"man is condemned to be free" and "for man, existence precedes essence" (Sartre and Beauvoir 1946). What these two maxims amount to is that we must choose who we want to be. Any attempt to escape from this ontological self-responsibility can only be sustained through self-deception, hence why the existentialists referred to such acts as "bad faith." Wellbeing in this eudaimonic tradition arises from actualizing an identity that is self-concordant (Sheldon 2013)—"know thyself" and "become who you are," to borrow the Hellenic maxims. Aristotle's emphasis on reason and the philosophical life is a product of the fact that *his* nature was defined by these things. Other people's natures will encourage different callings.

An Integrative Approach

The preceding analysis served two purposes. The first was to clarify the conceptual landscape. Prudential theory is a dense and challenging area, one that is not well understood outside of philosophical circles. At the very least, I hope the map I provided will help SW-B scholars identify where they fit and communicate more effectively with advocates of other schools of thought. The second purpose was to demonstrate that hybrid accounts of wellbeing (Woodard 2015), or something of that sort, seem increasingly necessary to understand the concept in all its richness. In the next few chapters, I elaborate a new hybrid account of SWB that is sensitive to prudential issues and utilizes Bishop's inclusive approach as a methodological stance. To differentiate my theory from others I refer to it by its two components. The *subjective wellbeing production function* (SWBPF) defines the components of SWB as an end. It is comparable to Bishop's "positive causal network." The left-hand-side variable is the flow state of SWB, which emerges once a positive causal network is fully realized. The right-hand-side variables are positive causal network "fragments" that must be present for SWB to permeate lived experience. They are necessary conditions for SWB, but it is their being networked that is the cause of SWB. The *coalescence of being* describes the eudaimonic process by which SWB is attained. By way of an introduction, I sketch both the SWBPF and coalescence below. I also draw out some key implications for prudential theory to bookend the analysis in the first half of this chapter. I then elaborate the SWBPF in detail across chapters 4–8. The coalescence of being is the topic of chapter 9.

The Subjective Well-Being Production Function

The notion of a production function is borrowed from economics, where it is used to express in mathematical terms what determines the output of a firm. The most common form of the production function is the Cobb-Douglas production function, which is as follows:

$$Q = AK^{\alpha}L^{\beta}$$

where
Q = quantity of output
K = capital (i.e., machinery)
L = labor
A = the productivity of labor and capital (i.e., "total factor productivity")
and α and β are parameters that capture the rate at which the marginal product of capital and labor respectively diminish.

The production function approach to wellbeing would similarly involve specifying some mathematical model of what factors contribute to increasing someone's SWB, to wit:

$$SWB = f(.)$$

I begin to populate this function in what follows.

Looking across the full breadth of research into SWB, three broad themes emerge. These are whether life is pleasant, whether it is fulfilling, and whether it is valuable.[3] These three themes point to a very general, first-order specification of the wellbeing production function. Call the idea that SWB is about a pleasant life the hedonic dimension of SWB. Fixtures of this dimension

[3] The Japanese concept of *ikigai* also incorporates all three of these dimensions of wellbeing (Matthews 2008).

include the primary concerns of hedonic psychology: a balance of positive over negative affect and hedonic satisfaction. Hedonic satisfaction is an evaluation of the *pleasurableness* of life. It is distinct from *existential* satisfaction, which concerns how valuable and fulfilling life is. Lester Burnham, the protagonist of the film *American Beauty*, is high in hedonic life satisfaction but low in existential satisfaction. He is wealthy and comfortable owing to his business success but suffers from ennui and despair owing to a sense of purposelessness and alienation from his family.

Hedonia is commonly contrasted with eudaimonia. I follow this trend and use eudaimonia to describe the cluster of variables that take in whether life is fulfilling. For this cluster I draw on the literature from eudaimonic psychology, specifically the three basic psychological needs emphasized by self-determination theory (Deci and Ryan 2000): autonomy, relatedness, and competence. Autonomy concerns how volitional you are in your decisions and the extent to which your behavior is intrinsically motivated. Competence concerns the extent to which you are instrumentally good at the things you care about. And relatedness concerns the quality of your social ties to people and groups you care about.

I call the final dimension conscience because it is concerned with feelings pertaining to virtue and morality, meaning, and identity, all of which are bound up with conscience. Virtue, meaning, and identity map onto the three principal concerns of existentialist philosophy: nausea, seriousness, and anguish. Nausea concerns whether life is meaningful and purposeful, seriousness whether one's ethics are experienced as authoritative and binding, and anguish whether one has a clear sense of self that effectively guides decision making. These themes were prominent in early continental psychology (Frankl [1946] 2008) and also appear in the writings of more recent positive psychologists (Baumeister 1992; Ryff 1989b; Seligman 2011). I use virtue, meaning, and identity rather than the bleaker language of existentialism because this makes all the variables in the SWBPF positively connoted. You want higher scores in everything. Virtue, meaning, and identity are also more expansive terms than seriousness, nausea, and anguish, as I will explain in chapter 8.

Putting these factors together, we arrive at a specification of the subjective wellbeing production function (SWBPF) that is sufficient for our needs for the time being:

$$SWB = f\left(Hedonia, Eudaimonia, Conscience\right)$$

And in turn,

$$Hedonia = g\left(positive\ affect, negative\ affect, hedonic\ satisaction\right)$$

$$Eudaimonia = h\left(autonomy, competence, relatedness\right)$$

$$Conscience = k\left(identity, meaning, virtue\right)$$

This specification of the wellbeing production function is obviously intended as a sketch. Other authors have advocated for demarcations different from the one I am proposing. Baumeister (1992), for example, places much of what I have under the headings of "eudaimonia" and "conscience" under the single heading of "meaning." I defend my specification over the course of the following chapters.

In the next section I outline the role self-actualization plays in satisfying all three of hedonia, eudaimonia, and conscience. This is not to suggest that self-actualization is some sort of meta-strategy for SWB that subsumes all others. There is a lot of value in studying strategies appropriate to the acquisition of any one of the dimensions of wellbeing, such as Sheldon et al.'s (2013) hedonic adaptation prevention model. I discuss such techniques throughout the book. Rather, it is to show how important self-actualization is independently for the acquisition of SWB, the extent to which the three dimensions of SWB are interrelated and interdependent, and the usefulness of adopting an integrative and practical perspective.

The Coalescence of Being

The coalescence of being is a model of self-actualization. Its core comes from self-discrepancy theory (Higgins 1987). Over the life course, you try to harmonize your "actual self" with your "ideal self" and "ought self." Your actual self is who you are now, including the things that you value and the things you find intrinsically motivating and pleasurable. Your ideal self is who you would like to be, and your ought self is who you have a responsibility to be.

Your ideal self can be crudely conceptualized as a constellation of values and their associated behaviors with which you *identify*. This means that you value them but do not necessarily have much intrinsic motivation

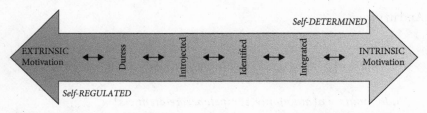

Figure 3.1 The motivation spectrum according to self-determination theory

toward pursuing them. The ought self is similar, but the values therein are specifically *ethical* values. According to the motivation spectrum of self-determination theory (SDT; Deci and Ryan 2000), "identification" is an autonomous rather than controlled form of motivation. It is relatively extrinsic in that self-regulation is required to pursue identified activities, but they can become more intrinsically motivated over time through the process of "internalization." SDT posits a spectrum of motivation running from extrinsic at one end to intrinsic at the other, depicted graphically in figure 3.1. The more extrinsically motivated a behavior, the more self-*regulation* it requires. The individual must exert willful control to conduct the activity. In contrast, the more intrinsically motivated an activity, the more self-*determined* it is. The individual will undertake the activity organically. Duress is the most extreme form of extrinsic motivation. The other principal class of extrinsically motivated behaviors is those that are introjected. This means that they are done for rewards contingent to the activity itself, such as parental approval. Unlike duress or introjection, identified behaviors are somewhat intrinsically motivated because the activity itself is valued, but some self-regulation is still required.

The spectrum of motivation can be illustrated with the example of exercise. Someone who pursues swimming because of parental pressure has *introjected* it. In contrast, many people value health and pursue activities, such as swimming, as a means of maintaining their health. Health here is *identified*. This identification provides some intrinsic motivation, but swimming for the unskilled and unfit will still be arduous and require willpower. People must push themselves to the end of their training sessions, for example. Swimming here retains an element of self-regulation even as an identified behavior. As such identified behaviors become assimilated into the self they start to connect to other values. For example, one might join a triathlon club to help with swimming. This will associate swimming with other values for community groups and athletic competitions. In this way, swimming becomes *integrated*, which is the stage of internalization before intrinsic motivation. Connections between swimming and a variety of identified and intrinsically motivated values and behaviors will make it feel more authentic and increase motivation over time. Eventually, swimming may even become entirely intrinsically motivated.

The basic idea in self-discrepancy theory is that you should *identify* who you want to be with the help of your innate motivational compass and then try to become that person. You must also negate the "feared self"—the individual you especially do not want to be (Silvia and Eddington 2012). This idea is reminiscent of the Hellenic maxim, repeated by Nietzsche and Norton, "become who you are." The process by which you bring your actual self into accord with your ideal self is guided by affective signals that accompany what the existentialists called the "disclosure of being." This is where *who you are* in reality is revealed to you in your actions or the observations of others. For example, if you desire to be fit and consequently swim one kilometer, this indicates to you that you are somewhat fit. You will experience positive affect as a result because you are revealed by your actions to be closer to who you ideally want to be. As you swim farther, faster, and more frequently, you will more thoroughly confirm this observation that you are fit, and this will make you happy and enhance your SWB.

If you do not complete the one-kilometer swim, this will result in negative affect (Silvia and Eddington 2012). There are a few ways to interpret this negative affective signal. If you are *depressed* because you didn't complete your objective, you may need to redouble your efforts. However, if you are instead *disenchanted* by swimming, it might simply be that swimming doesn't suit you—it is not in accordance with your "true self" (Sheldon 2002).[4] Your self (or daimon) is communicated to you by the degree of motivation you experience for certain values and activities and the corresponding affective signals you receive when undertaking those activities and affirming those values. Now, if *fitness* is core to your personality but swimming is not a self-concordant way to achieve fitness, you just need to find a more suitable sport. However, it could be that fitness itself is the unsuitable value, in which case you may need to abandon it. Qualitative differences in affective signals can

[4] Note that the conceptualization of a true self in self-determination theory and the coalescence of being is very limited. It corresponds principally to innate dispositions and talents. This is very different from notions of the true self in Aristotelian writings, notably that of Norton (1976), which tend to invoke a more richly realized personality. I discuss the notion of a true self in more detail in chapters 8 and 9.

communicate these nuances to you. For example, if swimming is boring but you feel a sense of achievement when your lap times improve, then swimming is likely the problem rather than fitness. In contrast, if you feel only apathy toward both swimming and its physical effects, then fitness is likely the wrong value for you. Perhaps you have introjected it under social pressure.

To correctly interpret your affective signals, you will need to do some introspection and rationally engage with your feelings (see Tiberius 2008 for a discussion of what this introspection might be like). This introspection is a major theme in narrative therapy (McAdams and Janis 2004) and some cognitive behavioral therapy exercises. It is also fundamental to the other great Hellenic maxim: "know thyself."

This process of harmonizing the actual and ideal selves through iterative engagement with the world and introspection is similar for the ought self, which concerns specifically ethical values. Perhaps you identify with recycling because you think that the world has finite resources and we should protect them for future generations. Recycling takes a bit of effort initially as you learn to sort your rubbish and motivate yourself to carry your loads to the neighborhood recycling bins, but it gradually becomes easy. You get a warm feeling from recycling that makes the effort worthwhile, and you integrate the trip to the bins into your weekly grocery run. You also start to organize with local groups to make recycling more straightforward and the community more aware of its benefits. Local government follows through on your suggestions, and the world is now a little bit more the way you'd like it to be.

Now imagine that one day you are watching a documentary on television that shows how glass recycling takes more energy than it saves, and that the other resources involved, namely sand, are abundant (Munger 2013). You find it persuasive. At this point, you might need to adjust your recycling values to not include glass (or encourage glass reuse rather than recycling), and this might bring you into conflict with some of your old comrades in the neighborhood recycling group. Here, not only will you need to introspect about your own values, but you will also need to develop arguments, especially rational arguments, with which to convince your colleagues of your own views. This will force you to systematize your thinking about your own values. This provides some psychologically realistic texture to Aristotle's notion of living in accordance with reason.

The preceding is a simple explanation of coalescence using crude examples, but it already reveals how self-actualization brings about SWB. First, guided by your affective signals, you mostly do things that you find intrinsically enjoyable and gradually eliminate extrinsically motivated activities and values from your life. This achieves a *balance of positive over negative affect* as your behavior gradually comports toward positive affect and moves away from negative affect. It also nurtures your sense of *autonomy*. As you become good at these pursuits following sustained engagement in them, you feel increasingly *competent* at things that you care about. This is exhilarating and provides a source of self-esteem that makes you resilient to depression and anxiety, thereby fostering your emotional wellbeing.

You also pursue ethical values that you find intrinsically attractive This is likely to bring you *meaning* and give you *purpose* because you are making the world a better place according to your own evaluation. You pursue these values because you want to be the kind of person who lives in accordance with them. This pursuit requires integrity and virtue, because without them you will constantly stray from your values and fail to live up to your ought self. As you pursue your values (ideal self) and try to make the world a better place (ought self) you necessarily come across and socialize with other people who share your values. You might even organize with them to oppose groups with antithetical values. This nurtures your need for *relatedness*. This process of self-actualization also sees you come to better understand yourself gradually because of the disclosures of being that you witness, the introspection and rational analysis of yourself that you undertake, and the emotional signals that you get from yourself. The result is that you come to know and be who you are, which gives *identity*. All the different dimensions of wellbeing have been accounted for: hedonia, eudaimonia, and conscience. Incidentally, we also see how self-actualization brings us to the fulfillment of Tiberius' (2018) "appropriate" values, which integrate emotions, motivations, and cognitions.

Finally, substantial progress in coalescence promotes the emergence of flow across many domains of conscious experience. The key criteria for flow are intrinsic motivation, a highly challenging task, the necessary skill to complete that task, and high-quality feedback. Pursuing self-concordant activities means that your day is filled mostly with intrinsically motivated activities. Calibration of ideal and ought self goals to be desirable but also achievable within the parameters of the actual self ensures that the individual has the requisite capability to achieve these otherwise challenging goals. Deepening one's mindfulness, metacognition, self-awareness, and introspective skills ensures that one derives high-quality feedback from life experiences. All the conditions for flow are thus met, and *across many day-to-day activities*. This is the "generalized flow state" of SWB, but it can only be achieved through coalescence, which is intimately bound up with the nine items of the SWBPF. Coalescence calibrates the various elements of the SWBPF such that they become networked and give rise to SWB. I will say more about the precise nature of generalized flow in chapter 9.

Preliminary Implications for Prudential Theory

It is possible to draw two important implications for prudential theory from the sketch of the SWBPF and coalescence of being just presented. First, self-actualization promotes all the different dimensions of the SWBPF and is implicated in wellbeing regardless of which definition of well-being you prefer. It deserves more attention from philosophers, as does the notion of applied wellbeing theory more generally. Philosophers should devote relatively more thinking not just to what wellbeing is but also to how you get it.

Second, engaging with self-actualization reveals interrelationships between the different accounts of wellbeing. For example, coalescence addresses the conscience dimension through the pursuit of values and goals with integrity. At first, the conscience dimension might not seem to have much to do with hedonistic emotions like exhilaration or enjoyment. Yet coalescence is guided by affective signals that include these and many other emotions, like despondency, euphoria, alienation, belonging, melancholy, glee, enchantment, and joy. Conscience and hedonia are thus interrelated. Similar things can be said for the basic psychological needs that make up the eudaimonia dimension. Pursuing activities that are intrinsically motivated and bring us into contact with groups that share our values helps us to feel *autonomous*, *related* to people we care about, and, ultimately, *competent*. Yet we rely on affective signals to help us sense whether we are undertaking an intrinsically motivated activity or a self-regulated one. We also require notions from the conscience dimension to understand our values and thereby help us to identify comrades. The dimensions are again interrelated.

It might seem like the affective dimension is the critical one here, as it is the guide to the deeper dimensions, but the relationship goes both ways. It is hard to understand why we feel good or bad about specific behaviors, values, and groups without drawing on the eudaimonic and conscience dimensions. For example, perhaps we enjoy videogaming with friends in the moment, but the next day we feel like we wasted that time. We have mixed emotional signals here to make sense of. Introspection might reveal that our ought self thinks we should dedicate more time to personally expressive or ethical activities, but our basic psychological need for relatedness is well nourished by gaming with friends. We see here that while affective signals guide our value fulfillment, we reason through our affective signals with reference to the aspects of eudaimonia and conscience that give rise to most of those values. As such, a narrow focus on the hedonic dimension of wellbeing would miss crucial issues related to the causation and intrinsic nature of wellbeing.

What sort of theory is my theory of SWB? The "generalized flow state" of SWB fits uneasily within a hedonistic notion of wellbeing because it is not a purely "mental" state and because other accounts of wellbeing are present in fundamental and inextricable ways. Coalescence is obviously a eudaimonic account of wellbeing because it emphasizes a prudent way of living and a kind of nature fulfillment in self-actualization through the harmonization of the actual, ideal, and ought selves into a self-concordant identity. Coalescence also places a strong emphasis on classical hedonistic tropes of pleasure and pain in the form of affective signals. You will also need to satisfy your preferences in order to achieve coalescence—these can be understood as the high-level goals inherent to the ideal and ought selves, which inform lower-level goals in minute detail (more in chapter 9). These preferences will initially be unclear to you and may even be wrong. Hence you will be inauthentic when you express them. However, as coalescence proceeds and you come to know thyself and become who you are, you will discard self-discordant preferences and refine self-concordant ones through introspection. Your preferences will thereby become "appropriate," as described by Tiberius (2018) in her value fulfillment theory of wellbeing. Fulfilling these values will make you satisfied with your life in a considered, authentic, and autonomous way, as in Sumner's subjectivist theory of wellbeing. You will need to live in accordance with reason because rational introspection is required to understand your affective signals. Rational reflection is also critical to resolve compartmentalization and inconsistencies in your identity. Similarly, you will also be a virtuous individual because without commitment to your ought self you will be unable to satisfy your conscience. Here we see themes from Aristotelian accounts.

Philosophers could sharpen my logic and perhaps identity exactly what sort of theory I am proposing, but I would suggest that this is at best a low-value exercise. The operative question is whether I have presented a good theory of SWB. Which category it fits into (and what categories are available to choose from) is of secondary importance. I have explicitly adopted the inclusive approach, so my aim is primarily to explain as much of the gamut of wellbeing scholarship as possible, rather than to demonstrate the superiority of one class of wellbeing theories over others. It is similarly of low value to debate where in my theory prudential value obtains—is it in the right-hand-side variables of the SWBPF, or the left-hand-side variables, or the prudential process of coalescence? It seems to me that the answer is all of them. Following Bishop (2015) and his network theory of wellbeing, I contend that PCN fragments have prudential value, as does a more or less actualized PCN, as does the process by which fragments are formed and joined up in the overall network. If all of these things are necessary for wellbeing, then we should seek to understand all of them holistically.

The Way Forward

The first half of this chapter pried open some space in the analytical philosophy of wellbeing for a new theory of SWB that is sensitive to prudential issues. I argued for a modification of the traditional criteria for judging the merit of a theory of wellbeing, namely descriptive, normative, and empirical adequacy. Philosophers have an implicit hierarchy wherein descriptive and normative adequacy are more important than empirical adequacy, and they judge a theory of wellbeing predominantly by whether it decisively resolves our commonsense judgments about what wellbeing is. I advocated instead for the inclusive approach, which comes from a philosophy-of-science point of view. It argues that a theory of wellbeing should be judged by its explanatory power. How many of the descriptive, normative, and empirical issues in wellbeing research can it make sense of? Adopting the vantage point of the inclusive approach, it is easy to see overlaps and complementarities between the various theories of wellbeing proposed by philosophers, especially in recent articulations wherein each theory borrows heavily from others. This doesn't mean that they are all good theories of wellbeing, but it does suggest that we could learn a lot by trying to integrate these theories rather than always differentiating them.

The second half of the chapter then sketched a theory that attempts precisely such an integration. It has two parts: the subjective wellbeing production function (SWBPF) and the coalescence of being. The first part is model of wellbeing as outcome: well-*being*. The second part is a model of the prudential way of achieving wellbeing. That is, a model of well-*living*.

Historically, theories of the prudential good have tended to emphasize either living or being. The hybrid account in the SWBPF/coalescence model is the first I have encountered that explicitly combines these two perspectives (though the account in Martela and Sheldon 2019 is close). The SWB state can only be successfully achieved through coalescence. However, coalescence does not on its own provide an account of the state of wellbeing—this requires the SWBPF. Both components are therefore necessary to give a full account of the prudential good. The next six chapters elaborate the elements of this two-part model in much greater detail.

4

The Subjective Wellbeing Production Function

> My soul is like a hidden orchestra; I do not know which instruments
> grind and play away inside me, strings and harps, timbales and
> drums. I can only recognise myself as symphony.
>
> —Fernando Pessoa, *The Book of Disquiet*

Introduction

This chapter outlines the subjective wellbeing production function
(SWBPF) in full. Chapters 5 through 8 then justify and explain each of its
constitutive elements in greater detail. I discuss in turn the capabilities of
constraint, hedonia, eudaimonia, and conscience, drawing extensively on
the relevant literatures in development studies, psychology, philosophy,
and economics.

Before continuing, I'd like to address a concern that some readers might
have at this stage that this project of developing a holistic model of wellbeing
is ambitious; indeed, overly ambitious given the state of our existing empirical understanding of wellbeing. On the one hand, I am sympathetic to this
perspective. When theory gets too far ahead of empirical confirmation it
opens the possibility of ultimately wasted effort when a large body of theoretical work is later refuted by empirical findings. On the other hand, I see a lot
of value is outlining a general theory of SWB for two reasons.

First, there is plenty of potential for wasted *empirical* effort when different branches of a research program are not coordinated and lack a
shared language. This is a risk for wellbeing scholarship because of its wide
interdisciplinary scope. There are currently several streams of research
that don't talk to each other much if at all. If they do communicate more

A Theory of Subjective Wellbeing. Mark Fabian, Oxford University Press. © Oxford University Press 2022.
DOI: 10.1093/oso/9780197635261.003.0005

in the future, researchers in each stream might discover that their work runs counter to a body of knowledge in some other silo. An example is Annas' (2004) paper on classical philosophical perspectives on happiness. This piece was prompted by an email notifying her that she had been included in the World Happiness Database (Veenhoven 1995), which is a repository of research in SW-B. Upon perusing that resource, Annas felt that Aristotelian perspectives were unrepresented in it. This concerned her because these Aristotelian perspectives called SW-B claims into question yet were unaddressed by SW-B scholars.

Second, there are numerous examples in other areas of social science research where the statement of a general theory aided the investigation of branches of that general theory and helped them to feed findings back into the trunk. An illustrative case is inquiry into the nature of the education production function. Several decades ago, the Coleman Report (1966) proposed that education was a function of student characteristics like general intelligence and effort, school characteristics like teacher quality and class sizes, household characteristics like income and parental conflict, and neighborhood characteristics like socio-economic status and culture. At the time, the effects size of each of these domains was ambiguous and the precise form of the education production function was unclear. Nonetheless, the statement of the entirety of the function clarified the research landscape and illuminated, among other things, what interrelationships might exist between relevant variables. This clarification at the aggregate or meta level was helpful to empirical scholarship of individual variables like the impact of school infrastructure on education outcomes (Hanushek 1986).

I am attempting something similar here with the subjective wellbeing production function. I lay out a general theory in the hopes that it will guide more specialized inquiry and help to feed results back into a general theory. While the theory I develop is derived from empirical findings, I present the SWBPF only as a hypothesis. Empirical work will be required to test its claims. How to go about this empirical work is the topic of chapter 10.

This chapter begins with the first-order structural equation of the SWBPF. It then discusses the second-order structural equations for each variable in the first-order structural equation. With the key variables thus specified, the chapter turns to discuss important parameters, namely emotional wellbeing, nihilism, personality, and reference points.

Structural Equations of the Subjective Wellbeing Production Function

Figure 4.1 shows the basic setup of the SWBPF. It depicts SWB as a function of three variables: hedonia, eudaimonia, and conscience. These correspond to whether life is pleasant, whether it is fulfilling, and whether it is valuable, respectively. Hedonia is in turn a function of positive affect, negative affect, and *hedonic* satisfaction. In the SW-B literature, positive and negative affect are widely regarded as being two separate spectrums rather than a single bipolar "mood" variable (Tugade and Fredrickson 2004; Kuppens et al. 2008). For example, you can be simultaneously in a state of high positive affect, such as exhilaration while watching the latest Hollywood action movie, and negative affect, such as stress at your impending deadlines. As such, positive and negative affect enter the model as separate terms.

Hedonic satisfaction refers to how pleasant you evaluate your life as being. Note that hedonic life satisfaction is distinct from *existential* satisfaction, which is captured by the eudaimonia and conscience terms. As such, for "life satisfaction" or some similar term to constitute a global measure of SWB it would need to capture both hedonic and existential satisfaction. You can evaluate your life as pleasant while still being unsatisfied with it and/or generally unwell. For example, your typical OECD university student of middle-class background afflicted with nihilism (see chapter 8) might say that they "can't complain" about their life because they are healthy, safe, comfortable,

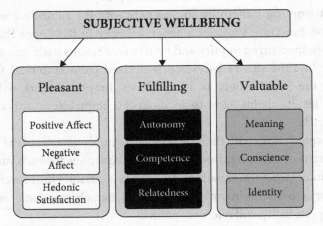

Figure 4.1 The subjective wellbeing production function

and entertained. They are high in hedonic life satisfaction. However, they may also feel lonely, empty, purposeless, dislocated, and unmotivated. They are low in existential satisfaction.

Eudaimonia *in the SWBPF* is a function of the three basic psychological needs emphasized by self-determination theory: autonomy, competence, and relatedness. Autonomy refers to how volitional one feels in one's behavior, competence to how capable one is at things one cares about, and relatedness to the depth of one's social ties to people one cares about. I say "in the SWBPF" for two reasons. First, eudaimonic accounts of well-being are characterized by an emphasis on living well, whereas the SWBPF is a model of being well. The second reason is that philosophical accounts of eudaimonia typically associate it with normative issues like virtue and rationality. The three basic psychological needs of SDT are only tangentially associated with normative issues. Eudaimonia is nonetheless an appropriate label for this dimension of SWB because self-determination theory self-identifies as a eudaimonic account of wellbeing explicitly in contrast to hedonic accounts (Ryan et al. 2008; Waterman 2008; Kashdan et al. 2008), and because self-determination theory contains many elements common to eudaimonic theories of wellbeing (Besser-Jones 2015). Basic psychological needs and intrinsic motivation play a central role in the coalescence of being, so the full SWBPF/coalescence model retains SDT's emphasis on living well.

Conscience is a function of meaning, virtue, and identity. These terms are heavily influenced by existentialist philosophy, especially its concepts of nausea, seriousness, and anguish. Existentialism was the first body of philosophical work to seriously investigate the loss of meaning and morality that followed the decline of religious and rural life in Europe during the industrial revolution. What Nietzsche called the "death of God" left behind what Frankl ([1946] 2008) calls an "existential vacuum." Without some notion of a cosmic order, people came to see their lives as pointless and their ethical system as without basis. As I will discuss in chapter 8 with reference to recent empirical research, such vacuums make people psychologically unwell. The existentialists developed an embryonic theory of self-actualization that could provide meaning and morality with a seriousness that they seem to lack in a secular world (Reginster 2009). The coalescence of being is an extension of this embryonic model. Fundamental to any theory of self-actualization is identity—a firm grasp of who you are and what you stand for. Adding identity to purpose and morality gives the three items of the conscience dimension: meaning, virtue, and identity.

Model Parameters

There are two important parameters that affect one of the first-order variables of the SWBPF. These are emotional wellbeing, which parameterizes hedonia, and nihilism, which parameterizes eudaimonia. There are two additional parameters that affect the entire SWBPF. These are personality and relative status effects. I will first discuss parameters that reflect the interrelationships between the three dimensions of wellbeing before turning to personality and reference group effects. These parameters determine how the variables of the SWBPF interact as a system.

I use the term "parameter" deliberately. These are not constraints. A parameter is a factor that sets the conditions of a system's operation. In this case, that system is the SWBPF. Parameters are perhaps most easily understood mathematically. For example, in the Cobb-Douglas production function, $Q = AK^{\alpha}L^{\beta}$, α and β are parameters, whereas Q (quantity), A (productivity), K (capital), and L (labor) are variables. The variables constitute the system, while the parameters play some deterministic role in how it operates. I have declined to provide a full mathematical specification for the SWBPF and its parameters because this should be revealed through empirical investigation utilizing flexible functional forms. I do not want to get bogged down in the details of these here.

Emotional Wellbeing

Hedonia is parameterized by emotional wellbeing, which is a function of eudaimonia, conscience, and attention. Emotional wellbeing refers in this case not to your present emotional state, which is captured by the affect variables, but to your emotional *disposition*. Emotional wellbeing was implicit in the discussion in chapter 3 of Haybron's (2008) critique of hedonism. It captures, among other things, your tendency toward depression, the resilience of your good moods to negative shocks, optimism versus pessimism, hope, and other factors that affect the volatility and *dynamics* of your mood—its tendencies in terms of stability and change.

Emotional wellbeing has two broad parametric effects. The first is that if your emotional wellbeing is low, you will struggle to achieve a high degree of positive affect and a low degree of negative affect. Low scores on eudaimonia and conscience are associated with depression and it is hard to put a depressed person into a good mood, even with things that have in the past elicited a strong positive affective response from them. Or consider another example: someone who has low self-esteem (an affective state) because they feel incompetent (an aspect of eudaimonia) will be hard to cure of their low self-esteem by way of mood interventions. The source or cause of the low self-esteem, namely that person's belief that they are incompetent, will need to be addressed first.

The second parametric effect of emotional wellbeing is that it affects the speed of adaptation of mood to negative and positive shocks. The lower someone's emotional wellbeing, the faster they will return to a low baseline following positive shocks. The effect of negative shocks will also be more persistent. Consider someone who is anxious because they have recently contradicted, in a grievous way, the morality they are trying to affirm as part of their ought self. Taking this person out dancing might distract them for a few hours, but the anxiety will rapidly return until the object of their guilt is addressed. Individuals low in eudaimonia and conscience will have transient and fragile good moods.

Emotional wellbeing is a function of eudaimonia and conscience because the affective signals such people receive from day to day will frequently draw their attention to their unmet psychological needs or the urgency of living according to serious values that define an identity and provide purpose in life. They will consequently have little cognitive ability to focus on potential sources of good mood and the things in their life that they find pleasing.

Alongside eudaimonia and conscience, the other principal component of emotional wellbeing is attention. Attention in this context is a catchall for various cognitive-behavioral strategies for managing mood. One is the very straightforward idea that focusing your attention on the positive things in your life will put you in a better mood than focusing on the negative things (Dolan 2014). This is the literal meaning of "attention" and forms a core part of the hedonic adaptation prevention model (Armenta et al. 2014). Other techniques in this suite come overwhelmingly from research in hedonic psychology and include savoring, gratitude, humility, and other positive activity interventions that I discuss in chapter 6. Finally, attention includes maintaining a positive and optimistic attitude where reasonable, which helps to avoid learned helplessness (Seligman 1992).

Nihilism

Eudaimonia is parameterized by nihilism. This is a cognitive state wherein the individual finds it difficult to make the psychic movement toward transcendence. In existential philosophy, transcendence involves creating meaning and identity and experiencing one's values as serious (Beauvoir [1949] 2011). The cynical worldview at the heart of nihilism, which perceives the world and life as *objectively* (as opposed to subjectively or intersubjectively) pointless, may well be factually accurate (religions of course disagree, but it is hard to assess their claims factually). Nihilism is hard to escape once you have succumbed to it because it is not irrational. Transcending nihilism requires the individual to bring meaning and value into the world and thereby define their identity. This requires some conviction that the things the individual does "matter" (in the sense that they have a point) simply because the individual "cares" about them (Heidegger [1927] 1962). But this care is always under assault from the nihilistic instinct that things aren't worth caring about because everything turns to dust in the end. The extent to which these instincts dominate conscious attention is what is captured by the nihilism parameter.

It is worth noting that most people do not suffer from nihilism. They are held up out of it by culture and other mechanisms that socialize us into value systems and identities that are palpable enough to stave off nihilism (Peterson 1999). Nihilism is on the march lately in the West, reaching a peak in the postmodern 1990s, because many traditional sources of normative order have dissolved in the last two centuries. The existentialists identified the roots of twentieth-century European nihilism in the decline of religiosity during the Enlightenment and industrial revolution (Nietzsche [1891] 1978). This was compounded by the emergence of atomizing metropolises that replaced the thick and tight cultural systems of rural, communitarian life (Simmel [1903] 1950). The First World War and Great Depression then swept away much residual order in economic and geopolitical life. The traditional sources of socialization into palpable normative systems were weakened in the space of a mere century or so. Totalitarianism, whether fascism or communism, with its clearly defined normative codes, penchant for grand demonstrations of social solidarity in parades and the like, and organization of individual life through work groups, party clubs, and central planning, seductively filled this vacuum (Jung [1928] 1933; Fromm [1941] 1994).

A similar phenomenon is arguably taking place today, especially in the United States (Fabian et al. 2020). The end of the Cold War and the slow death of the War on Terror with their clear ideological enemies, the decline of regional towns as a result of globalization and automation, the free-fall decline of religious belief, and the collapse of traditional gender roles all point to a normative vacuum. The evidence is in the growing polarization of American society, especially between the values of rural and urban America. An existential crisis is brewing. People are desperate for identity, especially group identity, hence the rise of identity politics and racialized economics (Sides et al. 2018). They are also desperate for normative seriousness, hence the political animosity and the wildfire popularity of Canadian psychoanalyst turned culture war commentator Jordan Peterson, who speaks directly to nihilistic themes—the subtitle of his most popular book is "an antidote to chaos" (Flanagan 2018). Finally, they are desperate for community and social identity, but these depend in part on shared values that have dissolved (Hochschild 2016; Carney 2019; Putnam 2001; Putnam and Romney Garrett 2020). Nihilism did not affect the United States so much in the past, which explains the relatively light engagement with it to date. It will become a bigger issue in the coming decades.

Nihilism undermines the acquisition of each of the three components of eudaimonia: autonomy, competence, and relatedness. Most obviously, it undermines the veracity and authority of the normative systems that underpin groups. For example, a nihilist would struggle to see the value in organizing a protest movement because their normative quests appear subjective and ultimately meaningless. As a result of this nihilism, the ways in which we are "related" to each other come to feel arbitrary and fictitious.

A nihilistic individual can feel competent, but the power of this self-belief to give rise to feelings of wellbeing is undermined by the nagging question "What is the point in being competent at this?" The achievement of competence requires persistent effort in the same direction. Such motivation is hard to sustain in the face of nihilism.

The relationship between nihilism and autonomy is less straightforward. The existentialists argued that nihilism arises out of our ontological freedom (Sartre and Beauvoir 1946). Consciousness gives us a sense that we have free will. In the moment of decision, we perceive ourselves as completely at liberty from any kind of determinism. Not even a gun to our head or the threat of eternal hellfire takes away our capacity to choose the bullet or damnation.

Sometimes we don't know what to do with this freedom—we don't know what the correct choice is in a situation. Yet we also know that this decision will define who we are into the future. This is what the existentialists called "anguish." Anguish makes our autonomy salient, but it also cuts us off from identity and confronts us with the need to effectively justify our decisions. Anguish leads us to ask the question "Who is it that is making this decision? Who am I? What defines me?" A failure to answer these questions in a coherent and definitive manner undermines feelings of autonomy.

One might ask whether it would be more straightforward to parameterize eudaimonia with conscience rather than introducing the additional concept of nihilism. A high score in conscience helps to overcome nihilism, after all. Yet nihilism and conscience are distinct. You can be strong in the conscience dimension and still suffer from nihilism. Like emotional wellbeing, nihilism is a psychological tendency or disposition. An individual high in nihilism is fragile with regard to their sense of identity, virtue, and meaning and is prone to bouts of existential anxiety. You can also be high in conscience and low in nihilism. This describes most people raised in a thick normative system that they slot comfortably into, like many contemporary Japanese or Amish. The normative community provides values with a sense of seriousness, imbues daily life with meaningfulness, and socializes the individual into an identity that is valued and reinforced by the group. Slotting into this normative community grants a sense of competence and nourishes feelings of relatedness. Eudaimonia is promoted. Finally, you can be in the unfortunate state of being high in nihilism and low in conscience. The "suicidal nihilist" of popular culture (such as Batman's villain the Joker) is a clear example, but a less dramatic one is the midlife crisis.

Personality

There is a growing body of empirical evidence to suggest that personality has a strong effect on SW-B (De Neve and Cooper 1998; Steel et al. 2008). Individuals high in openness and extraversion have been repeatedly found to have more positive moods on average, while individuals high in neuroticism and introversion have more negative moods (Bouchard et al. 1990; Steel et al. 2008; Lucas and Diener 2009). Personality has also been found to play a mediating role in adaptation to changing circumstances. For example, individuals high in conscientiousness struggle to adapt to unemployment (Boyce et al.

2016). By extension, changes in personality over time can predict changes in SW-B. For example, individuals who become less conscientious while unemployed adapt faster to unemployment (Boyce et al. 2013; Boyce, Wood, Delaney, et al. 2017). Recent research exploring the link between hope and optimism has found that these qualities predict emotional wellbeing, SW-B, and long-run life outcomes, like sustained effort to exit poverty (Bailey et al. 2007; Hutz et al. 2014; Graham 2017). The complex interplay between personality, personality change, and SWB is only now becoming a topic of extended, in-depth inquiry, but if recent publication rates are any indication, this is a rich vein of research (Boyce, Wood, and Ferguson 2017).

Relative Status and Reference Group Effects

A final parameter to consider is how to model relative status effects. There is now an abundance of empirical evidence that suggests people care almost as much about their relative income as they do about their absolute income (Knight and Gunatilaka 2014; Frijters and Mujcic 2012; Clark, Frijters, et al. 2008). There is also a long history in sociology and anthropology of inquiry into more generalized "status anxiety" (Veblen 1899; Bourdieu 1979). Hedonic psychology and happiness economics have demonstrated that people's life evaluations are determined in part by comparisons to their neighbors (Brown et al. 2008; Bhuiyan 2018; Clark and Senik 2014b). This is one origin of the ubiquitous phenomenon of "keeping up with the Joneses." Relatedly, SW-B scholars have observed what Graham (2012) calls a "happy peasant and frustrated achiever" phenomenon. When the poor or otherwise marginalized compare themselves to other people in similar situations, their relative poverty does not burden them as much as it might affect a poor worker in a rich neighborhood. In contrast, people who exit poverty through hard work often report relatively lower levels of life satisfaction that those who remain poor. This is perhaps because they compare their present situation not to their poor origins but to the wealthy people they would like to be.

Relative status effects could also reasonably be expected to affect the eudaimonic variables of autonomy, competence, and relatedness. Autonomy is perhaps the most robust to reference effects, but it is not immune. I may perceive myself as less autonomous if I perceive others as having more opportunities than me, even if I can largely do what I want.

Competence is often measured relative to other people and verified by authoritative peers. Art is an extreme example. It is notoriously prone to trends and cliques, and one's reputation as an artist depends significantly on the opinion of others rather than on one's technical brilliance. Even in areas where competence can be more objectively benchmarked, like sports, reference points play a role. Professional athletes set a standard for competence, and the quality of your immediate sporting community will likely impact how you perceive your own ability.

The effect of relative status on relatedness can be understood through the lens of "popularity contests." One might have a good level of relatedness in absolute terms but be dissatisfied with it because in relative terms one is unpopular or not the queen bee. To lean on popular culture tropes, one might be an accepted member of the cheerleading squad, but because one is not the head cheerleader and dating one of the star players of the football team one feels dissatisfied with one's level of relatedness. Such sentiments are not healthy. They smack of extrinsic aspirations—goals that are pursued for reasons contingent to the associated activities, like fame, money, or status (Kasser and Ryan 1993, 1996). As discussed at length in chapters 7 and 8, the pursuit of extrinsic aspirations is negatively associated with psychological wellbeing and even their attainment is at best only weakly positively associated with psychological wellbeing. Regardless of whether it is healthy or not to care about popularity in this manner, people *do care*, and this affects their level of relatedness.

What about conscience? Values are typically sustained intersubjectively by communities, but this is distinct from a relative status effect. Relative status effects in this context refer to changing your assessment of your level of meaning, virtue, and identity because of how much of these things someone else has. One way this could manifest is feeling less value in your life because some other group (and its values) is flourishing more than your own. An example is growing rural resentment toward urban elites in the United States (Cramer 2016). Another is feelings of status threat among white Christians (Mutz 2018) and antipathy toward immigrants and people of color, who are perceived as less deserving of economic success (Hochschild 2016). Such sentiments have encouraged some groups to organize politically around certain identities (white, rural, etc.) to promote their values and justify the meanings they ascribe to their daily experiences.

In summary, it seems reasonable to conjecture that relative status exerts parametric effects on every dimension of the SWBPF. In the next section

I discuss the capabilities and information constraints. Individuals attempt to increase their subjective wellbeing subject to a constraint imposed by their capabilities and their knowledge of what would make them well. The coalescence of being is a model of how this knowledge is learned.

The Capabilities Constraint

In most SW-B scholarship, the conventional objectives of economic development are taken to exert a *causal* influence on life satisfaction (see, for example, Clark et al. 2018). I take a different view. I argue herein that income, health, education, political enfranchisement, environmental quality, and suchlike are a *constraint* on an individual's ability to achieve SWB, rather than a direct source of that SWB. This notion of a capabilities constraint is in keeping with Sen's (1999b) distinction between capabilities and functionings. Functionings are specific ways of being and doing—for example, being a mechanic who works on rally cars. They are particular lives. An individual's capabilities constitute the option set of functionings available to that individual. Increasing someone's capabilities opens new ways of being and doing, but these beings and doings only provide SWB if they are actualized. Capabilities thus allow you to achieve the things that give you SWB but they do not themselves provide SWB. This is the distinction I make between welfare and wellbeing. Someone's welfare is the sum of their capabilities. Their SWB is to be found in the functionings that they choose to manifest with these capabilities. Of course, if your capabilities constraint is binding in the sense that you lack the option to live the life best suited to you, then your SWB will suffer.

This notion of a capabilities constraint is essentially an elaboration or extension of the consumer problem in neoclassical microeconomics. Income in this literature is not a source of utility but rather something you need in order to purchase goods you prefer. It is these goods that are the actual cause of your utility. This idea can be extended beyond income to other broad capabilities. As your health improves, for example, your capabilities expand. Perhaps you are now able to run a marathon. However, unless you actually want to run a marathon, this has little effect on your SWB. So too for other capabilities, even things like political enfranchisement. If the degree of enfranchisement you experience in your society is sufficient for you to genuinely undertake all the activities you desire, then the fact that your enfranchisement is not as good as possible does not have a significant impact on your SWB.

The most important ramification of taking capabilities as a constraint on rather than a cause of SWB is that it formalizes the idea that people need to *act* on their capabilities to achieve wellbeing. Capabilities theorists tend to treat capabilities as ends and to treat resources like income as means to those ends. This makes sense from a justice point of view, or if you see options as definitive of wellbeing (I will return to these ideas in chapter 11). But it is a deficient framework if we are thinking about SWB. In that case, SWB is the ends, and capabilities are mere means to that end. Further increases in means beyond the amount required for the functionings that are most appropriate for a particular individual have little effect on SWB because these means are superfluous. The person already has everything that they need to self-actualize.

If an individual remains unwell despite high capabilities, it is perhaps because they don't know *what* functionings to actualize to achieve wellbeing. This is an information constraint. It is related to the idea that preferences and values must be laundered in some way before their satisfaction becomes a source of SWB. These preferences are represented in the coalescence of being by the ideal and ought selves. Individuals continually adjust these preferences over the life course as coalescence progresses. This is a learning process that alleviates the information constraint.

Capability shocks can be readily understood through the constraint lens. If someone is operating at their capabilities frontier, meaning that they are making maximal use of their capabilities, and they experience a negative capability shock, this will likely have substantial impacts on their SWB. For example, athletes arguably suffer more from injuries than the average person because these injuries impede their ability to engage in sport. As sport is fundamental to their most appropriate functioning, this has a profound impact on their SWB. In contrast, if someone whose physique is not intimately bound up with their best functioning experiences an injury, this will likely reduce their SWB, if only through a pain effect, but the effect will be relatively weak. Similar inferences follow for positive shocks that expand the capabilities frontier. An aspiring professional athlete will experience an increase in their health as they train. Their SWB will consequently increase as this added health allows them to become a more capable athlete. In contrast, if a generally healthy person whose principal hobby is videogaming experiences a health shock (perhaps they are cured of asthma), this will not have a huge effect on their SWB because it doesn't change what functionings they actualize.

An interesting issue that emerges from this discussion is the potential to substitute one capability for another. Substitution is most feasible when an individual is not operating at their capability frontier across all its dimensions and they thus have some slack in one dimension. They could conceivably start to utilize this slack when a different dimension experiences a contraction. For example, someone with high environmental quality who suffers a shoulder injury (health shock) and can no longer play racquet sports can substitute hiking through that pristine environment. They may have avoided this activity previously because they enjoyed badminton marginally more than hiking, but now that badminton is precluded they choose to hike, and so they experience only a minor decline in overall SWB. A shock to many capabilities simultaneously, like a natural disaster, might prohibit such substitution and thus lead to a large decline in SWB.

Conclusion

The benefit of specifying an integrated subjective wellbeing function is that it clarifies what the relevant variables and parameters are and indicates how they might fit together. Researchers working on aspects of the function can then understand their work in relation to that of other scholars and can feed their findings, notably their coefficient estimates, into the overarching model. In this way, disparate research streams can be brought together to discover the nature of the complex phenomenon of SWB without a large number of researchers having to work across the entire spectrum of the phenomenon. This is necessary in the context of SWB research for two reasons. First, because SWB has such a wide interdisciplinary scope. And second, because many of these disciplinary streams individually require a high degree of disciplinary specialization, which impedes cross-disciplinary pollination. This chapter outlined the SWBPF. Detailed explication of variables and extensive references to supporting literature were absent. In the next four chapters I provide this missing content.

5

The Capabilities Constraint

Even if we act to erase material poverty, there is another greater
task, it is to confront the poverty of satisfaction—purpose and dignity—that afflicts us all . . . gross national product does not allow
for the health of our children, the quality of their education or the
joy of their play. It does not include the beauty of our poetry or the
strength of our marriages, the intelligence of our public debate or
the integrity of our public officials. It measures neither our wit nor
our courage, neither our wisdom nor our learning, neither our compassion nor our devotion to our country. It measures everything,
in short, except that which makes life worthwhile. And it can tell
us everything about America except why we are proud that we are
Americans.

—Robert Kennedy, remarks at the University of Kansas

Introduction

This chapter has two objectives. The first is to advocate that capabilities are
a constraint that individuals try to improve SWB within rather than being
direct causes of SWB. The second is to justify the items emphasized in the
capabilities constraint, namely income, health, education, enfranchisement,
and environment. The argument proceeds in the following manner. I begin
by briefly discussing the notion of a budget constraint on utility in microeconomics. This idea directly informed the emphasis on income growth
and productivity in economic policy advocacy and early development economics. I argue that the more recent emphasis on capabilities and especially the way capabilities were operationalized in the Human Development
Index, Millennium Development Goals, Sustainable Development Goals,
and the Stiglitz, Sen, and Fitoussi commission report (2009) essentially

A Theory of Subjective Wellbeing. Mark Fabian, Oxford University Press. © Oxford University Press 2022.
DOI: 10.1093/oso/9780197635261.003.0006

involves broadening the budget constraint to a capabilities constraint. I draw on this operationalization literature to justify the content of the capabilities constraint.

The focus on capabilities in development policy is appropriate because the capabilities constraint is so often the main impediment to the SWB of the poor. In wealthier contexts this might not be the case. SWB is determined by functionings rather than capabilities. People must know what functionings to actualize to achieve SWB. The poor are often so constrained that it is obvious what functionings are missing from their lives, notably food and healthcare. The wealthy more often have the means to actualize their most appropriate functionings; they just don't know what those functionings are. This is a knowledge problem that I conceptualize as an additional *information* constraint. Ironically, having more resources can make it harder to overcome this information constraint because the individual has more choices to consider. This is why I say that expanding capabilities expands *welfare*, not SWB. Welfare refers to capabilities—the life choices available to someone.

Wellbeing in Neoclassical Economics

The most basic building block of neoclassical microeconomics is a model of the individual consumer trying to maximize their utility subject to their budget constraint. Utility here is defined in the vaguest terms as anything "good" for the individual. More specifically, it is defined mathematically as anything that can be associated with a plus sign (+). Disutility is represented by a negative sign (−). In introductory textbooks, the utility function takes the following Cobb-Douglas form:

$$U = x^\alpha y^\beta$$

where x and y are two goods (or baskets of goods) and α and β are parameters that capture the rate at which the marginal contribution of these goods to utility diminishes as consumption increases. Goods are assumed to have prices, P_x and P_y. The individual's budget constraint is given by their own income. Expenditure must be less than or equal to income, and expenditure is given by the total quantities of x and y consumed multiplied by their respective prices. The budget constraint can thus be written:

$$I = P_x x + P_y y$$

Consumers are assumed to maximize their utility subject to their budget constraint, and so the "consumer's problem," as it is called, is given by the following objective function:

$$\max U = x^\alpha y^\beta \, s.t. \, I = P_x x + P_y y$$

An obvious inference that can be drawn from this model is that relaxing an individual's budget constraint will increase their utility—more income means more consumption, which means more utility. The additional utility gained will diminish as consumption increases, but nonetheless there is a straightforward mathematical association between income and utility by way of greater consumption. This relationship forms a key foundation of cost-benefit analysis and interpersonal welfare comparisons using prices and income as proxies for preference satisfaction. I will discuss these issues in some detail in the context of wellbeing policy in chapter 11. For now, I simply want to note that it is the consumption of "goods" (broadly conceived) that provides utility, not income. The causes of utility are in the utility function, not the budget constraint.

The consumer's problem is the formal background to the traditional emphasis on income growth in development economics. This is one reason priority was given to developing measures of income, prices, and GDP before any other metric of "wellbeing" (Coyle 2015). Income growth is a central element in several structural changes that take place in the early stages of development, notably the agrarian transition and industrialization (Foster-McGregor and Verspagen 2016; Thirlwall and Pacheco-López 2017). It also has tremendous power to improve the quality of life by financing healthcare, infrastructure, technology, and other aids (Deaton 2013). Given this significance, it is only natural that development economists started with GDP. However, a series of objections were raised to its preeminence as a measure of wellbeing, development, and social "progress" over the second half of the twentieth century. Four stand out. These concerned issues of freedom, rights, sustainability, and distribution. I discuss each of these in turn below.

Development as Freedom

Amartya Sen is associated with the argument that GDP is not a good measure of development because it is a poor proxy for whether people can "do what they want to do and be who they want to be" (Sen 1999a). While income measures whether someone can consume the goods they want, the notion of "goods" here is restricted to material goods that can be bought in commercial markets ("commodities"). Non-commercial goods, like dignity, career choice, living in a non-discriminatory society, and so on, are challenging if not impossible to measure using income, but are nonetheless important markers of wellbeing. Moreover, a society that is getting richer but providing fewer of these goods arguably should not be regarded as "developing."

Sen proposed a richer notion of development than simply income growth. He called it "development as freedom," which speaks to the idea that a society makes progress when it increases the possibilities open to its citizens (Sen 1999a). Income is an insufficient concept to measure such development. For example, imagine a society where everyone is getting wealthier but some opportunities are denied to an underclass of citizens on the grounds of caste, race, gender, or sexuality, such as for Dalits in post-independence India. This underclass may be richer, but few new life choices are opening for them. They are actively oppressed. It is contentious to suggest that this society overall is making progress.

Sen (1999b) provides a formal framework for understanding this definition of development. He begins by distinguishing between "wellbeing" and "advantage" (p. 3). He defines wellbeing in terms of achievement: "how 'well' is his or her 'being'?" Advantage, on the other hand, "refers to the real opportunities that the person has, especially compared with others." Critically, "the opportunities are not judged only by the results achieved, and therefore not just by the level of well-being achieved." To illustrate, consider a person with very restricted options who nonetheless manages to live out the life that is uniquely wellbeing-maximizing for them. This person is not free to be who they want to be and do what they want to do because they can only choose to be this one particular person. They have little *freedom* of choice (p. 9). Sen argues that the progress or justice of a nation should not be judged by whether its citizens are able to find wellbeing therein. Instead, it should be judged by whether citizens have a range of options available to them from which they can choose the one that will give them the most wellbeing.

This analysis leads to the important distinction between capabilities and functionings. Sen (1999b) approaches this distinction formally, but for ease of exposition I will dispense with the mathematics. Functionings are modes of being—they are the things one chooses to be and do. Capabilities refers to the option set of functionings: "[if] $Q_i(X_i)$ represents the freedom that a person has in terms of the choice of functionings . . . Q_i can be called the 'capabilities' of person i given those parameters $[x_i]$" (p. 9). In other words, capabilities are all the possible functionings a person has available to choose from. They then actualize only a chosen subset of those functionings. In Sen's philosophy, wellbeing derives from how an individual values the particular functionings they choose to actualize—in other words, from the utility of those functionings to them. So while capabilities are an objective list theory of justice and development, this seems to ultimately be a preference-satisfaction account of wellbeing. Different functionings will thus give rise to different amounts of wellbeing to different people. This makes it readily compatible with neoclassical microeconomics, just not with its tendency to measure preference satisfaction in terms of income alone.

Sen's theory was first operationalized in the Human Development Index (HDI), which was used as a complement to GDP by the UN and other major development organizations. HDI incorporates not only income but also education and health. The former is measured by years of schooling, the latter by life expectancy. HDI was believed to better capture people's capabilities than just using income (Hirai 2017). Education opens a range of doors unrelated to income, such as the ability to apply for jobs with specific educational requirements. Health is similar. An elderly individual might be better able to play with their grandkids if they are not infirm as well as old, for example. A key reason for the early adoption of these variables despite education and health constituting only a limited proxy for human development was the ease of data collection.

Linking Economic Models and the SWBPF

In this section I build a bridge between neoclassical economic theory and the model of SWB I outlined in chapter 4 using the capabilities framework.

Capabilities are an expansion on the notion of a budget constraint, and functionings are an expansion on the notion of a utility function. In neoclassical consumer theory, the budget constraint captures the option set available to the individual. In Sen's notion of development as freedom, capabilities serve the same purpose, only the qualitative nature of the constraint is richer. It ceases to be entirely a matter of income, covering instead the broader notion of whether an individual can be who they want to be and do what they want to do. Who they then choose to be and what they choose to do are their functionings, and it is by these functionings that they derive utility. Functionings are characterized by qualities like consumption, career choice, family life, hobbies, and so forth. Depending on the individual's preferences for these things, certain functionings will provide greater utility/wellbeing. Standard microeconomic theory about diminishing marginal returns to these characteristics likely still applies. For example, concentrating entirely on career and thus retaining little work-life balance could be expected to result in less total wellbeing for most people owing to greater diminution of marginal returns to career at such high levels of investment.

Expanding the budget constraint to a capabilities constraint retains from neoclassical theory the notion that expanding a constraint doesn't *cause* utility or wellbeing. Rather, it opens more possibilities for consumption or functioning, and it is these that cause increases in utility or wellbeing. It is for this reason that I say that expanding capabilities increases welfare, but not (subjective) wellbeing. Welfare is about access to wealth, resources, assets, opportunities, and so on; hence its central place in theories of justice and the fair distribution of scarce resources. Wellbeing in Sen's philosophy is about value fulfillment, and in this book it is about SWB (which is itself substantially about value fulfillment). Welfare and wellbeing are connected, but not identical. Wellbeing requires the *leveraging* of welfare. You need to choose the best options from among your capabilities to realize an ideal and ought self that is self-congruent and gratifying. If you don't know how to do that because your coalescence has not progressed enough, acquiring more welfare won't meaningfully increase your wellbeing.

In neoclassical economic theory it is assumed that the individual knows what they want to consume and that they optimize their consumption to maximize utility accordingly. The formal expression of this assumption is that preferences are almost always taken as exogenous in economic welfare modeling. The amount of welfare an outcome corresponds to is determined by how many preferences it satisfies rather than by the quality of those preferences, and the alteration of preferences in a "desirable" direction is not used as an objective of policy. Recent findings in behavioral economics show that this assumption of welfare-maximizing preferences on the part of agents is not strictly true (Kahneman 2011; Sugden 2018). As Pareto emphasized, people need opportunities to learn what their preferences are before their behavior, their "revealed preferences," can be reasonably employed as a proxy for utility. The same basic logic holds for wellbeing. Having more capabilities means that people can access functionings they couldn't access before. However, unless people know which functionings are most appropriate for them, this increase in capabilities doesn't necessarily translate into greater wellbeing. Learning must first take place, which is where the coalescence of being comes in.

That capabilities are a constraint on wellbeing rather than a cause of it has been somewhat overlooked to date perhaps because abundance is a recent phenomenon. Until around the second half of the twentieth century, even the middle class in relatively wealthy countries lived a meager existence, and few people were middle-class. This is still the case in developing countries today, and the blue-collar middle class has fallen back onto hard times in many developed countries in recent decades owing to deindustrialization (Graham 2017; McClelland 2013). When the capabilities constraint is tightly binding on wellbeing, as it is in these cases, there appears to be a causal relationship between capabilities and wellbeing. Poor people do not have the means to live the lives they would like to live. As soon as they get those means, their wellbeing improves, but we should not confuse this capability expansion with the root cause of wellbeing. There are plenty of middle-class and wealthy people in developed and developing countries who are miserable. Their ailment is often an information problem.

Conceiving wellbeing among capability-rich people in advanced nations as a problem of information rather than scarcity has implications not only for modeling SWB but also for using it as an indicator of development. It provides a hypothesis for why further economic development in advanced economies like Australia, Denmark, and Canada appears to have little impact on life satisfaction—people already have what they need to be who they want to be and do what they want to do (Stevenson and Wolfers 2013). The challenge for SWB in these countries is not scarcity but self-knowledge.

This inference is corroborated by some empirical evidence (Ng and Diener 2014). Graham and Lora (2009) found that the most important determinants of SW-B among the poor in Latin America are income and social support networks, while for the rich they are work and health. Similarly, Graham (2017) found evidence that the poor in the United States suffer from "bad" stress associated with desperation, while the rich suffer from "good" stress associated with striving for goals. These findings support the notion that the poor are heavily constrained in terms of their capabilities and must consequently fixate on life-sustaining activities. The rich, in contrast, have capabilities aplenty and can focus on more transcendental activities like career. Relatedly, Diener and Fujita (1995) found that resources such as health, wealth, and attractiveness barely correlate with SW-B unless they are relevant to people's idiographic strivings.

In terms of modeling, if capabilities are a constraint on rather than a cause of SWB, then the popular practice of running regressions with life satisfaction as the dependent variable and capabilities as explanatory variables bypasses a causal analysis. Direct causation is in a deeper substrate of analysis, one tied to coalescence. It is unsurprising, then, that these regressions have low explanatory power, with R^2 of around 0.15 at best (Clark et al. 2018, p. 20). Several such investigations have been conducted to date and were certainly useful (Argyle 1999; Van Praag and Ferrer-i-Carbonell 2004). Improving their explanatory power further also has value. However, if the field of SWB wants to move closer to a causal analysis, different data sets and models will be required.

The focus of this chapter has so far been on justifying the treatment of capabilities as a constraint on the SWBPF rather than variables within it. In the rest of the present chapter I justify the specific capabilities I include in the constraint, namely income, health, education, enfranchisement, and environmental quality. This is obviously an exceedingly narrow list. There are vastly more "beings" and "doings." It is also conceptually a bit wonky. Income, for example, is not a "being" or a "doing." Nor is environmental quality. Capabilities theorists would tend to consider income as a means or resource that makes available certain capabilities, like "being well-nourished" (Robeyns 2017). They would also emphasize the role of "conversion factors" that translate resources into capabilities. For example, if a disabled person has the money to buy a wheelchair but their local shops lack accessibility, then this wheelchair does not effectively grant the capability of "being mobile" or the doing of "going to the shops." Some aspects of what I call enfranchisement are arguably best conceptualized as conversion factors. For example, freedom from discrimination on the basis of sexuality is a conversion factor that allows homosexuals to translate income into going to a gay nightclub.

So if my five items are so wrongheaded, why do I nonetheless persist with them? First, it is to provide a *sketch*. By considering how the five items I identify feed into the options available to individuals, we get a sense of what social, economic, and political conditions are necessary to the realization of SWB. This will be important to my argument in chapter 11 that policy should focus only on indirectly improving SWB by improving welfare. Second, it is because the history of applying the capabilities approach in public policy has focused on these items. One purpose of this book is to translate wellbeing ideas across disciplines and fields, especially with regard to policy applications. An account of actions capabilities theorists have championed helps with this objective.

Nussbaum, Political Enfranchisement, and the MDGs

The Human Development Index added education and health to income. The next extension to the capabilities framework in action concerned political enfranchisement. Around the time the HDI was being implemented and refined in the 1990s, Sen was collaborating with Martha Nussbaum on related work concerning the gender dimensions of development. In Nussbaum's influential book *Women and Development: The Capabilities Approach* (2000), she argued for ten "central human capabilities" that should underpin development policy. These were (pp. 78–80):

1. Life expectancy
2. Bodily health
3. Bodily integrity (i.e., freedom from assault)
4. Being able to use the senses, to imagine, think, and reason
5. Emotions—being able to have attachments to things and people outside ourselves
6. Practical reason—being able to form a conception of the good and engage in critical reflection about the planning of one's life
7. Affiliation—being able to live with and toward others; also dignity
8. Respect for other species
9. Play
10. Control over one's environment, both political and material

Nussbaum was especially concerned about the special constraints facing women, particularly in developing countries, with respect to these central capabilities. Owing to the historical disenfranchisement of women, they often face gendered obstacles that limit their freedom. These are well understood, but worth reiterating briefly. Among other constraints, women in Europe were explicitly paid lower wages than men for the same work before and after the First World War, limiting their economic freedom (Summerfield 2012). In some countries and communities women are required to cover up or face opprobrium and criminal charges. This limits their cultural freedom to engage in a range of activities, like going to the beach. Until recently, women in Saudi Arabia were not allowed to drive, severely constraining their mobility and freedom. Women were historically excluded from voting and are still ineligible to vote in the Vatican. This limits their political freedom. More broadly, they were simply excluded from a range of opportunities. Women were only allowed to graduate from Oxford University in 1920, even if they met all the academic requirements (Oxford University Archives 2007). They could not be members of the Berlin Philharmonic Orchestra until the 1980s. Finally, women's sexual freedom has often been curtailed through practices like enforced marriage and genital mutilation.

The arguments and methodology that Nussbaum used to derive her list have come in for criticism (Clark 2002; Gasper 2004). I don't want to get bogged down in these dense debates here. I will instead try to sidestep them with two claims. First, most of Nussbaum's items can be conceptually subsumed under the health, education, and enfranchisement headings. Those that can't either are not capabilities or are better conceptualized as part of the information constraint and the coalescence process. Second, Nussbaum's items were operationalized in the Millennium Development Goals (MDGs) by adding various goals associated with political enfranchisement to the HDI. This lends credibility to the idea that "enfranchisement" is sufficiently broad a category in the capabilities constraint to account for Nussbaum's concerns.

Life expectancy, bodily health, being able to use the senses, and emotions are all health items. Bodily integrity is a composite of health and enfranchisement (freedom from violence and oppression). Affiliation and play are about enfranchisement. Respect for other species is an ethical precept, not a capability. That leaves practical wisdom. It could be part of the education capability. That would seem to shear it of its Aristotelian roots as a virtue that allows for eudaimonic living. For this reason, I think practical wisdom is instead synonymous with or at least related to the information constraint. It is learned or acquired through the coalescence process. Indeed, listing practical wisdom as a capability both underplays its importance and sidesteps the need to explain how it is acquired. Practical wisdom is what allows you to effectively leverage your capabilities to achieve SWB. Its acquisition thus does not open up more options for you, as a capability would, but rather allows you to navigate your existing options more effectively.

The MDGs both expanded the indicators for health and education employed in the HDI and added new items for political rights. The MDGs covered the eradication of poverty, universal primary education, the reduction of infant mortality, and efforts to combat HIV/AIDS, malaria, and other headline diseases. These correspond to the HDI's focus on income, education, and health. The MDGs also targeted maternal health specifically along with gender equality and the empowerment of women. This enfranchisement of women was pursued through three subgoals (United Nations 2015a):

- Eliminate the gender disparity in education between girls and boys at the primary, secondary, and tertiary levels.
- Increase the share of women in wage employment in the non-agricultural sector.
- Increase the proportion of seats held by women in parliaments worldwide.

Broadly speaking, the emphasis here is on political freedom and non-discrimination, which is why I refer to these items and the broader set of capabilities to which they belong as "enfranchisement." When someone is enfranchised in terms of their capabilities, it means that they are culturally, politically, and legally at liberty to pursue their preferences. They may still lack the health, education, income, and environment necessary to do so, but they are not actively disenfranchised by others, the community, or the state. This is broader than the specific MDGs concerned with women's empowerment. It emphasizes the right to be who you want to be and do what you want to do.

Sustainability and the SDGs

The seventh Millennium Development Goal was to ensure environmental sustainability. This objective has increased in prominence in recent years, and efforts to achieve it have accelerated. The clearest demonstration of this is the replacement of the MDGs with the Sustainable Development Goals

(SDGs; United Nations 2015b). These extend earlier initiatives born under the HDI and MDGs—for example, there is now a goal to achieve peace, justice, and strong institutions, which speaks to political enfranchisement—and place greater emphasis on environmental issues. There are new goals concerned with sustainable cities and communities, climate action, responsible consumption and production, organic life on land and in the water, and infrastructure development. This strong emphasis on environmental capabilities in the contemporary development literature speaks to the need to include environmental factors in the capabilities constraint.

The most obvious way that environment constrains wellbeing is in negative terms through the effects of pollution, climate change, congestion, and overcrowding, which make life unpleasant and difficult. What about in places where environment in terms of air and water quality and population density is relatively good, like Australia or the United Kingdom? Here we come across other issues that relate more subtly to the notion of capabilities. For example, both Australia and the United Kingdom have problems around good-quality, affordable housing that is proximate to opportunities like interesting, well-paid work, effective schools, and enjoyable leisure activities. Owing to a range of policy settings that constrain sensible and equitable real estate development (Daly and Coates 2018), many young Australians face a trade-off between living in affordable, pleasant housing that is far from many opportunities, or living in run-down or poorly built, often crowded neighborhoods close to opportunities. These less pleasant neighborhoods can also feature other environmental bads like high crime rates, noise pollution, and limited amenities like parks. Some of these trade-offs are unavoidable to some degree, at least without major technological changes around things like telecommuting—you typically can't live next to both a major commercial enterprise and a national park, for example. Others, however, are surmountable through advances in urban planning and design, as advocated by the SDGs and as explored in the burgeoning literature on wellbeing and geography (Glaeser 2012; Arampatzi et al. 2018; Okulicz-Kozaryn 2015).

Distribution and Social Capital

Before concluding, the issues of welfare distribution and social capital must be addressed, and reasons given as to why they are not factors in the SWBPF or the capabilities constraint.

Alongside environmental outcomes, the SDGs also target reductions in inequality in society. Such inequality, particularly when considered through the lens of just distribution, is a long-running theme in welfare economics (see, for example, Atkinson 1970; Fleurbaey and Maniquet 2011). Why then do I not include some account of the distribution of capabilities in the capabilities constraint? It is because inequality is included elsewhere in the SWBPF, specifically through the parameter for reference group effects and low-rank aversion. This is more appropriate than including it in the capabilities constraint for two reasons. First, because being of low rank in a reference group appears to exert a direct impact on SWB, with the severity varying by person. Second, because having more or less resources than others does not affect your SWB so long as you have sufficient capabilities to realize your best functionings. An exception is when inequality reflects social power imbalances, but the pernicious effects of this in terms of scarce resources and exclusion from opportunities by vested interests is captured through the enfranchisement variable.

Some recent work on measuring development has promoted the "four capitals" framework, which takes in built, human, environmental, and social capital (Arrow et al. 2012; Costanza et al. 2012). I have accounted for the first three of these in income, education and health, and environmental capabilities, but political enfranchisement is insufficient to capture the full scope of social capital. Absent are things like networks, cultural markers, and the ability to blend into key cultural group, like the ruling class. Why do I not account for social capital in the capabilities constraint?

It is because social capital is picked up through the relatedness variable. Individuals attempt to adopt the cultural markers of particular networks in order to join them. Success in this endeavor, which depends in part on whether the group's identity is self-concordant with the individual's identity, results in the ability to blend into that group. Much of what remains unaccounted for in terms of social capital is picked up by political enfranchisement. Of particular note here is the notion of equality of opportunity. If the ruling class, for example, is less a meritocratic group and more a matter of hierarchies enforced by laws, institutions, and discrimination, such as was the case under the apartheid regime in South Africa, then individuals without social capital do not have the capability to advance themselves. But it is precisely such factors that are captured in the political enfranchisement aspect of the capabilities constraint, so no additional variable is required. There are, of course, some aspects of social capital that are still unaccounted for. For example, if an appropriate functioning for you is playing in the local weekend soccer league, then you need that league to exist. Such community infrastructure is arguably a component of social capital (Putnam 2001). So social capital is arguably a capability, or at least a conversion factor. However, we are here crossing over into a realistic list of capabilities, which would include thousands of items (all the many beings and doings that humans are capable of). Recall that the five items I populate the constraint with were only ever intended as a sketch. Anyone applying the SWBPF model in a realistic setting should consider the context-specific capabilities and conversion factors that are relevant, and social capital may well be one of them.

Conclusion

Capabilities should be thought of constraints on wellbeing rather than direct causes of it. It is functionings that give rise to wellbeing. Different functionings will suit different people, and the completion of a difficult process—the coalescence of being—is required to discover which functionings are best for you. Given this delineation, capabilities should not be entered directly into the SWBPF. By extension, it is quixotic to continue to search for the determinants of wellbeing in correlations between SWB indicators and elements of the capabilities constraint, especially in advanced nations wherein the capabilities constraint is relaxed for many people. If we want to discover the causes of SWB we need to dig deeper.

Capabilities can be effectively operationalized using income, health, wealth, political enfranchisement, and environmental quality. What this limited taxonomy loses in nuance and comprehensiveness it more than makes up for in parsimony and ease of use. This is important in the context of the empirical investigation of wellbeing, which has historically been plagued by data availability issues. Operationalizing capabilities in this way keeps the SWBPF connected to the development economics literature, to development policy in practice, and to the relatively rich data collection efforts associated with these.

6

Hedonia

> It is impossible to live a pleasant life without living wisely and well
> and justly. And it is impossible to live wisely and well and justly
> without living a pleasant life.
>
> —Epicurus

This chapter has three objectives. First, to demonstrate that hedonia is distinct from eudaimonia and conscience but insufficient on its own to describe SWB holistically. Second, to explicate the nature of hedonia based on theoretical arguments and empirical evidence. And third, to discuss various techniques that are useful specifically to the promotion of hedonia, as distinct from eudaimonia, conscience, or SWB in general.

SW-B scholars argue that hedonism in the traditional sense of pleasure or mood is insufficient to describe SWB because it misses an evaluative component. This is why SW-B incorporates both affect measures for experienced wellbeing and life satisfaction for evaluative wellbeing. I review the extensive statistical evidence from SW-B research for this claim. I then explain why the three-variable model of SW-B (positive affect, negative affect, and life satisfaction) is inadequate to describe SWB holistically. I first elaborate on the nature and importance of emotional wellbeing, drawing on arguments from Haybron (2001, 2008). This extends the theory of experienced wellbeing in SW-B research. I then separate evaluative wellbeing into "hedonic satisfaction" and "existential satisfaction." The former is an evaluation of how pleasant one's life is and properly belongs in the hedonia dimension. The latter refers instead to how fulfilling and valuable one considers one's life to be and thus encompasses the eudaimonia and conscience dimensions. There is statistical evidence that "life satisfaction" is heavily influenced by items from the hedonia dimension relative to existential satisfaction.

A Theory of Subjective Wellbeing. Mark Fabian, Oxford University Press. © Oxford University Press 2022.
DOI: 10.1093/oso/9780197635261.003.0007

To describe the nature of hedonia I draw mostly on literature from hedonic psychology and happiness economics. I discuss hedonic adaptation, the peak-end rule and other cognitive biases or quirks associated with affective systems, the neuropsychology of emotion, and the determinants of emotional resilience. I also discuss findings from experience sampling studies of what behaviors people find most and least enjoyable.

In the final section of this chapter I canvass a range of techniques that can improve hedonia. These include positive activity interventions like gratitude and humility, the hedonic adaptation prevention model, bringing in the good, mindfulness, flow, cognitive-behavioral therapies, and crude hedonism. I also explore some practices that will encourage negative affect, including learned helplessness, rumination, and leaning into the hedonic treadmill. Managing hedonia is a sensible topic to cover given evidence that happiness is associated with a range of better life outcomes, including greater longevity, stronger immune systems, less hypertension, and higher productivity (Diener and Biswas-Diener 2008; Jacobs-Bao and Lyubomirsky 2013).

Distinguishing Hedonia from Eudaimonia and Conscience

SW-B scholarship has done a great deal of statistical work demonstrating that affect and mood (experienced wellbeing) is distinct from life satisfaction (evaluative wellbeing). The main evidence used to support the claim is that events and changes in circumstances tend to affect experienced and evaluative wellbeing variables differently (Lucas et al. 1996, 2003; Diener et al. 1999; Frey and Stutzer 2008). For example, high incomes increase evaluative wellbeing but not experienced wellbeing (Kahneman and Deaton 2010). A second piece of evidence is that experienced and evaluative wellbeing have different correlates (Luhmann et al. 2012; Diener et al. 2010). For example, child-rearing tends to lower experienced wellbeing, particularly by increasing negative affect, while often increasing evaluative wellbeing (Powdthavee 2008). Recreational use of hard drugs has the opposite effect, at least in the long term.

There is also substantial evidence that negative and positive affect should be entered as two separate items in the SWBPF, rather than as a single "mood" or "happiness" variable going from low to high (Stone and Mackie 2013, p. 39). This observation goes back at least to Bradburn (1969), who found that positive and negative affect are not opposite ends of a single spectrum but are distinct from each other. His findings have been replicated multiple times (Kahneman et al. 1999; Diener et al. 1999; Gere et al. 2011). The distinctiveness of positive and negative affect can be grasped intuitively by imagining someone who is experiencing both kinds of affect simultaneously. For example, someone might be stressed about their workload but also happy to be catching up with an old friend. There is some evidence that positive affect is qualitatively unidimensional (it is usually described as "joy") whereas negative affect has multiple qualitative dimensions like stress, anxiety, depression, and bereavement (Argyle 2001, p. 10).

The empirical evidence for these two propositions—that experienced and evaluative wellbeing are different and that negative and positive affect are distinct—is strong enough that a high-level panel of the National Academies of the United States concluded:

> Although life evaluation, positive experience and negative experience are not completely separable—they correlate to some extent—there is strong evidence that multiple dimensions of SW-B coexist. Experienced wellbeing is distinct enough from overall life evaluation to warrant pursuing it as a separate element in surveys; their level of independence demands that they be assessed as distinct dimensions. (Stone and Mackie 2013, p. 4)

In the section that follows, I present arguments and evidence for extending the conceptual framework developed by SW-B. I argue that emotional wellbeing is needed to give a complete account of mood and that life satisfaction must be disaggregated into hedonic and existential satisfaction for us to understand the dynamics of SWB.

Hedonic Versus Existential Satisfaction

By and large, SW-B research uses a single item in its investigations of evaluative wellbeing—life satisfaction. To better understand the causal structure of this arguably global metric it is helpful to disaggregate it into concepts that are theoretically separable. One such disaggregation is to differentiate between judgments of whether life is pleasant versus judgments of whether life is fulfilling and valuable (see Annas 2004; Deci and Ryan 2006; Waterman 2008).

What I call hedonic and existential satisfaction are not mutually inclusive. Some examples will help to illustrate the differences. In chapter 4 I gave the example of a middle-class university student in an OECD country afflicted with nihilism. They are physically healthy, secure, with a bright future ahead of them. They have had every advantage in life and can expect to continue to live in good conditions with food, clothing, and entertainment in perpetuity. They certainly live in such circumstances now. However, they may also suffer from ennui—a kind of existential boredom. They lack meaning and purpose, have an ambiguous understanding of their own virtue and how to enhance it, and don't know who they are or who they want to be. This kind of person would score high on hedonic satisfaction and low on existential satisfaction. If you asked them about their life, they might say, "Everything is fine but, you know, there's just something missing."

The opposite case is exemplified by a freedom fighter hiding from the state. They have a cause that they believe in that gives them seriousness, meaning, and identity. They have comrades who nourish their sense of relatedness. They are actively fighting for autonomy and, if the revolution is going well, they will feel competent. But their day-to-day circumstances might be extremely unpleasant, and so their hedonic satisfaction will be low.

Two other examples would be someone with a high-paying but ultimately lame job, and the archetypal long-suffering artist, beloved by philosophers. The former would have a pleasant but hollow life, while the latter's life would be a struggle but a passionate one.

Separating the hedonic and existential dimensions of evaluative wellbeing can give us a richer framework for thinking about the causes of SWB change. Consider someone nearing the completion of their PhD in an OECD nation. Assuming that this person is on a typical scholarship, they are likely low in affect owing to the stress of writing up their dissertation, but moderately high in hedonic life satisfaction owing to their modest, secure income in a developed nation. They have a clear goal in mind, they have a collegiate community (hopefully), they work on what they want to work on, and, as they are nearing completion, they feel increasingly competent.

After the completion of the PhD, this situation will likely change. We might expect affect to improve markedly as their source of stress fades. Hedonic satisfaction might increase as the individual moves to a higher-paying job. The impact on existential satisfaction is less clear-cut. Having a PhD in hand is a constant reminder that you are competent and accredited by your peers. However, the individual may lose a major source of meaning after graduating and may have to find paid work where they have less autonomy. Depending on their job market outcomes, how the individual makes sense of their life in terms of goals, identity, autonomy, competence, and relatedness may change dramatically. Someone deeply committed to academic pursuits who fails to secure the necessary job may experience reduced SWB despite earning higher pay in the private sector or having better work-life balance in a government job. The answer to why their SWB dropped overall is to be found in the eudaimonia and conscience dimensions. Poor performance there might be offset by improvements in the hedonia dimension associated with higher disposable income and less grueling work hours.

These examples demonstrate not only the possibility of conceptually hedonic and existential satisfaction, but also the usefulness of doing so for understanding the causal origins of changes in wellbeing. Sticking with life satisfaction as a global metric for evaluative wellbeing is advantageous in that it facilitates quick data collection and provides a single, comprehensive reference point. These advantages will be salient in some contexts. In other contexts, specifying a more disaggregated concept and employing multiple measures will allow us to appreciate important nuances.

There is empirical evidence to suggest that hedonic and existential satisfaction are two different constructs. Clark and Senik (2011) report a correlation between life satisfaction and four different aspects of eudaimonic wellbeing of between only 0.25 and 0.29. Diener et al. (2010) develop a psychological wellbeing (PWB) scale that is supposed to reflect aspects of SWB that I associate with eudaimonia and conscience. They report a correlation of 0.62 between their PWB scale and life satisfaction scale responses. The correlation between their PWB scale and measures of positive and negative affect is 0.62 and 0.51, respectively. Huppert and So (2013) developed similar tool for measuring "flourishing." They found a correlation of only 0.34 between their metric and life satisfaction scale responses in European Social Survey data. These studies are not targeting exactly the split I propose between hedonic and existential satisfaction. Nonetheless, their findings suggest that hedonic and existential satisfaction are distinct and that life satisfaction scales mostly pick up the former.

Emotional Wellbeing

Recall from chapter 4 that emotional wellbeing is a parameter that affects hedonia. It refers not to one's emotional state, which is captured by the positive and negative affect variables, but instead to one's emotional disposition, volatility, and stickiness. Disposition refers to how inclined you are to react positively or negatively to emotional shocks. Volatility refers to how large a change in your mood accompanies a proportionate shock (you could call this emotional elasticity). And stickiness refers to how quickly you adapt to shocks and their impact on your mood. Stickier individuals stay with moods for longer. Individuals low in emotional wellbeing will have weaker and more transient responses to positive shocks and stronger, longer-lasting responses to negative shocks. Vice versa for people high in emotional wellbeing. These different facets of emotional wellbeing are summarized in table 6.1.

It is important to distinguish between affective state and disposition to appreciate the full causal structure of hedonia. To illustrate, consider Buddhists like Mathieu Ricard (2014) who have trained their minds to navigate away from emotional responses (Dorjee 2014). They are both low in negative affect and less likely to experience sustained negative affect because they are high in emotional wellbeing. I discuss a range of techniques that bear on emotional wellbeing, like mindfulness and bringing in the good, in what follows. The extent to which the individual practices these techniques, whether with full cognizance of what they are doing or inadvertently, is captured by the notion of "attention" in the SWBPF, of which emotional wellbeing is a function.

Emotional wellbeing is also a function of eudaimonia and conscience. Self-determination theory notes that individuals whose lives do not nourish their basic psychological needs for autonomy, relatedness, and competence are more

Table 6.1 Emotional Wellbeing (EWB)

Facet of EWB	Meaning
Disposition	Susceptibility to emotional shocks
Volatility	Intensity of response to emotional shocks
Stickiness	Duration of emotional response to shocks
High emotional wellbeing	Easily fall into good moods but not bad ones Experience good moods deeply but bad moods weakly Stay in good moods for sustained periods while exiting bad moods quickly
Low emotional wellbeing	Have difficulty experiencing positive affect but easily slip into bad moods Have intense experiences of negative affect but only weak experiences of positive affect Struggle to exit bad moods but easily fall out of good ones

likely to manifest symptoms of depression, anxiety, and poor mood and less likely to present with symptoms of psychological wellbeing (Roth et al. 2017; Ryan et al. 2016; Laurin et al. 2015; Britton et al. 2014; Weinstein and Ryan 2011). Similar results have emerged from logotherapy—a school of clinical psychology that investigates the role of meaning in psychological wellbeing. People low in meaning and purpose are more likely to be depressed, anxious, and despondent (Weinstein et al. 2010; King and Hicks 2012; Ryff 2012; Slattery and Park 2012). Large sample studies conducted by SW-B scholars find inverse results for people high in meaning and purpose (Yalçin and Malkoç 2015). Research in terror management theory finds that people who feel like their values are not serious become distressed and anxious (Solomon 2012; Salzman and Halloran 2004; Dechesne and Kruglanski 2004). Some research on religion suggests inverse effects for people who feel deeply connected to their values (Emmons 1999). Finally, developmental psychologists find that young adults who struggle to define themselves are more prone to depression, anxiety, and low mood and that these symptoms are alleviated as these individuals learn who they are (Summer et al. 2014; To and Sung 2017).

The Nature of Hedonia

Hedonic judgments of present affective state and related matters like felt pleasure and pain are characterized by a range of curious cognitive phenomena. These include the peak-end rule, reference points and their interactions with prospecting, the focusing illusion, adaptation, the hedonic treadmill, and homeostatically protected mood. I review these matters in this section, drawing on literature from the last three decades of research in hedonic psychology (Kahneman, Diener, and Schwartz 1999). Perhaps the single most important contribution of SW-B research to date has been the identification of these empirical phenomena.

The Peak-End Rule and Hedonic Experience

Kahneman (1999) laid out the core features of hedonic experience according to then state-of-the-art empirical evidence. He differentiated between "subjective happiness," which "is assessed by asking respondents to state how happy they are," and "objective happiness," which "is derived from a record of instant utility over the relevant period." An example of an objective happiness recording instrument is to ask patients undergoing a colonoscopy to report their pain on a scale of 1–10 every minute. Leaving aside conceptual debates about whether pain can be used to study happiness, experiments conducted by Kahneman and other researchers in this vein provide fascinating insights into the nature of hedonia.

Some of the most interesting findings from this era of hedonic psychology concerned the discrepancy between how people experienced pleasure and pain and how they remembered it. For example, the main determinants of how painful (pleasurable) people remember an experience to have been are the peak of pain (pleasure) associated with that experience and how much pain (pleasure) they felt at the end of the experience (Schreiber and Kahneman 2000; Frederickson 2000). People seem to remember long and painful events with low peak pain as more pleasant than shorter and less painful events with higher peak pain (Kahneman et al. 1993). Similarly, they have more pleasant memories of long and painful events with relatively pleasant conclusions than shorter and less painful events with very unpleasant ends (Do et al. 2008).

Reference Points, Focusing Illusions, and Loss Aversion

Alongside his work on hedonic psychology, Kahneman is well known for his work on prospect theory (Kahneman and Tversky 1979; Tversky and Kahneman 1986). The two streams of research intersect when it comes to the importance of reference points for hedonic evaluations. Prospect theory holds that "the carriers of decision utility are gains and losses *relative to a reference level*, which is often the status quo" (Kahneman 1999, p. 17, emphasis added). What this implies is that people's assessments of how happy or sad they will be made by a change in circumstances is coloured by their present circumstances (Kahneman 1999, p. 17):

A given state can be assigned quite different utilities depending on the state that preceded it, and quite different states can be assigned approximately the same utility if they represent the same change relative to the reference level.

Kahneman (1999) uses the example of paraplegics to illustrate the implications of prospect theory. Most people are surprised to learn that people who become paraplegics appear to recover close to pre-accident levels of life satisfaction within two years (Brickman et al. 1978 was the seminal study of this phenomenon). Kahneman posits that this is because people focus on the event of *becoming* a paraplegic, where the reference point is being able-bodied, and pay insufficient attention to the experience of *being* a paraplegic, where the reference point is being a paraplegic. The research on paraplegics is questionable in light of scale-norming and disabled people's high willingness to pay to reverse their conditions (Loewenstein and Ubel 2008). Nonetheless, the example helps to illustrate why prospect theory is relevant to evaluations of wellbeing.

Two other ideas from prospect theory are worth mentioning: loss aversion and focusing illusions. Loss aversion refers to the fact that people tend to weight losses more than gains when making decisions. A famous example is that people want more money to sell an item than they are willing to offer to buy the same item. In the context of life satisfaction, individuals are hypothesized to weight losing what they have more substantially than making further improvements in their quality of life.

Focusing illusions are things that become salient during judgments of happiness that then bias those judgments by anchoring responses. A famous example is that citizens of the U.S. Midwest anticipated that they would be happier if they lived in California because the weather there is better (Schkade and Kahneman 1998). However, residents of California and the Midwest report similarly high levels of SW-B. California perhaps has some drawbacks, like high house prices and long commutes, that offset the effect of good weather. The findings of this study and at least one other famous study of focusing illusions (Kahneman et al. 2006) might fall afoul of scale-norming and ceiling effects. Other studies, however, are more robust. For example, Strack et al. (1988) found that priming respondents to think about how many dates they had been on recently caused them to significantly reevaluate their life satisfaction relative to a control group. Similar anchoring effects have been observed for priming people with health issues or the quality of their marriage (Schwarz et al. 1991; Smith et al. 2006).

In the model presented in chapter 4, these phenomena are captured by reference group effects. This is insufficient to capture the full complexity of cognitive biases in reporting SWB, but my interest is in specifying a *subjective wellbeing function*, not a *cognitive evaluation function* for SWB. I discuss the latter in chapter 10.

The Hedonic Treadmill, Adaptation, and Homeostatically Protected Mood

A major topic of inquiry in SW-B research is the adaptation hypothesis (Sheldon and Lucas 2014). This is the claim that people get used to changes in their circumstances. Consequently, the effects of those changing circumstances on SW-B fade with time and people return to a long-run "set point." Adaptation is clearly visible in life satisfaction panel data. Oswald and Powdthavee (2008) and Powdthavee (2009) find substantial adaptation to disability, and Powdthavee and Stutzer (2014) find similar effects for income growth. Other studies have found relatively rapid adaptation to childbirth and marriage and slower adaptation to the death of a spouse and divorce (Clark, Diener, et al. 2008; Dyrdal and Lucas 2013; Lucas et al. 2003; Stutzer and Frey 2006; Specht et al. 2011). Some circumstantial changes, such as cosmetic surgery and unemployment (Clark 2006; Powdthavee 2012), are severe enough to have lasting effects, but some degree of adaptation is typically observed even for these items. As with other findings in this area, the strength and speed of adaption may be mismeasured due to scale-norming. Nonetheless, it seems reasonable at this juncture to claim that adaptation is a real and significant phenomenon.

Set point theory is a relatively more recent addition to the adaptation hypothesis. It posits a baseline level of SW-B (in terms of both affect and life satisfaction) that people return to as they adapt to shocks (Lucas et al. 2004; Lucas and Donnellan 2007; Lykken 1999; Heady 2010; Heady et al. 2014). This set point is a kind of average level of SW-B that is apparent when looking at life satisfaction scale data. There is some evidence that set points are substantially genetically determined and that they vary substantially with personality (Lykken and Tellegen 1996; Røysamb et al. 2014). Extroverts tend to have higher set points than introverts and other people high on neuroticism. Finally, there is some evidence that set points, at least those for mood, are homeostatically protected (Cummins et al. 2014; Capic et al. 2017). This means that our neurochemistry brings us back to a mild level of background positivity following both positive and negative shocks. A failure of mood to rebound implies homeostatic defeat, which is typically associated with ongoing stressors like poverty. Cummins (2014) posits an evolutionary driver of homeostatically protected mood. Being depressed or ecstatic for sustained periods of time is maladaptive: depressed people lack motivation and ecstatic people are easily distracted from tasks required to maintain life. Consequently, we are wired to feel such things only temporarily, while the rest of the time we feel pretty good. This is optimal for motivation.

Alongside homeostasis, adaptation is conjectured to be driven by two forces: changing reference points and the hedonic treadmill (Layard 2005). Reference points like relative rank have been shown to influence people's satisfaction with their circumstances (Frijters and Mujcic 2013; Boyce et al. 2010; Brown et al. 2008; Bhuiyan 2018). One might think that an improvement in objective life circumstances would result in an improvement in SWB. However, structural changes in life circumstances can also change people's reference points such that they now assess their position within some new ranking. For example, imagine an individual from a working-class background who becomes CEO of a midsized company. We might expect their high income rank to result in high SW-B. Yet it is possible that this individual will now judge their income by where it sits in a ranking that consists only of other CEO salaries, not the salaries of the general population. Their SW-B might consequently decline. This hypothesis is one explanation for why lottery winners seem to adapt to their newfound wealth (Brickman et al. 1978) despite some persistent positive effects (Lindqvist et al. 2020). Another commonly conjectured manifestation of such changing reference points is rising aspirations. The idea here is that as people achieve long-held visions of success, they develop new aspirations that cause them to acclimatize to their existing achievements (Sheldon and Lyubomirsky 2012).

It should be noted that the psychological processes underpinning status anxieties like those just discussed can be treated with cognitive discipline (Lyubomirsky and Ross 1999). While there may be an unconscious, natural inclination among humans to care about status and thus to acclimatize to new income and reference points, you can actively avoid such acclimatization. This is important for how we think about SWB, especially in the policy realm. If humans adapt to changes, then this might defeat the purpose of some policies designed to raise SWB. On the other hand, if we see humans as mostly capable of resisting adaptation, then it makes many policy and other changes more desirable. Goethe is supposed to have said: "If you treat an individual as he is, he will remain how he is. But if you treat him as if he were what he ought to be and could be, he will become what he ought to be and could be." In a policy context, assuming strong adaptation might result in treating people as they are. Assuming they can avoid adaptation with training is more like treating people as they ought to be and could be. These different attitudes underpin different policy paradigms. The former leads to a "deficit model" of citizen psychology that justifies paternalism and technocracy. The later leads to more participatory paradigm with a focus on empowering citizens (see Hertwig and Gruner Yanoff 2017 for a discussion in the context of behavioral policy).

The hedonic treadmill is about getting used to *sensations* rather than circumstances. Sensations here are to be understood broadly to include things like the prestige associated with a more senior position at work. Kahneman (1999) uses comparisons to the psychology of color and absolute length to explain treadmill effects and differentiate them from reference group effects. In experiments pertaining to people's perception of the intensity of color, people's sensory mechanisms adapt to the brightness and richness of hues and experience them less intensely under repeated stress. In length experiments, people are given two lines in each phase of an experiment: short and medium, and then medium and long. In the first phase, people will describe the medium line as, for example, "neither long nor short." In the second, they will describe it as, for example, "short" or "very short." This is a context effect. The different outcomes in these two experiments are "produced by different processes: colour adaptation reflects a change in the sensory mechanism, whereas the context effect observed in size judgments is derived by the requirements of effective communication" (Kahneman 1999, p. 11). Reference points are context effects. The hedonic treadmill is about sensory effects. The hedonic treadmill is like acclimatizing to a hot bath— scalding at first, then pleasant. The temperature of the water doesn't change and neither does the individual's reference point. Instead, their sensory instruments adjust.

Hedonic Psychology and Economics

Economists have played a prominent role in SW-B research. Their efforts have focused predominantly on the relationship between SW-B and income and unemployment. More recently, they have become interested in the role of emotional factors like hope, optimism, and stress in economic decision-making. These are all important issues for the SWBPF. Income is part of the capabilities constraint and is an important determinant of pleasurable consumption. Work is a major source of competence, meaning, and relationships. Affective signals, including stress, play an important role in the coalescence of being.

Graham (2017) provides a thorough review of the existing literature on the relationship between hope, optimism, stress, and SW-B and economic outcomes (see also De Neve and Oswald 2012; De Neve et al. 2013). People who are more hopeful and optimistic have lower discount rates and invest more in the future than pessimistic and anxious people. They also appear to be more resilient to negative shocks, in terms of both their behavior and their SW-B (Favara and Sanchez 2017). This finding parallels findings in the study of learned helplessness and learned optimism (Maier and Seligman 1976).

As mentioned earlier, poor people and rich people appear to experience different kinds of stress, on average. The poor suffer from "bad stress" associated with insecurity and desperation (Graham, Chattopadhyay, and Picon 2010). They rely on social networks to mitigate these effects. In contrast, wealthy people experience "good stress," which is associated with goal pursuit and striving more generally (Graham and Lora 2009).

Extending earlier work on loss aversion, Graham (2017) finds that previously rich, typically white, typically regional or semirural communities in America that have declined because of deindustrialization express large declines in SW-B. In contrast, historically poor, typically black, typically inner-city communities are optimistic about the future and report relatively high SW-B despite being poorer on average than many of the declining white communities.

Finally, Graham finds that inequality can have positive effects on optimism, investment, and work ethic if it is perceived to be the result of genuine economic opportunities (Graham 2011). In this case, people believe that hard work will see them get ahead (Graham and Nikolova 2015). By contrast, inequality has a dampening effect if it is perceived to be a function of inequality of opportunity and extractive institutions. If people think the deck is stacked against them and there is no way to get ahead, they will exert relatively less economic effort.

The effects of unemployment have already been touched on: unemployment results in large decreases in SW-B that are not entirely adapted to over time. Sustained unemployment also seems to have a scarring effect. Even after the long-term unemployed return to work, their SW-B stays somewhat depressed (Knabe and Rätzel 2011).

Research into the relationship between income and wellbeing deserves a sustained discussion because of the central place it occupies in the happiness economics discourse (Clark and Senik 2014a). The seminal paper in this lit-erature was Easterlin's 1974 study of the relationship between life satisfac-tion and GDP using Gallup data. He found that while income explained differences in satisfaction *within* countries, it did not explain differences *between* countries. This finding became known as the Easterlin Paradox, and it continues to animate SW-B scholars. Easterlin speculated that the par-adox might be due to adaptation and reference group effects. Relatively rich people *within* countries counted themselves wealthy even if they were poor by global standards. Similarly, poor people in wealthy countries did not com-pare themselves to even poorer people in other countries and so reported low levels of satisfaction.

Research in the late 2000s took a lot of the wind out of the Easterlin Paradox's sails. Most importantly, Stevenson and Wolfers (2009, 2013) used updated Gallup data from the World Values Survey to demonstrate that there is a consistent linear relationship between the log of income and life satisfac-tion, and that a satiation point for income does not exist. A similar result was found by Veenhoven and Hagerty (2006). As income grows, life satisfaction continues to improve, albeit at a decelerating pace. Stevenson and Wolfers argued that the Easterlin Paradox was an artifact of bad data from the early Gallup surveys. These typically suffered from sampling bias associated with only interviewing wealthy people in poor nations (only they had telephones) and not including enough poor nations.

Stevenson and Wolfers do concede that the relationship between income and happiness is linear only on the log scale, meaning that the richer you get, the more money you need to get an increase in your life satisfaction. This means that while there is no satiation point, beyond middle income there are likely cheaper, easier, and more sustainable ways of generating bigger improvements in SWB than earning more money. This aligns with the arguments of chapter 5 that further relaxing an individual's capabilities con-straint once they already have the means to be who they want to be and do what they want to do is unlikely to have much effect. Stevenson and Wolfers' studies also do not refute either adaptation or reference group effects.

Easterlin has recently presented fresh evidence from China in favor of the idea that economic growth has limited effects on wellbeing. China's spectac-ular economic growth from 1990 to 2015 does not seem to have translated into improvements in life satisfaction (Easterlin et al. 2017). This is a striking observation, but the methodology leaves a lot to be desired. Easterlin et al. present evidence from several data sets, and some show a positive trend in life satisfaction over time. Like much research in happiness economics, the analysis is also only correlational. It is quite possible that economic growth in China has had a large positive impact on wellbeing that is offset by other factors, like rising levels of pollution and political repression. The analysis also relies on scale responses in a context where scale-norming is likely. It is perhaps time to retire the study of the direct relationship between income and life satisfaction and consider the relationship from within a more holistic model of SWB.

One important new angle on the relationship between income and SW-B is new research exploring changes in SW-B as a result of macroeconomic fluctuations (Boyce et al. 2018). Economists have recently begun exploring the differential impacts of recessions and booms on SW-B (De Neve et al. 2018). Initial findings suggest that recessions have larger negative effects on SW-B than booms have positive effects. This may pertain to loss aversion, capabilities constraints already being relaxed, adaptation, and changing reference points. It could also be explained by scale-norming and ceiling effects, but the differential is so large that it seems unlikely that the whole result could be explained by these measurement issues. De Neve et al. (2018, p. 366) note that "a 10% economic contraction corresponds to a 0.135 standard deviation drop in life satisfaction, but an equivalent 10% expansion . . . only to a statistically ill-defined increase of around 0.023 standard deviations."

Results from Experience Sampling and Time Use Surveys

This section briefly reviews our current understanding of what activities (as distinct from techniques) affect mood and emotional responses. The findings are drawn from studies using experience sampling (Stone et al. 1999; Hektner et al. 2007) and day reconstruction methods (Kahneman and Krueger 2006). The former involves paging respondents over short, regular intervals (hourly, for example) and having them report their mood and current activity. The latter asks respondents to describe their mood and activities over the course of the previous day. Both methods are considered valid and effective measurement tools (Kahneman et al. 2004a).

Using the day reconstruction method and a large sample of women in Ohio, Kahneman et al. (2004a) found that people had the highest levels of affect while engaged in sex, socializing, relaxing, eating, exercising, practicing religion, and watching television. They reported relatively lower levels of affect while talking on the phone and napping, and while engaged in chores including cooking, shopping, and computer tasks. The lowest levels of affect were reported for housework, childcare, commuting, and working. Similar results are reported by Argyle and Lu (1990).

White and Dolan (2009) and Dolan (2014) used experience sampling methods to extend this analysis by distinguishing between activities that give pleasure and those that give purpose. They find that some relatively less pleasurable activities like household chores and working are high in purpose, while some pleasurable activities like watching television are low in purpose. Two items that were relatively high in both pleasure and purpose were spending time with kids and volunteer activities. White and Dolan's research is an interesting extension of Aristotelian ideas regarding the differences between hedonia and eudaimonia. Their research opens the study of the *experience* of pleasure and purpose *in the moment*. Most philosophical and psychological accounts consider these two dimensions of wellbeing from the life evaluation standpoint instead.

Techniques for Achieving Hedonia

In the remainder of the chapter I survey a range of techniques for improving hedonia, especially mood. For this I draw largely on the literature from hedonic psychology and cognitive-behavioral therapies. Some of these techniques, notably mindfulness, have more general benefits beyond hedonia, but for the most part these techniques are what I call methods of mood management. In the closing passages of the chapter I discuss why mood management is insufficient for achieving deep, holistic, and resilient SWB. The techniques surveyed are positive activity interventions, gratitude, humility, prosocial behavior, compassion, maximizing versus satisficing, experimental disclosure, the hedonic adaptation prevention model, bringing in the good, and mindfulness. This is meant to be a thorough list of presently studied techniques, but there are doubtless some techniques that I have overlooked.

Positive Activity Interventions

Positive activity interventions (PAIs) are "simple, self-administered cognitive and behavioral strategies that can increase subjective well-being (happiness) by promoting positive feelings, positive thoughts, and positive behaviours" (Shin and Lyubomirsky 2014, p. 350). Examples of positive activities include writing letters of gratitude, counting one's blessings, practicing optimism, using one's strengths in a new way, affirming one's most important values ("experimental disclosure"), and meditating on positive feelings toward oneself and others. These are all distinct from simply doing something pleasant, like eating some cake.

The mechanism by which PAIs work to improve affect is theorized to be a combination of stimulating positive emotions and thoughts and satisfying basic psychological needs, specifically for autonomy and relatedness (Frederickson et al. 2008; Boehm et al. 2012). Many PAIs encourage prosocial behavior and an awareness of others and their role in our lives, which encourages and reinforces feelings of relatedness. PAIs are also an active therapy, which provides patients with a sense of autonomous control over their psychological state. PAIs protect against negative affect by discouraging rumination and loneliness (Sin and Lyubomirsky 2009).

The effectiveness of PAIs is moderated by several factors. First, consistent application of PAI techniques over long time horizons is more effective than short courses of treatment. In the context of PAIs like gratitude and kindness that basically involve being a good person, this finding suggests that *acting* like a good person for a little while doesn't have the same effect on wellbeing as actually *being* a good person. You need virtue! Second, practicing a variety of PAIs, varied randomly by the patient themselves, is more effective than mechanically practicing the same PAI as instructed by a therapist. The implication here is that one must *authentically* feel gratitude, be optimistic, et cetera. Finally, the activity must fit the person (Nelson and Lyubomirsky 2012). For example, collectivists may respond more powerfully to social PAIs like kindness than to internal PAIs like counting one's blessings.

Gratitude

The most well-known PAI is gratitude (McCullough et al. 2002). In Western psychological science, gratitude is defined as "the recognition of a positive outcome from an external source, including a sense of wonder or thankfulness for the benefit received" (Nelson and Lyubomirsky 2016). Gratitude is distinguished from "appreciation" by the presence of an interpersonal component. That is to say, if you are grateful for the good things in your life or for something like a beautiful sunset, psychological science says you have appreciation. Gratitude refers more specifically to thankfulness for positive things you receive from *other people*, especially in the form of altruistic acts that are privately costly for the Samaritan (Bartlett and DeSteno 2006). Gratitude does not involve feelings of indebtedness, though it does encourage reciprocity.

Contemporary research distinguishes between gratitude as an emotional *state* that you enter when you recognize altruistic acts and gratitude as a *trait* (Wood et al. 2010). A person with a grateful disposition (trait) feels the emotion of gratitude more frequently and with greater intensity. More generally, grateful people orient themselves toward appreciating the positive in the world. Grateful people thus experience both gratefulness and appreciation on a regular basis. Interventions to boost gratitude include counting one's blessings (Emmons and McCullough 2003), keeping a gratitude journal where you write down the things you are grateful for, and simply encouraging people to notice when people do them favors and react by saying thanks (Emmons 2008).

The mechanisms through which gratitude affects well-being are unclear (Wood et al. 2010). Indeed, it is still somewhat of an open question whether SWB leads to gratitude or gratitude leads to SWB. However, experimental studies suggest gratitude interventions for SWB stimulate outcomes that no-intervention (typically wait-list) control groups don't achieve. There is presently some empirical support for the following causal theories. First, focusing on positive rather than negative things inevitably increases the salience of positive feelings in one's conscious mind. This is particularly relevant for appreciation, which encourages individuals to actively enjoy the things they have rather than pine for what they don't or ruminate on their shortcomings. Second, gratitude instigates cognitive processes that see people reframe negative things in positive ways, such as "My layoff made me appreciate the support my family provides" (Nelson and Lyubomirsky 2016). Finally, gratitude dovetails with a range of prosocial behaviors and outcomes. Cultivating gratitude makes you more aware of things others do for you, which opens your eyes to your social networks and encourages you to help them in turn. This inspires a virtuous cycle of mutual support. In general, gratitude deepens social relationships, satisfying our need for relatedness (Algoe 2012). The effects of gratitude on sociality are strong enough to have inspired research dedicated to exploring the links between gratitude and avenues for the evolution of altruism and other prosocial behaviors in humans (McCullough et al. 2008).

Humility

A construct related to gratitude is humility. In psychological science, humility is defined by five observable indicators: (1) a secure, accepting identity, (2) freedom from distortion, (3) openness to new information, (4) other-focus, and (5) egalitarian beliefs (Chancellor and Lyubomirsky 2013). This broad definition is strikingly divergent from tradition. Contrast the definition given by psychological science with the *Oxford Dictionary*: "humility: the quality of having a modest or low view of one's importance." Synonyms include "modesty," "humbleness," "meekness," and "unassertiveness." It is in the context of such classic definitions that Nietzsche ([1888] 2000, essay 3) and Norton (1976) attacked humility as a self-abnegating quality. In the definition used by modern psychological science, humility is transfigured from this arguably unhealthy quality to being inextricable from the kind of self-awareness that is required for any sort of self-renovation.

The second half of the definition—other-focus and egalitarian beliefs—is especially questionable. Not only does it have little historical basis, but it also seems to associate humility with a pinch of left-wing idealism. It is unsurprising in this context that humility scholarship struggled to find a coherent measurement strategy through most of the twentieth century (Davis et al. 2010). Individuals on the left and right wings of politics have very different ways of understanding egalitarianism. As explained by Haidt (2012), the left wing emphasizes *relative* equity—how far apart people are in terms of resources like wealth. The right wing instead emphasizes *proportional* equity. This means getting what you deserve. Consequently, where the left wing sees unemployment payments as critical for egalitarianism, the right wing seems them as fundamentally inegalitarian, for example. In this context, unless survey questions measuring egalitarianism are phrased with great care, left-wingers may score high on questions where right-wingers score low, and vice versa, not because of different degrees of concern regarding equality but because of different intuitions regarding the meaning of the term. This makes the concept hard to measure and can easily bias results. Humility scholars insist that "a complete lack of a hallmark should disqualify one from possessing humility" (Chancellor and Lyubomirsky 2013, p.822). They suggest that anyone who "[approves] of inequalities among social groups in status, wealth and power" is not humble. Depending on survey design, this might preclude almost all economists, for example, from having humility. Most economists think some wealth inequalities are important to incentivize people with relatively high levels of productivity. Perhaps this doesn't amount to a difference among "social groups." But then we can point to the large economic literature explaining the gender wage gap as a function in part, certainly, of prejudicial discrimination (Bertrand et al. 2015), but also of items like occupational choices (Pan 2015), pregnancy and child-rearing (Bertrand et al. 2010), risk appetites (Booth et al. 2014; Gneezy et al. 2009), and negotiating styles (Kolb 2009). Someone who regards a gender wage gap produced by such forces as unproblematic shouldn't automatically be disqualified from humility.

Given this political and definitional baggage,[1] I will restrict my discussion here to empirical results pertaining to the first half of the new definition of humility: a secure, accepting identity, free from distortion and open to new information. I will use the phrase "well-adjusted" to describe this collection of traits. Being well-adjusted is a prerequisite for many of the techniques described in this chapter, and certainly for the coalescence of being.

A secure, accepting identity is largely about ego stability and consistent self-esteem. Volatility of self-esteem is associated with higher incidence and intensity of anger and hostility (Kermis 2005). Low self-esteem is associated with depression, delinquency, and a tendency to externalize problems (Donnellan et al. 2005). How to bring about ego stability and self-esteem is a complex question, but some necessary conditions can be drawn from studies in humility.

First, ego stability should not be confused with a self-image cast in iron that the individual never deviates from despite stress from the external world. Instead, individuals' self-relevant beliefs should "express flexibility and abstractness" (Campbell et al. 1996, p. 142). This is because abstract self-relevant thoughts can shift with changing circumstances and information, whereas identities founded on specific goals or facts collapse easily following failure to meet those goals. Empirical evidence suggests that the achievement of goals improves emotional wellbeing, but failure to achieve goals leads to

---

[1] One other point that deserves a footnote is that these definitional issues might be fueling empirical findings in a deceptive way. For example, there is a substantial body of work attesting to an upward spiral between gratitude and humility (Kruse et al. 2014; Ruberton et al. 2016). Yet this seems inevitable if you define humility as a fundamentally *social* virtue. There would be nothing wrong with this if researchers were examining the relationship between other-focus and egalitarian beliefs and gratitude. The problem comes when they tie in being well-adjusted. At that point, the implication is that saying thanks and being more appreciative of your life give you a more secure, accepting identity, free from distortion and open to new information. While one could invent theory to justify this result, it seems much more reasonable to assume that the result is an artifact of the definitions the empirical studies start from.

sadness (Lyubormisky et al. 2011). Of course, an identity based on abstract and flexible facts or goals is harder to precisely define, apply, be confident in, and pursue, so there is a trade-off here. From a pragmatic point of view, then, what is important is to be *realistic* in one's self-appraisal and open to changing one's mind in the face of new information. This mitigates the likelihood of failure and allows for flexibility, without precluding the clear articulation of one's identity.

Second, one should have a compassionate regard for one's self-image. This means that you are honest about your deficiencies and weaknesses, including your ability to change them (Neff and Vonk 2009). There is a risk in this attitude that you become lazy about changing those aspects of yourself that you don't like. Such an outcome should be avoided. But equally, hating yourself for things that you cannot change is a toxic and counterproductive attitude. Compassionate self-regard is fundamentally about being reasonable with yourself. This is distinct from being soft on yourself, which simply perpetuates cognitive dissonance.

Finally, freedom from distortion is predominantly about being honest with yourself. Individuals free from distortion can claim responsibility for their mistakes and avoid taking credit for work done by others, and they do not exaggerate or denigrate their own achievements. An undistorted self-image is critical to the coalescence of being. However, it is a difficult quality to cultivate. Notably, there is empirical evidence for self-enhancement in people's self-perception, even among otherwise well-adjusted individuals. For example, most people see themselves as above average, even in the face of contrary evidence (Kruger and Dunning 1999).

Prosocial Behavior

Gratitude and humility both sit within a broader category of prosocial techniques for improving emotional wellbeing. There is some evidence that prosocial behavior makes both the kind person and the recipient happy, and this happiness in turn encourages the recipient to reciprocate or otherwise "pay it forward" (Aknin et al. 2012; Dunn et al. 2008). One hypothesized channel for this is that prosocial behavior and a prosocial environment enhance our sense of relatedness. Another proposed channel is purely chemical, where prosocial behaviors provoke a dopamine or other pleasant neurochemical response. This makes sense if prosocial behavior is something we have evolved to improve our survival (Wilson 2015). Positive feelings associated with prosocial behavior would encourage us to engage in such behaviors, thereby improving our fitness.

Compassion

A specific kind of prosocial behavior that has received a measure of attention recently is compassion, specifically as articulated in Buddhist philosophy. In recent work to define compassion so that it can be operationalized for empirical study, the following five characteristics were identified: (1) recognizing suffering, (2) understanding the universality of suffering in human experience, (3) feeling empathy for the person suffering and connecting with the distress (emotional response), (4) tolerating uncomfortable feelings aroused in response to the suffering person and thereby remaining open to and accepting of the person suffering (non-judgment), and (5) motivation to act/acting to alleviate the suffering (Strauss et al. 2016). There are three orientations of compassion: compassion for others, receiving compassion from others, and self-compassion (Jazaieri et al. 2013). There is a tendency among many people to avoid compassion because it seems to threaten self-interest or because compassion is considered a limited resource that should be reserved for one's immediate kin.

The benefits of compassion for others have already been discussed under prosocial behavior, and the benefits of self-compassion were covered during the analysis of humility. What remains to be examined is receiving compassion from others. Some people may fear such compassion because they do not consider themselves worthy of it (Gilbert et al. 2011). Others may actively reject it because it implies that there is something wrong with them. In this context, increasing an individual's capacity to receive compassion might make them more open to receiving help when needed, or pay more attention to the concerns of others about their present behavior. Empirical work in compassion is in its infancy and so effect sizes for these benefits are not available.

An important point to make about compassion is that most contemporary psychological studies of it are tied to Buddhist philosophy and conducted by committed Buddhists. These authors underline that it is unclear whether the practice and benefits of compassion can be isolated or even exist independently of broader Buddhist practice and values (Dorjee 2014). Notably, compassion is a learned skill in Buddhism that helps the individual to practice loving kindness, notice and alleviate suffering, and ultimately move toward enlightenment. It is thus intricately associated with Buddhist ethics and philosophy. In the absence of this broader context, compassion becomes mostly about simply being a kind person.

Maximizing Versus Satisficing

Studies of the behavioral tendencies of happy people have revealed that they tend to look for and quickly take "good enough" options when making decisions rather than investing time and resources to find the best possible option (Abbe et al. 2003). This is the distinction between satisficers and maximizers. Several studies have demonstrated that maximizing is negatively associated with happiness (Schartz et al. 2002). This is not because maximizers make worse decisions. Indeed, the opposite seems to be the case. It is because they agonize over those decisions, even after they have been made (Lyubomirsky and Ross 1999). There is a cost in cognitive resources to this, not to mention an unnecessary anxiety burden.

Experimental Disclosure

Experimental disclosure involves writing and talking about life events as a form of therapy. In theory, disclosing the fact of such events and any feelings associated with them may allow people to free their mind of unwanted thoughts, help them to make sense of upsetting events, teach them to better regulate their emotions, habituate them to negative emotions, and improve their connection with their social world. Experimental disclosure is what happens on a psychiatrist's couch. One meta-analysis found statistically significant effects from experimental disclosure on emotional wellbeing, but the effect size was trivial, explaining only 0.56 percent (half of 1 percent) of the variance in measured outcomes (Frattaroli 2006).

The issue might be that the ambit of experimental disclosure is too broad. There is evidence that writing and talking are required for processing *negative* events, whereas simply thinking about *positive* ones has similar effects (Lyubomirsky et al. 2006). Writing and talking involve "organising, integrating and analysing one's problems with a focus on solution generation

or at least acceptance" (p. 693). This processing can satisfy the desire to understand the meaning of an event, enhance understanding of its significance
and create a narrative that links into the individual's identity (Singer 2004;
Smyth et al. 2001). Processing takes the emotion out of events, which allows
them to be reflected on without triggering distress. Obviously thinking is involved in both writing and talking, but the structured nature of the latter two
obviates deleterious rumination in a way that thinking on one's own does not
(Hixon and Swann 1993). Thinking rather than writing or talking about positive events is useful precisely because it limits processing and allows the individual to instead wallow in the positive emotional valence of pleasant past
experiences (Lyubomirsky et al. 2006).

The Hedonic Adaptation Prevention Model

This idea of retaining the emotional valence of positive experiences so that
they can be replayed and reducing it for negative experiences so that they
fade from consciousness is the basic idea behind the hedonic adaptation
prevention (HAP) model (Armenta et al. 2014). The HAP model was developed to counteract the natural tendency of individuals to adapt to positive
experiences while accelerating adaptation to negative ones (Sheldon and
Lyubomirsky 2012). One of its principal insights is that experiences that generate a variety of positive thoughts and feelings have a more prolonged effect
than those that generate only a single positive effect (Fritz et al. 2017). For
example, the effect of most material goods tends to fade because they provide only one sensation. By contrast, a new and enjoyable job can provide
a plethora of positive things to reflect on, such as colleagues, location, the
work itself, pay, and a meaningful mission. In general, experiences have been
found to produce longer-lasting positive emotional valence than goods (Van
Boven and Gilovich 2003).

Two other techniques frequently covered in discussions of the HAP model
are appreciation and living in the moment. Appreciation in this context is the
same as in gratitude, namely that reflecting on what's good in life brings positive emotions to the fore, reducing cognitive space for negative emotions.
Living in the moment breaks down into four items: savoring, basking, marveling, and awe. When something good is happening to you, focus your attention on the positive feelings and do not think of the future. This is savoring, and
it prevents the emotion from fading. If you can act on the experience by, say,

throwing a party, that's even better, and referred to as capitalization. Basking is the same technique as savoring applied when positive things are happening to *other people* that you have positive feelings for. Marveling and awe are essentially savoring applied to things that are amazing or staggering, typically in nature, like a beautiful sunset or sublime athleticism (Bryant and Verof 2006).

It is worth noting that two behavioral tendencies that are in a sense the opposite of the HAP model are rumination and leaning into adaptation. Rumination is "a mode of responding to distress that involves repetitively and passively focusing on symptoms of distress and on possible causes and consequences of these symptoms" (Nolen-Hoeksema et al. 2008, p. 400). Critically, "rumination does not lead to active problem solving to change circumstances surrounding these symptoms." People who ruminate remain "fixated on the problems and on their feelings about them without taking action." Unlike in the HAP model or experimental disclosure, ruminators do not process their experiences, construct a healing narrative, or look for solutions. They consequently build up the presence of negative emotions in their conscious experience rather than dissolving them. Leaning into adaptation involves a tendency to always focus on the future, the negative, the next step, or what remains to be maximized (Lyubomirsky et al. 2011). Unsurprisingly, such leaners adapt rapidly to improvements in their circumstances and consequently remain dissatisfied with life.

Bringing in the Good and the HEAL Method

Hanson's (2013) "bringing in the good" and associated HEAL method is another integrated strategy for improving affect balance. Bringing in the good is the deliberate internalisation of positive experiences in implicit memory. Like the HAP model, it is a suite of techniques that help individuals to focus on and thereby increase the intensity and duration of good feelings. Bringing in the good also emphasizes the possibility of using positive experiences to overwrite negative associations embedded in memory. For example, consider someone who suffers anxiety because of past bullying that occurred when they attempted to join a new social circle. This individual can focus on positive feelings associated with an enjoyable social experience in the present and use those feelings to actively replace the association between social interaction, bullying, and negative feelings they have in their subconscious. The HEAL method has four steps (Hanson 2013, p. 61):

1. *Have a positive experience.* This involves either noticing a pleasant experience underway, such as a feeling of wonder, or creating one yourself by, for example, thinking about things you are grateful for.
2. *Enrich it.* Stay with the feeling for a sustained period (ten seconds or longer) and try to bring it to the center of consciousness.
3. *Absorb it.* Meditate on the feeling so that it occupies not just your consciousness but mind (and potentially body) more generally.
4. *Link positive and negative material.* Bring negative associations into consciousness alongside your positive experience, thereby replacing those negative associations with the present positive ones.

Mindfulness

Mindfulness is a concept in Buddhist philosophy and practice that Jon Kabat-Zinn adapted for use as a treatment for stress (Kabat-Zinn 2003). It has also recently been adapted as a treatment for preventing depressive relapse (Barnhofer et al. 2009). Kabat-Zinn's original definition of the term was "paying attention on purpose, in the present moment, and nonjudgmentally." The definition employed in the Philadelphia mindfulness scale is "the tendency to be highly aware of one's internal and external experiences in the context of an accepting, non-judgemental stance towards those experiences" (Cardaciotto et al. 2008, p. 205).

These Western definitions of mindfulness are substantially more limited than the Buddhist one. Traditional definitions situate mindfulness within a broader suite of activities that help the individual practice Buddhist ethics, let go of the self, and attain enlightenment. The therapeutic effects of mindfulness derive from its ability to grant patients control over their conscious thoughts. In particular, mindfulness grants the ability to recognize emotions as not existing independently of mind. As we exercise some control over our minds, we can choose to let go of negative thoughts. This is referred to as renunciation (Ricard 2003). It can help individuals to avoid ruminative thoughts and control stress. Furthermore, the non-judgmental aspect of mindfulness allows people afflicted with stress and depression to manage these emotions without them provoking feelings of self-hate or hopelessness (Keng et al. 2011).

Some studies suggest that mindfulness can aid in values clarification and improve behavioral self-regulation (Roemer et al. 2009; Shapiro et al. 2006).

Attentional control is fundamental to self-awareness, which is in turn critical for self-actualization. To understand who you are, you must be aware of your actions and decisions on a moment-by-moment basis. It is in the moment that your self-concept is disclosed. If you are unable to regulate your behavior in line with your values, or if you are incapable of recognizing when you are acting in or out of line with your values, you cannot self-actualize. Non-judgment in the moment is important here, as judgment will cause you to expunge things in your conscious experience that you don't like and double down on those that you do like. This can be a hindrance to self-actualization if you avoid confronting the fact that you are behaving out of line with your avowed self. You especially want to be non-judgmental in the discovery phase of self-actualization, when you are still trying to figure out who you are. In the affirmation stage, compassionate judgment becomes increasingly necessary. Judgment allows you to regulate your subconsciously triggered behaviors so that they are in line with your avowed self. Non-judgment of actions that are incongruent with your avowed self impedes self-actualization.

This way of using mindfulness is somewhat antithetical to the way Buddhism applies the technique. In Buddhism, mindfulness allows the practitioner to

> recognise the emotion at the very moment that it forms, understand that it is but a thought, devoid of intrinsic existence, and allow it to dissipate spontaneously so as to avoid the chain reaction it would normally unleash. (Ricard 2003, p. 133)

Consistent application of mindfulness in Buddhism allows the user to gain control of the mind and, through it, the substance of conscious experience. The end goal is to completely empty the consciousness of self:

> If we want to be free of inner suffering once and for all, it is not enough to rid ourselves of the emotions themselves; we must eliminate our attachment to the ego. Is that possible? It is, because as we've seen, the ego exists merely as mental imputation. A concept can be dispelled, but only by the wisdom that perceives the ego is devoid of intrinsic existence. (Ricard 2003, p. 130)

Where Buddhism seeks to dissolve the ego, the coalescence of being seeks to build, strengthen, and multiply its ephemeral strands until it is no longer ephemeral but deep, dense, precisely articulated, aware of itself and its nature over time, and consistent in that nature. As we will see in later chapters, the purpose here is not to become free of inner suffering *once and for all*, but rather to become able to make sense of suffering and transfigure it into a source of meaning and joy in life (Nietzsche [1887] 1974). Mindfulness is a technique that can be used to bring about either the dissolution or the consolidation of the self. This book argues for the latter.

This chapter argued that hedonia is a function of positive affect, negative affect, and hedonic satisfaction. It further argued that hedonia is distinct from eudaimonia and conscience—more broadly, that hedonic satisfaction and existential satisfaction can and should be conceptually separated. It then discussed the importance of conceiving emotional wellbeing as a parameter that determines affective tendencies, namely emotional disposition, volatility, and stickiness. Emotional wellbeing is a function of attention, eudaimonia, and conscience. It is an important channel linking the three dimensions of wellbeing—hedonia, eudaimonia, and conscience—together.

The second section of the chapter discussed some prominent characteristics of hedonia. The first was the peak-end rule and the curious tendency of people to remember hedonia differently to how they experience it. This led to a discussion of two other prominent clusters of cognitive-behavioral theories associated with hedonia: first, reference points and the related phenomena of focusing illusions and loss aversion in wellbeing assessment; second, adaptation by way of homeostasis and the hedonic treadmill. This section also discussed the literature in happiness economics, notably the impact of hope, desperation, and inequality on investment decisions, declining marginal returns from income to SW-B, and the deleterious impact of unemployment.

The third section reviewed what we have learned about hedonia from time use surveys. Perhaps the main takeaway point here is that pleasure and purpose are experienced differently and are often traded off against each other. Work, for example, is typically good for purpose but not necessarily pleasure, and vice versa for watching television. We should be careful about overlooking either pleasure or purpose when thinking about SWB. Other results were what you would expect: people don't like doing chores and commuting, and they enjoy leisure and spending time with friends and family.

The final section of the chapter reviewed a range of techniques for mood management drawn largely from the cognitive-behavioral therapies literature. These assist the individual to achieve hedonia by encouraging constructive habits of behavior and mind. In many cases, they are formalizations of ancient wisdom (especially stoicism) and common sense, like being a good person, looking on the bright side, and not sweating the small stuff. Other techniques are somewhat more complicated, like self-compassion and staying in the moment of positive events.

The techniques of mood management are important, but they have a somewhat shallow relationship to SWB because they rarely consider the deeper causes of emotions and mood in eudaimonia and conscience. Emotion is a sophisticated signaling device. Fear, for example, sends our mind a message that we need to leave because we are in danger. In a similar way, positive and negative emotions accompany the process of self-actualization. For example, a sense of achievement accompanies the completion of authentic goals, whereas only a sense of relief accompanies the completion of extrinsically regulated goals. The coalescence of being uses these emotional signals as guides in the quest to overcome despair and achieve eudaimonia. As one progresses on that quest, the positive emotional signals one receives increase in frequency, duration, and intensity, while negative emotions do the opposite. This is because you are engaging in fewer activities, hold fewer values, and associate with fewer people who are "wrong" for you. When you associate with "appropriate" things you get positive emotional signals. You also rarely get negative emotional signals because you rarely associate with the "wrong" things.

The key point to underline here is that while mood and emotion management is important, if one lacks conscience or does not live in a way that nourishes basic psychology needs then negative moods and emotions will be more prevalent. Competence in self-administered cognitive-behavioral therapy can only address *symptoms* of emotional ill-being here, not *causes*. It is thus necessary to approach SWB, including emotional wellbeing, holistically, meaning a sophisticated and thoroughgoing engagement with eudaimonia and conscience. This task is taken up over the coming chapters.

7

Eudaimonia

> It matters not how strait the gate,
> How charged with punishments the scroll,
> I am the master of my fate;
> I am the captain of my soul
>
> —William Ernest Henley, *Invictus*

Introduction

The primary purposes of this chapter are (1) to further justify distinguishing eudaimonia as a dimension of wellbeing and (2) to justify and elaborate its content, namely autonomy, competence, and relatedness. The chapter also explains the differences between eudaimonic ideas in psychology and philosophy. Finally, it expounds a range of ideas from self-determination theory that are helpful for understanding the coalescence of being. These include the spectrum of motivation, internalization, and self-congruence.

The chapter proceeds as follows. I begin with the literature in psychology that attests to the conceptual differences between the hedonic and eudaimonic dimensions of wellbeing. Early SW-B scholarship hesitated to engage with the importance of relationships, autonomy, and competence to SWB (Kashdan et al 2008). SW-B scholars thought that these items were perhaps better conceptualized as causes of wellbeing rather than constitutive of it. They were also concerned that "eudaimonia" was not a theoretically unified construct, with many different theories all using the same term (this remains the case). Following critiques and bridging efforts from eudaimonic psychologists, the SW-B and eudaimonia literatures are now steadily merging, at least in psychology. In some of this new work, SW-B is regarded as symptomatic of need satisfaction (Martela and Sheldon 2019). SW-B is seen as a potential outcome measure for tracking whether an individual is living well, namely in a way that nourishes their basic needs. I instead posit affect, satisfaction, and basic

A Theory of Subjective Wellbeing. Mark Fabian, Oxford University Press. © Oxford University Press 2022.
DOI: 10.1093/oso/9780197635261.003.0008

needs together as aspects of SWB rather than some being constitutive of it while others are merely symptoms. My principal reason for doing so is that it seems intuitive that SWB is higher when someone with their basic needs met is also having a pleasant experience or leading a pleasant life. Hedonia and eudaimonia therefore have separate but interrelated positive impacts on SWB. This is in keeping with the notion of SWB as a network.

Having established eudaimonia as a standalone dimension of wellbeing, I turn to explain the difference between philosophical and psychological conceptions of it. These accounts are unified by two characteristics: an emphasis on wellbeing as a *process* rather than an *outcome*, and their claim that the most prudent way to attain wellbeing derives from human nature. The philosophical and psychological accounts diverge from there. Philosophical accounts are grounded in a view of humans as rational and ethical creatures and consequently emphasize the role of practical wisdom and virtue for living well. Psychological accounts instead emphasize the evolutionary origins of the human organism. We have evolved to autonomously seek to expand our self, notably in terms of skills and knowledge, and to integrate into groups that aid our survival. Psychological accounts consequently argue that the prudent way to live involves nurturing basic psychological needs that emerge from this organismic basis.

The most influential of the psychological accounts of eudaimonia is that of self-determination theory. It is to this body of work that the second half of the chapter is dedicated. I explain the nature of the three basic psychological needs emphasized by SDT and review empirical evidence that nurturing these needs is fundamental to SWB. I then briefly review the evolutionary basis of SDT and the notion of humans being wired for organismic integration, which gives them their basic orientation toward growth and internal consistency. A critical aspect of this organismic perspective is the nature of motivation—why do we do some things and not others? I explain SDT's influential theories of intrinsic and extrinsic motivation and their relationship to behavior and SWB. Finally, I review SDT research on self-concordant goals, which forms an important component of the coalescence of being.

Eudaimonia as Distinct from Hedonia

In chapter 6, on hedonia, I elaborated conceptual arguments and reviewed statistical evidence from the SW-B tradition that hedonia and eudaimonia are distinct aspects of wellbeing. Here I review additional arguments and evidence, this time from the eudaimonic tradition.

Among the first papers in psychology claiming that affect and satisfaction were insufficient concepts to capture holistic wellbeing were Ryff 1989a and 1989b. Ryff argued, as I did in chapters 1 and 2, that SW-B research had proceeded in the absence of theory and that this had caused that literature to miss important dimensions of wellbeing (1989b, p. 1069):

> The premise of this study is that there has been particular neglect at the most fundamental level in . . . the task of defining the essential features of psychological well-being. It is argued that much of the prior literature is founded on conceptions of well-being that have little theoretical rationale and, as a consequence, neglect important aspects of positive functioning.

After reviewing theoretical work in the history of philosophical and psychological thought on wellbeing, Ryff posited a six-factor model of wellbeing. It included the following: self-acceptance, positive relations with others, autonomy, environmental mastery, purpose in life, and personal growth. She then conducted a statistical analysis, the results of which suggested that these dimensions were important aspects of wellbeing and that affect and life satisfaction were insufficient to capture them (Ryff 1989b). Three of the dimensions emphasized by Ryff—relations, autonomy, and personal growth—are central themes in SDT's account of positive human functioning. Autonomy and personal growth feature in accounts of psychological wellbeing that self-identity as eudaimonic.

A notable body of work in this tradition is that of Waterman (2013). He published a series of papers (1990, 1992, 1993, 2007a, 2007b) developing the notion of eudaimonic wellbeing as grounded in "personal expressiveness" (similar to some "nature fulfillment" accounts of eudaimonia in philosophy, notably Haybron 2008). Waterman provided statistical evidence that this aspect of wellbeing was poorly represented in SW-B research. A key finding of Waterman's work was that while experiences of eudaimonia are always accompanied by positive affect, the reverse is not true. This finding relates to existential satisfaction. It is possible to be periodically happy and even generally satisfied with your life while still experiencing feelings of meaninglessness, existential boredom, and stagnation, all of which negatively impact SWB. It is not possible to address these deep determinants of ill-being simply by treating mood. In contrast, someone whose life nourishes their basic psychological needs will almost certainly have positive affect and be satisfied with their life because nourished needs give rise to these symptoms.

Waterman's efforts eventually culminated in a discussion between him and prominent researchers within SW-B in the *Journal of Positive Psychology* (Kashdan et al. 2008; Biswas-Diener et al. 2009; Waterman 2008). In their papers, the SW-B scholars expressed reservations about eudaimonic wellbeing for several compelling reasons. First, it is difficult to operationalize. Second, there are many conceptions of it that aren't entirely compatible. Third, there was confusion about whether eudaimonia was an outcome rather than a cause or ingredient of SWB. Finally, the differences and complementarities between eudaimonic philosophy and eudaimonic psychology were unclear, confusing, and poorly understood. However, the authors ultimately concluded that SWB scholarship needed to pay more attention to the factors highlighted by eudaimonic scholars, including relationships, meaning, autonomy, and personal growth. The eudaimonic perspective has grown in prominence in hedonic psychology and happiness economics since (OECD 2013; Stone and Mackie 2013). This book is an attempt to provide the synthesis and clarity that Kashdan et al. (2008) were concerned is lacking in eudaimonic accounts of wellbeing.

Waterman was supported in his efforts by a handful of other scholars, especially Vittersø and others associated with the "functional" approach to psychological well-being (Vittersø 2013, 2014; Vittersø et al. 2009, 2010), and researchers in SDT. Following an influential publication in the *Journal of Happiness Studies* merging SDT and eudaimonic perspectives in psychology and philosophy (Ryan et al. 2008), SDT has consistently been described by its leaders as a eudaimonic approach to wellbeing (Ryan and Deci 2017, p. 612).

While that description remains debatable, this volume argues that basic psychological needs should be differentiated from affect and satisfaction as independent dimensions of SWB. In SDT's eudaimonic account, basic psychological needs are conceptualized as constitutive of wellbeing while affect and satisfaction, among other things, are merely indicators of it. To recall Sheldon's (2013) phrasing, basic needs are the *ingredients* of wellbeing, while SW-B is a way of checking whether wellbeing is present. In contrast, I argue that basic needs, affect, and satisfaction are all ingredients in SWB. Measuring it is a matter of specific instruments, like the Basic Psychological Needs survey (Gagné 2003), life satisfaction scale questions, or the wellbeing profile (Marsh et al. 2020).

For now, I can only justify this view theoretically. If SWB is a state, then it seems intuitive that someone who is presently experiencing pleasant (unpleasant) circumstances and/or emotions is better (worse) off than someone who is in neutral circumstances. This is true even if both individuals have the same level of eudaimonic wellbeing. For example, someone whose life nourishes their basic needs has a higher level of SWB while they are eating their favorite food than ten minutes prior to that consumption, ceteris paribus. The food has little to do with their basic psychological needs, but it puts them in a better mood. Similarly, if you could transplant someone whose basic needs were met in a meager setting to a setting in which they had a higher standard of living, they would assess their new life as more pleasant. They would relax more easily on their plusher couch, have better gut health and vitality because of the higher-quality food that they eat, and have better moods thanks to the superior weather. All these would go to their SWB even though their basic needs are met identically in both cases. There are of course exceptions. Ascetics, for example, not only place little value on pleasure but might want to actively avoid it to attain their spiritual goals. Pleasure would distress them. However, these are *exceptions* to the rule; they do not *disprove* it. We should not abandon a good theory simply because there are a small number of outliers that complicate it.

Eudaimonia in Philosophy and Psychology

The term "eudaimonia" has a long history stretching back to Aristotle. Commensurate with these illustrious origins, eudaimonia has been the object of extensive study in philosophical circles and only more recently in psychology. Chapter 9 integrates some aspects of the philosophical accounts into the coalescence of being. This chapter focuses on the psychological accounts, notably the one emanating from SDT. It is worthwhile in this context to briefly delineate the psychological account of eudaimonia from the philosophical account, and to consider overlaps and potential complementarities between the two.

In both philosophical and psychological accounts, eudaimonia concerns what it means to "live well." This notion of *living* well means that eudaimonia is more about wellbeing as a *process* rather than wellbeing as an *outcome* (Besser-Jones 2015). However, outcomes tend to sneak in, such as in SDT's argument that nourishing basic psychological needs *leads to* positive affect, satisfaction, vitality, et cetera. The term "flourishing" is sometimes used to connote the outcome of eudaimonic wellbeing. Alongside an emphasis on living well rather than being well, eudaimonic accounts of wellbeing think that it must be explained in terms of the distinctive qualities of human beings.

Aristotle emphasized the unique human capacity for reason and morality. He consequently defined eudaimonia as activity of the soul in accordance with reason and virtue (Aristotle 1999, 1.7). This emphasis on "practical wisdom" as fundamental to wellbeing is inherent in most contemporary philosophical conceptions of eudaimonia (Annas 2011; Russell 2012; LeBar 2013) but absent from psychological accounts. Psychologists tend to be skeptical of emphasizing reason because there is extensive empirical evidence that we don't behave in accordance with reason, that in fact it plays a relatively minor role in our psychology and behavior, and that this is true even of people who have high levels of SW-B and reasoning ability. We are influenced by unconscious biases (Bargh and Chartrand 1999; Kahneman 2011), and some of these are conjectured to have important buffering effects on self-esteem and other aspects of SWB (Johnson et al. 1997). Many of our behaviors are unconscious and automatic (Doris 2002; Kahneman 2011). And our reasoning tends to come after instinctive judgments, which are what actually guide our behavior (Haidt 2001, 2012).

Rather than reason and virtue, psychological accounts instead ground their conception of eudaimonia in basic human needs, the kinds of lives that nourish these needs, and the positive states that flow from living and satisfying the needs in this way (Ryan and Deci 2017; Ryff and Singer 2008). The psychological accounts argue that humans have evolved to be a particular kind of organism that is programmed to behave so as to satisfy these basic needs. The organism will experience ill-being if it deviates from this nature and wellbeing if it aligns with it.

Basic Psychological Needs

SDT posits three basic psychological needs: autonomy, relatedness, and competence. A basic need is defined first and foremost by its direct causal relationship with optimal development, psychological integrity, health, and wellbeing. This causal relationship must go in both directions: the frustration of needs must cause ill-being indicators such as depression just as their nourishment causes wellbeing indicators such as positive affect (Ryan and

Deci 2017, p. 251). If the satisfaction of an item is only positively associated with wellbeing, then SDT describes it as a wellbeing enhancer but not a basic need. Beneficence is one example (Martela and Ryan 2016). As a logical consequence of this definition, basic psychological needs are posited as objective determinants of wellbeing. Someone who is not nourishing these needs will be unwell, regardless of how effective their mood management or the extent to which they are satisfying their preferences. There is substantial empirical evidence that basic psychological needs are universal features of human psychology that cut across cultures and genders (Ryan and Deci 2017, chap. 22).

Autonomy is the need to self-regulate one's experiences and actions. An autonomous individual feels volitional, self-congruent, and integrated (DeCharms 1968; Ryan 1993; Shapiro 1981). They are not externally controlled. The behaviors of an autonomous individual are self-endorsed and typically self-concordant in the sense that they align with the individual's authentic motivations and values. Autonomy in SDT is not about independence, self-reliance, freedom from all social influences, detachment from others, or individualism (Ryan and Deci 2017, p. 568). This is critical for understanding the relationship between autonomy and relatedness and responding to collectivist critiques. Social relativists have previously criticized SDT by claiming it is an excessively Western and individualistic doctrine that does not hold in collectivist cultures (Iyengar and Lepper 1999; Markus and Kitayama 2003). This is erroneous. Succinctly, an individual can autonomously promote the needs of the group and autonomously comport toward other individuals. There is no conflict between autonomy and relatedness and nothing in self-determination theory that makes it incompatible with collectivist cultures. I will return to these matters in chapter 9.

Competence is about being good at the things you want to be good at. It refers to a need for mastery and effectiveness. It is implicated in a wide range of behaviors, from athletics and videogames to scientific research and puzzle solving. However, it is also easily thwarted by excessive challenge, pervasive negative feedback, and overwhelming social comparisons (such as to professional athletes or the ultra-rich).

Relatedness concerns having healthy and satisfying relationships with valued others. More generally, it is about social connectedness. It is nourished both by being cared for by others and by being valuable to others, typically because of contributions to the group. Relatedness is closely associated with a "sense of belonging" (Baumeister and Leary 1995) and a sense of being integral to social organizations—what Angyal (1941) called "homonomy."

There is extensive cross-cultural empirical evidence to support the hypothesis that nourishing the basic psychological needs improves wellbeing in terms of positive affect, life satisfaction, ease of motivation, vitality, and self-esteem, as well as the absence of psychopathology, depression, anxiety, compartmentalization, defensiveness, and personality rigidity (Chen et al. 2015; Church et al. 2013; Sheldon, Elliot et al. 2004, 2009). These results have been extended to specific domains including the workplace (Deci et al. 2001; Ilardi et al. 1993; Baard et al. 2004) and schools (Jang et al. 2009). Variation in the degree to which basic needs are nourished predicts differences in wellbeing between individuals, and variation in the degree to which each need is nourished predicts changes in wellbeing within individuals (Sheldon et al. 1996; Reis et al. 2000; La Guardia et al. 2000; Lynch et al. 2009).

The Evolutionary Basis of Self-Determination Theory

Beyond basic needs, SDT has contributed a range of ideas to the wellbeing discourse that are important for understanding the coalescence of being. I will address three of these ideas in detail in the rest of this chapter: the evolutionary basis of SDT, the motivation spectrum, and the notion of self-concordant goals.

Evolutionary perspectives have swept across the psychological sciences in recent decades. The basic principle of evolutionary psychology is that there is such a thing as "human nature," including in terms of psychological processes and features, and that this nature is the product of evolutionary forces (Barkow et al. 1992). Evolutionary psychology has brought a kind of discipline to the psychological sciences by requiring that postulated aspects of human nature be grounded in evolutionary processes. If some postulated quirk of human psychology can't be understood as an evolutionary adaptation, then its veracity is called into question.

SDT is grounded in a view of human nature that neatly addresses the evolutionary basis of the theory's basic tenets. SDT posits a process of *organismic integration* that is inherent to human beings (Ryan and Deci 2017, p. 29):

Individuals are thought to possess an inherent, active tendency toward the extension, progressive transformation, and integration of structures, functions, and experiences. By continuously stretching their capacities, expressing their propensities, and integrating new skills and knowledge into existing structures, people develop in the direction of greater effectiveness, organisation and relative unity in functioning. Regulation of action based on a synthesis of experiences and values provides the basis for a coherent and vital sense of self and integrity.

A succinct summary of organismic integration is that humans have a tendency toward personal growth, but the concept runs deeper than that. The three basic psychological needs emerge directly from organismic integration. Humans have adapted to be inquisitive beings who seek to improve their competence, as this is critical for survival. They must learn navigation, the crafting and use of tools, language, self-defense, and a range of other skills to flourish. The psychological need for competence evolved around the acquisition of these skills. Humans are also aided in their survival by collective action and have consequently evolved a tendency toward social behavior (Baumeister 2005; Greene 2014; Wilson 2015). This is the evolutionary basis of the need for relatedness. The need for autonomy emerges in parallel to intrinsic motivation as a rudder guiding behavior toward adaptively advantageous growth and integration (Ruiz-Mirazo et al. 2000; Santelices 1999). Environments and groups that thwart the basic needs undermine the tendency of humans toward organismic integration. This naturally gives rise to distress in the form of depression, anxiety, and psychopathology as the psychophysiology of the human animal reacts to its odds of survival being diminished (Slavin and Kriegman 1992).

Organismic integration also undergirds the psychological tendency to avoid and overcome compartmentalization. Integration requires different aspects of the self to be coherent. If different aspects of the self are inconsistent they will pull the individual in different directions, leading to goal conflict, undermining motivation, and causing distress.

The Motivation Spectrum

SDT is foremost a theory of motivation: an account of why humans undertake certain actions and not others, and why they feel certain behaviors to be relatively effortless to engage in while others require willpower or even duress. The principal device for understanding motivation in SDT is the notion of a spectrum of motivation running from extrinsic to intrinsic (see figure 7.1). Tasks that are motivated in ways closer to the intrinsic end of the spectrum are easier to undertake because they are more self-determined. In contrast, the more extrinsically motivated a behavior, the more self-regulation is required to engage in it. Extrinsically motivated activities are undertaken either to avoid extrinsic punishment or to attain rewards that are contingent to the activity itself, such as approval. Intrinsically motivated behaviors are those where the activity is its own reward, so to speak.

Intrinsic motivation and the associated need for autonomy emerge out of the postulate of an organismic tendency toward integration. This tendency is grounded in primordial, subconscious inclinations toward certain activities—a minimalist "innate self." Activities that align with this core of inclinations come naturally—they are intrinsically motivated. Individuals can gradually bring behaviors and values from the extrinsic end of the motivation spectrum to the intrinsic end through the process of internalization, described later.

The spectrum of motivation begins at one end with "controlled" behaviors that are extrinsically motivated and entirely self-regulated. These are behaviors motivated by external agents, typically via duress, such as domestic violence. The individual does not undertake such behaviors autonomously. They cause distress to the controlled individual and are draining, reducing vitality.

Introjected behaviors are one step closer to intrinsic motivation. Like controlled behaviors, they are motivated by factors contingent to those behaviors, but unlike in controlled behaviors that are motivated by *external* duress, these contingencies are *administered by the individual themselves* (Deci and Ryan 2000, p. 236). The prototypic examples are contingencies of self-worth like pride, shame, and guilt. The latter two are related to moral opprobrium, which links them to contingencies of positive regard by others (Tangney and Tracy 2012). Another important and common example is activities undertaken for contingent love, especially from parents and peers. Individuals can autonomously introject behaviors, but the high degree of

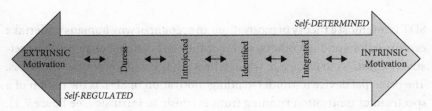

Figure 7.1 The motivation spectrum according to self-determination theory

self-regulation required to pursue them makes such behaviors difficult to motivate and even harder to internalize.

Identified behaviors are another step closer to being intrinsically motivated. Individuals engage in them not for their own sake but because they recognize their *value*. They thus require less intense self-regulation than introjected behaviors. A common example is improving your diet. While many people dislike dieting or are reluctant to spring for expensive but healthful food items, they do so because they value the effects on their health and appearance. This makes motivating oneself to eat right easier. Because of the more palpable element of volition in these behaviors, they are meaningfully more autonomous than introjected behaviors. However, they are not engaged in for their own sake, so they are not intrinsically motivated behaviors either.

Integration is where the positive valuations that underpin identified behaviors are connected to other items in the individual's broader value system. They thereby become part of the individual's core identity and thus become more intrinsically motivated. For example, as a dieting individual interacts with food blogging communities and their cooking and taste is appreciated by their family and friends, they may start to enjoy diet-related activities more. This is because these activities are assimilated more thoroughly into their lifestyle and connected to intrinsic values like social interaction with valued peers. Dieting moves from being done for health, appearance, and taste to something that is done more for its own sake.

A richer but more complex example is the increasingly common pursuit of mathematical competence among social scientists. Until recently, there was a common lay attitude that some people had a mind for the arts and humanities while others had a mind for the sciences. Intrinsic motivation for mathematics was a common way of demarcating between these individuals. Recently, advances in quantitative social science have seen its methodologies come to dominate disciplines previously characterized by the power of intuition and eloquent argumentation. Now people with "arts and humanities" minds who want to influence policy or simply mount a compelling argument must be able to present formal models of their theories and statistical evidence to back them up. They are consequently undertaking training in mathematics. Their desire to be competent social scientists causes them to *identify* with mathematics. They value it. Pursuing competence in it nonetheless demands substantial willpower and self-regulation from them. Over time, as they encounter branches of mathematics that are especially useful to them, like the mathematics of causal inference, this identification deepens. As they develop competence and apply mathematics in their research it will contribute to other values they hold, like knowledge, clear argumentation, and publication. More importantly, they will be able to use mathematics to do social science, where the latter is an intrinsically motivated activity for them—unlike, say, learning calculus. Mathematics will thereby become *integrated*. They may never develop full intrinsic motivation toward mathematics, but it will require less willpower to engage in than when they first got started.

"Internalization" is the process by which behaviors move from identification through integration to intrinsic motivation. It occurs when identified behaviors nurture the basic psychological needs for autonomy, competence, and relatedness. When these needs are not nurtured the identified behaviors tend to be aborted. For example, individuals will affiliate with identified groups so long as those groups provide them with support and other goods and accept them as a valued member of the collective. If this does not take place, the individual will experience ostracism and ultimately abandon the group, barring unusual circumstances. Similarly, individuals will undertake valued activities unless they prove consistently incompetent at them. A classic case here is New Year's resolutions. Finally, individuals will undertake identified behaviors provided they grant a sense of autonomy. For example, quitting smoking because you deem it good for your cherished health is easier than quitting because your university has banned smoking from campus and the activity is thus highly inconvenient. It is notable in this circumstance that experimental evidence suggests that the provision of contingent rewards can undermine intrinsic motivation (see Deci et al. 1999 for a meta-analysis).

Intrinsic and Extrinsic Values and Self-Concordant Goals

A final insight pertaining to wellbeing emerging from research in SDT is that all goals are not created equal. Specifically, goals targeted because they are associated with extrinsic and contingent rewards like money, fame, and image do not produce the same SW-B benefits at attainment as goals associated with intrinsic rewards like personal growth and intimacy (Kasser and Ryan 1993, 1996). Indeed, attaining extrinsic goals can even be negatively associated with SW-B (Kasser and Ryan 2001). Furthermore, the mere pursuit of so-called extrinsic aspirations can be harmful to SWB, as this pursuit does not nurture basic psychological needs. In contrast, the process of attaining intrinsic aspirations does nurture basic needs, and so pursuing such goals is SWB enhancing regardless of whether the goals are achieved or not (Howell et al. 2011; Sheldon, Ryan et al. 2004; Sheldon and Krieger 2014). Experimental evidence suggests that this poor relationship between extrinsic aspirations and SWB holds even in social contexts like business schools and corporate law firms that espouse extrinsic aspirations like money and power and celebrate their achievement (Kasser and Ahuvia 2002; Vansteenkiste et al. 2006).

Sheldon has expanded these insights into a more general theory of goal self-concordance (Sheldon and Elliot 1999). The self-concordance model posits that people will derive greater wellbeing from goals that fit their personalities or, more daringly, their innate selves (Sheldon and Vansteenkiste 2005). Now, innate qualities vary across persons and are very difficult to measure, but intrinsic motivation can act as a proxy in empirical work (Sheldon and Cooper 2008; Sheldon and Schuler 2011). Part of the power of the self-congruence model is its relationship to self-actualization. Pursuing discordant goals brings negative affective signals that discourage us. In contrast, the pursuit and achievement of concordant goals brings positive affect. Intrinsic pursuits are also easier to motivate and thus sustain. They leave us feeling exhilarated rather than drained. These signals help us to "bootstrap ourselves into our own futures, arriving at the future of our choice" (Sheldon 2013, p. 126). This turn of phrase from Sheldon is reminiscent of the Hellenic maxim "become who you are."

Conclusion

SDT's nuanced theory of goal pursuit and attainment is important because it underscores that there is a right way and a wrong way to go about wellbeing. The prudential good is a combination of prudential outcomes and prudential pursuit of those outcomes. Pursuing extrinsic aspirations is unlikely to be beneficial to either the process or the outcome of wellbeing. Relatedly, SDT's findings concerning extrinsic aspirations also underscore that "preference satisfaction" is an insufficiently nuanced way to conceptualize wellbeing. The satisfaction of some preferences is unlikely to result in wellbeing. Preference satisfaction accounts of wellbeing are often aware of such issues and deal with them through the notion of "laundered" preferences (Hausman 2015) or "appropriate" values (Tiberius 2018). SDT's research on internalization and self-congruence contributes to a realistic and psychologically rich understanding of what laundering involves and what "appropriate" means.

SDT's sophisticated combination of organismic principles, motivation, and the notion of basic psychological needs bridges objective list and subjectivist accounts of wellbeing. The basic psychological needs are posited as objective indicators of wellbeing. However, the need for autonomy and the motivation spectrum make it clear that individuals approach these objective ends in thoroughly subjective ways. What goals, values, and behaviors an individual is intrinsically motivated to pursue will be unique to that individual. What specific competencies and relations nourish the individual's basic psychological needs will be substantially, indeed mostly, dictated by their subjective makeup and assessments.

In the next two chapters I expand on SDT's insights and combine them with ideas from continental philosophy and other theories in psychology. I further develop the connection between eudaimonia and hedonia by giving a deeper account of the role affective signals play in helping people identify their intrinsic self and navigate toward it. I merge SDT's theory of internalization with ideas from self-discrepancy theory to produce a simple mechanism that describes the central processes of self-actualization. I will bring in ideas from philosophy and social psychology pertaining to the nature of introspection and social verification to give a deeper account of what living in accordance with practical reason might mean. I will also enrich the links between SDT and meaning. As our understanding of it is somewhat nascent, meaning is often presented as something that can simply be chosen, as though it just happens. In reality, meaning is a tricky and challenging thing to achieve. By combining SDT with other theories from philosophy and psychology, I can give a preliminary account of how meaning emerges and thickens into a palpable feeling.

8

Conscience

> There is but one truly serious philosophical problem and that is su-
> icide. Judging whether life is or is not worth living amounts to an-
> swering the fundamental question of philosophy.
>
> —Albert Camus

Introduction

As with the chapters on hedonia and eudaimonia, the primary purpose of
this chapter is to justify the distinction of the conscience dimension in the
SWBPF and elaborate its subcomponents, namely meaning, identity, and
virtue. These themes motivated existentialism, a prominent school of continental (European as opposed to Anglophone) philosophy that existed
from around 1850 to 1950. This period had to deal with the aftermath of the
Enlightenment's disenchantment of the world—what Nietzsche called "the
death of God." The tremendous progress of reason during the Enlightenment
made it difficult to believe the teachings of Christianity. Europeans were consequently searching, increasingly frantically, for stable sources of meaning,
identity, and palpable norms. The loosening force that the Enlightenment
exerted on European culture was exacerbated by technological change.
Industrialization altered the nature of work and led to the emergence of the
industrial metropolis. People moved from "tight" cultural communities
that characterize agrarian life to "loose" metropolitan ones. Tight communities are characterized by thick cultural norms that structure daily life and
are strictly enforced. In contrast, loose communities have thin norms and
permissive cultures (Gelfand 2018). Cities allowed people unprecedented
free expression in the anonymity of crowds while making it difficult to really stand out. Drawing identity from the collective was thus made harder by

A Theory of Subjective Wellbeing. Mark Fabian, Oxford University Press. © Oxford University Press 2022.
DOI: 10.1093/oso/9780197635261.003.0009

cities while they simultaneously undermined the ability of people to be recognized for their uniqueness (Simmel [1903] 1950).

The existential problems of "anguish," "nausea," and "seriousness" were the inevitable, organic products of this milieu. These variables correspond to the absence of identity, meaning, and virtue, respectively. Succinctly, nausea refers to the sense of meaninglessness that characterizes the world after the death of God. Seriousness refers to the feeling that ethics and values more generally lack significance and authority over the individual's conduct because there is no cosmic order to enforce them. And anguish refers to the inability of the individual to attain a sense of themselves because they are always becoming as they make decisions.

People's need to mitigate these fonts of ill-being contributed to the rise of fascism and totalitarianism. These ideologies provided thick norms based on race or class and enforced by the state. Similar forces are today contributing to the polarization of politics and the rise of nationalist populism in the United States and Europe. Now is thus a timely moment to revisit the insights of existentialism, which have been almost entirely absent from the SWB discourse. While empirical research has recently caught up to the themes of existentialism, the full depth of that philosophical movement is not yet appreciated.

The chapter is set out as follows. First, I review Kierkegaard's notion of "despair," which is arguably the first systematic articulation of existentialism's core problems. Despair in existentialist thought is not the opposite of hope or optimism. It has a distinct and specific meaning, vaguely similar to nihilism. I then distinguish nausea, seriousness, and anguish as articulated by the French existentialists. These three problems are contained within Kierkegaard's notion of despair, but it is easier to work with them as three separate concepts rather than one unified but relatively clumsy idea. I quote extensively from existentialist texts throughout this analysis in a manner that might strike non-philosophers as odd. I do this for three reasons. First, such textual engagement is customary in continental philosophy. Second, my interpretation of existentialist ideas is an oversimplification made necessary by the nature of the present work and I want to ensure that the full complexity of the ideas is at least somewhat present. And finally, because most scholars in SWB studies are not familiar with these works, I want to make clear what it is that I am interpreting to avoid charges of misrepresentation.

In the second part of the chapter I review a raft of research in modern psychology attesting to the importance of nausea, seriousness, anguish, and related issues for understanding SWB (Sumner et al. 2014). I then elaborate the precise meaning of identity, meaning, and virtue. High scores in these variables reflects a triumph over despair, but they are more than merely the inverse of the existential problems. The conscience variables help us to understand not only how to escape despair but also how to flourish.

In the third part of the chapter I canvass solutions to despair proposed in the philosophical literature. Specifically, I examine Kierkegaard's faith-based solution, Norton's eudaimonistic approach, and the roots of the coalescence of being in the work of Nietzsche and the French existentialists. This philosophy provides a skeleton upon which I foist theories and evidence from recent research in psychology to articulate the coalescence of being in chapter 9.

The Existential Problems

The problems and themes of existentialism were arguably first articulated in the modern era by the Danish philosopher Søren Kierkegaard, especially in his *The Sickness unto Death* ([1849] 2008). He uses a single term to encapsulate these problems: "despair." From the outset, despair is characterized as concerning human "being" (Kierkegaard [1849] 2008, p. 9):

> Despair is a sickness of the spirit, of the self, and so can have three forms: being unconscious in despair of having a self (inauthentic despair), not wanting in despair to be oneself, and wanting in despair to be oneself.

To understand Kierkegaard's notion of despair, it is necessary to engage with his definition of the "self." This is given in very arcane terms (Kierkegaard [1849] 2008, p. 9):

> Spirit is the self. But what is the self? The self is a relation which relates to itself, or that in the relation which is its relating to itself. The self is not the relation but the relation's relating to itself. A human being is a synthesis of the infinite and the finite, of the temporal and the eternal. In short a synthesis. A synthesis is a relation between two terms. Looked at in this way a human being is not yet a self

To translate: "self," for Kierkegaard at least, is reflexive consciousness, that is, self-awareness. "Spirit" in Kierkegaard's philosophy is thus "I." The reason self is a "relation that relates to itself" is that consciousness can stand apart from the rest of a person; we can reflect on ourselves. Indeed, we seem to be able to change ourselves through conscious effort.

The final part of the definition, which refers to a human being as a synthesis of the temporal and the eternal and thus "not yet a self," is the most important. The "temporal and the eternal" refers to the fact that individual humans grasp that they are both the same person over time (Usain Bolt, for example) and also that they are a different person at each point in time (Usain Bolt before and after breaking the world record for the 100-meter sprint, for example, or before and after retirement). The reason we are "not yet a self" is that we are always *becoming*. We as individuals are defined by the choices we make over time. Consciousness and free will mean that these choices are never predetermined. Who we are in the next moment is always an open question, and we are always engaged in an ongoing process of self-actualization.

The French existentialists would later summarize the relationship between consciousness and becoming in one of their two slogans: "existence precedes essence." The idea here is that we are born a human being, but it is the nature of human beings to be constantly constructing an individual identity through their unique choices: "man first of all exists, encounters himself, surges up in the world—and defines himself afterwards" (Sartre and Beauvoir 1946, p. 3).[1]

Consciousness is a powerful thing. As the French existentialists would later emphasize, it makes us ontologically free—we are at liberty to define ourselves, in particular our values. Consciousness means that we are not automatons (Kierkegaard [1849] 2008, p. 9). We are not complete slaves to our genetic programming and to our instinctive reactions to external stimuli. Yet while consciousness is powerful and liberating, it also brings with it the sickness of despair. To understand why, it is helpful to disaggregate despair into three subcomponents analyzed by the French existentialists, namely anguish, seriousness, and nausea.

Anguish

Anguish emerges first. As a conscious being, we are always cut off from ourselves in the moment of decision because we are *defined* by our choices (Sartre [1943] 2005, p. 62). As such, *we lack an identity* that we can hold

---

[1] See also Nietzsche ([1886] 2000, p. 250): "[Man is] the as yet undetermined animal."

fixed over time. We cannot definitively answer the question "Who am I?" because we are always becoming. Furthermore, we are *capable of agonizing over decisions*—this is a kind of ill-being. Agonizing is particularly common in the early stages of self-development because immature identities often contain conflicting values, rationales, and desires. These incompatible elements are compartmentalized. The individual only realizes their inconsistency when confronted with a decision that pits them against each other. This internal incoherence means that our "self" cannot provide clear guidance about what we should do in certain circumstances. We will consequently be conflicted and paralyzed with doubt. Anguish takes in these two issues: the absence of a fixed identity and the ability to agonize over decisions when the self is not unified (Sartre [1943] 2005, p. 53).[2]

Kierkegaard's three forms of despair all concern anguish. The first form—*being unconscious in despair of having a self*—refers to those individuals who are not aware that they are moral agents and masters of their own destiny. They do not suffer from anguish, but only because they do not comprehend the significance of their choices. The second form, *not wanting in despair to be oneself*, refers to people who flee the responsibility associated with being a moral agent—what the existentialists would later refer to as "bad faith." Eichmann, who was "just following orders" as he sent thousands of Jews to their deaths, is the archetypal example (Arendt [1963] 2003). The final form—*wanting in despair to be oneself*—refers to individuals who want to define themselves and use integrity to guide their decision-making but cannot because consciousness means that we are always becoming, inescapably.

Seriousness

The third form of despair brings two other subcomponents of despair into the picture alongside anguish: seriousness and nausea. As mentioned, seriousness is the feeling that our values lack authority. In the writings of the French existentialists, the primary force undermining seriousness is the death of

---

[2] Sartre ([1943] 2005, p. 53) describes anguish thus:

If our analysis has not led us astray, there ought to exist for the human being, in so far as he is conscious of being, a certain mode of standing opposite his past and his future, as being both this past and this future and as not being them. We shall be able to furnish an immediate reply to this question; it is in anguish that man gets the consciousness of his freedom, or if you prefer, anguish is the mode of being of freedom as consciousness of being; it is in anguish that freedom is, in its being, in question for itself.

God. Without a cosmic order to undergird and enforce morality, moral rules come to appear arbitrary and in any case are easily ignored, as they do not attract retribution from cosmic justice (Sartre and Beauvoir 1946, p. 6):

> The existentialist, on the contrary, finds it extremely embarrassing that God does not exist, for there disappears with Him all possibility of finding values in an intelligible heaven. There can no longer be any good *a priori*, since there is no infinite and perfect consciousness to think it. It is nowhere written that "the good" exists, that one must be honest or not lie, since we are now upon the plane where there are only men. Dostoevsky once wrote that if God does not exist, then everything is permitted; and that, for existentialism, is the starting point.

Kierkegaard wrote before the death of God as declared by Nietzsche ([1887] 1974, p. 181) and was a deeply religious Christian (of the Lutheran rather than Thomistic variety).[3] So the chief force undermining seriousness in his philosophy is not the absence of God, but an absence of *faith*. Without *belief* in a cosmic order, the individual is necessarily confronted by the capriciousness of norms ([1849] 2008 p. 83):

> It recognizes no power over itself; therefore, in the final instance it lacks seriousness and can only conjure forth an appearance of seriousness, even when it bestows upon its experiments its greatest possible attention.

This is because an individual in the third form of despair is responsible not only for creating their own values but also for enforcing them upon their own behavior. Consciousness means that this enforcement is never absolute, because we are always capable of contradicting ourselves. Our values thus appear whimsical, made-up, superficial, and open to caprice. Kierkegaard makes this point eloquently in the following passage ([1849] 2008, p. 84):

> The self is its own master, absolutely (as one says) its own master; and exactly this is the despair, but also what it regards as its pleasure and joy. But it

---

[3] Thomists are followers of St. Thomas Aquinas. A defining characteristic of their religiosity is that they believe Christianity has largely rational foundations, rather than being founded on faith (see Fesser 2017). An analysis of their views is outside the scope of this book. Suffice it to say that *with some nuances*, the arguments laid out later in this chapter about the psychology and sociology of conscience are readily applicable to Thomists.

is easy on closer examination to see that this absolute ruler is a king without a country; that really he rules over nothing; his position, his kingdom, his sovereignty, are subject to the dialectic that rebellion is legitimate at any moment.

Sartre makes a similar point when he underlines that past pledges on the part of conscious beings exert little binding force on decisions in the present (Sartre [1943] 2005, p. 57):

> But what he apprehends then in anguish is precisely the total inefficacy of the past resolution. It is there doubtless but fixed, ineffectual, surpassed by the very fact that I am conscious of it. The resolution is still *me* to the extent that I realize constantly my identity with myself across the temporal flux, but it is no longer *me*—due to the fact that it has become an object *for* my consciousness. I am not subject to it; it fails in the mission which I have given it.

Existentialism argues that we struggle to hold ourselves to our promises because consciousness means that we can always decline to follow through (see Callard 2018 for a similar argument from an analytical, decision-theoretic perspective). What this means is that we are always capable of contravening our avowed ethical prerogatives. God's cosmic order was a way around this issue because it promises eternal suffering to any who go against the rules. But if values are subjective and if the cosmic order does not exist, then the only immediate consequences of contravening your values is you being disappointed in yourself. Indeed, there may be no consequences if you decide that your past values were erroneous. This ease with which we can generate, assert, and then contravene values speaks to their lack of seriousness. If we are the only authority over our values and conduct, then our values exert little binding power.

A critical corollary point to draw out here is that in existentialist philosophy (exempting Kierkegaard's, owing to his theism) values are subjective. Values are not written into the firmament. They do not exist out there on some Platonic shelf waiting to be discovered by someone with enough moral reasoning. Reasons can be given to justify certain values, but the extent to which these reasons are experienced as binding over individuals is dictated by how compelling those individuals feel those reasons to be, not by some cosmic order. This is the link that connects anguish and seriousness most directly. We are the source of values, but we also cannot ever justify these values by reference to something other than ourselves. As Sartre ([1943] 2005, p. 62) notes: "As a being by whom values exist, I am unjustifiable."

Nausea

Nausea is closely related to seriousness. Nausea is the feeling of meaninglessness (literary explorations are available in Camus [1942] 2013 and Sartre [1938] 2000). In the absence of any cosmic order to imbue the world with transcendental purpose, the world comes to merely *be*; it does not *matter* (Reginster 2006). Meaning and purpose are closely related to value. When something is valuable, striving for it becomes somewhat meaningful. If values are made up and capricious, then it is hard to sustain a sense of purpose when pursuing them, especially in the absence of pleasure or other crude rewards. A cosmic order not only supplies values—it also makes things *transcendentally* valuable. The goods of a cosmic order are valuable across time and space. Playing your part in God's plan, for example, contributes to the grand design of the universe and secures you an eternal place in paradise. Without faith in a cosmic order, the best an individual can hope for is to pursue a life that is meaningful to them for the duration of their lives.

Nausea was a major theme of Nietzsche's philosophy. He argued ([1887] 1974, p. 75) that it was a fundamental part of the human condition:

> Gradually, man has become a fantastic animal that has to fulfil one more condition of existence than any other animal: man *has* to believe, to know, from time to time, *why* he exists; his species cannot flourish without a periodic trust in life—without faith in *reason in life*.

Nietzsche argued that the most pervasive and powerful source of meaning to date was religion, in particular the ascetic ideal. Religion imbues the universe with meaning—the cosmic order. The *meaning of life* becomes about comporting oneself to God's plan, or to nirvana, or to whatever else a religion dictates. This meaning is *external*—it lies outside the individual. This is why Nietzsche argued that "men of faith . . . are necessarily dependent people, the sort of people who cannot posit *themselves as a goal*, who are utterly incapable of positing goals out of themselves" (Nietzsche [1885] 1990, p. 54). He counseled the opposite approach: embrace the meaningless of existence as a joyous liberty, an opportunity to affirm your own values and become a manifestation of those values (Nietzsche [1889] 1990, p. 182):

> It is absurd to want to *devolve* human existence onto some purpose or another. We have invented the concept of "purpose": there are no purposes in reality. . . . The fact that nobody is held responsible any more, that being is not the sort of thing that can be traced back to *causa prima*, that the world is not unified as either a *sensorium* or a "spirit," *only this can constitute the great liberation*—only this begins to restore the *innocence* of becoming.

Nietzsche was the first of the existentialists to appreciate that the existential problems all emerge from *ambiguity*—from the fact that we want to know *with certainty* who we are, what is right, and what we should do. When the universe does not provide these answers, we become anguished and nauseated. The typical response to this ambiguity, as terror management theory demonstrates empirically (discussed later), is to search around in one's cultural environment for sources of identity, meaning, and seriousness. The existential problems emerge with greatest force in ages characterized by the breakdown of such cultural environments, with the early metropolitan period in Europe and deindustrialized communities in the present-day United States being prime examples. Existentialism argued that this quest for certainty would either fail or be engulfed in totalitarianism (fascist or socialist). Until humanity is comfortable with ambiguity it will oscillate between nihilism and ideology. The normative ambiguity of existence must be embraced as a joyous opportunity and responsibility to define our own values. This is a bitter pill to swallow because we are not wired to accept normative uncertainty, as I will explain later.

Scientific Evidence for the Importance of the Existentialist Perspective

In this section I want to review cross-disciplinary literature and empirical evidence that attests to the importance of the themes of existentialism for understanding SWB. This serves several purposes. First, it strengthens the case for including the conscience cluster in the SWBPF. It shows that multiple lines of inquiry have converged on meaning (nausea), identity (anguish), and virtue (seriousness) as central aspects of SWB. It also provides some empirical support for the claims of the existentialists. Many of the literatures I will be referring to are quantitative and experimental in nature. Second, it makes existentialist themes more accessible. Existentialism, like much philosophy, is written in at times impenetrable language that turns off a lot of parties who would otherwise be interested in its insights. The literatures to which I refer here are typically written in a more straightforward manner. Finally, these literatures provide extensions to the ideas of existentialism that motivate the distinction of meaning, identity, and virtue from nausea, anguish, and seriousness.

I begin with the literature on meaning and purpose. This is because of all the themes of existentialism, it is nausea that has received the most attention in other literatures, including recently in SW-B scholarship (OECD 2013; Diener et al. 2010; Seligman 2011). I move from nausea and meaning to seriousness and virtue, which are studied as part of contemporary inquiries into culture, norms, and community disintegration, including as part of the literature on eudaimonic wellbeing. The final literature I examine is that coming out of terror management theory (TMT), which argues that humans have a primordial aversion to death and normative uncertainty. They respond to this terror by comporting themselves toward meaning-making communities. TMT speaks powerfully to anguish, which is fundamentally about the ambiguity of norms that could undergird our sense of self and guide our decisions.

Nausea

The literature arguably most engaged with the role of meaning in SWB is the logotherapy tradition in clinical psychology. Logotherapy was pioneered by Victor Frankl, most famously in his short work *Man's Search for Meaning* ([1946] 2008; see also Frankl 1969, 1975, 1978, 2000, 2010). It emphasizes, echoing Nietzsche, that humans need meaning, that the absence of meaning can cause depression and other psychological ills, and that meaning-based therapies can help people suffering from a range of mental illnesses. Logotherapy has been championed in America by Victor Wong (see Wong 2010). Several studies in this literature speak to the relationship between meaning and wellbeing (see Steger 2010 for a review). A relationship has been found empirically between positive affect and meaning (Keyes et al. 2002; King et al. 2006; Steger et al. 2006). Empirical studies have also found a correlation between meaning in life and life satisfaction (Bonebright et al. 2000; Ryff 1989b; Steger 2006; Steger and Frazier 2005; Steger et al. 2008). More broadly, meaning has been linked to a range of desirable traits including autonomy, self-control, and sense of control (Steger et al. 2008; Garfield 1973; Newcomb and Harlow 1986; Reker and Peacock 1981), ego resiliency (Tryon and Radzin 1972; Shek 1992), and positive perceptions of the world (Simon et al. 1998).

There are other literatures concerning meaning and wellbeing. Religion is empirically associated with higher levels of subjective well-being (Ellison 1991; Witter et al. 1985; Lim and Putnam 2010; Dolan et al. 2008). Scholars of religion have argued that a key driver of this association is religion's capacity to give people a sense of transcendental meaning (Emmons 1999; Emmons et al. 1998; Steger 2005). This echoes Kierkegaard's argument that faith is the way out of despair (discussed later) and the argument of Nietzsche and the French existentialists that nausea emerges most powerfully after the death of God.

Baumeister has written about the role of meaning in wellbeing at book length (1991). He subsumes into the notion of meaning many of the themes that I separate out into eudaimonia, identity, and virtue, but he also speaks to the narrower definition I employ. He draws important links between meaning and man's nature as "the cultural animal" (see Baumeister 2005 for a longer treatment). A critical advantage that *Homo sapiens* possesses over other animals (and perhaps even over other members of the *Homo* genus— see Harari 2011) is that we are capable of symbolic language. That is, we are capable of sharing meanings for abstract concepts that we project through culture and its attendant tropes, notably art and ritual. This capacity is wired into us and has allowed our species to survive and flourish (Peterson 1999). Given this evolutionary background, it is reasonable to suspect that our neurochemistry is inclined to make us feel good when we interact with meaning and encourages us to seek out, create, and interact with meaning.

With all this empirical work being done, one might ask why we need existentialist philosophy at all to help us appreciate the importance of meaning to wellbeing. Yet existentialism is more theoretically deep than these literatures and brings novel insights. In particular, because other literatures did not typically emerge as a direct response to *atheistic nihilism*, they sometimes proceed as though the acquisition of meaning is a relatively straightforward affair. There is an implicit sense that people can just go out and do something meaningful or reinterpret their suffering as meaningful (Esfahani

Smith 2017). A major contribution of existentialism is to reveal why meaning is hard to achieve in a nihilistic universe populated by loose, secular cultures. Furthermore, existentialism provides the basic building blocks of the process—namely the coalescence of being—by which meaning can be wrested from such a hostile world. Similar things can be said for its contribution to our understanding of seriousness and anguish.

Seriousness

The last twenty-odd years have seen great progress in the study of sociobiology (the biological underpinnings of social behavior) and the evolutionary psychology of moral cognition. A motivating question of much of this research is: how can altruism exist? The driving force of evolution is the selfish gene and its competition with other selfish genes. Such a gene is understandably altruistic toward kin because kin share a lot of genetic material. But why would it care about entities that aren't kin, including other members of its species? What gives rise to cooperation at the level of the group? This question is particularly stark in humans, where a group can number millions of members and where such groups can form along seemingly arbitrary lines like hobbies and nationalities (a social construct if ever there was one). An additional complexity in humans is that we are so clearly selfish to a substantial degree. We are not ants or bees—we do not operate as if by some sort of hive mind—nor are we a herd, and our groups are much larger than packs. What determines when we switch from selfish to altruistic?

Breakthroughs have come in the last few decades out of the idea that natural selection can take place at both the level of the individual and the level of the group (Wilson 2015). While selfish individuals typically outcompete altruistic individuals, altruistic groups outcompete selfish groups. It is thus potentially fitness-enhancing to be able to cooperate and behave altruistically, and we should not be surprised to observe cooperative groups and species flourish in the long run.

A quick note here that "altruistic" refers to cooperation and other-regarding behavior rather than strictly to privately harmful behavior. Of course, cooperation often involves some privately harmful behavior in the short run, but this cost might be paid in the expectation of a net positive outcome in the long run due to reciprocity or collective benefits, or it might be paid to gain psychic rewards from aligning with your ideal self. Unlike ants, individual humans only very rarely engage in net negative behaviors like jumping on a grenade to save their squad.

Morality is part of the elaborate psychic and cultural architecture that we evolved as a species to help us cooperate in ever larger groups. The evolutionary chain is very simplistically the following. We first developed *shared intentionality* (Tomasello et al. 2005). This is the ability to grasp what someone else wants to do, which is necessary for any cooperation. Shared intentionality allows for behaviors like one person pulling down a branch while another picks the fruit. Both parties then share the meal. The next evolutionary step came after we started to form ever larger groups to achieve ever more lucrative collective tasks, like hunting mammoths and sacking villages. We developed *group-mindedness*, which is the cognitive architecture required for culture (Tomasello et al. 2005). In the words of Haidt (2011, p. 235), it grants us "the ability to learn and conform to social norms, feel and share group-related emotions and ultimately, to create and obey social institutions, including religion."

The way this cognitive architecture manifests in moral judgment is superbly explored in Joshua Greene's *Moral Tribes* (2014), particularly his analysis of results from what is jokingly called trolleyology. This is the study, through laboratory experiments, of the decision-making processes involved in the now infamous trolley problem, an ethical hypothetical where a runaway train is about to hit five people. You, a bystander, can pull a switch that will divert the train onto a different track, where it only kills one person. Most people pull. In brain scanners, their frontal lobe—the part of the brain responsible for conscious processing (as opposed to instinct)—is typically very active. The great mystery of trolleyology was that when people were instead given the chance to push a fat man off a bridge to stop the train, most people thought this was impermissible. In the brain scans, their brain stem and amygdala—elements of our brains carried over from our animal ancestors—were more active than their frontal lobe. Why did people change their decision given that the outcome is the same in both cases: one dead instead of five?

The answer lies in the different regions of the brain. The frontal lobe is responsible for the cool calculation of conscious processing. It is not emotional and tends toward utilitarianism. The parts of the brain that light up in the bridge case, however, are responsible for instinctive decision-making. In the primordial era of our species we had good reason to develop a cognitive module that instinctively prevented us from lashing out at our peers. The explanation is that it is hard to get a reputation as a trustworthy cooperator if you tend to smack your peers (or, in the trolley case, push them off a bridge). Conscious processing came later for a range of reasons, one of which is its ability to help us cooperate in *very large* groups, as evinced by its ability to justify a utilitarian decision to kill someone to save five others.

This distinction between quick, intuitive, system 1 moral instinct and slow, thoughtful, rational system 2 moral theorizing is a major theme of Jonathan's Haidt *The Righteous Mind* (2011). He explores it therein using the metaphor of an elephant and its rider. The elephant is system 1—our ancient normative instincts. The rider is system 2—our much more recently evolved rational faculties. Instincts are depicted as an elephant rather than a horse because elephants are larger and smarter than horses. When the elephant moves, the rider can do little to control it, even if an instinct seems irrational. Indeed, Haidt presents research that suggests it is often more apt to think of the rider as serving the elephant and not the other way around. Notably, instinctive normative *feelings* come first, and we then use our frontal lobe to rationalize these feelings. As Haidt (2011, p. 38) explains:

> What the rationalists were *really* doing was generating clever justifications for moral intuitions that were best explained by evolution. Do people believe in human rights because such rights actually exist, like mathematical truths, sitting on a cosmic shelf next to the Pythagorean theorem just waiting to be discovered by Platonic reasoners? Or do people feel revulsion and sympathy when they read accounts of torture, and then invent a story about universal rights to help justify their feelings?

Evidence for this comes from work on moral dumbfounding. This is a common phenomenon where people exert sustained effort to try to rationalize a moral instinct, but even when they cannot do so, they still don't change their mind. In one example, people are presented a hypothetical case where a brother and sister commit incest while using extensive birth control, then agree that it was lovely and satisfying for both, but they won't do it again. Many respondents condemn their behavior, but then cannot rationalize their condemnation. They first hunt for some sort of victim. When they can't find one, they say things like "It's just not done, you know." But they rarely change their minds and condone the behavior. Another piece of evidence comes from studies employing hypnosis. Some participants are hypnotized to feel disgust when they hear a benign code word. Out of hypnosis, they are then told a story that includes their code word about, for example, some guy named Simon who puts in a lot of volunteer work to run a school theater production. Triggered respondents concoct fantastical reasons why Simon is actually a terrible person, such as that he is a popularity-seeking snob (Haidt 2011, p. 62). Control group respondents display no such prejudices. Haidt catalogues a range of other studies using different methodologies that replicate these results.

The key lesson, Haidt argues, is that "judgement and justification are separate processes" (2011, p. 50). Furthermore, "we do moral reasoning not to reconstruct the actual reasons why we ourselves came to a judgement; we reason to find the best possible reasons why *somebody else ought to join us* in our judgement" (2011, p. 52). The point to underline is that morality is an evolution that is tied to social opprobrium and approval. This might explain why people have been found to behave more ethically in laboratory experiments where they believe they are being watched (Burnham 2003; Burnham and Hare 2007; Ernest-Jones et al. 2011; Haley-Jones and Fessler 2005; Nettle et al. 2013), though it must be noted that this body of literature is heavily embroiled in psychology's replication crisis (Dear et al. 2019). This parallels the arguments of Lerner and Tetlock (2003, p. 433), who write:

> A central function of thought is making sure that one acts in ways *that can be persuasively justified or excused to others.* Indeed, the process of considering the justifiability of one's choices may be so prevalent that decision makers not only search for convincing reasons to make a choice when they must explain that choice to others, *they search for reasons to convince themselves* that they have made the "right" choice.

It is unsurprising in this context that the negative moral emotions of shame, guilt, and low self-esteem, which can be associated with ill-being, are tied to moral trespass. These emotions and their physical cues, like blushing with embarrassment, help us to track social signals, show contrition, and ultimately to learn, obey, operate in, and act to change normative codes within normative communities. Leary (2012) has argued that self-esteem is a kind of sociometer that provides you with an affective gauge of how attractive you are as a partner or comrade. This perspective explains the omnipresence of gossip in our society—social judgment requires obsessive commentary on people's reputations. It also explains why God, that moral adjudicator par excellence, needs to be all-seeing (Wilson 2002). Once again, we see that negative affect can find its origins in the eudaimonia or conscience dimension.

The takeaway point from all this discussion of evolution, culture, and moral cognition is that "morality is a set of psychological adaptations that allow otherwise selfish individuals to reap the benefits of cooperation" (Greene 2014, p. 23). Haidt's (2011, p. 314) definition of a moral system makes a similar point:

> Moral systems are interlocking sets of values, virtues, norms, practices, identities, institutions, technologies, and evolved psychological mechanisms that work together to suppress or regulate self-interest and make cooperative societies possible.

So on this account, moral rules do not seem to be objective facts like physical laws (and, by extension, neither are values). They are instead the intersubjective product of our current social and environmental circumstances. They help us to prosper in those circumstances. Little wonder then that our morals have evolved so much since the Renaissance, as society has changed rapidly. Little wonder too that different cultural groups existing in different environments have developed different moral codes. Now, if value is subjectively created and intersubjectively maintained in this way, then we run straight into the problem of seriousness as articulated by the existentialists.

Anguish

There is a relatively small body of empirical work that connects the evolutionary psychology of moral cognition with the themes of existential philosophy by way of the human aversion to ambiguity and our need for seriousness. This is the literature from terror management theory, which grew out of a desire to experimentally engage with postulates in existential philosophy and anthropology (Burke et al. 2010). A motivating question for TMT is why symbols and rituals around death are so omnipresent in human culture and religion. The foundational idea of TMT is that consciousness makes humans unique among animals in that they can foresee their own death. This provokes in humans a profound, primordial terror. We have evolved a range of defense mechanisms to prevent this terror from becoming debilitating.

The most prominent of these is culture, which explains the world and imbues it with meaning and value (Greenberg et al. 2004, p. 16). Furthermore, culture, especially culture that speaks to death and the afterlife, connects us to an entity (the group) that lives on after we die. The march of science in modernity has undermined our ability to buy into many of these cultural systems, notably religion. This is one reason the death of God opened an existential vacuum.

Experimental results in TMT are typically derived using what is called a mortality salience condition. Participants are randomized into a control group and a treatment group, and the treatment group is manipulated in such a way that death thoughts become more prominent in their mind, either consciously, unconsciously, or both. Tests are then administered to determine what effect mortality salience has on different variables. Results indicate that people in mortality salience conditions have a higher need for closure than controls, suggesting discomfort with ambiguity—in other words, anguish (Dechesne et al. 2000).

Two defenses to mortality salience have been identified in existing research. The first is proximal defenses, which are observable immediately following the salience manipulation but then fade quite rapidly. These include avoiding rooms with mirrors or writing short stories about oneself. Mirrors and reflective stories are behavioral options inserted into experiments by researchers that are theorized to get at the approach or avoidance of self-focus. Another common proximal defense is *suppression*. Experimental evidence shows that mortality salience often doesn't reach the level of consciousness but increases at the subliminal level after manipulation (Florian and Mikulincer 2004, p. 61). Proximal defenses suggest that humans have psychological systems designed to inhibit death thoughts.

The second defense mechanism is distal defense, which has a delayed onset. The principal form of this defense is an exaggerated regard (disdain) for similar (dissimilar) others. For example, after a mortality salience condition, participants were more aggressive toward other participants with divergent political views (measured by how much hot sauce they administered to them)[4] than were individuals in a control condition. Distal defenses indicate a connection between social identity and the management of death-related thoughts.

---

[4] This is a standard approach to measuring aggressiveness in psychological studies. It is a meaningful form of pain, but not physically severe enough to trigger obstruction by an ethics committee.

Results in terror management research are mirrored by results in identity consolidation (IC) theory, which focuses on people's responses to personal uncertainty, which is more specific than general ambiguity. Personal uncertainty is also distinct from focal uncertainty. Focal uncertainty refers to situations where the individual doesn't know how to express themselves, such as not knowing the most appropriate way to dress and act during a college orientation week (Sorrentino and Roney 2000; Sorrentino et al. 2009). Such situations provide an opportunity for autonomous self-determination and can end with one feeling that one is "being oneself." In contrast, personal uncertainty refers to "a kind of identity crisis that arises from awareness of conflict or lack of clarity about self elements" (McGregor 2004, p. 183). In such cases, there is no clear identity to guide behavior, and multiple selves can offer conflicting advice, leading to dissonance, debilitation, and potentially multiple approach-avoidance conflicts. This is similar to the way anguish and its paralyzing effects are described in existentialist philosophy.

IC theory posits four overarching strategies that people use to cope with personal uncertainty: integration, self-worth myopia, group identification, and conviction. These strategies have parallels with those observed in terror management. They are rewarding because they bring about self-regulatory efficiency, but they can also lead to narcissism, intergroup bias, and zealous extremism (McGregor 2004).

The *integration* strategy for overcoming personal uncertainty involves building some life narrative and fitting new situations into that narrative. Such stories can make a life meaningful (McAdams 1993; see Nehamas 1985 for an existentialist account). Coherent stories also make information of fundamental importance to their narratives more accessible and psychologically consequential (McGregor and Holmes 1999). Experimental results indicate that people confronted with existential dilemmas react by planning activities and projects that are higher in integrity than control participants (McGregor et al. 2001). Undertaking such activities reduces personal uncertainty.

Self-worth is actually two techniques for managing personal uncertainty. The first is defensively enhancing one's self image when confronted by destabilizing information (Tesser 2000). Individuals reminded of their self-worth immediately after personal uncertainty priming are less likely to engage this defensive technique (Steele et al. 1993). The second technique is self-worth myopia, which involves reducing the elements of one's self-concept that are salient at any one time to make inconsistencies across multiple selves less obvious and thus less troubling.

Group identification involves borrowing values from a group. This reduces the need for unpleasant self-analysis in times of personal uncertainty and buttresses identity in times of crisis. We feel calmer when our beliefs are affirmed by those around us and their behaviors mirror our own. As in terror management research, experimental evidence in IC theory suggests that personal uncertainty encourages intergroup bias (McGregor et al. 2009; McGregor 2010; Van Den Bos 2009a, 2009b).

The final strategy is conviction and extremism. The basic idea here is to double down on one's present beliefs when confronted by threats to personal certainty (McGregor 2009). Individuals high in self-esteem demonstrate greater conviction in their beliefs when confronted with personal uncertainty than controls or people low in self-esteem (McGregor and Marigold 2003). However, it is unclear whether this is because their views are more fully developed, in which case it is appropriate that they be more convinced of them, or if the conviction is unwarranted and merely acts to buttress self-esteem.

These results in TMT and IC theory underline the importance of seriousness and anguish to wellbeing. People are distressed by ambiguity. They respond by doubling down on existing sources of meaning and seriousness, especially group norms. They are similarly distressed by inconsistent identities and respond to this with deeper compartmentalization or attempts to resolve inconsistencies.

There is an additional, important idea in TMT related to this last point about compartmentalization or personal growth. This is that culture, by which is meant collectively held and reinforced value systems, can only effectively manage despair at the level of the individual if that culture is intrinsically chosen and integrated into the self by that individual. In cases where a culture does not fit the individual, dissonance will prevent the cultural worldview from managing despair (or its sociological parallel, anomie), provoking the individual to reassess that worldview until they have something that does work. In this process, it is possible for an individual to reach a point where they have an acceptable cultural worldview but it is still weak in terms of its internal consistency. At this point, individuals may be inclined to engage in further values exploration, but this threatens the integrity of their cultural worldview and provokes existential anxiety. This tension between anxiety on the one hand and dissonance on the other can lead to developmental arrest and moral amplification of the type demonstrated by extremists (Haidt and Algoe 2004; McGregor 2003). As Pyszczynski et al. (2012, p. 389) explain:

Ironically then, a secure worldview and sense of self-worth allows us to venture forth to uncharted mental territories where discoveries can emerge that question those very security-providing structures, requiring us to revise those structures to accommodate our self expansions. . . . Unfortunately, we often fail to allow this dialectic process to continue its forward momentum; rather, we give up the potential pleasures of intrinsically motivated growth-promoting activity in exchange for the comfort and security that clinging to existing forms of psychological organisation of self and world provides.

So personal growth is enjoyable and worldview instability is unpleasant, but a degree of instability is required for growth. It follows that if an individual could develop an internally consistent and rationally accessible identity and worldview while also fostering a comfort with ambiguity, then they could frequently engage in personal growth without being overwhelmed by anxiety. The solid structure of their identity and worldview would absorb new ideas rather than being destabilized by them.

This hypothesis is supported by three clusters of empirical evidence. The first is that when people are primed to be creative in mortality salience conditions they engage fewer defensive mechanisms and are more comfortable engaging with existential questions (Routledge and Arndt 2009). The second is that individuals who go through near-death experiences find themselves more comfortable with mortality. They consequently tend to move to affirm personal values rather than group ones and they engage in more growth-inducing activities (Martin et al. 2004). The third is that individuals with a low need for closure are more comfortable reflecting on issues raised by mortality salience manipulations than individuals with a high need for closure. The latter tend to increase belief in bogus but relevant theories, like horoscopes, when doing so reduces mortality salience (Dechesne et al. 2000, 2003).

As we shall see, the coalescence of being is precisely an existential stance characterized by frequent personal growth that provokes little anxiety. Coalescence achieves this by starting from an acceptance of ambiguity and then providing a paradigm through which to build a rich, deep, and consistent identity.

A final empirical literature worth discussing in relation to anguish is the research on identity development. There is a large body of work exploring the importance of developing a clear sense of self through late childhood, adolescence, and early adulthood (Luyckx et al. 2006). This process can simultaneously involve depression, anxiety, openness, and curiosity, with failure prolonging depressive and anxious episodes (Luyckx et al. 2008). Themes from the literature on adolescent psychology are present in the more adult-focused literature on narrative therapy. This practice involves assisting patients to develop life stories and integrate traumatic or distressing events into identity through narratives that makes sense of them and provide meaning and closure (McAdams and McLean 2013; Angus and McLeod 2004). There is a proliferating body of literature in clinical psychology and contemporary explorations of SWB in public policy contexts that explores the role of ethnic identity in SWB and personal narratives (Crocetti et al. 2008; Stronge et al. 2016; Muriwai et al. 2005; Yap and Yu 2016). All of this speaks to the importance of identity to SWB and the challenge that anguish can pose.

Distinguishing Conscience from Despair

In this section I combine insights from existentialism with the theories and findings from psychology outlined previously to distinguish "conscience" from despair, and meaning, identity, and virtue from nausea, anguish, and seriousness. I use "conscience" rather than "despair" in the SWBPF in part so that it has a positive connotation. High scores should be good things. High scores in conscience can be thought of as the inverse of despair, but this does not entirely exhaust the concept. Conscience goes beyond despair in some ways, and these are worth outlining clearly.

Some of the characteristics outlined in what follows will become clearer after the coalescence of being has been elaborated. This is because the theory of coalescence emerges out of the philosophy and psychology of despair. A thoughtful reader may have noticed, for example, that the three variables in the conscience dimension are mutually reinforcing and interactive, which makes them difficult to empirically tease apart.

Meaning

Someone who is high in meaning is not nauseated. They feel like they have purpose in life, though they may recognize that this purpose is not transcendental (i.e., it does not connect into some cosmic order). This purpose does not need to go beyond the individual in question to provide SWB. For example, someone who busies themselves for a decade building a matchstick replica of the *Titanic*, which has little benefit to anybody but the individual, might nonetheless find the endeavor meaningful. Similar activities that provide meaning to individuals but have little to no positive spillovers on others, such as personal improvement practices, are easy enough to find. However, there is some evidence that endeavors that connect someone to groups and ideals beyond themselves more easily give rise to feelings of meaning and purpose than more self-serving activities (Emmons 1990; Seligman 2012). This jibes with the social psychology literature reviewed earlier on the association between groups, symbolic language, norms, and meaning.

Someone who is high in meaning also has goals that provide them with a high degree of motivation. This motivation need not be fully intrinsic, but it will be at least identified in nature. Introjected goals are unlikely to feel meaningful, and extrinsically motivated behavior may enhance feelings of despair.

The definition of meaning just given aligns neatly with the three themes of the empirical literature on subjective experiences of meaning in social and clinical psychology. These are coherence, purpose, and significance (King and Hicks 2020). Psychometric studies indicate that these three aspects feed into a global sense of meaningfulness (George and Park 2017; Kraus and Hayward 2014). Coherence refers to the sense that one's life "makes sense" (Heintzelmann and King 2014). Science can provide this, but it struggles with many issues that humans seem strongly drawn to, such as consciousness, connection to higher powers, death, and other topics where religion has historically provided coherence. In chapter 9, I explain how an iterative process of engaging with the world and introspecting on the feedback received thereby can give rise to a coherent worldview and self-concept through the application of reason to emotional data. Purpose refers to "the feeling that one's life is guided by personally valued goals" (King and Hicks 2020, p. 567). This chapter has underlined how difficult it is to rescue a sense of purpose from despair. Coalescence, which I begin to sketch in the next section of this chapter, explains why some things feel meaningful while others do not, and how feelings of meaning can thicken over time. Finally, significance refers to the feeling that one's life will have a lasting impact on the world.

What is missing from the empirical literature is a deep appreciation of the intimate connection between meaning and *value*. Scholars of meaning and purpose of course appreciate the importance of value and discuss it often, such as in their statement that purpose refers to "the feeling that one's life is guided by personally valued goals." But a theory of how value arises and is sustained amid an ambiguous universe is lacking. The analysis of despair just given underscores how necessary this broader theory of value is, but it is understandable that scholars have avoided it to date. Value is inherently difficult to tackle empirically, for a start. Nonetheless, meaning must be defined in a way that is conscious of this connection in order to make sense of SWB holistically. Chapter 9, on coalescence, goes into greater detail on these issues.

Identity

The defining characteristic of someone high in identity is a clear sense of self. They have met the first Hellenic maxim for flourishing: know thyself. Such individuals know their values and why they hold those values. They are familiar with their dispositions, talents, intrinsic motivations, and innate weaknesses. They know where they have come from and where they are going. When seeking to change themselves they will proceed in ways that they know are effective in the context of their own psychology. For example, some people might know that they are more likely to effect change if they go for a big push (like going cold turkey from a bad habit), while others will know that their best bet lies in making incremental changes.

A clear sense of self allows individuals to navigate difficult decisions. Core values are highly integrated, and their attendant behaviors are automated (see chapter 9). This means that a high-identity individual rarely experiences anguish. They can make many normatively complex decisions on autopilot. Their values and the reasons underpinning those values are also easily accessible to consciousness when necessary. High-identity individuals can therefore reason their way through complex problems in a manner that maintains their integrity. This limits the need for and presence of compartmentalization and prevents agonizing decisions from resulting in major changes to their self-concept. As a result, such individuals only experience a limited amount of anguish when confronted with tough choices.

Identity also allows for the navigation of feelings of self-worth because it provides a rationally accessible body of evidence regarding your value. An individual who has harmonized their actual, ideal, and ought selves knows what they can and cannot achieve. When they are confronted by self-esteem issues or the like, such as in a midlife crisis, they can reason their way out (Rauch 2018). They understand why they made certain decisions in life and can therefore justify their behaviors.

Finally, a clear sense of self improves an individual's ability to navigate the social world. They will understand where their affinities lie and what draws them to associated groups. They will be able to pick up on subtle cues regarding what makes a group click, and they will understand what they can contribute to a variety of social situations.

Virtue

Virtuous individuals experience their values as serious. Their ethical principles exert a binding force on their behavior and they feel compelled to act with fealty toward them. Martin Luther expressed this subjective feeling well when he declared at the Diet of Worms that: "I cannot and will not recant anything, for to go against conscience is neither right nor safe. Here I stand, I can do no other, so help me God, Amen."

Virtuous individuals feel that they are good people. This self-assessment is based on the alignment of their behavior with their ethical principles and the subjectively compelling arguments that they can muster in defense of those principles. Virtuous individuals respond to feeling of guilt, shame, and low esteem that call into question this self-assessment by genuinely considering whether they might have behaved badly or simply are bad.[5] They will process these feelings through the prism of their ethical principles, which will be more sophisticated if they are high in identity. Virtuous individuals will not find this process of ethical self-questioning traumatic because they are comfortable with ambiguity and resolved to be good people. They practice self-compassion and so they will forgive themselves moral trespass so long as they act henceforth in an ethical manner. The accessibility of their ethical principles will allow them to quickly and relatively painlessly navigate their way through ethical complexity to resolutions. These may involve either adjusting their ethical principles and/or behavior or developing a subjectively compelling argument as to why their behavior or nature is not bad. Either way, the feelings of guilt, shame, and low self-esteem will be ameliorated.

Finally, virtuous people will have ethical goals that provide some degree of intrinsic motivation and a great deal of identified motivation to behave

---

[5] A useful quip to remember when asking yourself whether you are a good person is that bad people don't ask themselves that question.

morally. They will not experience moral behavior as entirely a matter of self-regulation. Moral behavior is too often conceived as requiring self-abnegation or selfless behavior. Such behavior can only lead to ill-being because it is not rooted in relatively intrinsic forms of motivation (see Oakley et al. 2012 for a book-length treatment of "pathological altruism"). At the same time, it is obviously true that ethical behavior, which tends to be connected to other-regard and altruism, often involves an element of private cost. Self-determination theory's spectrum of motivation provides an explanation for how ethical behaviors can first be identified and then gradually become integrated. They thereby become increasingly intrinsically motivated and easy. They nourish feelings of autonomy, competence, and relatedness, promoting SWB. There is a means here of connecting ethical behavior and the psychology of self-interest is an extremely powerful way. I will elaborate on this somewhat in chapter 9, but it demands a longer and more deliberate treatment (see Besser-Jones 2014 for an excellent example).

Philosophical Solutions to the Existential Problems

In the rest of this chapter I canvass some of the philosophical solutions to anguish, seriousness, and nausea as articulated in existentialist philosophy. I analyze three solutions: faith in Kierkegaard, eudaimonism in Norton, and the basic principles of the coalescence of being in Nietzsche and the existentialists. This analysis serves two purposes. First, it clarifies the three existential problems further. Second, it illuminates what a practical theory of SWB needs to be able to do to overcome despair and thereby make holistic SWB possible. This provides a launch pad for the practical theory elucidated in this work, namely the coalescence of being. I describe coalescence in much greater detail in chapter 9, drawing principally on literature from empirical psychology rather than philosophy. In that chapter I will explain not just how coalescence overcomes despair, but also how it promotes conscience and all the other variables in the SWBPF.

Faith

Kierkegaard takes the existence of a cosmic order for granted, and sees despair as arising out of either an ignorance of this fact or an inability or refusal to *believe* in it. I emphasize "believe" because Kierkegaard accepts that God and the cosmic order are never verifiable—faith is fundamentally "in the absurd," that is, it is not rational. He argues that it is the "strength of the absurd" that allows faith to overcome despair. He is quite disparaging toward efforts to ground religiosity in reason (Kierkegaard [1843] 2005, p. 40):

> Would it not be best all the same to stop with faith, and is it not disturbing that everyone wants to go further? . . . Would it not be better to remain standing at faith, and for the one who stands there to take care not to fall? For the movement of faith must be made continuously on the strength of the absurd, though in such a way, be it noted, that one does not lose finitude but gains it all of a piece.

Faith works to address the existential problems by arresting the psychic dialectic out of which despair arises. The self is then held fixed by God (Kierkegaard [1849] 2008, p. 164). An individual who has faith in the Holy Scriptures receives transcendental values from outside their self, and these values then determine their behavior in an authoritative way. Religious values are written into the firmament and this gives them a transcendental character. Moral laws are clearly defined in scripture and enforced by cosmic justice, which provides serious ethics. The individual has a place in God's plan, and by fulfilling their ordained role they can contribute to God's holy and beneficent goals. The apprehension of such a transcendental purpose overcomes nausea. Religion's serious, transcendental normative order overcomes anguish because the appropriate decision for an individual to make in any given situation is prescribed in the ethical commandments of scripture and the individual's role in God's plan. While they experience anguish, they can readily find answers in the Word and prayers for guidance. The veracity of this scripture is given additional symbolic authority by the strong cultural forces that typically underpin religious communities, including elaborate and ever-present rituals and iconography that make norms easily identifiable and interpretable, and in-group reciprocity and tight enforcement of social norms that reinforce the notion of cosmic justice for believers and heathens (Wilson 2002; Gelfand et al. 2011).

The "Knight of Faith" also need never anguish over the broader question "Who am I?" because they receive the answer in contemplation of the Word. For Kierkegaard's Knight of Faith, the internal psychic dynamics of personality development are supplanted by the individual's comportment toward an external identity that they receive from an eternal God. Through prayer, introspection, and consultation with priests, the individual comes to sense God's intentions for them, which provides the "identity" that they are supposed to live. As this identity is part of the grand cosmic plan, it is given all at once, which mitigates the sense of perpetual becoming and overcomes anguish. Finally, this identity is transcendental, being part of God's grand design. This provides meaning and seriousness. In this way, despair is arrested (Kierkegaard [1843] 2005, p. 45).

The Crisis of Faith

While Kierkegaard is correct to the extent that faith can manage despair and dampen its effects, he is incorrect to suggest that it *annihilates* despair. The movement of faith begins with an individual introspecting, reaching out to God, engaging with religious texts, and communing with priests to discover their ordained place in God's plan. Once this is discovered, despair is held at bay so long as the individual maintains their faith that they have correctly identified their role in God's plan and that God and His cosmic order in fact exist. Faith in both items must be maintained on the strength of the absurd because neither is a testable hypothesis. (I will leave Thomistic proofs of God to one side—suffice it to say that they seem to me to be precisely hypotheses rather than proofs.)

The possibility of a *crisis* of faith in this context seems substantial. The march of science since the Enlightenment has called so much of revelation into question that sustaining belief in the rest of the Bible, Koran, or other religious texts is increasingly difficult. Conviction regarding one's own role is also ever open to the problem of the satanic verses: how is one to know whether it was God who sent you a message and not Satan? Finally, the Knight of Faith seems to be just as open to the anguishing assaults of unexpected events as any other individual. By way of a simple example, consider a religious mother in the Bible Belt of the United States. Following (some interpretations of) scripture and natural law, she regards homosexuality as a sin and the care of her offspring as a duty. She then discovers that her daughter is a homosexual. She can only salvage her identity from this crisis by reinterpreting some aspect of her faith. This instance of inner normative conflict is an archetypal example of anguish. This hypothetical case closely parallels the real life story of John Gustave-Wrathall, who founded an LGBT community within the Mormon Church to lobby for scriptural reform. He thereby reconciled his faith and sexuality in a way that nurtured his feelings of autonomy, competence, and relatedness.

Owing to the possibility of a crisis of faith, faith is no different from the coalescence of being. Both involve positing values and affirming them. However, faith requires the reason for these values to be grounded in the absurd, whereas the coalescence of being accepts from the outset no ultimate justification for values. Coalescence, following Nietzsche, takes normative ambiguity as a fundamental fact of existence. It posits that values are not written into the firmament but are instead created by acts of will and sustained by the individual's motivations and integrity, both of which are critical to attain SWB. Coalescence does not rely on faith; it relies on subjectively compelling arguments and feelings.

Eudaimonism

How can a *secularist* solve the existential problems? Eudaimonism is one approach. I use the term "eudaimonism" to refer to a specific technique wherein the individual affirms their internal identity against external intrusion. Eudaimonism relies on a eudaimonic account of wellbeing, and its themes are common in the Aristotelian tradition. Norton (1976), an Aristotelian, provides arguably the most thorough account of how eudaimonism works to address the existential problems. His is the only account of eudaimonism that I am aware of that specifically engages at length with existentialist philosophy. He is also referenced extensively by Ryff (1989a) in her influential model of psychological wellbeing. Therefore, I will focus my analysis on his account rather than on less extreme theories of eudaimonism that are not formulated with reference to existentialism. More classical eudaimonism in the style of Annas (2004) is founded on the notion of objective goods. The evolutionary psychology literature that I surveyed earlier runs counter to this possibility. Norton's eudaimonism does not have this requirement.

Where faith requires the individual to comport toward an external standard of behavior embedded in scripture, Norton's eudaimonism advocates for an entirely inward-looking approach. The central tenet of eudaimonism is that everyone has an innate "true self"—their daimon (Norton 1976, p. 14). "Eudaimonia" is the positive feeling that attends living in accordance with this true self (p. 5). It can be interpreted as the feeling that attends the absence of despair and is often translated as "happiness."

It should be noted that *Norton's* eudaimonism is strictly about living in accordance with one's true *individual* nature. I emphasize "individual" because some readings of eudaimonism take it as involving the fulfillment of our *human* natures (Haybron 2008, p. 174). According to Norton, it is the nature of humans to have a daimon and living in accordance with it brings wellbeing, but each individual daimon is unique, and so nature fulfillment is a fundamentally subjective enterprise.[6]

How does eudaimonism overcome anguish and nausea and secure seriousness? The power of eudaimonism in this regard comes from the fact that an individual's daimon constitutes a complete identity. It contains an individual's past, present, and future. Only their present can exist at any one time (this is their "actuality"), but the daimon also contains all their potentiality, which the individual must actualize if they are to "become who they are" (Norton 1976, p. 229):

> As we have noted previously, the mature lifetime of the integral individual is a single act, spread over time by the condition of existence that a thing cannot present itself all at once. But in a profound sense, integrity hereby abolishes time by containing its past and its future in its present . . . The past and future of the eudaimonic individual are contained in his present in the mode of that moral necessity conferred upon his life by his chosen principle of personhood.

The individual "discovers" their true self through introspection around the end of adolescence, and then lives their life in accordance with this true self. Certainly not all their true self is present at once, but their commitment to living in accordance with their daimon, that is, their integrity, means that their values and behaviors are determined once and for all from the moment they orient themselves toward their daimon (Norton 1976, p. 223):

> Eudaimonia's "wholeheartedness" means that the whole person is present in each of his acts. This is so because the individual's choice of his ultimate

---

[6] The most important quote from Norton in this regard is the following (1976, pp. 9–10):

> Our consideration of "personal truth" reveals that the great enemy of integrity is not falsehood as such but—ironically—the attractiveness of foreign truths, truths that belong to others. . . . When an individual allows himself to be deflected from his own true course, he fails in that first responsibility from which all other genuine responsibilities follow, and whose fulfilment is the precondition of the least fulfilment of other responsibilities. . . . Philosophically, this is formulated as the principle of ultimate varieties of value.

possibility establishes a principle of entailment whereby his future and his past are implicit in his present, and thereby are within his present act. Because his "there" is within his "here," he is devoid of that condition of semi-distraction that is the common attendant of personal life.

The "condition of semi-distraction" Norton refers to here is anguish. Eudaimonism resolves anguish by providing the individual with a deterministic identity from the beginning of adulthood. Their decisions are guided by their adherence to the daimon they seek to actualize, annulling anguish in the moment, and their daimon is a richly conceived identity, annulling any anguish pertaining to the question "Who am I?"

Eudaimonism brings about seriousness through the combination of two factors. The first is the moral imperative of living in accordance with the daimon. Norton argues that the daimon represents each individual's personal perfection, and so they are morally obliged to actualize it (Norton 1976, p. 141). This commitment to perfection provides the *content* of an individual's values, but it does not grant them seriousness; that comes from the necessity of *integrity*. Norton emphasizes that eudaimonism requires an individual to act with fealty to their daimon at all times (p. 193):

> The actualization of personhood is progressive, requiring, in Nietzsche's words "long obedience in the same direction." To re-choose is to annihilate all accomplished actualization stemming from original choice; it is a re-beginning out of a lapse into indeterminacy.

In Norton's philosophy, the individual has both an ethical and selfish interest in affirming their daimon. If they transgress its character they will be plunged back into "a life without identity or necessity." The positive feeling of eudaimonia will dissipate, and they will be left unwell. So they must act with integrity. They must show fidelity to the identity (the daimon) that they have chosen to actualize over the life course. This injects seriousness into ethics by making the individual an effective authority for enforcing their own values upon themselves. The individual will resist those aspects of her psyche that suggest transgressing the daimon and will stick to the plan that is the daimon.

It is somewhat unclear how Norton's eudaimonism overcomes nausea, but I take it to be largely a matter of intrinsic motivation. The daimon is fundamentally internal and comporting toward it is accompanied by the positive feeling and state of eudaimonia. It is therefore reasonable to expect that the individual will be intrinsically motivated to live in accordance with their daimon, and this motivation will be reinforced by positive affective signals. Contemporaneous theories in psychology, notably Maslow's hierarchy of needs (Norton's book is dedicated to Maslow), suggested that this kind of self-actualization is sufficient for achieving a sense of meaning. This view is sustained in more modern theories like SDT (Ryan and Deci 2000).

The Shortcomings of Eudaimonism

There are several flaws in the arguments pertaining to eudaimonism's ability to overcome despair. The first is the notion that "perfection" is sufficient to ground ethics. This error runs all the way back to Plato. Perfection has a normative but not ethical quality. It registers in the *aesthetic* sense, not the *moral* sense. For example, we can recognize that Floyd Mayweather is close to a perfect boxer. But while we may *value* this instrumentally, we do not give Mayweather *moral* credit for it. We do not think Mayweather is a "good" person because he is a "good" boxer. Indeed, Floyd Mayweather is widely regarded as a bad person due to his history of domestic violence, which has nothing to do with perfection. A pithy explanation of the problem with Norton's argument is in Tony Martin's joke on *The Late Show*: "My mother's obsession with the good scissors always scared me a bit. It implied that somewhere in the house there lurked the evil scissors." That something is instrumentally good does not mean that it is morally good. I am here using a definition of perfection grounded in instrumentality, but the point stands if you interpret perfection to refer instead to mere actualization of one's daimon, which may not have much instrumental quality whatsoever.

The research in the evolutionary psychology of moral cognition canvassed earlier suggests that ethical impulses evolved to help us cooperate in groups. These studies suggest that utilitarian and deontological considerations, particularly regarding issues of fairness and reciprocity, are fundamental to our moral cognitions. Norton's eudaimonism and its ethics of personal perfection can't engage with any of this, which limits the extent to which it can provide serious and practical ethics or underpin conscience.

The second flaw in eudaimonism is the idea that you can discover your "true self" *in totality* at the end of adolescence. This does not accord with present theories in developmental psychology.[7] It is reasonable enough to claim the existence of an innate self, however limited. Empirical evidence suggests a substantial role for genetic determinism of identity through a range of channels (Pinker 2002). Notably, our physical and intellectual characteristics and aptitudes influence the paths we can take in life. You cannot, for example, be a professional basketball player if you are short. Personality in general seems substantially genetic, as do tastes and talents (Polderman et al. 2015). However, there is a long way to go from this innate self to an actual self that constitutes an identity that is sophisticated, refined, and deep enough to withstand anguish.

Developmental psychology nowadays emphasizes genetic *predispositions* rather than *predeterminants* (Carver 2012). Metaphorically, we are born a lump of clay with certain dimensions like weight, but our final form is shaped through individual interaction with environmental factors. An elegant summary is provided by neuroscientist Gary Marcus (2004, pp. 30–40): "Nature provides a first draft, which experience then revises. . . . '[B]uilt-in' does not mean unmalleable; it means '*organised in advance of experience.*'" Developmental psychology also emphasizes the existence of "multiple selves" that we must harmonize as our personality develops (Showers and Zeigler-Hill 2012). Adolescence is punctuated by a growing awareness of these multiple selves and "a dramatic rise in the detection of contradictory self-attributes that lead to conflict and confusion" (Harter 2012). This picture is radically different from that developed by Norton. He posits that adolescents find themselves misunderstood by *others* and subsequently embark on a quest of *self-discovery* (Norton 1976, p. 111). Present developmental psychology instead argues that adolescents can't understand *themselves* and consequently set out on a quest of individuation that is part self-discovery through introspection and part *self-creation* through the affirmation of desired character traits (Higgins 1991). This process of identity formation is ongoing throughout life, so Norton's notion that we can choose an identity at the end of adolescence is questionable. Eudaimonism's ability to overcome anguish is thus limited.

The discussion in the preceding paragraph points to a third approach to overcoming despair that sits *between* faith and eudaimonism. I call it the coalescence of being, or coalescence for short. It combines introspection (the

---

[7] Norton should be given credit for trying to ground his theory in the work of contemporary developmental psychologists, notably Piaget, but the science has moved on since.

internal) and environmental, especially social, engagement (the external). It also involves both self-discovery and self-creation. I turn now to briefly pick up its origins in the work of Nietzsche and the French existentialists. I elaborate it in full with reference to more modern psychological literatures in chapter 9.

The Coalescence of Being in Philosophy

The most fundamental tenet of coalescence is the following, from Nietzsche ([1886] 2000, p. 343): "Above all, we should not want to rid the world of its rich ambiguity." As discussed, there is a desire in humans for fixed meaning: a grand cosmic plan, serious values. But these things don't seem provable, if they exist at all. Similarly, we seem to want objective truth, but this is inaccessible, so there is no hope of certainty.[8] As long as we look for certainty, we will suffer. Step one then is to embrace the lack of certainty that characterizes our existence, especially with regard to values (Nietzsche [1887] 1974, sec. 346):

> We have become cold, hard, and tough in the realisation that the way of this world is anything but divine; even by human standards it is not rational, merciful, or just. We know it well, the world in which we live is ungodly, immoral, inhuman.

This is liberating. If objective normative truth existed, then it would exert a binding power. We could not help but comport to it. Yet this would undermine our ability to be our authentic selves. Accepting that the universe is devoid of objective value gives us latitude to define our own values and

---

[8] Note that when I speak here of the inaccessibility of truth I am referring to the problem of induction, rather than the notion, common in postmodern circles, that objective truth does not exist. There is an objective world, and we can utter true statements about it. For example, a seventeenth-century European might say that "all swans are white." They base this claim on the thousands of times they have observed swans and the fact that they were always white. They then travel to Australia and discover that some swans are black. There is no social construction here. Our original claim is refuted. We believed that all swans were white because we had not observed the entire population of swans. This is the problem of induction: we can never know whether truth claims we make on the basis of observation are simply a function of too small a sample. Pure mathematics does not fare any better because mathematics begins either with axioms that are not drawn from reality or with empirical facts that suffer from the problem of induction. The way out of this problem is to focus on falsification. If we subject a claim, like "all swans are white," to a battery of tough tests and we are unable to falsify it, then we can treat it as a *fact* (not truth) until falsifying evidence comes along. This is the scientific method according to Popper (1934). I am not denying objective truth; I am denying that we can access it.

affirm them in the world without inherent normative opprobrium. It is by relinquishing the need for certainty and instead embracing our capacity to will meaning and value that we overcome despair (Nietzsche [1887] 1974, p. 289):

> One could conceive of such a pleasure and power of self-determination, such a freedom of the will that the spirit would take leave of all faith and every wish for certainty, being practised in maintaining itself on insubstantial ropes and possibilities and dancing ever near abysses. Such a spirit would be the *free spirit* par excellence.

Note that ambiguity is distinct from *absurdity*. Ambiguity holds that the meaning of the world is not given but must be created through affirmation. Absurdity is the view that the world can never contain meaning or value.

What immediately follows from this liberating embrace of ambiguity is the need to adopt what Nietzsche calls "noble morality" as distinct from "slave morality." Very simplistically, slave morality is about adherence to an external normative code, such as that laid out in the Bible or some ethical axiom. It is called "slave" morality because it involves obedience to someone else's values. Noble morality is the opposite: it involves embracing your nature as a value-creating entity and acting with fidelity to your own good and evil: "The most basic laws of preservation and growth require the opposite: that everyone should invent his *own* virtues, his *own* categorical imperatives" (Nietzsche [1885] 1990, p. 134). A noble's ethical sense is attuned primarily to whether they are transgressing their own values rather than whether they are transgressing other people's values. It is from this notion and the following passage that I take the name "conscience" ([1888] 2000, p. 495):

> The proud awareness of the extraordinary privilege of *responsibility*, the consciousness of this rare freedom, this power over oneself and over fate, has in his case penetrated to the profoundest depths and become instinct, the dominating instinct. What will he call this dominating instinct, supposing he feels the need to give it a name? The answer is beyond doubt: this sovereign man calls it his *conscience*.

Nietzsche talks often of "profound selfishness." What he means is that you owe allegiance to your own values first and foremost. It does not mean that you don't care about society's values or those of your subculture. You can certainly adopt these as your own and enforce them upon yourself (most people do, at least to some extent), but you are the ultimate authority over what is right and good and nothing can absolve you or rob you of this responsibility. The French existentialists would later summarize this in one of their maxims: "man is condemned to be free." In the writings of Nietzsche and the French existentialists this freedom is both the source of despair *and* the font of SWB provided the individual can overcome that despair.

It should be noted that Nietzsche's selfishness is not about repudiating altruism and other-regarding conduct. It is simply about locating the reason for altruism within the individual's own ethical rubric and in identified, integrated, and intrinsic rather than introjected or extrinsic motivation. It thereby becomes a source of individuation and SWB (Nietzsche [1881] 1996, sec. 103):

> It goes without saying that I do not deny—unless I am a fool—that many actions called immoral ought to be avoided and resisted, or that many called moral ought to be done and encouraged—but I think the one should be encouraged and the other avoided *for other reasons than hitherto*.

If other-regard and morality more generally are instead practiced through extrinsic and introjected motivation, then it will be exhausting and lead to psychopathologies. Nietzsche's notion of noble morality sits with the insight of SDT that ethical precepts must be autonomously endorsed for them to be sustainable over the long term. This way of thinking about moral motivation explains the phenomenon of overly empathetic or agreeable people who are ground down by society or preyed upon by parasitic individuals. They engage in too much self-regulation in order to abide by other people's values, which leaves them drained.

A critical aspect of noble morality and the coalescence of being more generally is integrity. Integrity is "the right to make promises" (Nietzsche [1888] 2000, bk. 2, sec. 1). Nietzsche is alluding in this statement to the problem, first identified by Kierkegaard, that if the individual is the source of values, then these values are open to caprice. What is to stop the individual from changing their mind at the moment of decision? Our past self does not exert any binding power over our present self because consciousness always allows us to stand apart from it. Integrity as a virtue is a way out of this problem because it discourages the individual from contravening their avowed values. The *strength* of integrity lies in the fact that it is necessary if individuals want to achieve SWB. Integrity is required for seriousness, and seriousness is required for SWB, so individuals have a self-interest—a privately beneficial reason—to uphold their values.[9] Nietzsche makes this point more explicitly when he says that conscience is "to possess the right to stand security for oneself and to do so with pride, thus to possess the right to affirm oneself" ([1888] 2000, p. 496). Affirmation is critical to SWB, and without integrity one cannot affirm oneself because one's commitments are loose. Beauvoir ([1947] 2002, p. 27) makes a similar point when she says that "to will is to engage myself to persevere in my will."

Nietzsche makes one final comment about integrity that is worth elaborating on. He says (Nietzsche [1888] 2000, p. 494):

Man himself must first of all have become calculable, regular, necessary, even in his own image of himself, if he is to be able to stand security for *his own future*, which is what one who promises does!

The reference to "his own future" speaks to the relationship between integrity and SWB. Perhaps more important, though, is the notion of becoming "calculable, regular, necessary, even in his own image of himself." This is reminiscent of the Hellenic maxims "know thyself" and "become who you are." If you know yourself, then you are calculable—rationally accessible—in your understanding of yourself. If you are proceeding to be the person who you claim to be and want to be by affirming your values through integrity, then your identity is a *necessity*—you cannot deviate from it because then you would lose your integrity and, in so doing, lose your "self" and your SWB, which will dissolve in despair. There is an element here even of the Aristotelian notion of living "in accordance with reason." You have reasons for valuing the things you do, and you live in accordance with those reasons through integrity. If the reasons upon which your values are based are confronted by other

[9] This idea has profound implications for meta-ethics that have not been fully appreciated by philosophers to date, but the present work is not the place to elaborate. However, it is worth noting the following passage from Sartre ([1943] 2005, p. 646), which more fully explains how and why existentialist ethics moves away from the traditional notion of ethical behavior as "disinterested conduct." In this philosophy, individuals are the source of (other-regarding) values, and they affirm and live by these values in order to achieve wellbeing. Ethics is then best understood through the prism of self-interest and psychic payoffs to being a good person.

Thus existential psychoanalysis is *moral description*, for it releases to us the ethical meaning of various human projects. It indicates to us the necessity of abandoning the psychology of interest along with any utilitarian interpretation of human conduct—by revealing to us the *ideal* meaning of all human attitudes. These meanings are beyond egoism and altruism, beyond also any behavior that is called *disinterested*. Man makes himself man in order to be God.

reasons that some more salient part of your identity finds convincing, then you will have to adjust your identity. Until such time you will persevere in your will for the sake of goodness and your SWB.

Integrity is the bedrock of seriousness in existentialism and an important element in the process by which SWB is achieved. The other crucial element is what the French existentialists called "the disclosure of being." This is where one's identity, one's "being," is revealed (disclosed) in the world by our actions and in the impressions and assessments of others. By this revelation, one's desired self is brought into existence (Beauvoir [1947] 2000, p. 30):

> My freedom must not seek to trap being but to disclose it. The disclosure is the transition from being to existence. The goal which my freedom aims at is conquering existence across the always inadequate density of being.

Disclosure is important because in it we are revealed as who we are in actuality. If what is disclosed aligns with who we want to be, then we experience a rush of self-actualization. If what is disclosed diverges from our ideal self, then we will experience depression. Repeated disclosures of who we want to be give us the sense that we are moving toward—coalescing toward—our ideal self.

This alleviates anguish for two reasons. First, we get the sense that our commitments (to ourselves especially) are trustworthy—we have the right to make promises. This means that we are not entirely cut off in the moment of decision from our prior commitments. Second, as coalescence progresses we disclose an increasingly broad, refined, deep, and, critically, *consistent* identity across a range of environments and circumstances. By this we come to have a clearer sense of who we are, thereby mitigating the anguish that comes with not knowing our identity.

What remains to be explained is how Nietzsche and the French existentialists thought we could overcome nausea. The first step is to accept that transcendental meaning is not possible. Things are only meaningful because we care about them (Beauvoir [1947] 2002, p. 15). Though they never say it explicitly, the source of meaning in existentialist thought seems close to or at least related to intrinsic motivation. There are things that we care about because we, in a sense, can't help but care about them. Arguments about the inherent purposelessness of the universe bounce off intrinsic motivation. We approach some values, activities, and goals through a kind of primal movement of the spirit. The meaningfulness of these things to us requires no explanation (Beauvoir [1947] 2002, p. 158):

Let men attach value to words, forms, colours, mathematical theorems, physical laws, and athletic prowess; let them accord value to one another in love and friendship, and the objects, the events, and the men immediately *have* this value; they have it absolutely. It is possible that a man may refuse to love anything on earth; he will prove this refusal and he will carry it out by suicide. If he lives, the reason is that, whatever he may say, there still remains in him some attachment to existence; his life will be commensurate with this attachment; it will justify itself to the extent that it genuinely justifies the world.

As with seriousness, the capacity of these values to ward off nausea is grounded in their ability to bring us SWB. When we pursue our intrinsically motivated goals, we experience the feeling of purpose. When we *successfully* pursue these goals, we experience SWB (Beauvoir [1947] 2002, p. 136). The essence of the existentialist approach to nausea is simply to observe that caring about something has the power to make that thing meaningful. Humans are wired to care about things, to imbue them with symbolic significance, to see them as meaningful and their promotion as purposeful. This is the neural architecture that allowed us to craft the great religions of the world. Meaning is contrived, but admitting that doesn't rob it of its power. Things matter because we care about them. That is enough (Beauvoir [1947] 2002, p. 159):

The fact remains that we are absolutely free today if we choose to will our existence in its finiteness, a finiteness which is open to the infinite. And in fact, any man who has known real loves, real revolts, real desires, and real will knows quite well that he has no need of any outside guarantee to be sure of his goals; their certitude comes from his own drive.

Conclusion

Existentialism emerged in response to the profound challenge of ambiguity that confronted European society in the wake of the Enlightenment. It analyzed three problems: nausea, seriousness, and anguish. Nausea is today studied in the wellbeing literature under the rubric of meaning and purpose. Seriousness is being studied by psychologists working on moral cognition and by a range of social scientists studying the role of culture in perpetuating

and enforcing norms. However, it has not made its way into the wellbeing discussion. The notion of identity and the anguish that makes it hard to achieve
are almost completely absent from wellbeing discussions outside of adolescent psychology, though the notion of "finding yourself" remains a favorite
of pop psychology and self-help books. Existential philosophy can today add
texture to the scientific study of these phenomena.

More importantly, it can highlight that success in these normative
dimensions of wellbeing will require, for many people at least, negotiating
the very tricky issues of nihilism and subjective values. Meaning, virtue, and
identity are not things that we can just choose to have one day. They require
patient, thoughtful exertion over a sustained period. This exertion is difficult if one doesn't have all the necessary philosophical tools. Existentialism
provides many of these. On some subjects, especially the issue of moral rela-
tivism, existentialism was an incomplete philosophy, but this is not the place
to dwell on these matters. Suffice it that I have hopefully demonstrated two
things. First, that the existentialist themes identified in this chapter are an
important part of SWB that should not be overlooked. Second, that existential philosophy provides at least the beginnings of a powerful theory of how
self-actualization can overcome these problems and promote conscience.
In chapter 9 I complete this theory of self-actualization—the coalescence of
being—drawing on a wide range of literatures in psychology.

9

The Coalescence of Being

> To think is easy. To act is hard. But the hardest thing of all is to act in
> accordance with your thinking.
>
> —Johann Wolfgang von Goethe

Introduction

This chapter outlines the coalescence of being in full. The coalescence of being is a model of self-actualization—the process by which SWB is achieved. Understanding this process is critical for understanding SWB holistically. There are two reasons for this. First, if you pursue SWB the wrong way you will not attain it. By extension, knowing about the outcome or state of SWB is insufficient for advising people, in a clinical, pedagogical, cultural, or policy context, on how to be well. The coalescence of being describes the right way of pursuing SWB. Second, training an eye on process illuminates the extent to which the different dimensions of the SWBPF are interlinked in its causal structure.

I outline the coalescence of being in the following stages. I begin with the core of the process, which is the harmonization of the actual, ideal, and ought selves. This involves both introspection and engagement with the external world—self-discovery and self-creation. It is guided by affective signals. I draw on self-determination theory to flesh out what each of these selves represents and to explain the motivational underpinnings of coalescence. An important difference between coalescence and the existentialist notion of "becoming" is that coalescence explains how a core sense of self can grow and thicken over time. In the final part of this opening section, I show how coalescence brings about the conditions for zest and flow. These notions help to illuminate the nature of SWB as a mode of being.

A Theory of Subjective Wellbeing. Mark Fabian, Oxford University Press. © Oxford University Press 2022.
DOI: 10.1093/oso/9780197635261.003.0010

Having sketched the basic principles of coalescence, I move to flesh it out over several stages. The first question to answer is where intrinsic motivations come from. I find answers in the developmental psychology literature. I then go into detail on the nature of goal pursuit, which is inherent to the process of harmonizing the actual, ideal, and ought selves. I discuss why self-concordant goals make a greater contribution to SWB than just any old goal, and how we can know that we have achieved a goal. The discussion in this section extends the existentialist's notion of the disclosure of being, linking it with more recent empirical work in self-verification theory. I then turn to the automatization of behavior, which is one of the means by which the coalescence of being dampens anguish. This discussion draws heavily on the literature in personality systems integration theory. Finally, I explain how the coalescence of being improves each item in the SWBPF. This explanation begins with a lengthy discussion of relatedness. I explain in more detail the social aspects of coalescence and underline that it is not a narrowly individualistic doctrine. I also rebut critiques that it does not apply to collectivist cultures.

The Core of Coalescence

Part 1: Self-Discrepancy Theory and the Dynamic Accretion of Self

The innermost core of the coalescence of being comes from self-discrepancy theory (Higgins 1987). The foundational idea of self-discrepancy theory is that people seek to harmonize their *actual self* (the person they believe themselves to be), their *ideal self* (the person they would like be), and their *ought self* (the person they feel a responsibility to be). The ideal and ought selves can be fruitfully understood as collections of values and/or goals. In the case of the ought self, these values have a distinctly ethical tinge. All three self-concepts can contain multitudes—that is, very many different and even incompatible fragments of a self. A college football player might see their actual self as consisting of "athlete" and "nerd," for example, and ponder how to integrate these two sometimes dichotomous identities. An activist mother might feel an obligation from her ought self toward both climate change work and stay-at-home parenting. Such multitudes are especially common in adolescence, when coalescence is just beginning. At this stage especially, there may be a great many incompatibilities between elements of the ideal and ought selves. For example, one might ideally like to be a professional football player *and* a professional tennis player, but the demands of each will require abandoning one. Other times, harmonization will be a less dramatic matter of trading off between different values. If one only wants to be merely a football and tennis enthusiast, then one can do each three days a week after work.

A simple example of the core coalescence process is depicted graphically in figure 9.1. Imagine a young woman who dreams of being a judge (ideal self). Assuming she has the requisite work ethic and intellectual ability (actual self), this is a challenging but inspiring goal that provides motivation, meaning, and challenge. However, she feels pressure from her traditional parents to have children (ought self). While not entirely averse to the proposal, she worries about the impact of motherhood on her career. Of course, she could ignore her parents' wishes, but this might result in an unpleasant schism that she would prefer to avoid. She ponders how to reconcile her actual self (ambitious with some fondness for children), her ideal self (hardworking judge), and ought self (mother), and eventually settles on finding a father who is happy to play the role of primary parent. In so doing, she harmonizes her parents' desire for grandchildren with her own preference for career.

Higgins (1987) postulated that people would be distressed by discrepancies between their self-concepts, and that this distress would be communicated to them by negative affect and associated emotions. Higgins further postulated that discrepancies between actual and ought selves would lead to anxiety, while discrepancies between actual and ideal selves would lead to

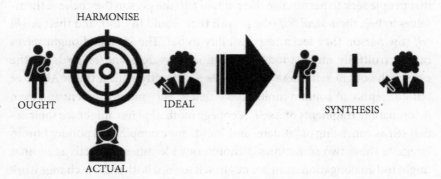

Figure 9.1 The core of coalescence—harmonizing the actual, ideal, and ought selves

depression. Resolving discrepancies and promoting harmony would reduce these negative feelings and be accompanied by positive affect. This is one example of how taking note of the qualitative nature of the emotions we feel can help us to diagnose what direction to steer our coalescence so as to promote SWB. If we are experiencing anxiety we should investigate what ethical principles we are contravening, rather than examining what ambitions we are failing to achieve. More on this shortly.

Higgin's basic ideas are supported by empirical evidence, though the association of anxiety with ought-self discrepancy and depression with ideal-self discrepancy has been hard to measure cleanly (Silvia and Eddington 2012). This is in large part because depression and anxiety are often correlated, so people are both depressed and anxious, and discrepancies with ideal and ought selves are similarly highly correlated, often larger than 0.7 (Gonnerman et al. 2000; Phillips and Silvia 2010; Tangney et al. 1998). People who don't converge with their ideal self usually also don't converge with their ought self. The constructs have been demonstrated to be meaningfully different, but it seems that attaining convergence with either of them requires the same skill set across both constructs.

Another important finding from recent empirical work is the discovery of a fourth construct: the undesired self. This is a representation of the self at its worst, sometimes called the 'feared self,' " which is a fundamental avoidance goal, a self that people strive to prevent (Silvia and Eddington 2012). On average, discrepancies from undesired selves have much stronger relationships with emotion than ideal or ought self discrepancies. However, ideal and ought self discrepancies exert a more powerful emotional effect the further an individual is from their undesired self (Carver et al. 1999; Heppen and Ogilvie 2003; Woodman and Hemmings 2008). This means that escaping anxiety and depression is often a function of transcending your feared self, whereas the movement toward positive emotion requires moving toward ideal and ought selves. More colloquially, the first step on the road to well-being is to ensure you do not become what you hate. The rest of the path is moving toward what you love. As Adam Smith (1759) said, "Man naturally desires, not only to be loved, but to be lovely; or to be that thing which is the natural and proper object of love."

Self-discrepancy theory stresses that the self is a dynamic, integrative system that develops in interaction with its social and natural environment through a process that is punctuated and guided by affective signals (Showers and Zeigler-Hill 2012, p. 116). Such a process of action, feedback, introspection, and adaptation is a recurring theme in the psychological theories that the coalescence of being draws upon. The self is composed of several parts that don't necessarily enter consciousness or act in harmony (Damasio 2010). However, there is an executive function that is capable of reflexive thinking, typically under provocation from emotional messages emanating from the broader mental system. Morf and Mischel (2012, p. 22) provide a rich and succinct definition of the self in this conceptualization:

> The self and its directly relevant processes (e.g. self-evaluation, self-regulation and self-construction) may be conceptualised fruitfully as a coherent organisation of mental-emotional representations, interacting within a system of constraints that characterise a person (or a type) distinctively . . . but it is also a motivated, proactive knowing, thinking, feeling action system that is constructed, enacted, enhanced and maintained primarily in interpersonal contexts within which it develops. Through this organised system the person experiences the social, interpersonal world and interacts with it in characteristic self-guided ways, in a process of continuous self-construction and adaptation.

Modern psychological science stresses that the healthy self is determined both volitionally and by its environmental context. In the language of existentialism, it requires both the internal and the external. Self-discrepancy theory highlights the role of the actual self, including innate characteristics, and an ideal self as a vague goal that must be refined and worked toward. Self-discrepancy theory therefore gives a role to both self-discovery and self-creation. Affective feedback and social commentary are posited as the means by which we come to "know thyself." They give us information about both our actual self—who we are right now—and whether our ideal self is a good fit for this actual self. What this means will become clearer as this chapter progresses.

Self-discrepancy theory highlights the importance to SWB of progressing dynamically over time toward a desired self—this is the foundation stone of coalescence. We are not just "becoming" aimlessly. Instead, we exercise some control over our preferred being and can sense our progress toward or away from it. This ideal self must be within the realm of possibility circumscribed by the actual self—it would be fruitless to dream of being a pilot if you are blind, for example. It must also be respectful of ethical and social demands emerging from the ought self. It might strike you as self-indulgent to pursue art if you feel a strong obligation to contribute to the public good, for example.

Part 2: Insights into Motivation and Integration from Self-Determination Theory

Self-determination theory provides some texture regarding the nature of the actual, ideal, and ought selves that is grounded in SDT's theory of motivation. This is depicted in figure 9.2. The actual self is characterized by intrinsic motivation. Recall from chapter 7 that intrinsically motivated activities are "activities that people do naturally and spontaneously when they feel free to follow their inner interests" (Deci and Ryan 2000, p. 223). They are freely and autonomously engaged in for their own sake. The ideal self is composed of values, goals, and behaviors that are *identified* and in the process of being *integrated* into the actual self. The ought self, meanwhile, is composed of *introjected* (social pressure) and *identified* (ethics) values, goals, and behaviors. They typically require self-regulation to enact, even if they are autonomously endorsed. In the case of ethical values, this regulation emerges from the fact that ethical behavior is often privately costly at first blush. Instincts of crude self-interest must be overcome to affirm these values.

Coalescence begins with individuals noticing discrepancies between their actual selves and the values inherent to their ideal and ought selves. They then *identify* behaviors that will dissolve this discrepancy. Undertaking these behaviors—affirming their values, in the language of existentialism— brings with it affective and social feedback. The individual *introspects* on this feedback. If it is positive, they will likely persist with their behavior and the values underlying it. Over time, it will become *integrated* with other values and behaviors associated with their actual, ideal, and ought selves, increasing the extent to which it is intrinsically motivated. As Pyszczynski et al. (2012, p. 385) observe, "The heightened positive affect or exhilaration resulting

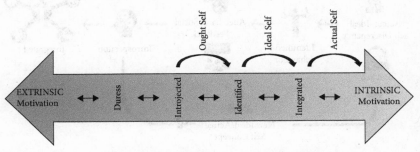

Figure 9.2 The internalization process in the coalescence of being

from integrative processing acts as an incentive for one to approach challenging tasks in the future and as a reinforcer for such engagement once it has
occurred." Internalization guided by affective signals thus promotes personal
growth over time.

Figure 9.3 illustrates this internalization process graphically. It begins with
a young woman who reflects on her intrinsic motivation (actual self) for
scientific discovery. She thinks that becoming an astronaut would help her
pursue this value, and so astronaut becomes her ideal self. This is a high-level
value in the sense that it informs a great many subgoals, subvalues, and sub-
behaviors. For example, astronauts are exceptional athletes. To bring herself
closer to her ideal self, the girl decides to take up gymnastics. This is an identified behavior. It is not intrinsically motivated, at least not initially, but is
associated with her astronaut ideal self.

As she undertakes gymnastic training, she gets affective feedback. Perhaps
she finds herself consistently eager to train, loves the endorphin rush of
somersaults, and is pleased with her athletic progress. She also gets social
feedback—her peers in the gymnastic community are welcoming, supportive, and have similar athletic goals. Introspecting on this feedback, consciously or unconsciously, the girl decides to continue with gymnastics. It
gradually becomes integrated with other goals, values, and behaviors she
has. For example, her gymnastic skills might qualify her for a college athletics scholarship to pursue a degree in astrophysics, bringing her closer to
her ideal self as an astronaut. She might be aesthetically pleased by the strong

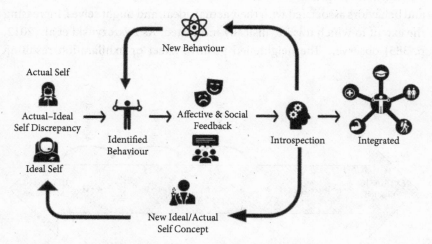

Figure 9.3 An illustrated example of the internalization process

physique gymnastics sculpts. Gymnastics also helps her find friends and lovers, and it boosts her health, allowing her to engage in other activities she enjoys, like hiking. This integration will make gymnastics increasingly intrinsically motivated.

Alternatively, the feedback might be negative. In this case, introspection is more challenging and more likely to involve conscious reasoning. The girl must determine whether she is simply doing gymnastics the wrong way. Maybe she has joined a gymnastics club with an unusually high number of unpleasant people, or perhaps she is spending too much time on the uneven bars, which she finds boring, and not enough time vaulting. A small corrective will work here. Alternatively, it might be that gymnastics is the wrong behavior. For example, what might be holding her back from becoming an astronaut is not her athletic potential but her lack of physics knowledge. A reallocation of time toward study—a new identified behavior—will help here. Finally, it might be that astronaut is the wrong high-level value. Introspection might reveal that what really excites this young woman about being an astronaut is the scientific research. In that case, she should perhaps reorient her ideal self toward being a laboratory scientist. This will lead to major changes in many of her behavior patterns as her overarching goal shifts.

This brief example highlights again how qualitative differences in affective and emotional signals can inform introspection and calibration of the self-concepts. From self-discrepancy theory we learned some ways to interpret depression and anxiety. From SDT we see that boredom and exhaustion imply introjected motivation and/or limited fit between identified behaviors and the actual self. In contrast, easy motivation and feelings of vitality imply intrinsic motivation. If this easy motivation is common across our behaviors, it implies that our values are well integrated. SDT can also help us to reason through our emotional signals by helping us to identify what basic psychological needs are involved. For example, if the main thing that stands out to us about gymnastics is how unpleasant everyone is, then we can infer that our needs for relatedness are not being met, and we should target this when choosing a new gymnastics club. This analysis goes some way to explaining what is involved in Tiberius' (2018) notion, discussed earlier in the book, of "appropriate" values integrating emotions, motivations, and cognitions.

This example illuminates both the social and egoistic elements of internalization. Individuals exist in a social world saturated with values. The desire for relatedness encourages individuals to comport themselves toward those groups with which they feel the greatest kinship. Individuals *identify* with the values of these groups. There is a social dimension here, namely group identity, and an egoistic one, namely the fit between group and individual. The greater the diversity of groups to which an individual can comport, the more individualistic the choice of group can be. However, a greater diversity of groups can make things difficult in the early stages of developing an identity because the individual does not know themselves. They may consequently waste time approaching many groups that are wrong for them. This is common in adolescence, wherein teenagers crave social acceptance but often bounce around different cliques looking for the one that fits them best.

When the individual and group are a bad fit, the individual is relatively extrinsically motivated toward the mores of the group. However, when the group is a good fit, this does not mean that the individual will immediately be intrinsically motivated to accept all the group's mores. Instead, the individual will begin by *identifying* with these mores and gradually internalize them until they are intrinsically motivated. Deci and Ryan (2000, p. 239) summarize this as follows:

> Research on internalisation of extrinsic motivations highlights the human readiness to internalise ambient values and regulations. Yet to fully integrate such values and regulations, and thus to become self-determined with respect to them, people must grasp their importance and synthesise their meaning with respect to other values and motivations. . . . [T]he holistic processing and self-compatibility checking that is necessary to act with self-concordance requires the experience of freedom from rejection by others, from indicators of incompetence, and from excessive pressures. In this sense, supports for relatedness, competence, and autonomy allow individuals to actively transform values and regulations into their own, and thus to be more self-determined.

A practical ramification of this for the coalescence of being is that the actual self parameterizes the individual's choice of groups (a source of relatedness) through the needs for competence and autonomy. If you can't do well in math, you can't join the mathletes no matter how much you think this is your "ideal" group. Similarly, if you dislike exercise, the football team will have a hard time convincing you to play linebacker despite their enthusiasm and your six-foot-six-inch frame because you will only ever be extrinsically motivated to play football.

Coalescence extends internalization metaphorically and literally to consider not just growth and integration but also destruction, externalization, exogenous shocks, and a clearer delineation between core and periphery. "Coalescence" evokes the formation of a star or planet. At the center is the core self, made up of more established elements like intrinsic motivations, innate biological characteristics, and talents. This region may be pockmarked with caverns and fissures representing compartmentalization and dissonance. These are logically inconsistent values, unsustainably introjected behaviors, and aspects of life that are difficult to harmonize. Occasionally a life event will detonate these contradictions like a volcanic eruption. For example, a firm believer in the beneficent effects of law may be forced to acknowledge that the law in their country is used for oppression as well as justice. At such moments, elements of the core self may need to be jettisoned—externalized—to restore integrity. At other times, an exogenous shock might impact the core self like a meteorite, requiring painful adjustments. Swirling around this core self is a periphery of values and behaviors in various stages of integration. Some activities might be undertaken under duress and will be pushed to the edge of the periphery. Introjected, identified, and integrated behaviors will come into the gravitational pull of the core self and swirl ever closer until they are fully intrinsic, joining and expanding the core self.

Figure 9.4 illustrates coalescence graphically for a hypothetical individual. Their core self is defined by their identity as a firefighter. In their youth, this individual was also very attracted to music. However, they struggled to reconcile this with the demands of a firefighting career. To find some harmony amid this incompatibility, they chose to relegate music to hobby status. They identified dance as the optimal way to engage with music in their limited time because it enhanced their fitness for firefighting. This meant that they gave up on playing the guitar, something they enjoyed and had previously invested a lot of time in mastering. Over time, they have made many friends in the dance community, enjoyed participating in competitions and festivals, and even met their life partner. Thanks to these social experiences and its compatibility with firefighting, dance has become increasingly integrated and is now almost a part of the individual's core self.

Sadly, an exogenous shock approaches: soon they will experience an injury that will limit their ability to dance and require that they change to a more administrative role at work. This exogenous shock will dislodge several aspects of the core self and send them rocketing out into space.

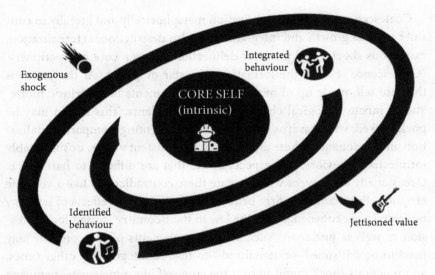

Figure 9.4 The coalescence of being

Doubtless this will be a painful experience and adaptation process, with major negative implications for the individual's SWB. The effectiveness of their adaptation will depend on whether they can find ways to integrate their new job tasks and alternative hobbies into their existing value system.

It is hopefully clear from this discussion how critical integrity is for coalescence and SWB. Achieving an ideal self requires long and sustained effort in the same direction, which is impossible without integrity. You can never become a skilled musician if you change instruments every year. Similarly, you will never become the "good person" you aspire to be if you do not apply in practice what you believe to be right in principle. Your actions must match your values for your actual self to align with your ideal self.

Finally, it should be noted briefly that coalescence does not require particularly ambitious conceptions of the ideal and ought selves, like "astronaut" or "judge." Indeed, they can just as well be mundane. What matters is that they are (1) *realistic*, in that they do not go beyond the parameters imposed by the actual/innate self; (2) *engaging*, so that they do not result in existential boredom; and (3) *authentic*, in the sense that they are self-concordant. For many people, full self-actualization will result in a very modest but also very pleasant, fulfilling, and valuable life.

Part 3: Flow as the State of SWB

Bertrand Russell's (1930) notion of "zest" and Mihaly Csikszentmihalyi's notion of *flow* help to describe what the endpoint of coalescence is like. This endpoint is of course SWB, but this term is descriptively quite empty. It helps to say that a person high in SWB has positive affect, a sense of meaning, and all the other items in the SWBPF, but this description still lacks ontological depth.

The notion of *subjective* well-being implies a *sense* or feeling, and yet it is inappropriate to describe SWB as either. Affective signals are feelings, and they guide coalescence. However, a coalesced individual high in SWB will experience a variety of affective states, such as frustration when working toward goals and exhilaration when they are achieved, that give little indication on their own as to the individual's overall SWB. Even the more expansive notion of life satisfaction is insufficient, because it gives an inadequate account of the tranquility of good conscience, the easy psychological stance granted by identity, or the quietude of steady meaning, among other things. I am even reluctant to describe SWB as a *mental* state because the self is embodied, and coalescence speaks to harmony between thought and action (see the quote from Goethe that opens this chapter). How then to describe ontologically the state of SWB that attends substantial progress in coalescence? Zest and flow provide clues and, in so doing, help to explain what Aristotle might have meant by eudaimonia, which is so much more than happiness or life satisfaction.

Zest is a notion developed by philosopher Bertrand Russell in his *The Conquest of Happiness*. He does not provide a succinct summary of it, but the following will do ([1961] 2006, p. 110, emphasis added):

> What *hunger is in relation to food, zest is in relation to life*. The man who is bored with his meals corresponds to the victim of Byronic unhappiness. The invalid who eats from a sense of duty corresponds to the ascetic, the gormandiser to the voluptuary. The epicure corresponds to the fastidious person who condemns half the pleasures of life as unaesthetic. Oddly enough, all these types, with the possible exception of the gormandiser, feel contempt for the man of healthy appetite and consider themselves his superior. It seems to them vulgar to enjoy food because you are hungry or to enjoy life because it offers a variety of interesting spectacles and surprising experiences.

Zest corresponds to the spontaneous enjoyment of life for its own sake. It is intimately connected with intrinsic motivation. It has parallels with flow but does not necessarily involve high challenge and high skill.

How does coalescence promote zest? The internalization process integrates *identified* activities and values and even transforms them into *intrinsic* ones over time. As the individual steadily orients themselves away from extrinsic activities and values and toward identified ones, intrinsic motivations and values come to preponderate in the individual's psyche and among their daily activities. This brings about zest—the spontaneous enjoyment of life as an intrinsically rewarding experience. Zest still feels too close to life satisfaction for my liking, but it is start.

What about flow? Flow is the feeling of being "in the zone" or "lost in the moment." The conditions for flow are high challenge, high skill, intrinsic motivation, and high-quality feedback. Flow has typically been studied by observing people engaged in absorbing (or not) activities, like painting or chess. In this regard, it seems very much to be a mental state. But Csikszentmihalyi's (1992, p. 214) original vision was grander than this. He considered flow a generalizable state:

> What this involves is turning all life into a unified flow experience. If a person sets out to achieve a difficult enough goal, from which all other goals logically follow, and if he or she invests all energy in developing skills to reach that goal, then actions and feelings will be in harmony, and separate parts of life will fit together—and each activity will "make sense" in the present, as well as in view of the past and of the future. In such a way, it is possible to give meaning to one's life.

The similarities with coalescence here are striking. In the outline just given, "astronaut" is the "difficult enough goal, from which all other goals logically follow." This goal informs the nested goals of gymnastics, physics knowledge, and education. Actions provoke affective and social feedback. These in turn provoke recalibrations like the shift to a more laboratory-oriented career until "actions and feelings are harmony." As integration proceeds across multiple domains, "separate parts of life will fit together," giving meaning to one's life.

Explaining this from the other direction—from coalescence to flow—gives a clearer picture of how coalescence results in the flow criteria being met in multiple life domains. Coalescence requires the harmonization of the actual, ideal, and ought selves. At its highest level of abstraction, the ideal self is an expansive goal toward which all activity is in some way directed. Crucially, it is *challenging*. If a person aims too low, they will succeed quickly and experience ennui—existential boredom. If they aim too high, affective feedback, especially the feeling of failure, will push them to work harder and/or recalibrate their ideal self over time. Provided that the individual has practical wisdom and is therefore capable of introspection, this feedback will be *high quality*. Through effort and application, competence grows. Eventually, the level of challenge inherent in the ideal self is well calibrated to the individual's level of *skill*. The ideal self also comes to be an intrinsically motivated goal over time. Initially it and its sub goals are merely identified, but affirmation, integration, and recalibration lead to disengagement from self-regulated behaviors and values and the accumulation of *intrinsically motivated* ones. All the conditions for flow are met: high challenge, high skill, high quality feedback, and intrinsic motivation. Furthermore, as all aspects of life feed into the ideal self, these flow conditions attend behavior from waking up in the morning to going to bed at night, year-round. Flow then becomes descriptive of the person's *life in general*, not just when they are pursuing specific activities.

Flow is attractive as a description of the state of SWB because Csikszentmihalyi (1992, p. 32) stresses that it is distinct from emotion and happiness. It is not some kind of generalized positive valence, nor even a mental state. It is simply a mode of being, a very positive one:

> It is the full involvement of flow, rather than happiness, that makes for excellence in life. When we are in flow, we are not happy, because to experience happiness we must focus on our inner states, and that would take away attention from the task at hand. If a rock climber takes time out to feel happy while negotiating a difficult move, he might fall to the bottom of the mountain. The surgeon can't afford to feel happy during a demanding operation, or a musician while playing a challenging score. Only after the task is completed do we have the leisure to look back on what has happened, and then we are flooded with gratitude for the excellence of that experience— then, in retrospect, we are happy.

Flow, then, is a kind of full engagement with life, similar to zest. It clearly transcends any of the individual items of the SWBPF, and is greater than the sum of those parts. It also not present when coalescence is embryonic.

It is only once coalescence has progressed sufficiently that someone's PCN fragments become networked that generalized flow can emerge. It can then thicken further, taking over more and more domains of lived experience.

There is a crucial connection to be made here between generalized flow and despair. Kierkegaard ([1849] 2008, p. 12) rightly noted that to be free of despair requires despair to be, in a sense, purged from consciousness:

> Not being in despair must mean the annihilated possibility of the ability to be in it. For it to be true that someone is not in despair, he must be annihilating that possibility every instant.

To be free of despair we must be rid of nihilistic questions: "Who am I? Is it right to do this? What is the point?" These questions must cease to pester us. It is in the generalized flow state that despair is so annihilated. We simply live, with zest, in a manner that is pleasant, fulfilling, and valuable. This is eudaimonia: a mode of being that is in accordance with (our) reason and (our) virtue. We cease to need to search justifications for our world, our selves, and our life. Given this ephemeral ontological quality, SWB might be difficult to measure directly. Instead, we can rely on the subjective reports of individuals and the empirical correlates contained within the SWBPF. We should not, however, mistakes these reports or these correlates for SWB *simpliciter*.

It is predominantly due to this tie-in to despair that I think ultimate prudential value, if such a thing is meaningful to speak of, lies in the generalized flow state. I think the elements of the SWBPF—elements of the SWB "network"—have prudential value. I also think that the coalescence process, a process of value fulfillment by which the elements become networked, has prudential value. If you don't go about building your network prudently you won't succeed in your endeavor. But ultimately, it is in the networking itself that the mother lode of value is to be found, because when the full network comes online you achieve flow across your conscious experience of your life. Incidentally, this is also why you cannot describe SWB as just an objective list of things that are good for people, like positive affective signals, practical wisdom, knowledge of your appropriate values, the items of the SWBPF, progress in coalescence, and so on. These things are independently good, but it is in their being *networked* that SWB *simpliciter* emerges. Specifying the items alone is not enough; we need to articulate the prudentially relevant interrelationships and interdependencies between these prudentially good things.

This synthesis of self-determination theory, self-discrepancy theory, flow, and zest is the core of the coalescence of being. The following sections of this chapter build on this foundation, providing greater detail. Up next is an analysis of where intrinsic motivations come from and how the coalescence of being understands notions of an innate self.

Insights into Innate Selves and Intrinsic Motivation from Developmental Psychology

One question that emerges from the preceding analysis is where intrinsic motivations initially come from. Are they innate? Relatedly, where does coalescence start? Does the individual awaken to self already heavily socialized? Are their social interactions egoistic, or can they engage from a young age with group identity?

SDT provides some guidance on these matters in their definition of self (Deci and Ryan 2000, p. 248):

> Our concept of self, because of its organismic basis, begins with intrinsic activity and the organismic integration process—that is, with the innate tendencies of human beings to engage in interesting activities and to elaborate and refine their inner representation of themselves and their world. The activity and integrative tendency move the organism toward a more unified set of cognitive, affective, and behavioural processes and structures . . . the inherent tendency for activity, the integrative process, and the fundamental needs are all aspects of one's *nascent self*, and gradually the self is elaborated and refined through the integrative process. As such, behaviours that are motivated by regulations that have not been fully integrated into the self are not considered *self*-determined.

According to SDT, then, the tendency to engage in interesting activities is innate, as is, presumably, what each individual finds interesting, at least initially, but how the individual develops over time depends on environmental interactions. As discussed in chapter 8, it is reasonable to conjecture that we are born with certain innate parameters and dispositions that incline us toward particular values, behaviors, and activities. However, the exact expression that these take over the course of our lives will be determined in large part by how we respond to environmental constraints and prompts.

A simple way to think about this is how aptitudes would have manifested during different historical epochs. For example, someone inclined to intellectual pursuits might become a shaman in prehistoric times, a priest in the medieval period, and an academic today. The expression of an intellectual disposition depends on social context. An even simpler example is that someone cannot be a professional athlete if no paid competition exists in which to compete.

Empirical research on the emergence of self in adolescence provides a more rigorous understanding of how the nascent self emerges and becomes accessible to consciousness. This research makes use of some early ideas in psychology from James (1890) and Piaget (1960). James' distinction between the I-self as the actor, knower, or recognizer and the me-self as the object of one's knowledge remains fundamental in the analysis of emergent identity. So too does Piaget's concept of egocentrism, which refers to a singular focus on the self (Harter 2012). The antithesis of egocentrism is perspective taking, which is the ability to take the viewpoint of others using mental images generated in the mind.

Toddlers have self-recognition (Rochat 2003). For example, when placed in front of a mirror with a spot of rouge on their nose, they rub the rouge, indicating that the coloring violates their understanding of what they look like. Very young children are also capable of describing themselves, their feelings, and their ownership of objects (Kring 2008; Thompson 2006). In addition, toddlers demonstrate agency and a rudimentary I-self in the sense that they recognize themselves as the same entity across time (Lewis 2008; Nelson 2003). These facts imply a degree of autobiographical memory (Fivush and Haden 2003). Furthermore, young children understand that they are a person recognized by others. This is the basis for the future development of perspective taking, a capacity toddlers lack (Rochat 2003; Thompson 2006).

Children develop metacognitive awareness around five to seven years of age (Rochat 2003). This is the ability to think reflexively about one's own thoughts. Perspective taking improves rapidly between the ages of eight and ten, enhancing self-awareness and preparing the child for the intense socialization of adolescence (Selman 2003). Social awareness develops next, and the early teenage years are unsurprisingly marked by heightened self-consciousness and concern with the appraisals of others. Multiple self-concepts are also the norm in adolescence, and thinking tends to be categorical and compartmentalized (Harter 1999). Individuals try to harmonize these cleavages over time (Higgins 1991). This harmonization begins in earnest in mid-adolescence, around thirteen to fifteen years old, in which there is "a dramatic rise in the detection of contradictory self-attributes that lead to conflict and confusion" (Harter et al. 1997).

The ability to "construct higher-order abstractions that provide a meaningful integration of single abstractions that previously represented contradictions" emerges in late adolescence (Harter 2012, p. 706). This is a critical skill for the harmonization of self-concepts. An example is resolving an apparent contradiction between a studious self-image and lackadaisical behavior in practice by asserting that you only study what you care about. Late adolescents are context sensitive when it comes to which aspects of themselves they present to the social realm. The ability to construct higher-order abstractions allows many beliefs, values, and standards to be clearly articulated and subsequently internalized, leading to more self-coherence and a greater sense of agency (Harter 2012).

From the preceding analysis it should be clear that we arrive at full consciousness with some identity already. The extent to which this is innate or genetic versus environmentally determined is somewhat beside the point. What matters is that we always have an "actual" self, and that in our earliest encounters with it we apprehend it as discordant, confused, and vague. Using our emerging sense of agency, we explore different facets of this actual self in the social world, gradually developing conceptions of our ideal and ought selves and comporting ourselves toward them. Greater self-coherence comes about over time as a result. This brings us back to the basic point about self, which is that it is a reflexive relation that is constantly under construction, largely through interaction with the social world: "the self is an interpersonal self-construction system" (Morf and Mishel 2012, p. 27).

Goal Setting, Achievement, and Recalibration: The Vehicle of Coalescence

The coalescence of being is closely related to the psychology of goal setting. Who you want to be is a goal, and attaining it involves goal setting and approach. I expand on the relationship between goals and SWB in this section.

There is a literature empirically demonstrating that people with clear goals on average have higher SWB than people who are, in a sense, aimless (Deci and Ryan 1985; Oyserman and Markus 1990; Locke and Latham 1990). However, this average effect obscures a lot of interesting detail pertaining to authenticity. For example, Emmons (1986, 1999) observed that it is important not just to have goals but to attach some personal importance to them. This implies that goals that are autonomously chosen and meaningful rather than simply interesting will have a greater impact on SWB. In line with this, Sheldon has consistently replicated results showing that goals have stronger effects on wellbeing when they are *self-concordant* (Sheldon and Kasser 1995; Sheldon and Elliot 1998, 1999; Sheldon and Houser-Marko 2001; Sheldon 2002).

There are two requisites for a goal to be self-concordant. The first is that it must be pursued autonomously. This pursuit might begin through identification, but the SWB payoffs are strongest in the latter stages of internalization. The second is that goals are aimed at intrinsic pursuits like personal growth, affiliation, and community rather than extrinsic pursuits contingent to activities themselves, like financial success, image, and popularity (Sheldon, Ryan, et al. 2004; Kasser 2003). This ensures that the goals and associated activities nourish basic psychological needs for autonomy, competence, and relatedness. Recall from chapter 7 on eudaimonia that there are relatively higher SWB payoffs to achieving intrinsic pursuits rather than extrinsic ones.

A critical link between the literatures on goal setting, the coalescence of being, and positive psychology is the finding that people only have strong affective responses to goals that relate to ego and identity. Such goals are sometimes referred to as contingencies of self-worth (Crocker and Park 2012). Successes and failures in goals that do not have substantial ego involvement do not provoke affective responses, but people have few such goals (Crocker and Park 2012, p. 322). The differences in affective response to success and failure in contingent and non-contingent domains can be stark. For example, figures 9.5 and 9.6 (reproduced from Crocker and Park 2012, pp. 312–313) show self-esteem fluctuations for a student with little ego involvement in academic goals and a student with a large amount of ego involvement in academic goals. The lines track their self-esteem across a time span in which they receive acceptance and rejection letters from graduate programs.

The self-esteem of the student oriented toward academic goals is far more volatile in response to self-relevant information in the form of acceptance and rejection letters. In comparison, the self-esteem of the student with little ego involvement in academic goals does not fluctuate much.

The relationship between contingencies of self-worth is clear in the written responses of participants in the study just mentioned. Three

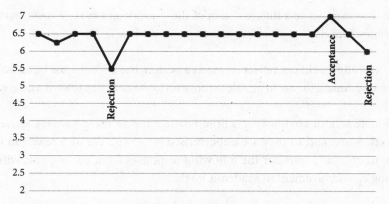

Figure 9.5 Student with little ego involvement in academic goals

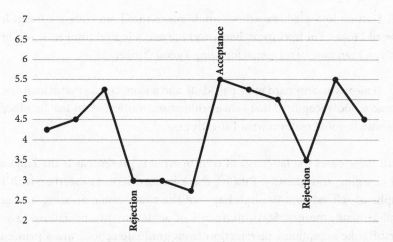

Figure 9.6 Student with substantial ego involvement in academic goals

students low in academic orientation wrote (reproduced from Crocker and Park 2012, p. 315):

> Getting into graduate school is a formality. It is a mere reminder of potential, rather than a reflection of hard work. It signifies a long, arduous road ahead in academia.
>
> . . .
>
> It means that I have been granted an opportunity to gain the knowledge and skills I need to be a competent and successful researcher. I will also be

able to experience a different area of the country and make a fresh start somewhere else.

. . .

It really would not reflect on me as a person, but it would just be an accomplishment for me to be able to move on to the next step toward a career.

Graduate school obviously has little relationship to these people's sense of who they are, and so they are unperturbed by acceptance and rejection letters. In contrast, consider the following responses from participants with a strong ego involvement in academic goals:

Getting into grad school (especially a really good one) would show me that I am one of the best students of an even more select group of students.

. . .

Getting into graduate school would mean that I am truly a scholar. It would mean I'm intelligent, hard-working and a logical thinker. It would mean I can now be respected for being a good thinker.

. . .

It means that my hard work pa[i]d off, and it would mean that at least one grad school recognised that I am a brilliant and motivated student. In other words, it would reaffirm what I already know.[1]

In all three cases the language of *confirmation* is present, as is the language of belonging and identity. Putting these written reports together with the graphs of self-esteem, the link between the coalescence of being and goal achievement emerges. Stark moments of achievement and failure in goal pursuit, like acceptance or rejection from graduate school, are a prime instance of disclosure. When we are disclosed as our ideal selves in our impact on the world and the eyes of others, we coincide with ourselves. When we are disclosed as something other than our ideal selves, we instead experience an "existential fail." Our identity collapses, negative affect rises to communicate to us that there is a problem, and we feel worthless (some self-compassion might be helpful here). The evidence provided here—two graphs and a few

---

[1] Anyone who has been to grad school and especially people who have experienced the academic job market for early-career researchers must feel a tinge of sympathy for these poor, naive fools. Graduate school is when the imposter syndrome really kicks in.

excerpts—is anecdotal, but data from the full samples in Park and Crocker's studies follows the themes outlined earlier. Park and Crocker summarize (2012, p. 315):

> As expected, within-person analysis of acceptances and rejections from graduate programs indicated that affect and self-esteem rose and fell together. . . . [F]urthermore, the more participants staked their self-worth on academic competence, the stronger their affective reactions to acceptances and rejections.

In other words, failure in non-contingent domains has limited effects on affect and self-esteem, and success in non-contingent domains provokes mild positive affect but no appreciable change in self-esteem. By contrast, success and failure in contingent domains provokes large changes in self-esteem and highly correlated commensurate changes in affect (Crocker and Park 2004). The implication is that moments of coalescence lead to large changes in emotion, while goal setting and achievement that are not self-congruent have little effect on emotion. Succinctly, affect tracks the disclosure of identity-relevant information. It is only weakly tied to identity-irrelevant feedback. This underscores the importance of studying affect and life satisfaction with an understanding of their possible deep determinants in eudaimonia and conscience. It should be noted in this context that few people have no contingencies of self-worth. For example, in a study of first-year college students, only 4 percent of students scored 3 or lower on seven 1–7 scales designed to assess what goal-related factors mattered to people's self-worth, and these 4 percent may well have had contingencies of self-worth not captured by the survey (Crocker 2002).

While the literature on contingencies of self-worth suggests that clear, authentic goals are important to SWB, evidence from other lines of research suggests that it is wise not to be *too* specific in one's goals. Pyszczynski et al. (2012) posit that making one's self-esteem contingent on more abstract standards can make them easier to satisfy. They give the example of being a top athlete versus being an Olympic medalist. There is not necessarily a difference in degrees here, as an Olympic medalist is certainty a top athlete. However, someone with the more abstract goal could derive a lot of confirmation and satisfaction from simply qualifying for the Olympics, while the latter requires something much more specific that can be interrupted by unrelated issues, like a poorly timed injury.

This recommendation of abstraction is supported by Freitas et al. (2001), who report six empirical studies showing that people engage in more self-esteem defense when they construe their actions at more concrete as opposed to more abstract levels. Another piece of supportive empirical evidence comes from Vess et al. (2011), who found that participants induced to adopt an abstract orientation are less reactive in terms of changes in self-esteem to negative feedback. However, Pyszczynski et al. (2012) also acknowledge that abstract contingencies of self-esteem can be harder to satisfy precisely because the requisite conditions are vaguer, which makes self-assessment and the tracking of progress harder. Some balance must be achieved between not setting oneself up to fail while nonetheless delineating clear targets that can provide feedback along the way to one's ideal self.

Psychological Perspectives on the Disclosure of Being

How do we know that we have achieved a goal? What experiences prompt the disclosure of being? A relatively straightforward source of information is objective measures. For example, if one's goal is to be able to run fast, then gradually reducing your personal best time on the 100-meter dash is clear evidence that you are getting faster. There is typically a range of objective metrics that can be associated with any desired identity.

Another source of evidence is other people, but the disclosure of being becomes more complicated when you move into the realm of social confirmation. There is no shortage of material advising us not to worry about what other people think. But we do worry, of course, and rightly so. There is evidence that we are prone to self-enhancement in our opinion of ourselves, so it is important that we give ourselves a reality check occasionally with the assessments of others (Sedikides et al. 2005). Furthermore, if we are trying to comport ourselves toward a group, then it is imperative that we check in with the group occasionally to make sure we're on the right track. This is particularly the case when what we are trying to excel at is relative, such as being the best chess player, or subjectively assessed, as in art circles. People's opinions can wound us, and we should be careful and exercise self-compassion when exposing ourselves to negative feedback. But such suffering is also the affective signal to disconnect from inappropriate goals and may simply see us move toward healthier social groups (like art circles with tastes closer to our own). We should not neurotically avoid it. Social dis/confirmation is an important source of evidence about our being.

The preceding analysis is indirectly supported by empirical evidence in social self-analysis, which concerns how people evaluate themselves relative to others (Alicke et al. 2012). Social appraisals have been found to exert more influence on self-appraisal when the perceiver is considered by the perceived to be relevant to their self-concept, an in-group member, desirable, valued, or otherwise important (Wallace and Tice 2012). Neuroscience studies align with this result. They show that when an appraiser is from a group you care about, their appraisals of you will activate the self-assessment part of your brain. This is not the case when they are from a group you don't care about or a random stranger (Devos et al. 2012, p. 158).

Self-verification theory explains how social assessments interact with the coalescence of being to create a self-reinforcing cycle (Swann 2011). Self-verification theory conjectures that self-views guide social interaction and, provided they are stable, make an individual's behavior more predictable to others. This predictability stabilizes the way others respond to the individual, which makes it easier to verify one's self-view through social interaction. Stable self-views thus encourage the emergence of a similarly stable and *coherent* social environment and vice versa, leading to a virtuous cycle wherein both self-concept and social environment become clearer and better fitted to each other. An important, empirically validated hypothesis that emerges from this theory is that people prefer social appraisals that align with their self-view even when these appraisals are negative (Swann and Buhrmester 2012). People move away from both incorrect and correct-but-negative appraisals over time toward groups that are both affirming and accurate in their social appraisals.

This chapter has now covered the basic methods of coalescence and provided some detail regarding its practice through the goal setting and social verification literature. I turn now to focus on the outcomes of the coalescence of being. I start with an in-depth discussion of automatization, which is important for understanding how coalescence dissolves anguish and how values become "appropriate."

Automatization and the Dampening of Anguish

The coalescence of being gradually automatizes decisions in many domains. This overcomes anguish because you rarely need to engage your conscious processing faculties in order to make a decision. Conscious, higher-order decision-making is taxing, and thus most efficaciously engaged only at times of substantial ambiguity or complexity (Kahneman 2011). Such ambiguity and complexity are the hallmarks of anguish, which intrudes upon us when we don't know what the *right* choice is. In trying to make that choice, we inevitably articulate a range of *reasons* for making one decision or another. As the coalescence of being progresses, the reasons we make one or another decision in certain circumstances and the consequences of those decisions become clearer. We can retrieve these reasons more easily from memory, and with habitual use they move almost to the level of instinct, thereby mitigating anguish. In addition, as higher-order cognitive engagement with a range of decision realms becomes less frequent, it frees up conscious attention to be focused elsewhere. The apparatus of conscious processing is consequently more fully available for use at moments of ambiguity where tough decisions need to be made. Such decisions tend to be meaningfully self-defining. With our rational faculties present, personal growth is more likely to result from these decisions because our autobiographical self is there to take note of what we choose and its ramifications.

Research in psychology provides a great deal of insight into how this automatization takes place. The first chunk of research comes from sports psychology (Fader 2016). When teaching athletes technique, top coaches will emphasize the distinction between conscious and unconscious processing, or what is nowadays called system 1 and system 2 thinking (or dual process thinking). System 1 is intuitive and instinctive. System 2 is conscious and deliberative (Kahneman 2011). Most things that we do physically are too complex for system 2 to handle, which is why we find it so hard to teach robots to walk (Simon 2017). Consider how a tennis player's arm seizes up for a few hundredths of a second on contact with the ball to stabilize the racquet head. If you tried to do that consciously, your arm would seize up long before and for a long time after the ball contacted your racquet, reducing your racquet head speed and the sensitivity of your reaction to contact, ruining your shot. However, bad habits that system 1 has learned are hard to correct without systematic attention from system 2. As a result, a key principle of teaching technique in sport is to engage the conscious brain during training but have it focus on only one or two technical changes at a time, like keeping the arm loose through the swing or trying to load the wrist more. After a few hundred (or hundred thousand) focused repetitions, the technical change becomes habit and focus can shift to other issues. In matches, the conscious brain is almost entirely turned off, and instinctive programming is allowed to take over. System 1 is much more capable of making the thousands of calculations per second required to perform complex operations like returning a 120 km/h forehand on the run while changing the direction of the ball and reversing its spin. In tennis, the conscious mind should be doing little beyond watching the ball during matches.

The same processes are at work in the coalescence of being. If there is something about yourself that you want to change you will need to repeatedly engage system 2. This allows you to focus on that thing and consciously, actively change it. Repetition in this environment allows habit to form, at which point system 2 can be disengaged. System 2 is a limited resource, so there is a degree of opportunity cost involved in using it to resolve one conundrum and not another. Having system 2 engaged all the time will also permeate your life with anguish, so there is a degree of urgency to commit things to instinct, and strong incentives to avoid activities that make uncertainty salient.

Instinct has the advantage of being able to take in a wider array of information than conscious processing, which can sometimes allow it to make better decisions, especially when under pressure (Kahneman 2011). A fascinating finding in this vein is that people introduced to new games often develop winning strategies via system 1 before they can articulate what these strategies are (Crowley et al. 1997). On the flip side, those who can articulate the strategy into system 2 then find it more cognitively accessible later and easier to generalize to similar games (Crowley and Siegler 1999). This has important parallels with the coalescence of being. Consciously processing the reasoning behind our decisions and values before committing those reasons to instinct allows that reasoning to be reengaged later when necessary and generalized to other domains. By way of a simple example, if one reasons that one won't eat veal because it is a child, then one can generalize this reasoning to suckling pig. Being able to generalize reasoning in this way is important for reducing compartmentalization and dissonance and promoting identification and integration.

This analysis is supported by studies in goal attainment. As Bargh (2004, p. 388) notes:

If in a given situation we tend to choose the same goal, the representation of that goal becomes more and more strongly associated with the mental representation of that situation. Thus, eventually that goal comes to be activated automatically when one enters that situation and then operates to guide one's behaviour towards the goal—without one consciously choosing or intending to pursue that goal at that moment, and even without the person aware of the real reasons for his or her behaviour in that situation.

It is also supported by findings in personality systems integration (PSI) theory (not to be confused with psi, which concerns telepathy). PSI theory distinguishes between two different volitional modes. The first mode, self-control, is responsible for inhibiting impulsive actions and maintaining focus on goals in active memory. The second mode is self-maintenance, which directs activity toward goals that are "either intrinsically appealing or congruent with a multitude of the person's inner values and autobiographical experiences" (Kuhl and Koole 2004, p. 416). Self-control and self-maintenance are functionally opposite, and similar to reflexive and reflective processing (Oyserman et al. 2012). Self-maintenance corresponds to instinct in the preceding analysis, guiding our behavior automatically toward the reasons, values, and goals that define our identity. Self-control is closer to conscious processing, helping us to correct bad habits and bring our actual self closer to our ideal self. Internalization from self-determination theory and the analysis of automation then explains how behaviors transition from being self-controlled to self-maintained, or in the language of SDT, automatic and automatized:

> We argued for a distinction between automatic and automatized behaviours. Automatic behaviours are those that are pushed by controlled processes and whose occurrence is not consistent with one's choices or reflections and cannot easily be brought into the realm of active choice. Automatized behaviours, in contrast, are ones that if reflected on, would fit with one's values or needs and could readily be changed when they no longer fit. (Ryan and Deci 2004, p. 468)

The automation of behavior is one aspect of the broader process of refining the self and is relevant to the integration of "multiple selves" (Showers and Zeigler-Hill 2012). We typically possess a range of personas that are broadly incompatible. The most common way of integrating these multiple selves is to determine which self-concept is most appropriate for what context. Showers and Zeigler-Hill (2012) offer the example of a "superdad" who is a nurturing father at home but a hard-assed executive at the office. The superdad will need reasoning to determine whether to engage his nurturing persona or his more cutthroat persona. Over time, these reasons will become automatized and his behavior will habitually swap between the personas as appropriate without effort. There are two things potentially at issue here. The first is that two different aspects of personality conflict: nurturing and hard-assed. The second is that aspects of personality that are positive or negative in one context may be the opposite in a different context, potentially leading to dissonance.

A formal but generalized framework for thinking about these issues is provided by "evaluative organization," which operates along a spectrum between evaluative compartmentalization and evaluative integration (Showers 1992a, 1992b, 2002). Evaluative compartmentalization sees positive and negative beliefs about the self separated into distinct constructs, with each one containing primarily positive or negative items. For example, a sprinter might have two self-concepts organized around their time at the track and their interpersonal behavior. The former contains mostly positive self-concepts, like "fast," "talented," "high-achieving," and "hardworking." The latter contains mostly negative self-concepts, like "moody," "distant," "boring," and "one-dimensional." Evaluative integration produces self-concepts that mix such positive and negative categories together so that the negative concepts are associated with their positive correlates. In the case of the sprinter, for example, part of the reason they are boring is because they are hardworking on the track and don't have much time left for culture and socialization. They are moody because their emotional state depends substantially on the quality of their most recent training session, but their emotional involvement in training is also what makes them high-achieving.

This is reminiscent of Nietzsche's notion of "giving style to one's character." He talked precisely about concerted effort to remove things you don't like about yourself (comportment to the ideal self and away from the feared self), but also about the transformation of unavoidable negative qualities into charming quirks. To wit (Nietzsche [1887] 1974, p. 232):

One thing is needed—to "give style" to one's character—a great and rare art! It is practiced by those who survey all the strengths and weaknesses of their nature and then fit them into an artistic plan until every one of them appears as art and reason and even weaknesses delight the eye. Here a large mass of second nature has been added; there a piece of original nature has been removed—both times through long practice and daily work at it. Here the ugly that could not be removed is concealed; there it has been reinterpreted and made sublime . . . for one thing is needful: that a human being should *attain* satisfaction with himself, whether it be by means of this or that poetry or art; only then is a human being at all tolerable to behold.

The similarities with automatization here are uncanny. "Second nature" is added by way of internalization, and first ("original") nature is removed by self-control ("long practice and daily work at it"). Integration is evident in the comment "Here the ugly that could not be removed is concealed; there it has been reinterpreted and made sublime."

Relatedness and Individualism in the Coalescence of Being

The process of coalescence is now quite well outlined. It is time to bring it back to the components of SWB. I will begin with relatedness. The connection between the two is quite straightforward. What is less clear is how a doctrine as individualistic and egocentric as coalescence can apply to people in collectivist cultures. I address this concern in what follows.

Healthy, satisfying relationships with others are critical to the wellbeing of most people. SDT posits relatedness as a basic psychological need. Social connections are one of the strongest positive correlates of life satisfaction identified to date in international panel data and cross-sectional studies (Helliwell 2020). There is evidence that the feeling of experiencing the same thing as someone else—I-sharing—is exhilarating and a feeling people seek out (Pinel et al. 2004). Collective action and group goal setting and achievement provoke similar feelings. Strong relationships, especially intimate ones, support self-esteem and aid terror management. Indeed, there is evidence to suggest that self-esteem evolved as an instrument for monitoring one's "relational value to others" (Leary and Baumeister 2000). People seek out group affiliations that are affirming of their self-worth.

The coalescence of being promotes relatedness in the following way. Individuals pursuing their ideal selves will comport toward groups that share their values and help them to realize their goals. Someone with environmentalist values might join a social democratic political party, for example. These groups will provide feedback to the individual that assists with the disclosure of being. Members of the party might, for example, comment on how passionate the individual is about green policy and how unwavering they are about reducing plastic use. Positive feedback will typically reinforce the individual's group affiliation and encourage them to reciprocate, building a mutual sense of relatedness between members.

Negative feedback can encourage disengagement and the search for new groups. It can also encourage behavior change so that the individual's actual self, which is communicated to them in the group's assessment, aligns with their ideal self, which the group's values represent. This is particularly true of feedback in the form of the social emotions of guilt and shame (Leary and Baumeister 2000). Of course, if it turns out that the group's values do not align with the individual's ideal self, this will result in disengagement. For example, the environmentalist might discover that the social democratic party wants to keep coal mines and steel plants open, which would be terrible for the environment. They consequently swap allegiance to the Green Party. Coalescence therefore has a mutually reinforcing relationship with relatedness. Good-fitting and supportive groups will provoke increasing engagement and alignment by the individual and, in turn, acceptance by the group.

The coalescence of being does not obviate a collective self or collectivist values. It is not even individualistic. It merely emphasizes that individual *autonomy* is a basic psychological need. Any collectivist system that enforces behavior that it is not autonomous and intrinsically motivated will generate ill-being. Such behavior results in compliance and protectiveness rather than confidence and prosocial ingratiation (MacDonald and Leary 2012, p. 363).

There is within the coalescence of being a detailed explanation of how an autonomously acting individual can hold collectivist values and put a group before their individual needs. To wit, the individual *autonomously* prioritizes the group, self-regulating their purely egoistic desires to instead affirm the identified values of the group in an autonomous manner. As Ryan and Deci (2004, p. 452) explain:

> Self-determination can be used to connote independent choices, but it can also describe acts of volitionally consenting to inputs such as obligations, inducements, urges, pressures or rising desires. As an example, consider a man who has fully assimilated and embraced collectivist cultural norms and practices. In a moment when he is pressured or tempted to act individualistically, he is likely to either implicitly or explicitly experience discrepancy and conflict. To be autonomous, he would have to find a meaningful way to coordinate the individualistic aim with his prior beliefs or revise either the aim or the prior beliefs. Anything less would represent less than full endorsement by the self and lack of integrity in behavior.

Whether behavior is autonomous or heteronomous has little to do with whether it affirms individual or collective goals (these are motivationally similar after identification). It depends instead on whether there is an external or internal locus of control. Healthy collectivism, like in a Spartan phalanx, is where group values are *identified* by individual members. They thus act autonomously when pursuing those values. Unhealthy collectivism, as in authoritarian regimes or manipulative cults, is where individuals pursue group values only through introjected motivation to receive approval or extrinsic motivation to avoid social censure.

Two empirical studies lend support to this analysis. Iyengar and Lepper (1999), in a study that was framed as critical of SDT's conception of autonomy, examined the aspirations, motivations, and achievements of American and Japanese university students. They found that in both groups, having goals *imposed* by others led to the lowest levels of intrinsic motivation and well-being. This would be introjection or extrinsic motivation. However, among the American students, decisions made personally resulted in the highest levels of intrinsic motivation, while those made on advice from trusted insiders ranked second. Among the Japanese, these positions were reversed. The key thing, then, is not collectivism or individualism, but whether the individual is controlled or self-determined. People can feel more autonomous when endorsing and enacting the values of people with whom they identify but they will only achieve autonomy if it is they who choose the values. If they are *forced* to follow collective values under duress or manipulation, then ill-being will eventuate.

Further support comes from Devine et al. (2008). Their study tracks households throughout Bangladesh. Both qualitative and quantitative survey techniques reveal that even in this highly collectivist society, and even among members who are discouraged or limited in their autonomy, such as women, issues of autonomy remain salient. Individuals expressed the desire to be consulted, to be financially independent, to have outside options thanks to a good education, and simply "to be free." Importantly, though, many people expressed their autonomy in terms of their relationships, not just with family members, but also with kin networks more broadly, and within community-based and development organizations. This is in line with the theoretical postulate that values might be collective but the processes underlying psychological well-being depend on autonomy and intrinsic motivation.

The coalescence of being nourishes the need for *relatedness* by pushing the individual out into the world to affirm their values. This will inevitably see them gravitate toward those with similar values, internalize collective values and behaviors, engage in collective action with and against groups, and promote their own interests through their group allegiances. I turn now to explain how coalescence promotes the other eight dimensions of the SWBPF.

The Coalescence of Being and Subjective Wellbeing

Autonomy is fundamental to coalescence because the actual self directs the individual's initial engagements in the world. Furthermore, the process of internalization brings initially relatively extrinsic behaviors into the core self over time. Feedback encourages the individual to disconnect from extrinsically motivated behaviors. The end result is a life in which most values are held and behaviors engaged in volitionally and for intrinsic reasons.

Coalescence involves the harmonization of the actual, ideal, and ought selves across many life domains, which brings about *identity*. Harmonization requires the elimination of dissonance and compartmentalization, and the integration of identified but external values and behaviors with intrinsic ones. Introspection is critical to this process, and introspection necessarily involves articulating the reasons you value and do the things that you do. This ensures that you *know* who you are and can explain that identity to yourself and others. Anguish is dampened because you can retrieve your reasons when confronted by tough decisions and because you have reduced the degrees of separation between multiple selves in your identity. Conscious introspection upon feedback helps you to track your progress toward your ideal and ought selves. While this progress is always ongoing and so you are always becoming, you also have a sense that you are *growing*. The core self becomes richer, deeper, more articulated. This is the "being" that the French existentialists wanted.

To maintain our sense of self over time we need to act with integrity. Abandoning one's values invites terror from normative uncertainty and dissolves identity. As such, there is a strong incentive to be consistent in behaviors and values over time, including one's *ethical* values and behaviors. This provides *seriousness*. Your values are binding on your behavior because if you transgress your principles you lose your SWB. When we are disclosed in our actions and the eyes of others as aligning with our ought self we can confirm that we are a "good person." What we mean by a good person is well articulated because of the time we spend introspecting on our ought self across a range of domains. Thus the coalescence of being ensures a sense of *virtue*.

Meaning in the coalescence of being comes from intrinsic motivation, zest, and flow. Intrinsically motivated behaviors are enjoyable for their own sake, and intrinsic values emerge from our core self. Such values and activities are not transcendentally valuable—they are not written into the firmament. But they are valuable *to us*, and this is enough to suffuse life with meaning and give us purpose. We matter if we choose to. In any case, we are distracted from any nihilistic thoughts by the omnipresence of flow. As we harmonize our actual and ideal selves the level of challenge inherent in our ideal self comes to be calibrated to the level of skill inherent in our actual self until the two are aligned. Internalization steadily transforms the behaviors that we undertake and values that we pursue day to day into intrinsically motivated ones. And mindfulness, introspection, and practical wisdom ensure that we attain high-quality feedback from our life at all times. Coalescence thus brings about the conditions for flow across a range of life domains, ensuring that we increasingly get lost in the moment regardless of what we are doing.

The extension of flow across our life domains also nurtures our need for *competence*. Our goals are challenging, so when we accomplish them we feel a sense of achievement. They are also calibrated to our skill level such that we are frequently successful and consequently have this sense of achievement on a regular basis. More simplistically, coalescence is essentially about achieving the goal of your ideal self. Therefore, success at coalescence implies a feeling of competence.

Finally, coming back to hedonia, we have *happiness*. How does the coalescence of being bring about positive emotion? This analysis will be split into two parts. The first deals with direct causal chains between coalescence and positive emotion. The second discusses the integrated nature of affective and personality systems.

The coalescence of being is an enjoyable process because the attainment of our ideal self is an exhilarating experience. Goals are affectively coded, and goal achievement is consequently satisfying, even if this satisfaction fades and the goal needs to be replaced by a new one (Silvia and Eddington 2012). As the coalescence of being reaches a high level, most of the things you do will provoke flow experiences, which are enjoyable. You will also correspond closely to your ideal self and this fact will be frequently disclosed to you, provoking positive emotions via feelings of self-worth. However, the positive emotion that accompanies the coalescence of being is meaningfully distinct from a high background level of positive affect. Goal achievement inevitably involves effort. The coalescence of being is full of suffering for your identity. But this effort and suffering are fundamental to flow, which cannot be achieved without the presence of high *challenge*. Life is thus punctuated by ups and downs, but you have a measure of control over the downs. You go through them willingly for the ups as you pursue competency and self-actualization.

SWB and coalescence are bound up together in other, more complex ways. Personality systems integration theory emphasizes that affective signals are critical for coordinating shifts between self-maintenance and self-regulation (intuitive and conscious processing) as circumstances demand (Kuhl and Koole 2004, p. 420). Simplistically, if automatic decision-making is leading the individual into unhealthy behaviors that reduce SWB they will receive negative affective signals. These prompt a shift from self-maintenance to self-regulation so that conscious processing can be engaged to determine what is unhealthy about present behaviors. Once this mystery is solved, healthier behaviors can be engaged. As eudaimonia and conscience rise from these, positive affect will result, and this signals to the personality system that it can automatize these behaviors and shift to self-maintenance. This process is assisted by the fact that affect is more intense when you are self-focused (Carver 2012, p. 53).

A more coalesced being—high self-concept clarity, in psychological parlance—is also associated with *emotional well-being*. Higher self-concept clarity has been linked to less negative mood among college students under conditions of high life stress (Cohen et al. 1997; Linville 1987; Dixon and Baumeister 1991). Research also suggests that individuals with low self-concept clarity experience greater volatility in their affective state (McConnell et al. 2009). Finally, as Showers and Zeigler (2012, p. 113) note, "Low self-concept clarity is associated with neuroticism, low agreeableness, low self-esteem, low internal self-awareness, chronic self-analysis and a ruminative form of self-focused attention."

Conclusion

The coalescence of being is a model of the self-actualization *process* by which the *outcome* of SWB is attained. Its central mechanism is the harmonization of the actual, ideal, and ought selves over time through the setting of goals and their achievement or recalibration. Succeeding in goal pursuit brings a sense of competence. Calibrating our goals to our skill level over time increases the frequency of flow experiences. Acting with integrity toward our ideal and ought selves brings meaning and seriousness. In our acts and in the eyes of others we disclose our actual selves, and this helps us to understand who we are, bringing identity and annulling anguish. The automatization of behaviors over time as we become more comfortable with ourselves, our goals, and our values dampens anguish further by reducing the frequency with which we are confronted by the need to consciously choose. The coalescence of being is most effective when we pursue intrinsically motivated goals that are self-concordant. This ensures autonomy. It also brings us into collectives with like-minded individuals, nourishing our need for relatedness. This whole process is punctuated and guided by affective signals. It is through our emotional responses to success, failure, and new endeavors that we come to understand what goals and values are right for us. However, we struggle to improve our SWB simply by treating these affective signals. Mood management is not enough for SWB. We must understand the association these signals have with the deep determinants of our SWB in the eudaimonia and conscience dimensions.

If coalescence is correct, it raises concerns about the prevailing ways of measuring SWB. Life satisfaction scales seem a particularly questionable instrument for measuring dynamic changes in SWB because coalescence involves frequent and profound scale-norming. The iterative process of conceiving an ideal self and affirming it in action and social appraisal inevitably involves conceiving a new scale on which to assess your life after each moment of disclosure. Success often provokes greater ambition, increasing life satisfaction *while also* shifting the scales up. Failure provokes a reassessment of the individual's self-concept and goals, which changes the qualitative meaning of each point on that person's scales. The raw number reported on a scale does not clearly communicate these meaningful changes. I explain this scale-norming challenge and how it might be rectified in chapter 10, which concerns how we can measure SWB as described in the SWBPF and coalescence of being. I pay special attention to SWB measurement in the context of economics and public policy.

10

Measuring Subjective Wellbeing

If you cannot measure it, you cannot improve it.

—William Thomson, Lord Kelvin

Introduction

This chapter analyzes how to measure SWB, especially for applications in welfare economics and public policy. It begins with a brief discussion of how SWB can be measured using relatively long surveys. It then discusses the contextual peculiarities of economics and public policy that make such long surveys impractical. SWB measures must be relatively cheap and quick to administer because otherwise they are hard to incorporate into the large-sample social surveys that are the workhorses of policy analysis. For applications like cost-benefit analysis, an SWB measure would ideally be unidimensional and at least interpersonally ordinal if not cardinal.

Life satisfaction scales show promise on these counts. Such scales ask respondents to evaluate their life and describe this evaluation using a number on some bounded scale. A representative example is the following, from the Household Income and Labour Dynamics of Australia (HILDA) survey: "All things considered, how satisfied are you with your life at this time on a scale from 1–10?" Such questions feature in just about every major longitudinal social survey. Sometimes Cantril's ladder of life is used instead, such as in the World Values Survey. This question involves presenting respondents with the image of a ladder, typically with ten steps. Respondents are then asked something like the following:

> Assume that this ladder is a way of picturing your life. The top of the ladder represents the best possible life for you. The bottom rung of the ladder

A Theory of Subjective Wellbeing. Mark Fabian, Oxford University Press. © Oxford University Press 2022.
DOI: 10.1093/oso/9780197635261.003.0011

represents the worst possible life for you. Indicate where on the ladder you feel you personally stand right now.

The major difference between conventional life satisfaction scale questions and the ladder of life question is the inclusion of the phrases "best possible" and "worst possible." It is hoped that these phrases will anchor respondents' scales to some fixed points over time.

I argue that while promising, life satisfaction scales are of questionable usefulness in many applications because of the largely overlooked or at least underappreciated issue of scale-norming. This is where the qualitative meaning of the points on a respondent's scale changes over time. Scale-norming makes comparing scale responses interpersonally and intertemporally tough without making strong assumptions. I present a formal model of the reporting function that maps latent life satisfaction to a scale response. This illuminates where scale-norming comes from and what processes need to be isolated when studying the reporting function in order to control for it. I then survey evidence for the existence and perniciousness of scale-norming and briefly discuss its implications.

Measuring Subjective Well-Being

SWB as I have defined it—a combination of both the SWBPF and the coalescence of being—is a complex, multifaceted construct. It is consequently difficult to measure. This difficulty is further compounded by the challenges associated with measuring a subjective construct and with measuring a latent construct. Some of these difficulties pertain to fundamental requirements for conducting empirical research. For example, when you have a construct that is empirically predicted by nine co-determined items and a slew of parameters, establishing discriminant validity is not straightforward.

Nonetheless, great progress has been made in recent years. There are established measures for most if not all the components of the SWBPF. This should be clear from the empirical literature surveyed in support of each component in chapters 4 through 9. While this book is a work of theory, it builds on empirical results and cannot be easily dismissed with "Where is your evidence?" Affect can be studied using the experience sampling methods discussed in chapter 6, simple day reconstruction questions like

"Did you experience a lot of worry yesterday?," and brain scans. SDT has a twenty-one-question survey for studying basic needs (Deci and Ryan 2000; Gagné 2003). Several meaning-in-life measures exist, and there is a lively discussion as to which one is most appropriate and in which circumstances (Hill et al. 2019; Damàsio et al. 2016; Morgan and Farsides 2009). Identity can be measured using the sense-of-self scale (Flury and Ickes 2007).

Virtue is tricky. Chapter 8 argued that values and ethics are sustained intersubjectively rather than being objective features of the universe. This makes it arguably impossible to test someone's virtue by seeing whether their behavior corresponds to axiomatic propositions. Some efforts in this direction are nonetheless interesting. Notably, Kaufman et al. (2019) have developed a "light triad" scale to complement the large body of work on the dark triad of personality. The dark triad is made up of narcissism, psychopathy, and Machiavellianism. The light triad consists of Kantianism, humanism, and faith in humanity. Kantianism here is defined as treating others as ends unto themselves rather than means to your own ends. Humanism is defined as valuing the dignity and worth of individuals. And faith in humanity is "believing in the fundamental goodness of humans" (p. 7).

These seem like admirable qualities in a person, but their possession is distinct from virtue. Virtue in the SWBPF is the sense that you are a good person. This is open to what you think "good" means. Some utilitarians, for example, might be distinctly not Kantian and have well-articulated reasons for their position. Furthermore, someone could feel that they are a good person while also having low faith in humanity. There are, for example, people who resolutely contribute substantially to communal pots in public goods games even as other players behave in increasingly selfish ways.[1] Indeed, given how selfishly people behave in public goods games, faith in humanity is arguably irrational (Zelmer 2003). A final limitation of the light triad scale for measuring virtue is that it is self-reported. People may perceive themselves as more virtuous than their real-life actions would suggest.

---

[1] The public goods game works as follows. Each round, all players are given some sum of money, say ten units. They choose some amount to keep for themselves and some amount to contribute to the communal pot. At the end of the round, the communal pot is doubled by the conductor of the game and its value evenly distributed among *all* players. As such, if the group wants to maximize its total payoff, then all players should contribute all ten units to the communal pot. However, if there is some payoff associated with being the overall winner, then individual players have an incentive to keep some amount for themselves each round. In simple versions of the game where contributions are anonymous and punishment is impossible, people tend to be increasingly stingy in their contributions over successive rounds (Zelmer 2003).

An alternative approach to measuring virtue might be to track social emotions like guilt, shame, and self-esteem. These relate to how others perceive you, which is an important source of information about whether we are moral. The problem here is that individuals might be associating with unsuitable groups because of introjection. Those groups would then not be a good guide to the individual's virtuousness. Indeed, someone who is defecting from what they perceive to be the bad behavior of a group may feel shame precisely because they behaved virtuously. More research is required to understand how to measure virtue, especially in the context of coalescence.

Speaking of, what about coalescence? How could you measure such a dynamic, subjective, and individual process? Measuring coalescence is made especially tricky by its iterative aspects. Many goals we pursue will turn out to be unsuitable for us and so progress toward them is not a good approach to measuring coalescence. Rather than looking at goal pursuit, determining whether someone is coalescing well might be best served by assessing whether they are effectively introspecting on affective and social signals associated with value fulfillment. This likely requires a qualitative approach. That's fine if you are a therapist, friend, or other agent trying to give good advice, but it makes things hard for a scientist inclined toward positivism and quantitative methods.

Bedford-Peterson et al. (2019) argue that Little's (2006, 2015) Personal Projects Analysis (PPA) system might be suitable for measuring something like coalescence. PPA elicits people's personal projects and asks them to rate those projects on a range of dimensions, including their prioritization and their prospects for successful pursuit. It also includes a module assessing the extent to which different projects are compatible. However, DeYoung and Tiberius (2021) argue that even PPA would need to be transformed from a self-report instrument to something like a semistructured clinical interview in order to effectively track whether an individual is fulfilling appropriate values. Such an interview would, among other things, allow researchers to identify values that the respondent doesn't even realize they hold. It also brings in a bystander's perspective on whether values are being *successfully* fulfilled. As discussed earlier, humans have a notorious positive bias in self-assessments (unless they are chronically depressed, in which case the opposite is often true—indeed, a common application of cognitive-behavioral therapy is to address counterproductive and inaccurate negative self-assessments [Wilding 2015]). So it seems there are ways forward in measuring coalescence, but we have work to do in terms of developing relatively straightforward quantitative metrics for it.

Presenting respondents with a survey containing dozens of Likert-scale questions to measure the different components of the SWBPF might be feasible and appropriate but is also arduous. Fortunately, there is at least one more succinct but nonetheless comprehensive instrument already established for measuring well-being: the Well-Being Profile, or WB-Pro (Marsh et al. 2020). The WB-Pro tracks fifteen factors that are thought to reflect well-being defined, as befits clinical psychologists, as the inverse of depression and anxiety. These are competence, clear thinking, emotional stability, engagement, meaning, optimism, positive emotions, positive relations, resilience, self-esteem, vitality, acceptance, autonomy, empathy, and prosociality. The WB-Pro has attractive psychometric properties, and while its full form involves a forty-eight-item survey, a more parsimonious fifteen-item survey loses little in the way of statistical credibility. The WB-Pro is grounded in extensive theorizing about the nature of psychological well-being. It is therefore robust to many of the critiques leveled against SW-B in chapter 2.

The overlaps between the WB-Pro, SWBPF, and coalescence are substantial. Autonomy, competence, and positive relations are the variables of the eudaimonia dimension. Positive emotions is arguably the most important variable in the hedonia dimension, and emotional stability and resilience are close analogues to emotional wellbeing. Meaning is one part of the conscience dimension, and empathy and prosociality are defensible proxies for virtue. Engagement is prominent once coalescence has brought about the conditions for flow across many life domains. Clear thinking is the product of introspection as coalescence progresses, and self-esteem the result of successful goal pursuit. Acceptance emerges once the actual, ideal, and ought selves have been harmonized. The one variable that does not overlap is optimism. Optimism is an important factor in wellbeing for clinicians because depressed people tend to assess their situations more realistically than healthy people (Moore and Fresco 2012). However, outside of this context, optimism seems more questionable. Someone is arguably more "well" if they are accurately assessing reality and their prospects within it. Such realism is particularly important in coalescence, where understanding oneself honestly is critical to advancement.

Many social scientists might be reluctant to include even the fifteen-item WB-Pro in a survey given funding constraints and worries about attrition among participants in such a time-consuming process. These researchers would value a unidimensional measure of SWB like life satisfaction or at least a parsimonious conception like affect plus life satisfaction. Marsh et al. (2020) argue, as I have, that such measures are of limited usefulness because they don't provide information about the causal structure of SWB. Life satisfaction and affect are useful indicators, especially at scale, but too shallow to facilitate diagnoses. They must be disaggregated to target interventions, whether therapeutic, economic, or otherwise. For example, there is relatively little value in implementing mood management techniques with someone whose low SWB lies in their low levels of relatedness. Even so, it would be useful to have a simple measure of SWB for experimental contexts where researchers are trying to identify a causal relationship between some intervention and SWB broadly considered. Such a simple measure would also allow for relatively straightforward comparisons between the effect sizes of interventions. Finally, there are a host of compelling reasons for wanting a single-item measure of SWB in the context of policy, particularly with regard to cost-benefit analysis and the movement to go "beyond GDP." I review these briefly in the next section.

Desirable Qualities of Wellbeing Measures in Public Policy

An interpersonal welfare comparison involves assessing whether some individual or group has more than some other individual or group. Such comparisons are advantageous to the analysis of policy outcomes and especially to the fairness of those outcomes. For example, when government is considering whether to build a light rail network or expand existing bus services, it is helpful to know with some clarity how the benefits and costs of each option will be borne by different parts of the population. If the light rail has a higher net present value than the bus network but almost all the benefits accrue to already wealthy and well-served groups, the bus option might be preferable (Adler 2019). Unfortunately, such welfare comparisons are difficult, both conceptually and practically. Indeed, arriving at something tractable to this end was arguably the raison d'être of rational choice theory and neoclassical economics.

Economists are often criticized for the unrealistic assumptions that underpin their models, but this overlooks their purpose. A map is only helpful if it presents a simplified version of reality. A detailed map is typically less useful than a parsimonious one. So too with models of welfare and decision-making in the context of public policy. Rational choice theory conceptualizes decision-making as a matter of preference satisfaction that can be modeled using the simple mathematical device of a utility function. Among other benefits, this approach allows the psychologically crude but powerful and practical architecture of cost-benefit analysis to be constructed (Adler and Posner 2006).

The key notion underpinning cost-benefit analysis is that prices and income measure roughly equal quantities of welfare. How can this be so? Individuals try to maximize their utility subject to the constraint imposed by their budget. They rationally allocate their scarce income to those things that will bring them the most utility at least cost. They communicate these preferences into the market as consumer *demand*. Producers try to maximize their profits by producing goods that people demand at lowest cost. They communicate the costs associated with producing relatively profitable goods into the market as producer *supply*. In competitive markets, the interplay of supply and demand across millions of consumers and producers moment by moment gives rise to market prices. These capture the marginal costs and benefits of consuming and producing any one good relative to any other good. In equilibrium, one good priced at $10 therefore gives the same utility to the population at large as another good priced at $10. If one of these goods were to increase in price to $10.05, rational consumers at the margin would substitute away from it to the cheaper good to maximize their utility. Such behavior is ubiquitous, though there are of course many exceptions, such as market failures and irrational decision-making arising out of cognitive biases (Kahneman 2011).

An important corollary of this logic is that while Jane and John might have different preferences and so spend $10 on different things, that $10 is worth roughly the same amount of utility to both of them. This ability to denominate any source of utility in a single metric makes income and prices a *unidimensional* measure of welfare. Furthermore, if John were to have $15 and Jane $10, John would have 150 percent of Jane's income, not just "more" income. This is what is known as *cardinal* comparability and is opposed to ordinal comparisons, which concern rank. For example, if John has $15, Jane has $10, and Jim has $5, then John > Jane > Jim. Cardinal comparisons consider proportionality. John has 1.5 times Jane's income and three times Jim's income. Evidence suggests that income is worth more in terms of utility to a relatively poor person than to a relatively rich person, so this cardinal comparison is not as straightforward as depicted here (Blackorby and Donaldson 1988). Economists have developed various tools for weighting income to relatively poor people to account for these factors (see Adler 2019 for a review). Some degree of cardinality is critical to these distributional analyses. Consider two societies of five people each. In the first, incomes are 5, 4, 3, 2, and 1. In the second, incomes are 50, 4, 3, 2, and 1. These societies are ordinally identical, but it is straightforward to see that the second society is vastly more unequal. Cardinality is required to engage with and account for these proportional differences.

A central reason we have historically used income and prices for interpersonal welfare comparisons is that they are interpersonally cardinal and unidimensional metrics. This should not be overlooked in efforts to go beyond income and prices in assessing the welfare and wellbeing impacts of various policies (Fleurbaey and Blanchet 2013 offer a sophisticated treatment of these issues). Advocates should be especially careful not to cast income and prices, and GDP more broadly, as somehow divorced from "wellbeing." They are a reasonable and attractive measure of *preference satisfaction*, which is one definition of wellbeing. They are certainly limited in many important ways, but so are alternative metrics, as we shall see shortly. The claim that life satisfaction scale responses are a more "direct" measure of utility than income and prices is erroneous. Income and prices are a measure of preference satisfaction, whereas life satisfaction scale responses are a measure of mental states. These are two different definitions of well-being (Angner 2009). Relatedly, the claim that life satisfaction is the same as "utility" as economists use the term (Diener et al. 2009) is incorrect. Utility in classical economics, such as the work of Jevons on political economy (1871), refers to use-value or the instrumentality of a thing. In contemporary welfare economics, utility refers to preference satisfaction (Hausman 2015). One must go back to John Stuart Mill (1863) to find a mental state account of utility.

Within economics, arguably the most popular and advanced alternative (or perhaps extension) to the income and prices framework for interpersonal welfare comparisons is the capabilities paradigm discussed in chapter 5. Capabilities is a *multi*dimensional approach to conceptualizing welfare. In the Human Development Index, for example, you have income, health, and education. Comparing two individuals in terms of their welfare within this framework requires the application of weights. Consider two individuals in America, one with an income of $30,000, perfect health, and a master's degree and the other with an income of $80,000, a bad knee that necessitates a wheelchair for journeys of more than a few steps, and a bachelor's degree. Who has more welfare? We can't answer this question without assigning weights to health, education, and income that will allow us to compare the two individuals in a unidimensional way. The advantage of prices in this context is that health and education can be denominated in dollars, which can then be folded into income. For example, if knee surgery costs $100,000 and a master's degree a further $50,000, these figures can be added to income to account for health and education disparities. It is worth noting in this context that GDP is highly correlated with capabilities (Schmidt-Traub et al. 2017). It is thus of questionable value to try to incorporate many things independently into welfare comparisons rather than trying to denominate them all in dollars, at least in cases where dollar denomination is straightforward. However, while "equivalent income" approaches remain the most common approach to welfare analysis in economics, welfare economists have developed a range of innovative responses to these weighting challenges, and the architecture for capabilities-based interpersonal welfare comparisons is quite advanced (Alkire 2016).

Some advocates argue that life satisfaction scales are an interpersonally cardinal and unidimensional measure of welfare, or at least as close to one as income and prices (Fujiwara and Dolan 2016; Frijters et al. 2019). There is compelling evidence that regression results from models where life satisfaction is the dependent variable are nearly identical regardless of whether scale responses are treated as ordinal or cardinal (Ferrer-i-Carbonell and Frijters 2004). It is also undeniable that the measurement of income is far from perfect, leaving space for a bad but relatively less flawed alternative to emerge (Coyle 2015). Life satisfaction scales have the added advantage here of being cheap and quick to administer (Diener et al. 2009) compared to income and price measurement.

While advocates acknowledge that life satisfaction scales do not capture experienced SWB (Clark et al. 2018), it is reasonable to argue that policy should focus on evaluative wellbeing, which they do measure at least somewhat effectively. However, while the promise of life satisfaction scales in this regard deserves further research, their potential in cost-benefit analysis, cost-effectiveness analysis, or any other form of interpersonal welfare comparison is limited in light of scale-norming. I explain this problem in detail in the next section.

Scale-Norming

Scale-norming is where the qualitative meaning of the points on a respondent's scale change over time (Frederick and Lowenstein 1999). For example, imagine a final-year PhD student. With a secure income, autonomy, rewarding work, and (hopefully) a collegial community, they say they are 8/10 in response to a life satisfaction scale question, such as the HILDA question presented at the beginning of this chapter. They associate a scale response of 9/10 with securing a tenure track job, and 10/10 with becoming a full professor. Now imagine that they do in fact secure the tenure track position. Assuming consistency of scale use over time, we would expect their response in period 2 to change to 9/10. If they instead say 8/10, we assume that they have adapted to their new circumstances or that those circumstances weren't so great, and so they have not increased their life satisfaction as anticipated. This might seem like a simple case of rising expectations in the long term offsetting short-term increases in life satisfaction. However, teasing such explanations for scale responses apart from scale-norming is precisely the problem. It is quite possible that if you asked the respondent directly "Are you more satisfied now (in time 2) than you were then (in time 1)?" they would say that they are, despite giving the same scale response, 8/10, in both time periods (see Köke and Perino 2017 for quantitative evidence of this phenomenon). As ambiguity about the future has dissolved, they may now associate 9/10 with publishing in good journals, as this will bring them closer to being a full professor. Their ranking of lives is identical between time 1 and 2, and they also feel more satisfied in time 2 than in time 1. What has changed is the way they map their subjective assessment of their life into a response category on the scale. This is scale-norming.

Stillman et al.'s (2015) study of Tongan migrants to New Zealand provides an illustrative example of scale-norming in the context of subjective assessments of wealth, which can be compared to objective measures, unlike life satisfaction. New Zealand uses a lottery system to allocate visas to would-be migrants from Tonga. Around 10 percent of applicants are successful and migrate to New Zealand, where they typically experience meaningful increases in their real incomes. Stillman et al. survey both successful and unsuccessful applicants two to five years after the lottery. One survey question is the "welfare ladder," as follows: "Please imagine a 10-step ladder where on the bottom, the first step, stand the poorest, and on the highest step, the tenth, stand the rich. On which step are you today?" In addition, the successful applicants (migrants) were asked which step of the ladder they were on when they were last living in Tonga. Despite their higher (on average) real incomes, the migrants report being no higher on the welfare ladder than the unsuccessful applicants. However, they report being 0.75 rungs higher on average than they were when last living in Tonga.

This again seems like a straightforward case of changing reference points. While the migrants are wealthier in New Zealand, they are also surrounded by wealthier people. They consequently adjust their evaluation of their old life downward. The question for welfare analysis is whether the migrants feel subjectively better off in New Zealand. Imagine if the question were phrased differently: "Are you on a higher step now than you were previously?" The answer is surely yes. Yet this improvement is obfuscated by the fact that the reporting scale used shifts between waves of the survey. This is scale-norming. Reference point changes, adaptation, and scale-norming are hard to tease apart, as I will discuss shortly.

Consider how the migrants' reporting on the welfare ladder would play out if it were a life satisfaction ladder instead. Assume that rather than increases in real incomes, the migrants had experienced increases in latent life satisfaction. However, they had also discovered new life satisfaction possibilities in New Zealand, which causes them to reconceptualize their scale. The outcome is then equivalent: *latent* life satisfaction increases by 0.75 steps, but the scale response doesn't change; the scale itself changes instead. If you asked the migrant "Are you more satisfied with life now than you were in Tonga?" the answer would again be yes.

This matters for welfare analysis. When thinking about social progress, good therapeutic outcomes, or intergroup welfare, reports of being "more satisfied than before" are arguably more important than seeing a numerical increase in a scale response. They are certainly more important if the numerical responses are only loosely anchored to changes in underlying subjective states. It is important to note in this context that life satisfaction scale questions and life satisfaction "relative to the past" questions often produce different answers. For example, the first four waves of the German Socio-Economic Panel (GSOEP) included a scale question for present satisfaction and a second question for satisfaction in the previous year. The correlation between the retrospective question and the actual response in the previous year is only 0.5. Similarly, waves 16 and 17 of the British Household Panel Survey (BHPS) include both a life satisfaction scale question and the following: "Would you say you are more satisfied with life, less satisfied with life, or feel about the same as you did a year ago?" This is a straightforward question about whether life is better now than before. The correlation between this question and life satisfaction scale responses is only 0.22.

Now, these divergences might not reflect scale-norming. They might reflect errors of memory, implicit narratives of change, effort justification, and a range of other issues (Bond and Lang 2019). Researchers frequently worry that answers to relative questions are biased by these issues (Odermatt and Stutzer 2019). Yet it is not clear that "bias" is an appropriate term here. Discrepancies between life satisfaction scale and "more satisfied than before" type questions might instead arise from different cognitive processes associated with answering these questions. The implications for welfare analysis are substantial. The next section develops a relatively formal model of the reporting function, which is the source of scale-norming. It then uses this model to distinguish scale-norming conceptually from related phenomena like adaptation and changing reference points. This allows for a more informed discussion of potential "biases" in life satisfaction reporting and the implications for welfare analysis.

The Reporting Function

The "reporting function" is a cognitive process that translates latent life satisfaction into a response on a scale question (Oswald 2008). It is depicted graphically in figure 10.1. To get a handle on it, consider the well-replicated result that extroverts report higher life satisfaction than introverts (Diener

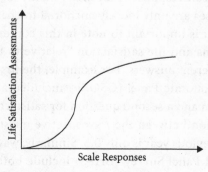

Figure 10.1 The life satisfaction reporting function

and Lucas 1999). Is this because extroverts have higher *latent* satisfaction than introverts? It's possible. Extroverts might have more friends on average than introverts, for example, and this extra relatedness might enhance their life quality. But it might equally be the case that extroverts *report* their satisfaction differently. That is, they execute the reporting function in a different manner.

Pavot and Diener (1993) gave one of the first informal descriptions of the reporting function. They describe the process of making a life satisfaction evaluation as involving the individual constructing a "standard" that they perceive as appropriate for themselves, and then comparing the circumstances of their life to that standard. Fleurbaey and Blanchet (2013) developed a more formal and sophisticated model of "subjective well-being as it can be retrieved with typical questionnaires." They begin with a vector, l_i, that covers "the diversity of states, activities and possibilities enjoyed or endured by an individual [i] over the course of their life" (p. 175). When someone answers a life satisfaction questionnaire, they consider l_i and there is some function, ξ_i, that maps this vector, including the individual's actual life, l_i^*, into possible responses to the scale question, r_i. As Fleurbaey and Blanchet explain:

> $\xi_i(l_i)$ must lie in a given scale, which can be a verbal scale (e.g. very satisfied/fairly satisfied/not very satisfied/not at all satisfied), or a numerical scale (e.g. from 0 to 10). The cognitive problem for the individual is to put the many dimensions of l_i into one of a few ordered categories.

The reporting function maps the entire vector l_i into the entire scale, r_i. So we can let $r_{it} \in \{1, 2, \ldots, k, \ldots, K\}$ denote the choice of response category to a single life satisfaction scale survey item with K response options. However, the individual's own life, l_i^*, maps into a single response category, r_i^*. The individual's response to a life satisfaction question is thus given by $r_i^* = \xi_i(l_i)$. The challenge for the respondent is to communicate the complexity of their life satisfaction assessments, l_i, within the constraints of the scale instrument. The challenge for researchers is to infer l_i^* relative to l_i from r_i^* despite the messiness introduced by the reporting function. Fleurbaey and Blanchet identify three separate but related problems that are likely to plague such exercises: the scope, ranking, and calibration problems.

The scope problem concerns what aspects of l_i are relevant for the individual to consider. For example, what time frame is appropriate—today, this week, the time since the last survey? Should the state of the household be considered or just the individual? What about the state of the world in general? The scope problem would give rise to scale-norming if respondents used inconsistent scopes across survey waves. On New Year's Eve, they may think in terms of the past year. In contrast, if surveyed right after missing the bus, they may fixate on the present moment. Similarly, if surveyed around election time, they might focus on how society is doing. If surveyed around Christmas or some other holiday celebration, they might instead consider their family's situation. The points on these different scales will have widely divergent meanings, which makes comparing responses on them questionable.

The ranking problem refers to the cognitive difficulty of arranging relevant possible lives (e.g., 1_a, 1_b, etc.), including the individual's actual life, l_i^*, into an ordinal pattern (e.g., 1_1–1_9). Another way of thinking about it is that if the scope problem involves deciding what items are relevant considerations for

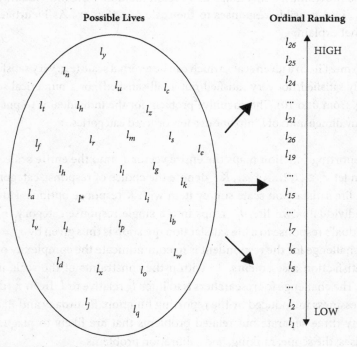

Figure 10.2 The ranking problem

Note: Respondents must arrange possible lives they could live, of which there are theoretically an infinite number, into an ordered ranking from least to most satisfying.

life satisfaction, the ranking problem is about the relative weights to attach to each of those considerations. The ranking problem is depicted graphically in figure 10.2. Note that there are likely to be very many relevant possible lives to consider, but only ten or so response categories. The complexity of this exercise may induce respondents to focus on salient aspects of their immediate situation and forget other relevant dimensions of their life. The "focusing illusion" is a famous example of this (Schkade and Kahneman 1998). Respondents may focus on, say, the poor weather in their area and fail to take into consideration relatively low local living costs. SW-B scholars hope that avoiding explicit primes through smart survey design will mitigate this issue (Stone and Mackie 2013, Bertrand and Mullainathan 2001). However, while avoiding explicit primes might prevent researchers from biasing responses through survey design, it is unlikely to prevent respondents from framing their life in terms of whatever is bothering them at the time of the survey. These preoccupations may differ between surveys in ways that give rise to scale-norming. For example, if the survey is taken during a difficult month at work, those difficult circumstances could crowd out the good salary, colleagues, and commute that dominate work assessments during the other eleven months of the year. During the good work months, the qualitative meaning of the points on the respondent's scale might be determined by household issues instead.

The calibration problem is about how the individual maps their ranking of many possible lives, including the position of their actual life, l_i^*, to response categories, r, on the scale provided. It is depicted graphically in figure 10.3. There is a strong framing effect present that arises out of the fact that the scale offered is closed. This contrasts with real life, where many considerations relevant to life satisfaction are open, like income, or have fuzzy limits, like pain or longevity. The closed scale forces respondents "to move from reasoning in terms of life content to a reasoning in terms of a statistical distribution" (Fleurbaey and Blanchet 2013, p. 181). The calibration problem is which distribution to choose. For example, should the respondent choose from among the lives available to all humans, including Jeff Bezos, or rather from among those that seem realistically possible for themselves? Different calibrations across respondents and over time could create arguably incomparable responses.

An empirical example of the calibration problem comes from Ubel et al. (2005). They tested how respondents assess their health relative to "perfect health" when explicitly asked about perfect health for "a 20-year-old" or

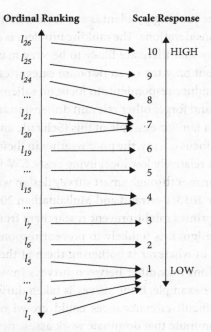

Figure 10.3 The calibration problem

Note: The calibration problem involves mapping the many possible lives individuals might consider when evaluating their own life into the limited number of response categories on the scale instrument.

"someone your own age." They found that unprimed respondents interpret perfect health somewhere between perfect health for a twenty-year-old and someone their own age. As people age, this scale meaningfully changes such that an eighty-year-old has a different scale in mind than a forty-year-old.

The calibration problem is one explanation for why introverts and extroverts differ in their life satisfaction, on average. Consider two individuals, A and B. Assume that they have identical latent life satisfaction, but A is introverted while B is extroverted. A might map their latent life satisfaction less generously into lower responses to a scale question than B. This is depicted graphically in figure 10.4. This is the same idea as two high school teachers who both make the same assessment of the quality of a student's work, but one then marks it more *generously* than the other. It's perfectly possible that two individuals giving exactly the same *ranking* of essays in a class might nonetheless differ in the *grades* given to those essays (Kaiser 2021). To understand why this is pernicious to interpersonal welfare comparisons,

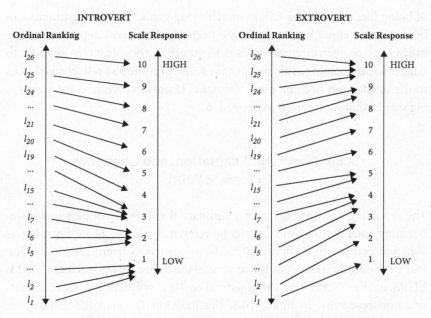

Figure 10.4 Differences in calibration styles, e.g., between introverts and extroverts

Note: Individuals who differ in their calibration style (for example, stringent or generous) may map identical subjective life satisfaction assessments into different response categories.

consider the following. Assuming introverts and extroverts simply map their satisfaction into responses differently, would the world have more wellbeing if all introverts were somehow converted to extroverts? Should more policy effort be directed at introverts given their lower scale responses? I think the answer to both questions is no. In the reporting function model outlined here, both A and B have the same *subjective* well-being. They make the same assessment of their wellbeing; they just report it differently.

To summarize, the problem with life satisfaction scales is that we want to know about l_i^* relative to l_i, but we can only ever observe $r_i^* = \xi(l_i)$. Furthermore, both l_i^* and $\xi_i(l_i)$ could change over time such that responses to life satisfaction scale questions become neither intertemporally nor interpersonally comparable, even ordinally. This may go some way to explaining why scale responses have low test-retest coefficients of 0.5–0.7 over even short periods of one day to two weeks (Krueger and Schkade 2008). The coalescence of being suggests that l_i^* and $\xi_i(l_i)$ should be expected to change over time. People adjust their values and perceptions of their life following disclosures of being like success and failure in achieving goals. These adjustments can be significant enough to trigger scale-norming. Furthermore, the more significant a change in circumstances is, the more reasonable it is to expect it to trigger scale-norming. This means that scales become less reliable as shocks to life satisfaction become more dramatic. Unfortunately, it is precisely the big shocks that we are most interested in.

Scale-Norming, Adaptation, and Changing Reference Points

The reporting function helps to illuminate the differences between scale-norming, adaptation, and changing reference points. Scale-norming is depicted graphically in figure 10.5. The *y*-axis tracks latent life satisfaction from 0 to infinity. The *x*-axis tracks annual waves of a survey, such as HILDA, BHPS, or the GSOEP (the three general social surveys most used in life satisfaction research). In figure 10.5, the individual's latent life satisfaction does not change across the five waves of the survey, staying consistently at 7. However, the scale they use does. In time 1, for example, they report 4/10, whereas in time 2 they report 6/10. Perhaps they calibrate their scale differently in these two survey instances. In wave 1 they may have calibrated their

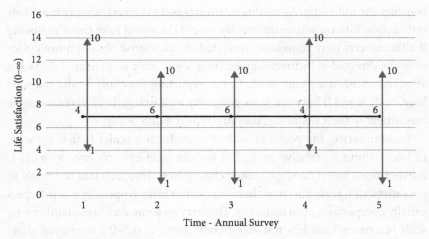

Figure 10.5 Scale-norming

Note: Scale-norming is where the qualitative meaning of the response categories on a respondent's scale (represented by the 1–10 vertical lines) changes over time. As a result, responses (the bold numbers) vary over time even as latent life satisfaction (the trend line) remains constant.

scale according to what is possible for humanity. This being a grand distribution, they naturally score relatively low on it. In wave 2 they may have calibrated their scale according to what is realistically possible for themselves. Here they do relatively better, hence their 6/10 response. The result of this scale-norming is apparent volatility in the respondent's life satisfaction, but this interpretation is entirely the product of incorrectly assuming identical scales across waves.

One possible source of scale-norming is ceiling effects. This is where someone already at the top of their scale experiences a further improvement in their life satisfaction. Not wanting to say that they are "completely satisfied," they instead scale-norm. Ceiling effects are depicted graphically in figure 10.6. The individual is 7/10 in the first wave of the survey. In wave 2, they experience an increase in their satisfaction, and translate this to their scale by increasing their response to 8/10. In wave 3, their satisfaction increases further to where they would say 10/10 on their scale from wave 1. But they can still see further possible improvements in their life satisfaction. They therefore do not want to suggest that they are completely satisfied. Instead of altering their response to 10/10, they alter their scale such that an 8/10 now corresponds to a 10/10 on their previous scale. A researcher observing only their responses would erroneously conclude that their life satisfaction has not increased, perhaps due to adaptation. Ceiling effects

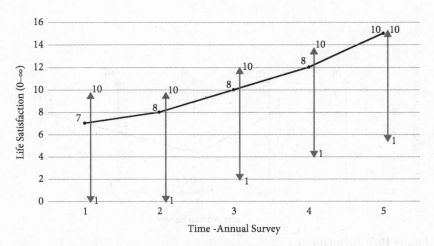

Figure 10.6 Scale-norming as a result of ceiling effects

Note: Ceiling effects are when a lack of space to communicate further changes at the extreme ends of a scale (here the upper end) triggers scale-norming.

would undermine the feasibility of using life satisfaction scales to measure social progress, as the better society was doing the more likely ceiling effects would be to kick in.

Ceiling effects are consistent with evidence from Rasch analysis of life satisfaction scales that suggest the scales are insensitive at high scores. Rasch analysis was deliberately designed to test the precision of scales whose psychometric validity had already been established. It is thus relevant to the claims of this chapter regarding life satisfaction scales. Rasch analysis produces a number of useful statistics concerning the internal workings of scales, but one that is particularly relevant here is "use validity." This estimates whether respondents have equal facility to use all the response categories available. Two RASCH analyses of the satisfaction with life scale (SWLS; Diener et al. 1985), using data from Norway/Greenland and Italy/South Africa, respectively, both find that its sensitivity deteriorates toward the upper end of the scale (Vitterso et al. 2005; Schutte et al. 2019). This is despite most respondents reporting life satisfaction in these high regions. This implies that statistical analyses of life satisfaction data are more likely to be biased the more satisfied the sample is.

Adaptation is depicted in figure 10.7. The individual suffers a negative shock to their life satisfaction in wave 3; perhaps they are inflicted with a facial scar. This drops their latent life satisfaction to 3 and their scale response to 3/10. Over the next two waves of the survey, they acclimatize to this shock

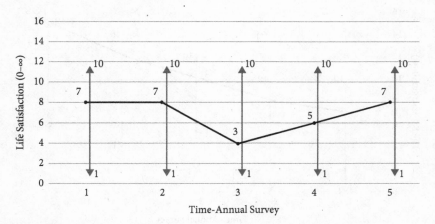

Figure 10.7 Adaptation

Note: Adaptation involves real changes in latent life satisfaction rather than reporting style. Even as the scale (the horizontal bars) remains fixed over time, life satisfaction varies due to acclimatizing to the shock in wave 2.

and their life satisfaction rises commensurately. Perhaps they become accustomed to their new visage and are no longer embarrassed by people's reaction to their face. In any case, by wave 5 they are back at their original satisfaction of 7 and scale response of 7/10. Importantly, no change in objective circumstances is responsible for the adaptation. The scar remains. There is also no scale-norming. The individual does not calibrate their scale differently pre- and post-injury, for example. Adaptation is a biological phenomenon where people get used to something such that it no longer affects them as it once did. It is about a change in feelings, not a change in reporting style.

Life satisfaction reporting is further complicated by changing reference points. This is where scale-norming causes a change in latent life satisfaction. Reference point shifts are the fundamental mechanism of many positive psychology interventions. Consider gratitude (Emmons and McCullough 2004). This technique involves reflecting on the positive things in your life to make them more cognitively salient. For example, during pandemic-induced lockdowns we might focus on how grateful we are not to be ill rather than our inability to go to the gym. This deliberate, conscious effort to adjust the standard by which we assess our life causes a real improvement in feelings. This reference point shift is depicted graphically in figure 10.8. The individual initially suffers a decline in latent life satisfaction with the onset of lockdown between waves 1 and 2. There is no scale change. They then

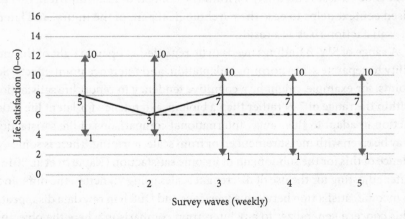

Figure 10.8 Changing reference points

Note: Reference points shifts are when scale-norming causes a change in feelings. This occurs between waves 2 and 3. The downward shift in the scale causes an improvement in latent life satisfaction. The dashed line indicates where latent life satisfaction would be had only scale-norming occurred rather than a reference point shift.

practice gratitude. This results in scale-norming in wave 3: the scale shifts downward, indicating a more generous reporting style. This scale-norming causes a real change in feelings, with latent life satisfaction rising. The dashed line indicates where life satisfaction would have been had there been scale-norming without an attendant change in feelings. The causal channel from scale-norming to changes in latent satisfaction is essential to the definition of reference points shifts. An individual could scale-norm while experiencing an unrelated change in life satisfaction. They could change their scope from themselves to their family while being happier about their progress in a hobby, for example. This would not be a reference point shift.

A concern for research using life satisfaction scales is that it is challenging to distinguish scale-norming, adaptation, and changing reference points without information beyond scale responses. Consider the long-running study of the SWB of people with spinal injuries. While adaptation to spinal injury and other injuries is far from complete (Lucas 2007), it does seem to occur to a substantial extent (Diener et al. 2006). Scale-norming might also be occurring (van Leeuwen 2012; Schwartz et al. 2018). People may report 7/10 before their injury and again three years after, but these 7s might correspond to different levels of underlying life satisfaction. Kahneman (1999) argues that the life satisfaction of people with spinal injuries could also be explained by changing reference points, as discussed in chapter 6. Scale-norming occurs, with the injured moving over time to assess their lives within the context of their injuries. This revised context helps to ease the psychological pain of the injury, and latent life satisfaction rises as a result.

A range of SW-B findings needs to be regarded as open in light of the inability to separate scale-norming, adaptation, and reference point effects. Set points, for example, might be a cognitive tendency to report life satisfaction within the range of 7–9 rather than a biological tendency for latent life satisfaction to adapt to this range. International comparisons of life satisfaction may be riven with measurement error from scale-norming. There is some evidence of this for the subdomain of income satisfaction (Kapteyn et al. 2013). After adjusting for the use of discrepant scales using vignettes, the difference in income satisfaction between Americans and Dutch in raw data disappears. This concern generalizes to any intergroup comparison where the objective context of the two groups is meaningfully different, such as rural-urban or between cultures. Kaiser (2021) reviews other evidence for scale-norming from similar vignette studies.

There are circumstances that arguably mitigate concerns about scale-norming when interpreting life satisfaction scale data. Plant (2020) provides an extended analysis of the reasons to be optimistic about the cardinality of life satisfaction scales against concerns of scale inconsistency across respondents and over time. Among other reasons to be optimistic, the very large sample sizes that are often used in SW-B research hopefully wash out much of the noise emerging from scale-norming to reveal broad patterns. If life satisfaction data shows a long-running and sizeable trend in a consistent direction, this can be taken as suggestive evidence. In clinical and similar contexts, if an intervention almost exclusively produces effects in a single direction, then this is at least suggestive evidence of sign if not magnitude. Finally, if life satisfaction results align with evidence from other measures of SWB, then the life satisfaction data bolsters an overall story. Scale-norming does not invalidate life satisfaction scales, but it does warrant caution when it comes to effect sizes.

Unfortunately, the accurate measurement of effect sizes is important in welfare analysis for policy. Welfare analysis requires a comparison between the latent life satisfaction, l_i^*, of individuals and the monotonic aggregation of such latent life satisfactions into group welfare, such as in social welfare functions. Scale-norming can easily muddle this process, producing unintended consequences. For example, frustrated achievers might seem to have lower satisfaction than happy peasants when in fact the rising latent life satisfaction of frustrated achievers is obfuscated by scale-norming.

Evidence for Scale-Norming from Response Shift Studies

While it did not typically use life satisfaction scales, a relatively large body of research exists in the quality-of-life studies literature on "response shift" that attests to the existence of scale-norming (Daltroy et al. 1999; Lacey et al. 2008, Schwartz et al. 2006). This literature does not seem to be widely known, at least among the younger generation of SWB scholars, and SW-B papers rarely consider whether their results are biased by scale-norming. This is perhaps because quality-of-life studies are used mostly in the medical space and do not often use life satisfaction scales. Or it may be because the results of these studies are inconclusive (though no less open to interpretation that life satisfaction scale research). In any case, with the push to incorporate SWB into public policy, now seems an appropriate time to popularize this research and port it over to life satisfaction scales. To this end, I briefly review the main findings of response shift studies.

The response shift literature is concerned with understanding whether people affected by medical conditions and treatment experience changes in quality of life. As in life satisfaction studies, a challenge to this research is people using different standards to evaluate their life before and after afflictions and treatment. McClimans et al. 2013 present an instructive example (p. 1862). A man in the early stages of chemotherapy was asked, "Were you limited in pursuing your hobbies or other leisure time activities?" He answered: "My hobby is working in the garden, that's very difficult, quite a bit." Four weeks later, he is asked the same question and replies: "I'm reading at the moment; gardening is not possible anymore, a little." It is unclear to what extent the chemotherapy has affected this individual's life. On a revealed preferences account, the man would clearly prefer to garden than read, otherwise he would have read when both options were available. However, it's possible that, having been forced to read by chemotherapy, the men discovered that he quite enjoyed reading and the activity compensated for lost quality of life from gardening. The response shift literature is interested in teasing apart changes in the man's quality of life from measurement issues. A 2010 paper by Ubel et al. links this literature directly to scale-norming. The paper argues (p. 465) that the response shift literature "lumps together sources of measurement error (e.g. scale recalibration) with true causes of changing quality of life (e.g. hedonic adaptation)."

Schwartz et al. (2006) conducted a meta-analysis of nineteen response shift studies. They found evidence for response shift (scale-norming) across the studies and significant heterogeneity in the sign of the effect. Encouragingly, the size of the effect was generally small. They write that (p. 1540):

> One may tend to conclude that response shifts are a common and significant phenomenon in QOL measurement, implying that people adapt their internal standards of QOL in response to changing health state. We found that overall the effect size of response shift phenomena published to date are relatively small according to Cohen's (1992) criteria. Even a small response shift may, however, result in an underestimation of the true QOL change, i.e. concluding that it is small when it is moderate, or moderate when it is large.

One concern with the response shift literature is that it mostly relies on the "then-test" methodology to determine the extent of scale-norming (Schwartz and Sprangers 2010). The then-test is any kind of retrospective pre-test/post-test design, such as Stillman et al.'s (2015) question to the Tongan migrants of "How did you feel when you last lived in Tonga?" Effective implementation of the then-test requires an experimental design with treatment and control groups. A significant discrepancy between the pre-test and then-test scores of the experimental and control groups suggests scale-norming. This is especially the case if objective indicators of quality of life would suggest a discrepancy, as with the rising incomes of the Tongan migrants to New Zealand. However, even in such case, there are three concerns with the then-test. Schwartz and Sprangers (2010, p. 457) explain:

> The first disadvantage of the thentest is that the basic premise of a shared internal standard by thentest and posttest has not been unequivocally supported (compare Sprangers et al. 1999 to Nolte et al. 2009). Second, the thentest is susceptible to recall bias, given its retrospective nature (Schwartz et al. 2004, Ahmed et al. 2005, Rapkin and Schwartz 2004). Third, there is the potential contamination due to other alternative explanations, such as social desirability responding, and effort justification (Howard and Dailey 1979). Further, the thentest is prone to implicit theories of change, where patients use a general heuristic for thinking about times past and infer what their initial state must have been (Norman 2003).

Schwartz and Sprangers (2010) offer recommendations for best practice in research design when applying the then-test. These are outside the scope of discussion here, but important for analyzing scale-norming in life satisfaction studies going forward.

One thing worth mentioning is that effort justification and theories of change are conceptually hard to distinguish from real changes in latent life satisfaction. An example of effort justification is people saying that their life is better after changing jobs even though it isn't, simply to validate their decision. An instructive example of theories of change comes from Ross (1989). He assessed people's study skills using objective measures and self-reports. He put students through a course designed to improve their study skills. Objectively, the course had no effect on skills. Student self-reports seemed to parallel this, with students who were objectively 6/10 also assessing themselves as 6/10. However, at the end of the course, Ross has students recall their study skills from the start of the course. Students who reported themselves as 6/10 at the end of the course would remember themselves as 4/10 from the start of the course. They downgraded their earlier assessment because of an implicit theory that the course would improve their study skills.

Ross' experiment makes clear how theories of change can be a concern in SWB assessment, but the presence of a theory of change does not necessarily invalidate a retrospective SWB report. Theories of change are fundamental to the coalescence of being, as is, arguably, effort justification. Consider the example from chapter 9 of someone who aspires to be an astronaut. Assume that they successfully pursue this goal over several years, with incremental steps toward it being accompanied by positive emotional feedback. The person ultimately succeeds in becoming an astronaut and says that they are very satisfied with life as a result. How could they, let alone an observer, know whether their professed satisfaction is not simply effort justification? Furthermore, their personal journey has been underwritten by a theory of change as they have steadily approached being an astronaut. As such, any life satisfaction question put to them during their coalescence was likely informed by "astronaut" as a standard of evaluation. How could SWB reports be separated from such theories of change? They may well be an inherent feature of the reporting function. We therefore need to conceptually differentiate between *erroneous* theories of change, depicted in Ross' (1989) study, and germane theories of change that provide a framework for SWB evaluations. Not an easy challenge!

SWB researchers need to commit more resources to the study of scale-norming. It is potentially a highly pernicious problem, especially for policy applications of life satisfaction, and our empirical understanding of it is limited. The small effects identified in the response shift literature might incline us toward optimism, but they may be a function of the medical context of quality-of-life studies. In the broader social science domain, some circumstances might trigger more dramatic scale-norming. Stillman et al.'s migrants, for example, may have shifted their scales by around 10 percent. Furthermore, in the context of social progress and coalescence, it's possible that scale-norming occurs regularly. This would compound measurement error over time. It would be helpful to study not only the size of scale-norming following various shocks, but also the reporting function itself. How do individuals differ in the way they execute the scope, ranking, and calibration problems across separate waves of a survey? For studying scale-norming, Schwartz and Sprangers (2010) provide an admirable analysis of methods for applying the then-test methodology robustly. For studying the reporting function, new methods will need to be developed. In this context, it is critical that SW-B scholars, who battled immense headwinds for decades to get life satisfaction scales established as credible instruments, not become headwinds themselves, defending the status quo of scale use against upstart new instruments. Deepening the credibility of SWB measurement will require open-mindedness and patience.

Conclusion

SWB can be measured, though perhaps without the precision necessary for certain applications. As demonstrated by the chapters of this book, each individual item in the SWBPF can be tapped using a variety of metrics, though virtue needs more work. The Well-Being Profile (Marsh et al 2020) is a promising tool for measuring both the SWBPF and coalescence together. The WB-Pro is comprehensive and yet reasonably parsimonious in its fifteen-item form. These metrics are not ideal for some experimental and policy settings where a unidimensional and interpersonally cardinal measure of SWB would be ideal. Life satisfaction scales present an attractive possibility in these contexts, but we must be wary of scale-norming and the challenges associated with understanding the underlying causes of SWB when we only measure life satisfaction.

Scale-norming is where individuals use qualitatively different scales to respond to questions across separate waves of a survey. It can potentially make responses neither interpersonally nor intertemporally comparable. Scale-norming is a by-product of the reporting function—the cognitive process that maps latent life satisfaction into a report on a life satisfaction scale question. This reporting function involves solving (at least) three separate cognitive problems concerning scope, ranking, and calibration. If different individuals solve these problems in incommensurable ways, then their life satisfaction reports become harder to compare accurately. The same outcome results if one individual solves these problems in different ways across separate waves of a survey.

More research needs to be conducted to tease scale-norming apart from adaptation and reference point effects. Where scale-norming is a measurement issue associated with scale metrics, adaptation is in contrast a biological phenomenon where individuals acclimatize to circumstances. Reference point shifts is where deliberately solving the ranking and calibration problems differently causes latent life satisfaction to change. All three effects—scale-norming, adaptation, and reference point shifts—can appear identical in life satisfaction data. It would be helpful to include some auxiliary questions in surveys where possible to assist with separating these phenomena. High quality then-tests like those discussed by Schwarz and Sprangers (2010) are a good place to start.

Issues around the measurement of SWB are one reason we should be cautious about giving SWB a more prominent role in public policy. I discuss others in chapter 11, which returns to the issue of whether SWB is the prudential good. I argue that even if SWB is the prudential good for individuals, it should not be the goal of government. There is a range of normative concerns associated with putting SWB front and center in policymaking that emerge from the nature of government and political legitimacy rather than the nature of the prudential good. Policy can nonetheless take SWB into consideration and promote it cautiously and indirectly, but we should retain a focus on objective circumstances rather than subjective states.

11

The Politics of Subjective Wellbeing

It is this Good which we are commanded to love with our whole heart, with our whole mind, and with all our strength. It is toward this Good that we should be led by those who love us, and toward this Good we should lead those whom we love. In this way, we fulfil the commandments on which depend the whole Law and the Prophets: "Thou shalt love the Lord Thy God with thy whole heart, and thy whole soul, and with thy whole mind"; and "Thou shalt love thy neighbour as thyself." For, in order that a man might learn how to love himself, a standard was set to regulate all his actions on which his happiness depends. For, to love one's own self is nothing but to wish to be happy, and the standard is union with God. When, therefore, a person who knows how to love himself is bidden to love his neighbour as himself, is he not, in effect, commanded to persuade others, as far as he can, to love God?

—Saint Augustine of Hippo, *City of God*

The purpose of this chapter is twofold. First, to explore some of the philosophical arguments made against accounts of wellbeing similar to the one I have put forward. I will offer rebuttals to many of these arguments, but only where individuals are concerned. There are many arguments against SWB as the prudential good that are compelling when the situation in question involves doing SWB *to* somebody, as in public policy. This exploration will likely be regarded as too brief and ultimately unconvincing by philosophers, but I am not trying to defend an account of the prudential good. Rather, I am trying to sensitize SWB scholars to prudential matters that arise in applications of SWB involving policy and the government. This brings me to the second purpose of the chapter, which is to argue that while there are compelling reasons to believe that SWB is good for people, government

A Theory of Subjective Wellbeing. Mark Fabian, Oxford University Press. © Oxford University Press 2022.
DOI: 10.1093/oso/9780197635261.003.0012

nonetheless should not, generally speaking, promote SWB, at least not directly. This two-part claim will likely surprise many readers. If SWB is the prudential good, why shouldn't government promote it? This begs the question. Why should government promote the prudential good? The idea that it is government's purpose to efficiently and equitably distribute well-being is an assumption at the heart of the social planner tradition that is ascendant in welfare economics and much analytical philosophy. Other frameworks for thinking about the proper role of government, notably the social contract and deliberative democracy traditions, repudiate this assumption.

I will argue that it is to some extent a practical necessity that government have some way of thinking about the efficient and equitable allocation of wellbeing. Cost-benefit analyses and social welfare functions of the sort developed by welfare economists, at least as an input into policy deliberation, are valuable tools. These tools require a definition of the prudential good to function. SWB, while it is prudentially good, is risky as a foundation for these tools. SWB-based cost-benefit analysis could lead to perverse distributional consequences, reorient the behavior of states toward neuro-governance, and open the door to technocracy and other ills that make social contract theorists recoil. The proper foundation of cost-benefit analysis remains income and prices or, in contexts where it is manageable, capabilities.

Some readers may be concerned that this will maintain a focus on materialism in government policy. The solution to this is not to replace income and prices in cost-benefit analysis with SWB, but to restrict the domain in which cost-benefit analysis is decisive to material ones like infrastructure provision. Other domains should rely more heavily on citizen input and other means of determining the relative value of different policy options. A useful heuristic for the broader "goal of government" is that government should promote welfare, not well-being: they should expand the options available to their citizens and work to ensure that the social, economic, environmental, and institutional conditions for wellbeing are met. This leaves ample scope to promote sustainability, fairness, mental health, "what matters to people," and other goals of SWB policy advocates.

Is SWB the Prudential Good?

As discussed in chapters 3 and 4, the model of SWB that I have put forward integrates many existing accounts of wellbeing. It has the most in common with nature fulfillment accounts, where wellbeing comes from fully actual-izing one's self; with eudaimonic accounts in psychology, where wellbeing is about living in a way that aligns with our organismic needs and motiva-tional systems; and with Tiberius' value fulfillment theory of wellbeing, which is a psychologically realistic preference satisfaction account of well-being. The model thus has several rich traditions of philosophical thought to draw on in support of the view that it describes something of prudential value. More broadly, the model explains (see chapter 9) how to reach a point where one subjectively assesses one's life as pleasant, fulfilling, and valuable. These broad themes and the more specific variables in the SWBPF are widely associated with wellbeing in both folk and academic theories of wellbeing (Carlquist et al. 2017; Pflug 2009; Phillips et al. 2017). Coalescence, mean-while, mitigates feelings of depression, anxiety and other maladies associ-ated with ill-being in folk and academic theories. So it seems that many if not all accounts of wellbeing are satisfied in some way by coalescence and the SWBPF. What is controversial is the claim that SWB and thus the pru-dential good is "ultimately" or "intrinsically" a (mental)[1] state, specifically generalized flow. As I've already argued extensively, I don't think that the dis-tinction between things that are intrinsic to wellbeing and things that are instrumental to it is significant if all are *necessary*. Nonetheless, it is illumi-nating to explore some of the arguments typically leveled against (mental) state accounts of wellbeing in the philosophical literature.

There are at least five such arguments. First, many commentators are put off by the idea that someone engaged in seemingly immoral acts, like slavery or racism, could be "well" on a mental state account. Second is the experi-ence machine. Nozick (1974) argued that people would not plug into a mere *simulation* of a good life and thus truth or reality seems to be an important component of the prudential good. A common variant of this argument is that someone who is happy based on an erroneous understanding of their circumstances is not well. For example, if a happily married man discovered that his partner had been cheating on him for years he might be distraught.[2] His SWB is thus based on an erroneous understanding of the facts. Third, we cannot measure subjective mental states. Fourth, people can mentally adapt to their circumstances. Someone might thus be in a pleasant mental

---

[1] As discussed in chapter 9, I am reluctant to describe SWB as a *mental* state because the flow state is embodied.

[2] I think this hypothetical speaks to a toxic sort of monogamy, but it is a common intuition pump in the literature, so I will persevere with it.

state even when they are objectively unwell. Finally, mental state accounts permit paternalism. Under such an account, benevolent governments, friends, families, and so on would be justified, indeed obliged, to ignore citizens' preferences if those preferences were not conducive to citizens' SWB. I take each of these critiques in turn.

Immoral but Well?

There is something unsettling about the idea that an evil individual could be well. There are three rejoinders to make here. First, many people we describe as "evil" are in fact unwell in a psychopathological sense. Serial killers, for example, typically have aberrant psychology, notably sociopathy (Oakley 2008). More mundane murderers often have schizophrenia or extremely low intelligence. In 2000, the Death Penalty Information Center estimated that between 12 and 20 percent of death row inmates in the United States were intellectually disabled (Entzeroth 2001). History's great mass murderers, notably the totalitarian dictators of the twenty-first century such as Mao and Stalin, may have been psychologically altered by their power. There is laboratory evidence that power reduces empathy and encourages the objectification of subordinates (Guinote and Vescio 2010; Guinote 2017). All this is to say that "evil" people are not "normal people." I concede that my definition of what is good for people only applies to people with normal psychology. A theory that functions for the average and a few standard deviations either side of it is fit for purpose. Sociopathic outliers do not constitute a counterargument.

The second rejoinder is the standard one against tying moral behavior into definitions of wellbeing, namely that nobody can convincingly prove what objectively good behavior is, so this is a vague criterion. It is convenient to declare that an individual is unwell because they engage in acts that I consider morally reprehensible, but this may well just be me applying my prejudices. Many Christians believe that homosexuals are mentally unwell. Conversely, some homosexuals point out that praying to an invisible entity is insane. Making the definition of wellbeing dependent on moral standards that are constantly in flux and open to debate seems at least impractical. Aristotelian accounts of wellbeing that emphasize the need for someone to be virtuous, with virtue determined objectively or rationally rather than subjectively, seem to have conceded that their account depends on ultimately arbitrary value judgments (Hursthouse 1999; Kraut 2009).

Third, immorality is present in SWB in the form of virtue. As discussed in chapter 8, individuals who believe themselves to be bad people will be distressed by that belief. People who do things that are uncontroversially considered evil, like selling children into slavery and suchlike, would be hard pressed to regard themselves as good people unless they are psychologically aberrant. Coalescence requires acting with fealty toward ethical values and the ought self. Some people will act with integrity toward values that might strike us as reprehensible—religious fundamentalist terrorist cells, for example. In some of these cases, the immorality is related to irrationality, which will give rise to compartmentalization, impede coalescence, and undermine SWB. A psychologically normal politician who hypocritically attacks homosexuality while secretly being homosexual himself, for example, will buckle under the weight of their dissonance. However, it is reasonable to expect that people possessing *internally* consistent ethical frameworks, surrounded by like-minded peers who provide relatedness, living in isolation from forces that might introduce external logic arguments, could be well indefinitely. Ancient practitioners of child sacrifice are an example. Our psychology requires values, goals, and meaning, but this psychological architecture can map onto a range of different value systems.

The Experience Machine

The first rejoinder to the experience machine critique is to note that it works best against sensory hedonist accounts of well-being. That is, accounts that define well-being as pleasure or some such. Most of us would not sign up to be kept in a permanent morphine high. The state described by the SWBPF is more sophisticated than sensory pleasure and impossible to simulate outside the "anything is possible" world of philosophical hypotheticals. Nonetheless, one could imagine such a highly sophisticated device, and people do seem to have some reservations about plugging into it, as discussed in chapter 3. This brings us to a second rejoinder, namely that if we were in the experience machine or some other simulation, we wouldn't know any better. It is only when reality is revealed to diverge from our beliefs that we become distressed. This means that it is not reality or truth that is critical to well-being, as Nozick argued, but an alignment between belief and experience. This notion is embedded in the disclosure of being and a fundamental part of coalescence. If your experience reveals that your actual self is not your ideal self, you will be unwell. This is what occurs in the case of the cuckold. The happy cuckold is not unwell because they live an uninformed life. Rather, they *become* unwell when they discover that they are not in a secure monogamous marriage but are in fact a cuckold. This is an information shock that upends identity and thereby destroys SWB. What's needed for wellbeing is not a correct understanding of the facts, but a logically consistent understanding of the facts that endorses one's desired self-image. Coalescence brings this about. Plugging into the experience machine cannot bring this about because one knows one's new reality is fake.

Measurement

The discussion in chapter 10 and the last forty-odd years of SW-B research demonstrate that we can measure SWB. The question is whether we can measure it with enough accuracy for our purposes. In this regard, economists tend to focus on interpersonal welfare comparisons, which require a high standard of measurement (Hausman 2015). I argued in chapter 10 that contemporary SWB measures do not meet this standard, principally because of scale-norming issues. However, welfare economists sometimes overlook the other angles social scientific research can take into SWB and the sufficiency of present measurement practices for these ends (Alexandrova 2017; Angner 2013). This book is a catalogue of many of the impressive findings from this research program.

Some welfare analysts might also be concerned that few policy applications of SWB have been studied using experimental methods that allow strong causal identification. Transitioning ideas from a psychologist's lab to policy is tricky and requires evaluation. Efforts are underway in this regard, particularly in the field of positive education (Lordan and McGuire 2018; Heintzelman et al. 2020; Jang et al. 2010). However, until our understanding of causal pathways matures, we should be cautious about such ventures. The potential for unintended consequences is severe when causal identification is lacking.

A recent paper by Oishi et al. (2018) provides an instructive illustration. They show that periods of relatively high progressive taxation are correlated with higher life satisfaction among the poor. Progressive taxation is also correlated with lower satisfaction among the rich, but this negative effect is swamped by the positive effect observed among the poor. Oishi et al.

conclude (p. 165) that "our analyses suggest that progressive taxation could be an important policy tool, not only as an antidote to growing income inequality in the United States but also as an instrument in combating the possible negative effects of inequality on perceived fairness, trust, and the happiness of the nation."

Leaving aside the vexed ethics and politics of taxation and inequality, this conclusion is problematic given that the analysis does not allow strong causal identification. Notably, Oishi et al. do not assess whether it is higher social security spending during periods of high taxation that is the real causal element in the higher rates of satisfaction that they observe. Social security payments raise the incomes of poor people, unlike progressive taxation, and income is well established as a key determinant of life satisfaction (Stevenson and Wolfers 2013). Social security payments could be relatively high even under a relatively less progressive tax regime (Stewart and Whiteford 2018), so a correlation between taxes and satisfaction here does not equal causation. Additionally, higher social security payments and more progressive income taxation could reasonably be expected to have different side effects on the economy at large. Taxation might reduce consumption, flowing on to lower investment and fewer jobs in retail and low-end services—the kind of jobs that poor people are disproportionately employed in. Unemployment has a well-established negative effect on subjective well-being (Winkelmann and Winkelmann 1998). If the taxation itself does not have a causal effect on the life satisfaction of the poor, the net result would be lower life satisfaction among the poor and general economic malaise. This example illustrates why we should be cautious about mental state interventions until our causal understanding matures. Due to the atheoretic approach of SWB scholarship to date, there are typically multiple mechanisms that can explain even an experimentally established association between SWB and some intervention. We need to deepen our theoretical understanding of SWB so that we can start to isolate each of mechanisms and understand their interaction.

Adaptive Preferences

A separate challenge for SWB accounts of the prudential good that relates to measurement is the issue of adaptation. If someone has gotten used to their circumstances they may express a high level of SWB even though their circumstances could be (much) better. Someone can practice gratitude and other techniques of mood management to make the most of a bad situation, possibly succeeding in achieving a high degree of SWB even while living in, for example, poverty or an oppressive dictatorship (though this seems unlikely given the deleterious impact of such regimes on motivation).

Adaptation has two undesirable consequences when SWB is the goal of government. First, it implies that policy resources should be directed to frustrated achievers rather than happy peasants (Graham and Lora 2009). Some achievers, despite being objectively well-off, have high aspirations or are perhaps unsatisfied by constitution and thus report low levels of life satisfaction. In contrast, some peasants, despite living in objectively meager circumstances, report high levels of life satisfaction, perhaps because they have gotten used to their poverty. If the goal of government is to maximize life satisfaction, then policy should focus on improving the satisfaction of the achievers—the peasants are already doing well. For example, it should not direct resources toward restoring vision to satisfied blind people. From the perspective of just distribution, this seems perverse. This argument was made most forcefully by Sen (1999a, 1999b) when he first advanced the capabilities paradigm.

The second undesirable consequence of adaptation in the context of SWB policy is that it shifts the role of government from improving circumstances to improving how people *feel about* those circumstances. Making SWB the goal of government means that government should pursue the most cost-effective means to promote SWB. In many cases, it will be cheaper to help people adapt to bad circumstances than to address those circumstances. For example, financing cognitive-behavioral therapy to address anxiety from climate change may be cheaper than effecting a transformation to a green economy.

This shift in objective is particularly perverse when government policy is a driver of bad circumstances. For example, Friedli and Stearn (2015) describe how welfare recipients in the United Kingdom are now required to attend positive psychology sessions if they want to continue receiving income support. Government believes that some welfare recipients cannot find work because they are not happy enough—they do not have a "positive attitude." However, it's possible that persistent unemployment is a function of the government's pro-cyclical austerity policies. SWB interventions for welfare recipients shift blame for unemployment from government actions to insufficient happiness among citizens.

These two undesirable consequences of adaptation together constitute a powerful argument against making SWB the goal of government, the foundation of cost-benefit analysis, or a measure of development. However, they do not undermine the claim that SWB is what is good for *individuals*. An individual living in challenging circumstances should absolutely practice mood management if it helps to lessen their misery. Adaptation and reference point adjustment is a sensible response to adverse shocks like divorce, physical impairment, and natural disasters. Of course, it is also important to meet adversity with courage and willpower to improve your circumstances. Adaptation should not be taken so far that it turns to acquiescence and hopelessness. However, a balance can be struck between maintaining long-term motivation to transcend a bad situation and mood management to ensure that the bad situation doesn't make you miserable in the meantime.

We should be especially careful to avoid discouraging adaptation to bad circumstances when people are genuinely powerless to address those circumstances. Transforming bad circumstances often requires collective action, and this is impossible unless affected individuals stay firm. The civil rights movement in the United States would have been even more of a struggle if the oppressed had focused on getting used to their oppression rather than engaging in activism. At the same time, it seems excessive to suggest that it would have been better for the average oppressed citizen's well-being to experience the violence early civil rights activists faced. For those activists, their identity and integrity demanded that level of sacrifice. For others, adaptation is the most well-being appropriate response.

Paternalism

The principal critique of (mental) state-based accounts of well-being among preference satisfaction enthusiasts is that state-based accounts justify paternalism. External actors like governments could override a person's preferences, claiming those preferences undermine that person's SWB. This is anathema to the liberal tradition in economics and political theory. As an illustration of how this might go, the Communist Party of China declared in a 2018 white paper that "the principal human right is to be happy" (PRC 2018). The white paper goes on to claim that China has therefore excelled in promoting human rights. This is despite Human Rights Watch (2018) underlining China's ongoing detention of human rights lawyers, detention and genocide of Uighurs in Xinjiang, ongoing oppression in Tibet, historical atrocities committed against Falun Gong practitioners, and oppression of democratic activism. This example highlights how "happiness" and other mental states can be used to justify policies that go against citizen preferences in controversial ways.

Advocates of SWB as the goal of policy might respond that the *subjective* nature of SWB undermines the ability of government to override people's preferences. How could the state know your *subjective* well-being better than you? In this vein, Clark et al. (2018, p. 4) write that life satisfaction "is democratic—it allows individuals to assess their lives on the basis of whatever *they* consider important to themselves." Similarly, Frijters et al. (2019) write that a life satisfaction scale "takes individuals seriously as political agents and sets them at the top of the judgement tree."

This claim is questionable given how SWB research is conducted in practice. SWB researchers elicit life satisfaction data from respondents using scale questions. They then place these reports on the left-hand side of a regression equation and populate the right-hand side with variables chosen *by the researchers* that the *researchers* think are associated with SWB. The marginal effects derived from regression analysis are then fed into cost-effectiveness formulas. At no point is the respondent asked why they are satisfied (or not) with their life. There are good reasons for this. Direct questions might act as priming mechanisms, triggering focusing illusions and anchoring effects. They might also encourage social desirability bias and other maladies. From a research perspective, then, there are reasons to avoid direct questions about the causes of SWB. However, *policy is not research*. What is technically appropriate in a research context must be balanced against what is normatively appropriate in a policy context. This methodology leads to technocratic and paternalistic policy and needs to be tempered with greater citizen involvement to ensure democratic legitimacy.

Deeper citizen involvement, perhaps through co-production or deliberative democratic mechanisms, would also allow the enumeration of "what really matters to people," a frequent slogan of the wellbeing public policy movement. When people are asked what really matters to them they don't say "life satisfaction." They list things like health, housing, employment, autonomy, and healthy communities. Why don't we measure those things directly, then? The answer, as discussed in chapter 10, is that such a multidimensional dashboard of indicators would be difficult to utilize in cost-benefit analysis. Life satisfaction, being a unidimensional and somewhat cardinal measure of wellbeing, is more straightforward to apply. But this then just replaces the monolith of income-aggregating preference information with the monolith of life-satisfaction-aggregating preference information. There is little here that is meaningfully democratic, and little meaningful engagement with the specific things that "really matter to people."

In contrast, the capabilities literature has already demonstrated the feasibility of developing, in partnership with communities, surveys that capture the many variables that people regard as crucial to their wellbeing. This research often discovers idiosyncratic items specific to the local context that are important to particular communities, such as the quality of fishing in recent months (see, for example, Durie 2006; Ganesharajah 2009; McGregor et al. 2003; Ruttenberg 2013; Yap and Yu 2016). Similar methods of co-producing notions and measures of wellbeing with stakeholders have been widely utilized in the medical sciences for decades (Batalden et al. 2016; Elwyn et al. 2020). Such surveys are, of course, of questionable usefulness to national statistical and financial agencies because they are multidimensional and highly context specific. But there is no reason the needs of such agencies should dominate how wellbeing public policy is done across the whole gamut of government. There is a tension here between features of wellbeing theories and measures that are attractive to policy actors, like democracy, legitimacy, and participation, and features attractive to scientists, technical experts, and treasury officials, like psychometric validity and suitability for cost-benefit analysis. An extensive discussion of these issues is outside the scope of this volume, but they should be prominent themes of wellbeing public policy efforts going forward.

As with some of the other critiques of state-based accounts of well-being, paternalism is a powerful argument against using SWB as the prudential good in *policy*, but it does not undermine SWB as what is good for *individuals*. Outside of extreme cases like schizophrenia, individuals know their own minds better than anybody else. The *subjective* aspect of SWB therefore mitigates mental state promotion justifications for paternalism at the micro level. A wicked stepmother cannot justify keeping you confined to the home "to protect you" if you tell them that you would feel better venturing forth. More practically, in contrast to government, it is difficult for family members or other close associates to coerce your behavior against your will but "in your best interest." Checking someone into rehab or prescribing medication for them, for example, requires informed consent. Having someone committed to a mental health institution for the long term is difficult if the individual does not want to stay there and is not a threat to others. Furthermore, it's more acceptable for personal acquaintances to act paternalistically than for states to do so. Indeed, it is arguably a duty for people to care about their loved ones when they engage in self-destructive behaviors.

Government Should Promote Welfare, Not Wellbeing

The preceding analysis suggests that while SWB is the prudential good for individuals, there are dangers associated with governments making SWB their goal. How can these two positions be reconciled? What is the goal of government if not wellbeing? One could first answer that government has a limited role associated with resolving collective action problems that has little to do with wellbeing. Collective action problems include most market failures, and so government has a role providing public goods, addressing externalities, easing imperfect information, and improving competition in concentrated industries. A central concern of the social contract tradition in political theory is how to design and establish the institutional architecture that allows government to execute these tasks without infringing on human rights or committing other injustices (Rawls 1971; Buchanan and Tullock 1962). This tradition has little need for a welfare criterion, being focused instead on matters of procedural justice.

The need for a welfare/wellbeing criterion comes from the social planner tradition (Arrow et al. 2011), which has at times been rebuked by social contract theorists (Buchanan 1964). The central concern of the social planner tradition is how to efficiently and equitably allocate resources to maximize total utility or some other expression of aggregate social welfare. Government is here conceived as a benign and benevolent technocrat rather than a harnessed leviathan, as in social contract theory. The social planner tradition proceeds by specifying a social welfare function that defines wellbeing and an ethical way of aggregating it. Government's job is to maximize this function. Cost-benefit analysis, as a product of the same welfare economics architecture, similarly involves aggregating individual well-being in some way to arrive at a comparison of the well-being implications of different policies. Within a social contract framework, the business of democracy, politics, government, and policy can continue without some agreed-upon definition of well-being. Not so for the social planner framework.

The social planner is a questionable paradigm for understanding the nature and objective of government, but the tools of social welfare functions

(SWFs) and cost-benefit analysis (CBA) are valuable aids to policy decision-making (Dobes 2018; Adler 2019). Even someone with a deliberative perspective on political legitimacy (Dryzek 2002) would struggle to deny that SWFs and CBA are helpful inputs into deliberative processes. Citizens confronted with a choice to vote either for a new light rail system or an expansion of the existing bus network, for example, would find it helpful to have someone compare the costs and benefits of each proposal in terms of dollars and cents. If one project clearly has a larger net present value than the other, this is useful information even if it not normatively conclusive. Similarly, SWFs allow for relatively easy comparisons of the distributional implications of different policies. Citizens intent on justice would find this information helpful even if they ultimately don't trust technocrats with the selection of distributional weights and other normative aspects of the analysis. All this means that having an agreeable definition of the goal of government to feed into SWFs and CBAs is valuable. This brings us back to our original question: what is the goal of government if not wellbeing?

I propose welfare. "Welfare" and "wellbeing" are typically used interchangeably in welfare economics, but history is not destiny and we should move away from this practice. As discussed in chapter 5, we should use "welfare" when referring to the option set available to individuals from which they choose the life that is best for them. "Wellbeing" is then used to refer to the value the individual gets from that specific life. This demarcation is closely analogous to Sen's (1999b) framework in the capabilities and functionings paradigm, which is itself an expansion of the consumer's problem of maximizing utility subject to a budget constraint. In all cases, the individual is taken as arbiter of which choices will best promote their own wellbeing. Their preferences are not the object of policy, which instead focuses on expanding the potential choices the individual can make and the individual's capacity to make those choices. For mostly technical reasons, such as the need for a unidimensional and interpersonally cardinal measure of welfare, CBA and SWFs still need to be grounded in income and price analysis, at least for now. The more ambitious goals of government can be framed in terms of capabilities, as in the Sustainable Development Goals.

Promoting welfare would of course indirectly promote SWB. Having a relaxed capabilities constraint is critical to coalescence. A wide option set to choose from generally increases the likelihood that we will be able to realize the functionings that bring us the most SWB. Conceptualizing welfare in terms of capabilities rather than merely income also shifts the ambition of government to providing the economic, social, environmental, and institutional conditions, broadly conceived, that allow people to flourish. Rather than targeting people's psychology directly, provide opportunity and let people realize their wellbeing however they might like.

Whither SWB Policy?

Having government focus on welfare rather than wellbeing is arguably only a minor reform to the status quo. SWB advocates will likely be left cold by this outcome. They might worry about sustainability, just distribution, happiness, and mental health. These are all items that SWB advocates think would be better promoted under a paradigm that moves away from materialistic concerns like GDP and ever more energy-intensive lifestyles. To these concerns I offer three rejoinders.

First, these items can and indeed have been successfully promoted using capabilities and preference satisfaction accounts of welfare. Their lack of political salience is a function of politics and culture, not technics. Steering policy toward sustainability and other such ends requires shifting the values of the public, not changing the analytical architecture that underpins policy analysis. Second, maintaining welfare and not wellbeing as the goal of government does not preclude SWB from playing a central role in policy analysis. I hope that this book, especially the work of happiness economists discussed in chapter 6, has illuminated the many insights SWB theory and data can provide on a range of policy-relevant social science questions. These insights can expand the perspectives of the public as well as analysts, thereby making CBA and other tools more sophisticated. Third, even in a welfare-not-wellbeing paradigm there is arguably a role for government to promote the practical wisdom or "means to reason" of citizens, notably through education. This opens a limited but relatively uncontroversial space for SWB policy. I discuss each of these rejoinders in greater detail in what follows.

SWB Goals Can Be Promoted Within a Welfare Paradigm

There is no reason to think that citizens don't care about happiness, mental illness, fairness, or sustainability. All these things can be accommodated within the existing preference satisfaction framework for welfare analysis

(Fleurbaey and Blanchet 2013) and capabilities framework for objective setting. Indeed, they already are. Layard et al. (2007) used traditional cost-benefit analysis to successfully argue for the inclusion of mental health services in the United Kingdom's National Health Service. Experts in CBA are at pains to explain that environmental and social outcomes belong in CBA because they are sources of utility (Dobes 2018). The Sustainable Development Goals, which emphasize environment and fairness, are the latest iteration of a capabilities-based approach to policy planning.

When these items are not included in policy objectives it is a matter of either politics or culture. Politically, vested interests often manipulate the policy process to promote their preferred outcome. This is why we don't see, for example, carbon taxes or congestion charges in widespread use even though they are textbook economic solutions to pollution. It is also implicated in the inability of governments to combat runaway inequality. Making SWB the goal of government wouldn't suddenly remove these political factors.

Culturally, people might not value things that are positively associated with SWB. This might be because SWB research is erroneous, or perhaps because citizens have self-defeating preferences. Even in the latter case, it would be hubristic for SWB researchers to bypass citizens' preferences claiming they are "wrong." If they are indeed erroneous it should be easy enough to demonstrate this to citizens. Educational efforts to change beliefs and values are required in this situation, not technocratic efforts to rig the methods of policy analysis. Government will start to promote SWB if citizens value SWB more than material concerns. More widespread knowledge of things like the counterproductive power of extrinsic goals, the deleterious effects of inequality on life satisfaction, and the importance of allocating time to relationships and meaningful activities rather than commuting (Whillans 2020) would inevitably lead to a shift in voter sentiment. "Economic value" (utility) is just a numerical representation of preference satisfaction. Moving to "an economy of wellbeing" or some such therefore simply involves having citizens prefer SWB over other policy objectives.

SWB Can Still Play a Role in Policy Analysis

Regardless of whether it is the goal of government or not, SWB theories and metrics can provide useful insights into policy issues. For example, Graham

(2017) observed higher levels of pain and stress and lower levels of optimism among individuals in counties that voted for Trump in the 2016 election. These negative SWB outcomes often contrast with economic indicators, especially at the individual level. The U-shaped relationship between satisfaction and age inverts conventional wisdom that middle-aged people are in the prime of life while the elderly are miserable (Rauch 2018). The current wave of research into the relationship between life satisfaction, positive affect, and productivity has significant implications for industrial relations and management practices (Krekel et al. 2019; Bellet et al. 2019). Relatedly, citizens seem to be at least partially in favor of improving mental health outcomes and other SWB-related issues. Any CBA of the most efficacious policies in such areas will need data from SWB studies as inputs. All this is to say that collecting SWB data, promoting SWB literacy in national statistical agencies, and studying topics at the intersection of SWB and policy is sensible and should be promoted. We should just stop short of making SWB the goal of government.

Alongside these perspective-enhancing inputs to policy discussion, SWB advocates can speak directly to citizens rather than government. Cultural advocacy like that of Layard and Ward (2020), which is explicitly rhetorical, is an important input into the public sphere and less problematic than technocratic policy entrepreneurship. Technocratic activism seeks to circumvent democratic mechanisms because such mechanisms are supposedly hamstrung by "bad" preferences. In contrast, the purpose of cultural advocacy is to change values and preferences and thereby change policy. If people value SWB, then convincingly showing them that their preferences do not serve it will change their preferences.

The role of SWB researchers is cast here in the manner proposed by deliberative democrats (Brown 2014). Policy is not developed through dialogue between politicians and enlightened technocrats. Instead, experts help citizens to deliberate wisely over their preferences. Citizens then communicate these well-deliberated preferences to politicians. This is a mode of expert engagement in policy that fosters citizen participation and wisdom, empowering citizens. There are plenty of reasons to be skeptical of deliberative democracy. Perhaps foremost among them is that citizens have scarce time, energy, or enthusiasm for deliberation in many cases (Lafont 2015). However, these reasons are arguably less pernicious than the reasons outlined earlier for resisting technocratic efforts to make SWB the goal of government.

SWB and Means to Reason

One area where SWB policy is less controversial is in enhancing people's skills with respect to their own SWB. Analysis throughout this book suggested that several skills are helpful, if not required, for making progress on the coalescence of being and achieving SWB. These include mood management, mindfulness, willpower, and identifying your actual, ideal, and ought selves. Possession of these skills could be considered a core capability, namely practical wisdom (Nussbaum 2000). Policies to promote them could then be justified within the capabilities paradigm. Such programs would likely involve informed consent and don't concern budgeting decisions. They thus sidestep many aspects of the critiques from paternalism and adaptation.

Positive psychology has developed a range of tools for improving people's skills and capacity to reason wisely about their lives with the aim of enhancing their SWB. Examples include the healthy minds curriculum, which teaches mood management techniques (Lordan and Macguire 2018); personal strengths training courses, which can promote self-esteem and also assist people in developing ideal selves (Peterson and Seligman 2004); mindfulness and meditation training courses (Meiklejohn et al. 2012); the future offering program, which builds an understanding of sacrifice and goal setting (Morisano et al. 2010); and the ENHANCE program, which is a general SW-B-promoting intervention (Heintzelmann et al. 2020). Many of these interventions are explicitly designed for school environments (Seligman et al. 2009) and can be grouped under the heading of "positive education." Schools and children are both settings where a degree of paternalism is appropriate. This avoids one of the main pitfalls of SWB policy.

Such training programs could be incorporated into existing educational curricula to ensure that they prepare students for life and not just work. Government could also make courses available to adults through facilities like local libraries. If this is deemed too expensive, government could instead operate knowledge warehouses that disseminate program information to interested parties, much like the What Works Centres do in the United Kingdom.

The main argument against this sort of thing is that such programs are costly and outside the appropriate scope of government. Citizens can already access these programs through popular literature, media, commercial ventures, academic webpages, and podcasts, often for free. It's not clear that governments have a role to play in providing these goods owing to some market failure, equity issue, or cognitive bias that prevents people from accessing them on their own. Wouldn't people rather just pay less tax? There is a clear need for more research in this space to assess the potential cost-effectiveness and accessibility of such policies.

Conclusion

This chapter argued that there are compelling if not necessarily over-whelming reasons to think that SWB is good for people. Nonetheless, government should be cautious about promoting it. Adaptation, paternalism, and measurement all pose problems for SWB that make it problematic as a goal of government. However, these concerns are not compelling at the individual level. Individuals should, and do, pursue SWB. They think it is good for them. Government should focus on welfare: the option set of possible lives that an individual can choose from. This ensures that governments focus on improving circumstances rather than how people feel about those circumstances. It also ensures that policy resources are directed foremost to those who have the least rather than to those who feel the worst. Finally, it ensures the social and economic conditions required for people to self-actualize. Coalescence is difficult when your option set is limited. All this does not preclude SWB from having a role in policymaking. SWB insights can inform policy analysis and the policy discourse. SWB researchers and knowledge brokers should do more to communicate with the public rather than with policymakers. Convincing the public to change their values and behavior to better serve SWB promotes SWB as a social goal without under-mining liberal political institutions that are critical to our wellbeing. SWB research can also assist in education, providing citizens with the practical wisdom necessary to make good choices and achieve a high level of SWB.

Conclusion

> Happiness is when what you think, what you say, and what you do are in harmony
>
> —Mahatma Gandhi

This book was motivated for the most part by the challenges associated with integrating SWB into public policy. Chapter 1 argued that SW-B scholarship has made substantial contributions to science over the past four decades. It has illuminated the distinction between evaluated and experienced wellbeing. It has raised new topics for inquiry, such as adaptation, set points, and the SWB reporting function. And perhaps most importantly, it has contributed to the development of an architecture for the empirical study of SWB by peeling the concept away from discussions of prudential value. Hedonic psychologists and happiness economists defined a new construct, SW-B, that could be studied without asking whether SW-B is "good for" people. They utilized an exploratory empirical methodology and discovered a fascinating landscape for analysis.

In all this, SW-B's operationalist epistemology was arguably a boon. But in the public policy and welfare economics domains, operationalism leaves SW-B scholarship open to long-standing and well-rehearsed critiques. This is in large part because wellbeing in these domains is intimately tied to prudential matters. Maximizing wellbeing in policy and welfare economics means maximizing prudential value, so to apply SW-B herein it must be asked whether SW-B is good for people. The answer is complicated. SWB is good for people, but SWB is a richer concept than SW-B. Furthermore, while SWB is what is good for individuals, it should not be the goal of government because the purpose of government is not straightforwardly to promote the prudential good. Making SWB the priority of government could lead to perverse redistribution toward millionaires, clumsy allocation of public

A Theory of Subjective Wellbeing. Mark Fabian, Oxford University Press. © Oxford University Press 2022.
DOI: 10.1093/oso/9780197635261.003.0013

funds in cost-benefit analysis owing to scale-norming and other errors of measurement, and an inappropriate focus on helping people adapt to bad circumstances rather than addressing those circumstances.

Nonetheless, SWB scholarship has valuable contributions to make to policy discourses, particularly with regard to empiricism. To make these contributions constructively and effectively, SW-B must replace its operationalist epistemology with a realist one. Chapter 2 argued that the first step in this enterprise is to posit a deep and comprehensive theory of SWB, including how it relates to the prudential good. Recall Alexandrova's (2017) "better implicit logic of construct validation":

A measure M of construct C can be considered validated to the extent that M behaves in a way that respects three sources of evidence:
1. M is inspired by a plausible theory of C. *This theory should be articulated as fully as possible and defended against alternatives.*
2. M is shown to track C *as C is understood and endorsed by the subjects to whom C is applied.*
3. Other knowledge about C is consistent with variations in values of M across contexts. *This knowledge should encompass the normative significance of C, including moral and political contexts of the use of C.*

The bulk of this book was devoted to item (1): providing a plausible theory of SWB that is articulated as fully as possible and defended against alternatives. Chapter 3 explained why analytical philosophy struggles to provide this theory. First, its natural inclination toward classification undermines its ability to integrate perspectives on wellbeing into a coherent whole. Yet an integrative perspective is what is required. Second, analytical philosophy has arguably been focused on developing a relatively narrow conception of wellbeing that can be plugged into the social planner framework as a maximand. One important issue this approach obviates is understanding wellbeing as both an outcome *and* a process. While theories of both exist in analytical philosophy, they are rarely integrated. Accounts of the process of wellbeing have also been shallow on practicalities.

Chapters 4 through 9 developed the integrative and expansive theory of SWB that chapters 2 and 3 argued was necessary. Chapters 4 through 9 merged the SW-B and analytical philosophy of wellbeing literatures with the broader literatures on SWB and wellbeing in clinical, social, moral, and developmental psychology, continental philosophy, and welfare economics.

The outcome of SWB in this theory is expressed in the subjective wellbeing production function (SWBPF), while the process is articulated in the coalescence of being. The combined analysis of the SWBPF and coalescence of being revealed that SWB (the left-hand-side variable in the SWBPF) can be described as a state of generalized flow occurring across most domains of life. We become increasingly enraptured in the experience of life because our activities are intrinsically motivated and challenging but achievable, and we possess the awareness, sensitivity, and introspective capacity to derive high-quality feedback about our experiences. The SWBPF outlines a set of variables that empirically predict subjective reports of being high in SWB. Chapters 4 through 9 explained how these variables interact to give rise to SWB.

The SWBPF consists of three dimensions: hedonia, eudaimonia, and conscience. These correspond roughly to whether one regards one's life to be pleasant, fulfilling, and valuable, respectively. Drawing on the literature in SW-B and philosophy, chapter 6 argued that hedonia is a function of positive affect, negative affect, and hedonic life satisfaction and is parameterized by emotional wellbeing, eudaimonia, and virtue. Someone who is broadly "well" is even more well if they are "happy"—experiencing positive mood. Appropriately, chapter 6 canvassed a range of techniques for improving moods, including savoring, gratitude, and mindfulness. However, the font of everyday mood and emotion lies in eudaimonia and conscience. Treating mood directly cannot bring about holistic wellness or even sustainable positive moods if basic needs are not met and/or an individual lacks value/s (Tiberius 2018).

Chapter 7 distinguished eudaimonia from hedonia using theoretical arguments and empirical evidence from clinical and social psychology. It also defined eudaimonia as a state wherein an individual's basic psychological needs for autonomy, competence, and relatedness are thoroughly nourished. This claim was supported by evidence from self-determination theory and related literatures.

Chapter 8 argued that the conscience dimension is a crucial element of SWB that needs to be better appreciated. Conscience concerns meaning and purpose, identity, and virtue (the sense that one is a good person). A critical challenge for many people in achieving conscience is despair: the feeling that the universe is without value (nausea) and lacks a moral order (seriousness), and the feeling that we are always becoming and so cut off from a fixed sense of self (anguish). Empirical inquiry in psychology has advanced our factual understanding of conscience in recent decades. However, existential philosophy, where many of these concepts were first developed, has depth to offer and should be more thoroughly integrated into SWB scholarship. Existentialism is particularly powerful in the context of growing secularism and individualism because existentialism arose as a response to the collapse of religion and collectivism in twentieth-century Europe. Furthermore, the pursuit of values is a prominent theme of wellbeing scholarship across analytical philosophy, psychology, and happiness economics. Existentialism has substantial contributions to make to these streams of scholarship because it developed a conceptualization of value specifically for the context of nihilism.

The dimensions of SWBPF are interconnected. Affective signals from the hedonic dimension guide the coalescence of being. This process in turn leads to the nourishment of the basic psychological needs in the eudaimonia dimension and secures the meaning, identity, and virtue that constitute the conscience dimension. In reverse, it is only by building a robust foundation for wellbeing in eudaimonia and conscience that the individual can achieve a life punctuated predominantly by positive rather than negative affect. Eudaimonia and conscience are connected as well. The nihilist, who knows little of themselves and perceives the world as pointless and morality as flippant, will struggle to motivate themselves and nourish their basic psychological needs. Meanwhile, individuals raised in environments that foster their basic psychological needs, particularly for relatedness, will be buffered against the debilitating effects of despair.

Individuals seeking to improve their SWB are constrained in this activity by their capabilities. These capture the extent to which individuals can be who they want to be and do what they want to do. Chapter 5 explained the contents of the capabilities constraint, drawing on the work of Sen (1999a, 1999b) and Nussbaum (2000) and the way their ideas have been operationalized in the HDI, MDGs, and SDGs. A summary list of capabilities was proposed that included income, health, education, political enfranchisement, and environmental quality.

A central claim of chapter 5 was that once an individual has sufficient capabilities to be who they want to be and do what they want to do, increasing their capabilities will have little impact on their wellbeing. If an individual appears to have a relaxed capabilities constraint but is nonetheless unwell, it is possibly because they lack quality information regarding who they should be and what they should do. Understanding this information shortfall in a comprehensive fashion necessitates having some model of how individuals come to learn what ways of being and doing are best for their unique selves. The coalescence of being, explored in chapter 9, provides insights into what this learning process involves.

The coalescence of being is a model of self-actualization, a long-running fixture of philosophical accounts of wellbeing that has until now been somewhat underspecified. The central process of coalescence is the harmonization of the actual, ideal, and ought selves. These correspond to who one is, who one wants to be, and who one feels a responsibility to be, respectively. The ideal and ought selves consist of goals and identified values. Positive affective signals will punctuate progress toward goals that are self-concordant, indicating that the individual is on the right path toward SWB. Negative affective signals require introspection and rational digestion. They may indicate that the individual is not pursuing their goals with enough rigor and is consequently falling short of sensibly desired ends. Or they may indicate that the ends are inappropriate. The ends may be self-discordant: a poor fit for the individual in question. The individual must then abandon these goals and reconceptualize their ideal and/or ought self.

As coalescence progresses, the individual will improve across all dimensions of the SWBPF. They will pursue predominantly intrinsically motivated activities, nourishing their sense of autonomy. They will comport toward activities and values that are associated with positive affect and abandon those associated with negative affect, ensuring hedonia in the long run. Their progress toward their ideal self will give them a sense of growing competence, and their progress toward their ought self will give them a sense of meaning and purpose, especially as they change the world to be more in line with their values. Pursuit of the ideal and ought selves will bring the individual into communities of like-minded individuals where they will be valued, nourishing their sense of relatedness. Introspection upon the affective signals that guide the individual along the path of coalescence will give the individual a rationally accessible understanding of themselves, providing identity and ameliorating anguish. Finally, coalescence requires integrity and fealty toward the principles inherent in the ideal and ought selves. This means that these principles come to exert a binding power over the individual's behavior that emerges out of that individual's own desires. This overcomes seriousness and nurtures virtue.

While this book has argued that wellbeing is ultimately a state of being, this classification is largely beside the point. If those interested in promoting

SWB sought to promote the variables in the SWBPF as a kind of objective list account of wellbeing, they would be indirectly promoting wellbeing. If they instead sought to promote the subjective report of wellbeing that the variables in the SWBPF empirically predict, they would similarly be indirectly promoting wellbeing. Finally, if they sought to assist people in achieving the eudaimonic wellbeing and value fulfillment associated with successful coalescence, they would likewise be promoting wellbeing. These observations suggest that it there is little marginal value in trying to hem the concept of wellbeing into ever more precise classifications.

Measuring SWB is challenging but not insurmountable. Metrics exist for each individual element of the SWBPF, except perhaps virtue. The Well-Being Profile (Marsh et al. 2020) overlaps substantially with the SWBPF and the coalescence of being and possesses attractive psychometric properties. Life satisfaction scales also constitute a cheap and simple metric that is sufficiently accurate to serve as a global measure of SWB for certain purposes. Scales become increasingly inappropriate the more complex the underlying causal drivers of an individual's SWB are. In such cases, SWB needs to be disentangled to allow for diagnoses and targeted interventions.

Life satisfaction scales also become increasingly inappropriate as greater precision is required. Interpersonal welfare comparisons in many policy contexts are the most prominent example. Life satisfaction scales appear attractive in such contexts because they are unidimensional and seem to generate interpersonally ordinal data. Unfortunately, what evidence we currently have for scale-norming suggests that it might significantly undermine the interpersonal and intertemporal comparability of scale responses. This makes scales a questionable metric for precision welfare analysis. More research is required to understand and potentially surmount the scale-norming challenge. The need for more research should not be discouraging, because there are good normative reasons not to rush into policy applications of SWB.

Governments should focus on promoting welfare, not wellbeing. Welfare is the option set available to citizens from which they can choose those life choices that will bring them the most wellbeing. Essentially, governments should focus on expanding capabilities. They should seek to ensure the social and economic conditions that facilitate wellbeing. There is plenty of scope within this paradigm to shift from material concerns like GDP to items like mental health and sustainability. There is also plenty of scope to apply SWB research, notably where it relates to people's practical wisdom—their ability to learn what ways of being and doing will bring them the most wellbeing and actualize those realities.

Now is a great time to be doing wellbeing research, especially *subjective* wellbeing research. Both the public and the policy community have an appetite for scholarly output. Individuals left cold by materialism are seeking a deeper understanding of how to live a good life. Governments are concerned that the income and prices framework of economic analysis that dominated the second half of the twentieth century, while powerful and mostly beneficial (Fabian and Bruenig 2018), has run its course. They are looking for a new paradigm to guide their decision-making. This appetite has penetrated the academic community as well. Wellbeing and happiness have become increasingly mainstream topics over the past few decades, thanks in large part to the efforts of pioneering SW-B scholars. Wellbeing research is welcome in top journals across many disciplines and is a priority funding area for several research councils. The convergence of all this enthusiasm represents an opportunity to unify wellbeing research in an interdisciplinary way, set it on solid foundations, and make it one of the central themes of academic discourse. I hope this book contributes meaningfully to this endeavor.

Works Cited

Abbe, A., Tkach, C., and Lyubomirsky, S. (2003). The Art of Living by Dispositionally Happy People. *Journal of Happiness Studies*, vol. 4, no. 4, pp. 385–404.

Adams, R. (1999). *Finite and Infinite Goods*. Oxford, UK: Oxford University Press.

Adler, M. (2013). Happiness Surveys and Public Policy: What's the Use? *Duke Law Journal*, vol. 62, no. 8, pp. 1509–1601.

Adler, M. (2019). *Measuring Social Welfare: An Introduction*. New York, NY: Oxford University Press.

Adler, M., and Posner, E. (2006). *New Foundations of Cost-Benefit Analysis*. Cambridge, MA: Harvard University Press.

Ahmed, S., Mayo, N., Corbiere, M., Wood-Dauphinee, S., Hanley, J., and Cohen, R. (2005). Change in Quality of Life in People with Stroke over Time: True Change or Response Shift? *Quality of Life Research*, vol. 14, no. 3, pp. 611–627.

Alexandrova, A. (2017). *A Philosophy for the Science of Well-Being*. Oxford, UK: Oxford University Press.

Algoe, S. (2012). Find, Remind and Bind: The Functions of Gratitude in Everyday Relationships. *Social and Personality Psychology Compass*, vol. 6, no. 6, pp. 455–469.

Alicke, M., Guenther, C., and Zell, E. (2012). Social Self-Analysis: Constructing and Maintaining Personal Identity. In M. Leary and J. Tangney (eds.), *Handbook of Self and Identity*, second edition, pp. 291–308. New York, NY: Guilford.

Alkire, S. (2016). The Capability Approach and Well-Being Measurement for Public Policy. In M. Adler and M. Fleurbaey (eds.), *The Oxford Handbook of Well-Being and Public Policy*, pp. 615–644. New York, NY: Oxford University Press.

Aknin, L., Dunn, E., and Norton, M. (2012). Happiness Runs in a Circular Motion: Evidence for a Positive Feedback Loop Between Prosocial Spending and Happiness. *Journal of Happiness Studies*, vol. 13, no. 2, pp. 347–355.

Angner, E. (2013). Is It Possible to Measure Happiness? *European Journal for Philosophy of Science*, vol. 3, no. 2, pp. 221–240.

Angner, E. (2009). Are Subjective Measures of Well-Being "Direct"? *Australasian Journal of Philosophy*, vol. 89, no. 1, pp. 115–130.

Angner, E. (2015). Well-Being and Economics. In G. Fletcher (ed.), *Routledge Handbook of Philosophy of Well-Being*, pp. 492–503. London, UK: Routledge.

Angyal, A. (1941). *Foundations for a Science of Personality*. New York, NY: Commonwealth Fund.

Angus, L., and McLeod, J. (eds.) (2004). *The Handbook of Narrative and Psychotherapy: Practice, Theory and Research*. New York, NY: Sage.

Annas, J. (1998). Virtue and Eudaimonism. *Social Philosophy and Policy*, vol. 15, no. 1, pp. 37–55.

Annas, J. (2004). Happiness as Achievement. *Daedulus*, vol. 133, no. 2, pp. 44–51.

Annas, J. (2011). *Intelligent Virtue*. New York, NY: Oxford University Press.

Antonakis, J. (2017). On Doing Better Science: From the Thrill of Discovery to Policy Implications. *The Leadership Quarterly*, vol. 28, no. 1, pp. 5–21.

Arampatzi, E., Burger, M., and Novik, N. (2018). Social Network Sites, Individual Social Capital, and Happiness. *Journal of Happiness Studies*, vol. 19, no. 1, pp. 99–122.

Arendt, H. ([1963] 2006). *Eichmann in Jerusalem: A Report on the Banality of Evil*. New York, NY: Penguin.

Argyle, M. (1999). Causes and Correlates of Happiness. In D. Kahneman, E. Diener, and N. Schwartz (eds.), *Well-Being: The Foundations of Hedonic Psychology*, pp. 353–373. New York, NY: Russell Sage.

Argyle, M. (2001). *The Psychology of Happiness, second edition*. London, UK: Routledge.

Argyle, M., and Lu, L. (1990). The Happiness of Extroverts. *Personality and Individual Differences*, vol. 11, no. 10, pp. 1011–1017.

Aristotle (1999). *Nichomachean Ethics*. Trans. W. Ross. Kitchener, ON: Batoche Books.

Armenta, C., Jacobs Bao, K., Lyubomirsky, S., and Sheldon, K. M. (2014). Is Lasting Change Possible? Lessons from the Hedonic Adaptation Prevention Model. In K. Sheldon and R. Lucas (eds.), *Stability of Happiness: Theories and Evidence on Whether Happiness Can Change*, pp. 57–74. London, UK: Academic Press.

Arrow, K., Dasgupta, P., Goulder, L., Mumford, K., and Oleson, K. (2012). Sustainability and the Measurement of Wealth. *Environment and Development Economics*, vol. 17, no. 3, pp. 317–353.

Arrow, K., Sen, A., and Suzumura, K. (2011). *Handbook of Social Choice and Welfare*. Oxford, UK: Elsevier.

Atkinson, A. (1970). On the Measurement of Inequality. *Journal of Economic Theory*, vol. 2, no. 3, pp. 244–263.

Baard, P., Deci, E., and Ryan, R. (2004). Intrinsic Need Satisfaction: A Motivational Basis of Performance and Well-Being in Two Work Settings. *Journal of Applied Social Psychology*, vol. 34, no. 10, pp. 2045–2068.

Bailey, T., Eng, W., Frisch, M., and Snyder, C. (2007). Hope and Optimism as Related to Life Satisfaction. *The Journal of Positive Psychology*, vol. 2, no. 3, pp. 168–175.

Bakker, A. (2005). Flow Among Music Teachers and Their Students: The Crossover of Peak Experiences. *Journal of Vocational Behaviour*, vol. 66, no. 1, pp. 26–44.

Bargh, J. (2004). Being Here Now: Is Consciousness Necessary for Human Freedom? In J. Greenberg, S. Koole, and T. Pyszczynski (eds.), *Handbook of Experimental Existential Psychology*, pp. 385–397. New York, NY: Guilford.

Bargh, J., and Chartrand, T. (1999). The Unbearable Automaticity of Being. *American Psychologist*, vol. 54, no. 7, pp. 462–479.

Barnhofer, T., Crane, C., Hargus, E., Amarasinghe, M., Winder, R., and Williams, J. (2009). Mindfulness-Based Cognitive Therapy as a Treatment for Chronic Depression: A Preliminary Study. *Behaviour Research and Theory*, vol. 47, no. 5, pp. 366–373.

Barkow, K., Cosmides, L., and Tooby, J. (1992). *The Adapted Mind: Evolutionary Psychology and the Generation of Culture*. New York, NY: Oxford University Press.

Bartlett, M. Y., and DeSteno, D. (2006). Gratitude and Prosocial Behaviour. *Psychological Science*, vol. 17, no. 4, pp. 319–325.

Batalden, M., Batalden, P., Margolis, P., Seid, M., Armstrong, G., Opipari-Arrigan, L., and Hartung, H. (2016). Coproduction of Healthcare Services. *British Medical Journal: Quality and Safety*, vol. 25, no. 1, pp. 509–517.

Baumeister, R. (1992). *Meanings of Life*. New York, NY: Guilford Press.

Baumeister, R. (2005). *The Cultural Animal: Human Nature, Meaning and Social Life*. Oxford, UK: Oxford University Press.

Baumeister, R., and Leary, M. (1995). The Need to Belong: Desire for Interpersonal Attachments as a Fundamental Human Motivation. *Psychological Bulletin*, vol. 117, no. 3, pp. 497–529.

Beauvoir, S. de ([1947] 2002). *The Ethics of Ambiguity*. Trans. B. Frechtman. New York, NY: Kensington.

Beauvoir, S. ([1949] 2011). *The Second Sex*. New York, NY: Vintage Books.

Bedford-Peterson, C., DeYoung, C., Tiberius, V., and Syed, M. (2019). Integrating Philosophical and Psychological Approaches to Well-Being: The Role of Success in Personal Projects. *Journal of Moral Education*, vol. 48, no. 1, pp. 84–97.

Beebe-Center, J. (1932). *Psychology of Pleasantness and Unpleasantness*. New York, NY: Van Nostrand.

Bellet, C., De Neve, J., and Ward, G. (2019). Does Employee Happiness Have an Impact on Productivity? Saïd Business School Working Paper 2019-13.

Benjamin, D., Cooper, K., Heffetz, O., and Kimball, M. (2020). Self-Reported Well-Being Indicators Are a Valuable Complement to Traditional Economic Indicators but Are Not Ready to Compete with Them. *Behavioural Public Policy*, vol. 4, no. 2, pp. 198–209.

Benjamin, D., Heffetz, O., Kimball, M., and Rees-Jones, A. (2012). What Do You Think Would Make You Happier? What Do You Think You Would Choose? *American Economic Review*, vol. 102, no. 5, pp. 2083–2110.

Bentham, J. ([1780] 2007). *An Introduction to the Principles of Morals and Legislation*. Mineola, NY: Dover Publications Inc.

Bertrand, M., Goldin, C., and Katz, L. (2010). Dynamics of the Gender Gap for Young Professionals in the Financial and Corporate Sectors. *American Economic Journal: Applied Economics*, vol. 2, no. 3, pp. 228–255.

Bertrand, M., Kamenica, E., and Pan, J. (2015). Gender Identity and Relative Income Within Households. *Quarterly Journal of Economics*, vol. 130, no. 2, pp. 571–614.

Bertrand, M., and Mullainathan, S. (2001). Do People Mean What They Say? Implications for Subjective Survey Data. *American Economic Review*, vol. 91, no. 2, pp. 67–72.

Besser-Jones, L. (2014). *Eudaimonic Ethics: The Philosophy and Psychology of Living Well*. London, UK: Routledge.

Besser-Jones, L. (2015). Eudaimonism. In G. Fletcher (ed.), *The Routledge Handbook of Philosophy of Well-Being*, pp. 187–196. London, UK: Routledge.

Bhuiyan, M. (2018). Life Satisfaction and Economic Position Relative to Neighbours: Perceptions Versus Reality. *Journal of Happiness Studies*, vol. 19, no. 7, pp. 1935–1964.

Bishop, M. (2015). *The Good Life: Unifying the Philosophy and Psychology of Well-Being*. New York, NY: Oxford University Press.

Biswas-Diener, R., Kashdan, T. B., and King, L. A. (2009). Two Traditions of Wellbeing Research, Not Two Distinct Types of Wellbeing. *The Journal of Positive Psychology*, vol. 4, no. 3, pp. 208–211.

Blackorby, C., and Donaldson, D. (1988). Money Metric Utility: A Harmless Normalization? *Journal of Economic Theory*, vol. 46, no. 1, pp. 120–129.

Boarini, R., Comola, M., Smith, C., Manchin, R., and De Keulenaer, F. (2012). What Makes for a Better Life? The Determinants of Subjective Well-Being in OECD Countries, Evidence from the Gallup World Poll. *OECD STD Working Paper*.

Boehm, J. K., Lyubomirsky, S., and Sheldon, K. M. (2012). [The role of need satisfying emotions in a positively activity intervention], unpublished raw data, cited in: Shin, L., and Lyubomirsky, S. (2014). Positive Activity Interventions for Mental Health Conditions: Basic Research and Clinical Applications. In J. Johnson and A. Wood (eds.), *The Handbook of Positive Clinical Psychology*, pp. 349–363. New York, NY: Wiley.

Bond, T., and Lang, K. (2019). The Sad Truth About Happiness Scales. *Journal of Political Economy*, vol. 127, no. 4, pp. 1629–1640.

Bonebright, C., Clay, D., and Ankenmann, R. (2000). The Relationship of Workaholism with Work-Life Conflict, Life Satisfaction and Purpose in Life. *Journal of Counselling Psychology*, vol. 47, no. 4, pp. 469–477.

Booth, A., Cardona-Sosa, L., and Nolen, P. (2014). Gender Differences in Risk Aversion; Do Single-Sex Environments Affect Their Development? *Journal of Economic Behaviour and Organisation*, vol. 99, no. 1, pp. 126–154.

Borsboom, D., Wijsen, L., and Alexandrova, A. (2021). Values in Psychometrics. Forthcoming in *Perspectives on Psychological Science*. https://journals.sagepub.com/doi/full/10.1177/17456916211014183

Bouchard, T. J., Lykken, D. T., McGue, M., Segal, N. L., and Tellegen, A. (1990). Sources of Human Psychological Differences: The Minnesota Study of Twins Reared Apart. *Science*, vol. 12, pp. 223–228.

Bourdieu, P. (1979). *Distinction*. London, UK: Routledge.

Bower, G. (1981). Mood and Memory. *American Psychologist*, vol. 36, no. 2, pp. 129–148.

Boyce, C., Brown, G., and Moore, S. (2010). Money and Happiness: Rank of Income, Not Income, Affects Life Satisfaction. *Psychological Science*, vol. 21, no. 4, pp. 471–475.

Boyce, C., Delaney, L., and Wood, A. (2018). The Great Recession and Subjective Well-Being: How Did the Life Satisfaction of People Living in the UK Change Following the Financial Crisis? *PLoS ONE*, vol. 13, no. 8, pp. 1–17.

Boyce, C., Wood, A., Delaney, L., and Ferguson, E. (2017). How do Personality and Social Structures Interact with Each Other to Predict Important Life Outcomes? The Importance of Accounting for Personality Change. *European Journal of Personality*, vol. 31, no. 3, pp. 279–290.

Boyce, C., Wood, A., and Ferguson, E. (2016). Individual Differences in Loss Aversion: Conscientiousness Predicts How Life Satisfaction Responds to Losses Versus Gains in Income. *Personality and Social Psychology Bulletin*, vol. 42, no. 4, pp. 471–484.

Boyce, C., Wood, A., and Ferguson, E. (2017). For Better or Worse: The Moderating Effects of Personality on the Marriage Life Satisfaction Link. *Personality and Individual Differences*, vol. 97, no. 1, pp. 61–66.

Boyce, C., Wood, A., and Powdthavee, N. (2013). Is Personality Fixed? Personality Changes as Much as "Variable" Economic Factors and More Strongly Predicts Changes to Life Satisfaction. *Social Indicators Research*, vol. 111, no. 1, pp. 287–305.

Bradburn, N. (1969). *The Structure of Psychological Well-Being*. Chicago, MI: Aldine.

Bramble, B. (2016). A New Defence of Hedonism About Well-Being. *Ergo*, vol. 3, no. 1, pp. 85–112.

Brickman, P., Coates, D., and Janoff-Bulman, R. (1978). Lottery Winners and Accident Victims: Is Happiness Relative? *Journal of Personality and Social Psychology*, vol. 36, no. 8, pp. 917–927.

Britton, P., Van Orden, K., Hirsch, J., Niemiec, C., and Williams, G. (2014). Basic Psychological Needs, Suicidal Ideation, and Risk for Suicidal Behaviour in Young Adults. *Suicide and Life-Threatening Behaviour*, vol. 44, no. 4, pp. 362–371.

Brown, G., Gardner, J., Oswald, A., and Qian, J. (2008). Does Wage Rank Affect Employee's Wellbeing? *Industrial Relations*, vol. 47, no. 3, pp. 355–389.

Brown, M. (2014). Expertise and Deliberative Democracy. In S. Elstub and P. McLaverty (eds.), *Deliberative Democracy*, pp. 50–69. Edinburgh, SC: Edinburgh University Press.

Bruni, L., and Porta, P. (2005). *Economics and Happiness: Framing the Analysis*. Oxford, UK: Oxford University Press.

Bruni, L., and Sugden, R. (2007). The Road Not Taken: How Psychology Was Removed from Economics, and How It Might Be Brought Back. *The Economic Journal*, vol. 117, no. 516, pp. 146–173.

Bryant, F., and Veroff, J. (2006). *Savouring: A New Model of Positive Experience*. New York, NY: Routledge (Psychology Press).

Buchanan, J. (1964). What Should Economists Do? *Southern Economic Journal*, vol. 30, no. 3, pp. 213–222.

Buchanan, J., and Tullock, G. (1962). *The Calculus of Consent: Logical Foundations of Constitutional Democracy*. Indianapolis, IN: Liberty Fund, Inc.

Burke, B., Martens, A., and Faucher, E. (2010). Two Decades of Terror Management Theory: A Meta-Analysis of Mortality Salience Research. *Personality and Social Psychology Review*, vol. 14, no. 2, pp. 155–195.

Burnham, T. (2003). Engineering Altruism: A Theoretical and Experimental Investigation of Anonymity and Gift Giving. *Journal of Economic Behaviour and Organization*, vol. 50, no. 1, pp. 133–144.

Burnham, T., and Hare, B. (2007). Engineering Human Cooperation: Does Involuntary Neural Activation Increase Public Goods Contributions? *Human Nature*, vol. 18, no. 2, pp. 88–108.

Callard, A. (2018). *Aspiration: The Agency of Becoming*. New York, NY: Oxford University Press.

Campbell, J., Trapnell, P., Heine, S., Katz, I., Lavallee, L., and Lehman, D. (1996). Self-Concept Clarity: Measurement, Personality Correlates and Cultural Boundaries. *Journal of Personality and Social Psychology*, vol. 70, no. 6, pp. 141–156.

Camus, A. ([1942] 2013). *The Outsider*. Trans. S. Smith. New York, NY: Penguin.

Capic, T., Li, N., and Cummins, R. (2017). Confirmation of Subjective Well-Being Set Points: Foundational for Subjective Social Indicators. *Social Indicators Research*, vol. 137, no. 1, pp. 1–28.

Cardaciotto, L., Herbert, J., Forman, E., Moitra, E., and Farrow, V. (2008). The Assessment of Present-Moment Awareness and Acceptance: The Philadelphia Mindfulness Scale. *Assessment*, vol. 15, no. 2, pp. 204–223.

Carlquist, E., Ulleberg, P., Delle Fave, A., Nafstad, H., and Blakar, R. (2017). Everyday Understandings of Happiness, Good Life, and Satisfaction: Three Different Facets of Well-Being. *Applied Research in Quality of Life*, vol. 12, no. 2, pp. 481–505.

Carney, T. (2019). *Alienated America: Why Some Places Thrive While Others Collapse*. New York, NY: Harper Press.

Carver, C. (2012). Self-Awareness. In M. Leary and J. Tangney (eds.), *Handbook of Self and Identity: Second Edition*, pp. 50–68. New York, NY: Guilford.

Carver, C., Lawrence, J., and Scheier, M. (1999). Self-Discrepancies and Affect: Incorporating the Role of Feared Selves. *Personality and Social Psychology Bulletin*, vol. 25, no. 7, pp. 783–792.

Chancellor, J., and Lyubomirsky, S. (2013). Humble Beginnings: Current Trends, State Perspectives and Hallmarks of Humility. *Social and Personality Psychology Compass*, vol. 7, no. 11, pp. 819–833.

Chen, B., Vansteenkiste, M., Beyers, W., Boone, L., Deci, E., Van der Kaap-Deeder, J., Duriez, B., Lens, W., Matos, L., Mouratidis, A., Ryan, R., Sheldon, K., Shoenens, B., Van Petegem, S., and Verstuyf, J. (2015). Basic Psychological Need Satisfaction, Need Frustration, and Need Strength across Four Cultures. *Motivation and Emotion*, vol. 39, no. 2, pp. 216–236.

Church, A., Katigbak, M., Locke, K., Zhang, H., Shen, J., de Jesus Vargas-Flores, J., Ibáñez-Reyes, J., Tanaka-Matsumi, J., Curtis, G., Cabrera, H., Mastor, K., Alvarez, J., Ortiz, F., Simon, Y., and Ching, C. (2013). Need Satisfaction and Well-Being: Testing Self-Determination Theory in Eight Cultures. *Journal of Cross-Cultural Psychology*, vol. 44, no. 4, pp. 507–534.

Clark, A. (2006). A Note on Unhappiness and Unemployment Duration. *Applied Economics Quarterly*, vol. 52, no. 4, pp. 291–308.

Clark, A., Diener, E., Goergellis, Y., and Lucas, R. (2008). Lags and Leads in Life Satisfaction: A Test of the Baseline Hypothesis. *Economic Journal*, vol. 118, no. 529, pp. F222–F243.

Clark, A., Flèche, S., Layard, R., Powdthavee, N., and Ward, G. (2018). *The Origins of Happiness*. Princeton, NJ: Princeton University Press.

Clark, A., Frijters, P., and Shields, M. (2008). Relative Income, Happiness and Utility: An Explanation for the Easterlin Paradox and Other Puzzles. *Journal of Economic Literature*, vol. 46, no. 1, pp. 95–144.

Clark, A., and Senik, C. (2011). Is Happiness Different from Flourishing? Cross-Country Evidence from the ESS. *Revue d'Economie Politique*, vol. 121, no. 1, pp. 17–34.

Clark, A., and Senik, C. (2014a). *Happiness and Economic Growth: Lessons from Developing Countries*. Oxford, UK: Oxford University Press.

Clark, A., and Senik, C. (2014b). Income Comparisons in Chinese Villages. In A. Clark and C. Senik (eds.), *Happiness and Economic Growth*, pp. 216–239. Oxford, UK: Oxford University Press.

Clark, D. (2002). *Visions of Development: A Study of Human Values*. Cheltenham, UK: Edward Elgar.

Cohen, J. (1992). A Power Primer. *Psychological Bulletin*, vol. 112, no. 1, pp. 155–159.

Cohen, L., Pane, N., and Smith, H. (1997). Complexity of the Interpersonal Self and Affective Reactions to Interpersonal Stressors in Life and the Laboratory. *Cognitive Therapy Research*, vol. 21, no. 4, pp. 387–407.

Cohen Kaminitz, S. (2018). Happiness Studies and the Problem of Interpersonal Comparisons of Satisfaction: Two Histories, Three Approaches. *Journal of Happiness Studies*, vol. 19, no. 2, pp. 423–442.

Coleman, J., et al. (1966). *Equality of Education Opportunity*. Washington, DC: National Center for Educational Statistics.

Costanza, R., Alperovitz, G., Daly, H., Farley, J., Franco, C., Jackson, T., Kubiszewski, I., Schor, J., and Victor, P. (2012). *Building a Sustainable and Desirable Economy-in-Society-in-Nature*. New York, NY: United Nations Division for Sustainable Development.

Coyle, D. (2015). *GDP: A Brief but Affectionate History*. Oxford, UK: Princeton University Press.

Cramer, K. (2016). *The Politics of Resentment: Rural Consciousness in Wisconsin and the Rise of Scott Walker*. Chicago, IL: University of Chicago Press.

Crisp, R. (2006). Hedonism Reconsidered. *Philosophy and Phenomenological Research*, vol. 73, no. 3, pp. 619–645.

Crocetti, E., Rubini, M., and Meeus, W. (2008). Capturing the Dynamics of Identity Formation in Various Ethnic Groups: Development and Validation of a Three-Dimensional Model. *Journal of Adolescence*, vol. 31, no. 2, pp. 207–222.

Crocker, J. (2002). The Costs of Seeking Self-Esteem. *Journal of Social Issues*, vol. 58, no. 3, pp. 597–615.

Crocker, J., and Park, L. (2004). The Costly Pursuit of Self-Esteem. *Psychological Bulletin*, vol. 130, no. 3, pp. 1275–1286.

Crocker, J., and Park, L. (2012). Contingencies of Self-Worth. In M. Leary and J. Tangney (eds.), *Handbook of Self and Identity*, second edition, pp. 309–326. New York, NY: Guilford.

Cronbach, L., and Meehl, P. (1955). Construct Validity in Psychological Tests. *Psychological Bulletin*, vol. 52, no. 4, pp. 281–302.

Crowley, K., Schrager, J., and Siegler, R. (1997). Strategy Discovery as a Competitive Negotiation Between Metacognitive and Associative Knowledge. *Developmental Review*, vol. 17, no. 4, pp. 462–489.

Crowley, K., and Siegler, R. (1999). Explanation and Generalisation in Young Children's Strategy Learning. *Child Development*, vol. 70, no. 2, pp. 304–316.

Csikszentmihalyi, M. (1992). *Flow*. New York, NY: Harper and Row.

Cummins, R. (2014). Can Happiness Change? Theories and Evidence. In K. Sheldon and R. Lucas (eds.), *Stability of Happiness: Theories and Evidence on Whether Happiness can Change*, pp. 75–100. New York, NY: Academic Press.

Cummins, R., Gullone, E., and Lau, A. (2002). A Model of Subjective Well-Being Homeostasis: The Role of Personality. In E. Gullone and R. Cummins (eds.), *The Universality of Subjective Wellbeing Indicators*, pp. 7–46. Dordrecht, NL: Springer.

Cummins, R., Li, L., Wooden, M., and Stokes, M. (2014). A Demonstration of Set-Points for Subjective Well-Being. *Journal of Happiness Studies*, vol. 15, no. 1, pp. 183–206.

Daltroy, L., Larson, M., Eaton, H., Phillips, C., and Liang, M. (1999). Discrepancies Between Self-Reported and Observed Physical Function in the Elderly: The Influence of Response Shift and Other Factors. *Social Science and Medicine*, vol. 48, no. 11, pp. 1549–1561.

Daly, J., and Coates, B. (2018). *Housing Affordability: Reimagining the Australian Dream*. Melbourne, VIC: Grattan Institute.

Damasio, A. (2010). *Self Comes to Mind: Constructing the Conscious Brain*. New York, NY: Vintage.

Damàsio, B., Hauck-Filho, N., and Koller, S. (2016). Measuring Meaning in Life: An Empirical Comparison of Two Well-Known Measures. *Journal of Happiness Studies*, vol. 17, no. 1, pp. 431–445.

Davies, W. (2015). *The Happiness Industry: How the Government and Big Business Sold Us Well-Being*. New York, NY: Verso.

Davis, D., Worthington, E., and Hook, J. (2010). Humility: Review of Measurement Strategies and Conceptualization as Personality Judgement. *The Journal of Positive Psychology*, vol. 5, no. 4, pp. 243–252.

Dear, K., Dutton, K., and Fox, E. (2019). Do "Watching Eyes" Influence Anti-Social Behaviour? A Systematic Review and Meta-Analysis. *Evolution and Human Behaviour*, vol. 40, no. 3, pp. 269–280.

Deaton, A. (2013). *The Great Escape: Health, Wealth and the Origins of Inequality*. Princeton, NJ: Princeton University Press.

Deaton, A., and Stone, A. (2016). Understanding Context Effects for a Measure of Life Evaluation: How Responses Matter. *Oxford Economic Papers*, vol. 68, no. 4, pp. 861–870.

De Brigard, F. (2010). If You Like It, Does It Matter If It's Real? *Philosophical Psychology*, vol. 23, no. 1, pp. 43–57.

DeCharms, R. (1968). *Personal Causation: The Internal Affective Determinants of Behaviour*. New York, NY: Academic Press.

Dechesne, M., Janssen, J., and van Knippenberg, A. (2000). Derogation and Distancing as Terror-Management Strategies: The Moderating Role of Need for Closure and Permeability of Group Boundaries. *Journal of Personality and Social Psychology*, vol. 79, no. 6, pp. 923–932.

Dechesne, M., and Kruglanski, A. (2004). Terror's Epistemic Consequences: Existential Threat and the Quest for Certainty and Closure. In J. Greenberg, S. Koole, and T. Pyszczynski (eds.), *Handbook of Experimental Existential Psychology*, pp. 247–262. New York, NY: Guilford.

Dechesne, M., Pyszczynski, T., Arndt, J., Random, S., Sheldon, K., van Knippenberg, A., and Janssen, J. (2003). Literal and Symbolic Immortality: The Effect of Evidence of Literal Immortality on Self-Esteem in Response to Mortality Salience. *Journal of Personality and Social Psychology*, vol. 84, no. 4, pp. 722–737.

Deci, E., Koestner, R., and Ryan, R. (1999). A Meta-Analytic Review of Experiments Examining the Effects of Extrinsic Rewards on Intrinsic Motivation. *Psychological Bulletin*, vol. 125, no. 6, pp. 627–668.

Deci, E., and Ryan, R. (1985). *Intrinsic Motivation and Self-Determination in Human Behaviour*. New York, NY: Plenum.

Deci, E., and Ryan, R. (2000). The "What" and "Why" of Goal Pursuits: Human Needs and the Self-Determination of Behavior. *Psychological Inquiry*, vol. 11, no. 4, pp. 227–268.

Deci, E., and Ryan, R. (2006). Hedonia, Eudaimonia, and Well-being: An Introduction. *Journal of Happiness Studies*, vol. 9, no. 1, pp. 1–11.

Deci, E., Ryan, R., Gagné, M., Leone, D., Usunov, J., and Kornazheva, B. (2001). Need Satisfaction, Motivation, and Well-Being in the Work Organizations of a Former Eastern Bloc Country: A Cross-Cultural Study of Self-Determination. *Personality and Social Psychology Bulletin*, vol. 27, no. 9, pp. 930–942.

De Neve, J., Diener, E., Tay, L., and Xuereb, C. (2013). The Objective Benefits of Subjective Well-Being. In J. Helliwell, R. Layard, and J. Sachs (eds.), *World Happiness Report II*, pp. 54–74. New York, NY: Earth Institute, Columbia University.

De Neve, J., and Oswald, A. (2012). Estimating the Effects of Life Satisfaction and Positive Affect on Later Outcomes Using Sibling Data. *Proceedings of the National Academies of Sciences USA*, vol. 109, no. 49, pp. 19953–19958.

De Neve, J., Ward, G., De Keulenaer, F., van Landeghem, B., Kavetsos, G., and Norton, M. (2018). The Asymmetric Experience of Positive and Negative Economic Growth: Global Evidence Using Subjective Well-Being Data. *Review of Economics and Statistics*, vol. 100, no. 2, pp. 362–375.

De Neve, K., and Cooper, H. (1998). The Happy Personality: A Meta-Analysis of 137 Personality Traits and Subjective Well-Being. *Psychological Bulletin*, vol. 124, no. 2, pp. 197–229.

Devine, J., Camfield, L., and Gough, I. (2008). Autonomy or Dependence—or Both? Perspectives from Bangladesh. *Journal of Happiness Studies*, vol. 9, no. 1, pp. 105–138.

Devos, T., Hyunh, Q., and Banaji, M. (2012). Implicit Self and Identity. In M. Leary and J. Tangney (eds.), *Handbook of Self and Identity: Second Edition*, pp. 155–179.

DeYoung, C., and Tiberius, V. (2021). Value-Fulfilment from a Cybernetic Perspective: A New Psychological Theory of Well-Being. Unpublished manuscript.

Diener, E., and Biswas-Diener, R. (2008). *Happiness: Unlocking the Mysteries of Psychological Wealth*. Malden, MA: Blackwell.

Diener, E. and Fujita, F. (1995). Resources, Personal Strivings, and Subjective Well-Being: A Nomothetic and Idiographic Approach. *Journal of Personality and Social Psychology,* vol. 68, no. 5, pp. 926–935.

Diener, E., Emmons, R., Larsen, R., and Griffin, S. (1985). The Satisfaction with Life Scale. *Journal of Personality Assessment,* vol. 49, no. 1, pp. 71–75.

Diener, E., Inglehart, R., and Tay, L. (2013). Theory and Validity of Life Satisfaction Scales. *Social Indicators Research,* vol. 112, no. 3, pp. 497–527.

Diener, E., and Lucas, R. (1999). Personality and Subjective Well-Being. In D. Kahneman, E. Diener, and R. Schwarz (eds.), *Well-Being: The Foundations of Hedonic Psychology,* pp. 213–229. New York, NY: Russell Sage.

Diener, E., Lucas, R., Schimmack, W., and Helliwell, R. (2009). *Well-Being for Public Policy.* Oxford, UK: Oxford University Press.

Diener, E., Lucas, R., and Scollon, C. (2006). Beyond the Hedonic Treadmill: Revising the Adaptation Theory of Wellbeing. *American Psychology,* vol. 61, no. 4, pp. 305–314.

Diener, E., and Seligman, M. (2004). Beyond Money: Toward an Economy of Wellbeing. *Psychological Science in the Public Interest,* vol. 5, no. 1, pp. 1–31.

Diener, E., Suh, E., Lucas, R., and Smith, H. (1999). Subjective Well-Being: Three Decades of Progress. *Psychological Bulletin,* vol. 125, no. 2, pp. 276–302.

Diener, E., Wirtz, D., Tov, W., Kim-Prieto, C., Choi, D., Oishi, S., and Biswas-Diener, R. (2010). New Well-Being Measures: Short Scales to Assess Flourishing and Positive and Negative Feelings. *Social Indicators Research,* vol. 87, no. 2, pp. 143–156.

Dixon, T., and Baumeister, R. (1991). Escaping the Self: The Moderating Effect of Self-Complexity. *Personality and Social Psychology Bulletin,* vol. 17, no. 4, pp. 363–368.

Do, A., Rupert, A., and Wolford, G. (2008). Evaluations of Pleasurable Experiences: The Peak-End Rule. *Psychonomic Bulletin and Review,* vol. 15, no. 1, pp. 96–98.

Dobes, L. (2018). Making Facts and Telling Furphies with Economic Modelling: Cost-Benefit Analysis in a Post-Truth Era. In M. Fabian and R. Breunig (eds.), *Hybrid Public Policy Innovations: Contemporary Policy Beyond Ideology,* pp. 83–96. London, UK: Routledge.

Dolan, P., Peasgood, T., and White, M. (2008). Do We Really Know What Makes Us Happy? A Review of the Economic Literature on the Factors Associated with Subjective Well-Being. *Journal of Economic Psychology,* vol. 29, no. 1, pp. 94–122.

Dolan, P. (2014). *Happiness by Design.* London, UK: Penguin.

Doris, J. (2002). *Lack of Character: Personality and Moral Behavior.* New York, NY: Cambridge University Press.

Dorjee, D. (2014). *Mind, Brain and the Path to Happiness: A Guide to Buddhist Mind Training and the Neuroscience of Happiness.* London, UK: Routledge.

Dyrdal, G., and Lucas R. (2013). Reaction and Adaptation to the Birth of a Child: A Couple-Level Analysis. *Developmental Psychology,* vol. 49, no. 4, pp. 749–761.

Dryzek, J. (2002). *Deliberative Democracy and Beyond: Liberals, Critics, and Contestations.* Oxford, UK: Oxford University Press.

Dunn, E., Aknin, L., and Norton, M. (2008). Spending Money on Others Promotes Happiness. *Science,* vol. 319, no. 5870, pp. 1687–1688.

Durie, M. (2006). *Measuring Maori Wellbeing.* New Zealand Treasury Guest Lecture Series. Wellington, NZ: Treasury.

Easterlin, R. (1974). Does Economic Growth Improve the Human Lot? Some Empirical Evidence. In P. A. David and M. W. Reder (eds.), *Nations and Households in Economic Growth: Essays in Honor of Moses Abramovitz,* 89–125. New York, NY: Academic Press.

Easterlin, R., Wang, F., and Wang, S. (2017). Growth and Happiness in China, 1990–2015. In J. Helliwell, R. Layard, and J. Sachs (eds.), *World Happiness Report*. New York, NY: United Nations, ch. 3, pp. 48–83.

Ellison, C. (1991). Religious Involvement and Subjective Well-Being. *Journal of Health and Social Behaviour*, vol. 32, no. 1, pp. 80–99.

Elwyn, G., Nelson, E., Hager, A., and Price, A. (2020). Coproduction: When Users Define Quality. *British Medical Journal: Quality and Safety*, vol. 29, no. 1, pp. 711–719.

Emmons, R. (1986). Personal Strivings: An Approach to Personality and Subjective Well-Being. *Journal of Personality and Social Psychology*, vol. 51, no. 5, pp. 1058–1068.

Emmons, R. (1999). *The Psychology of Ultimate Concerns: Motivation and Spirituality in Personality*. New York, NY: Guilford.

Emmons, R. (2008). *Thanks! How Practicing Gratitude Can Make You Happier*. New York, NY: Mariner.

Emmons, R., Cheung, C., and Tehrani, K. (1998). Assessing Spirituality Through Personal Goals: Implications for Research on Religion and Subjective Well-Being. *Social Indicators Research*, vol. 45, no. 1–3, pp. 391–422.

Emmons, R., and McCullough, M. (2003). Counting Blessings Versus Burdens: An Experimental Investigation of Gratitude and Subjective Well-Being in Daily Life. *Journal of Personality and Social Psychology*, vol. 84, no. 2, pp. 377–389.

Emmons, R., and McCullough, M. (2004). *The Psychology of Gratitude*. New York, NY: Oxford University Press.

Entzeroth, L. (2001). Putting the Mentally Retarded Criminal Defendant to Death: Charting the Development of a National Consensus to Exempt the Mentally Retarded from the Death Penalty. *Alabama Law Review*, vol. 52, no. 3, pp. 911–942.

Ernest-Jones, M., Nettle, D., and Bateson, M. (2011). Effects of Eye Images on Everyday Cooperative Behaviour: A Field Experiment. *Evolution and Human Behaviour*, vol. 32, no. 2, pp. 172–178.

Eronen, M., and Bringmann, L. (2021). The Theory Crisis in Psychology: How to Move Forward. Online First at *Perspectives on Psychological Science*. DOI: 10.1177/1745691620970586.

Esfahani Smith, E. (2017). *The Power of Meaning: Crafting a Life That Matters*. New York, NY: Crown.

Fabian, M., Breunig, R., and De Neve, J. (2020). Bowling with Trump: Economic Anxiety, Racial Identification, and Well-Being in the 2016 Presidential Election. Brookings Institution Report.

Fabian, M., and Dold, M. (2021). Agentic Preferences: A Welfare Criterion for When Preferences Are Clearly Endogenous to Nudges. Unpublished manuscript.

Fabian, M., and Pykett, J. (2021). Be Happy: Navigating Normative Issues in Behavioral and Well-Being Public Policy. Online First in *Perspectives on Psychological Science*.

Fader, J. (2016). *Life as Sport: What Top Athletes Can Teach You About How to Win in Life*. Boston, MA: Da Capo.

Favara, M., and Sanchez, A. (2017). Psychosocial Competencies and Risky Behaviour in Peru. *IZA Journal of Labor and Development*, vol. 6, no. 3, pp. 1–40.

Feldman, F. (2002). The Good Life: A Defence of Attitudinal Hedonism. *Philosophy and Phenomenological Research*, vol. 65, no. 3, pp. 604–628.

Ferrer-i-Carbonell, A., and Frijters, P. (2004). How Important Is Methodology for the Estimates of the Determinants of Happiness? *The Economic Journal*, vol. 114, no. 497, pp. 641–659.

Fesser, E. (2017). *Five Proofs of the Existence of God*. San Francisco, CA: Ignatius Press.

Fivush, R., and Haden, C. (eds.) (2003). *Autobiographical Memory and the Construction of a Narrative Self*. Mahwah, NJ: Erlbaum.

Flanagan, C. (2018). Why the Left Is So Afraid of Jordan Peterson. *The Atlantic*, August 9. https://www.theatlantic.com/ideas/archive/2018/08/why-the-left-is-so-afraid-of-jordan-peterson/567110/.

Fletcher, G. (ed.), (2015a). *The Routledge Handbook of Philosophy of Well-Being*. London, UK: Routledge.

Fletcher, G. (2015b). Objective List Theories. In G. Fletcher (ed.), *The Routledge Handbook of Philosophy of Well-Being*. London, UK: Routledge, pp. 148–160.

Fleurbaey, M., and Blanchet, D. (2013). *Beyond GDP: Measuring Welfare and Assessing Sustainability*. Oxford, UK: Oxford University Press.

Fleurbaey, M., and Maniquet, F. (2011). *A Theory of Fairness and Social Welfare*. Cambridge, UK: Cambridge University Press.

Flury, J., and Ickes, W. (2007). Having a Weak Versus Strong Sense of Self: The Sense of Self Scale (SOSS). *Self and Identity*, vol. 6, no. 4, pp. 281–303.

Foster-McGregor, N., and Verspagen, B. (2016). The Role of Structural Change in the Economic Development of Asian Economies. *Asian Development Review*, vol. 33, no. 2, pp. 74–93.

Frankl, V. ([1946] 2008). *Man's Search for Meaning*. London, UK: Rider.

Frankl, V. (1969). *The Will to Meaning: Foundations and Applications of Logotherapy*. New York, NY: Meridian.

Frankl, V. (1975). *The Unconscious God*. New York, NY: Pocket Books.

Frankl, V. (1978). *The Unheard Cry for Meaning: Psychotherapy and Humanism*. New York, NY: Touchstone Books.

Frankl, V. (2000). *Recollections: An Autobiography*. Trans. J. Fabry and J. Fabry. New York, NY: Perseus Books Group.

Frankl, V. (2010). *The Feeling of Meaninglessness: A Challenge to Psychotherapy and Philosophy*. Milwaukee, WI: Marquette University Press.

Frattaroli, J. (2006). Experimental Disclosure and Its Moderators: A Meta-Analysis. *Psychological Bulletin*, vol. 132, no. 6, pp. 823–865.

Frederick, S., and Loewenstein, G. (1999). Hedonic Adaptation. In D. Kahneman, N. Schwartz, and E. Diener (eds.), *Well-Being: The Foundations of Hedonic Psychology*, pp. 302–329. New York, NY: Russell Sage.

Freitas, A., Salovey, P., and Liberman, N. (2001). Abstract and Concrete Self-Evaluative Goals. *Journal of Personality and Social Psychology*, vol. 80, no. 3, pp. 410–424.

Frey, B., and Stutzer, A. (2002). *Happiness and Economics: How the Economy and Institutions Affect Wellbeing*. Princeton, NJ: Princeton University Press.

Frey, B., and Stutzer, A. (2008). Stress That Doesn't Pay: The Commuting Paradox. *The Scandinavian Journal of Economics*, vol. 110, no. 2, pp. 339–366.

Frederickson, B. (2000). Extracting Meaning from Past Affective Experiences: The Importance of Peaks, Ends and Specific Emotions. *Cognition and Emotion*, vol. 14, no. 4, pp. 577–606.

Frederickson, B., Cohn, M., Coffey, K., Pek, J., and Finkel, S. (2008). Open Hearts Build Lives: Positive Emotions, Induced Through Loving-Kindness Meditation Build Consequential Personal Resources. *Journal of Personality and Social Psychology*, vol. 95, pp. 1045–1062.

Friedli, L., and Stearn, R. (2015). Positive Affect as Coercive Strategy: Conditionality, Activation, and the Role of Government Workfare Programs. *Critical Medical Humanities*, vol. 41, no. 1, pp. 40–47.

Frijda, N. (1986). *The Emotions*. New York, NY: Cambridge University Press.

Frijters, P., Clark, A., Krekel, C., and Layard, R. (2019). A Happy Choice: Well-Being as the Goal of Government. *Behavioural Public Policy*, vol. 4, no. 2, pp. 42–53.

Frijters, P., and Mujcic, R. (2013). Economic Choices and Status: Measuring Preferences for Income Rank. *Oxford Economic Papers*, vol. 65, no. 1, pp. 47–73.

Fritz, M., Walsh, L., and Lyubomirsky, S. (2017). Staying Happier. In M. Robertson and M. Eid (eds.), *The Happy Mind*, pp. 95–114. Cham, CH: Springer International Publishing.

Fromm, E. ([1941] 1994). *Escape from Freedom*. New York, NY: Holt Paperbacks.

Fujiwara, D., and Dolan, P. (2016). Happiness-Based Policy Analysis. In M. Adler and M. Fleurbaey (eds.), *The Oxford Handbook of Well-Being and Public Policy*, pp. 286–320. Oxford, UK: Oxford University Press.

Gagné, M. (2003). The Role of Autonomy Support and Autonomy Orientation in Prosocial Behaviour Engagement. *Motivation and Emotion*, vol. 27, no. 3, pp. 199–223.

Ganesharajah, C. (2009). *Indigenous Health and Wellbeing: The Importance of Country*. Native Title Research Report No. 1/2009. Canberra, AU: Australian Institute of Aboriginal and Torres-Strait Islander Studies AIATSIS.

Garfield, C. (1973). A Psychometric and Clinical Investigation of Frankl's Concept of Existential Vacuum and Anomie. *Psychiatry*, vol. 36, no. 4, pp. 396–408.

Gasper, D. (2004). *The Ethics of Development*. Edinburgh, SCT: Edinburgh University Press.

Gere, J., Schimmack, U., Pinkus, R., and Lockwood, P. (2011). The Effects of Romantic Partners' Goal Congruence on Affective Well-Being. *Journal of Research in Personality*, vol. 45, no. 6, pp. 549–559.

Gelfand, M. (2018). *Rule Makers, Rule Breaker: How Tight and Loose Cultures Wire Our World*. New York, NY: Scribner.

Gelfand, M., Raver, J., Nishii, L., Leslie, L., Lun, J., Lim, B., Duan, L., Almaliach, A., Ang, S., Arnadottir, J., Aycan, Z., Boehnke, K., Boski, P., Cabecinhas, R., Chan, D., Chhokar, J., D'Amato, A., Ferrer, M., Fischlmayr, I., Fischer, R., Fülöp, M., Georgas, J., Kashima, E., Kashima, Y., Kim, K., Lempereur, A., Marquez, P., Othman, R., Overlaet, B., Panagiotopoulou, P., Peltzer, K., Perez-Florizno, L., Ponomarenko, L., Realo, A., Schei, V., Schmitt, M., Smith, P., Soomro, N., Szabo, E., Taveesin, N., Toyama, M., Van de Vliert, E., Vohra, N., Ward, C., and Yamaguchi, S. (2011). Differences Between Tight and Loose Cultures: A 33 Nation Study. *Science*, vol. 332, no. 6033, pp. 1100–1104.

George, L., and Park, C. (2017). The Multidimensional Existential Meaning Scale: A Tripartite Approach to Measuring Meaning in Life. *Journal of Positive Psychology*, vol. 12, no. 6, pp. 613–627.

Gilbert, P., McEwan, K., Matos, M., and Rivis, A. (2011). Fears of Compassion: Development of Three Self-Report Measures. *Psychology and Psychotherapy: Theory, Research and Practice*, vol. 84, no. 1, pp. 239–255.

Glaeser, E. (2012). *Triumph of the City: How Our Greatest Invention Makes Us Richer, Smarter, Greener, Healthier and Happier*. New York, NY: Penguin.

Gneezy, U., Leonard, K., and List, J. (2009). Gender Differences in Competition: Evidence from a Matrilineal and a Patriarchal Society. *Econometrica*, vol. 77, no. 5, pp. 1637–1664.

Gonnerman, M., Parker, C., Lavine, H., and Huff, J. (2000). The Relationship Between Self-Discrepancies and Affective States: The Moderating Roles of Self-Monitoring and

Standpoints on the Self. *Personality and Social Psychology Bulletin*, vol. 26, no. 7, pp. 810–819.

Graham, C. (2011). *The Pursuit of Happiness: An Economy of Well-Being*. Washington, DC: Brookings Institution Press.

Graham, C. (2011). Adaptation Amidst Prosperity and Adversity: Some Insights from Happiness Around the World. *World Bank Research Observer*, vol. 26, no. 1, pp. 105–137.

Graham, C. (2012). *Happiness Around the World: The Paradox of Happy Peasants and Miserable Millionaires*. Oxford, UK: Oxford University Press.

Graham, C. (2017). *Happiness for All? Unequal Hopes and Lives in Pursuit of the American Dream*. Princeton, NJ: Princeton University Press.

Graham, C., Chattopadhyay, S., and Picon, M. (2010). Adapting to Adversity: Happiness and the 2009 Economic Crisis in the United States. *Social Research*, vol. 77, no. 2, pp. 715–748.

Graham, C., and Lora, E. (2009). *Paradox and Perception: Measuring Quality of Life in Latin America*. Washington, DC: Brookings Institution Press.

Graham, C., and Nikolova, M. (2015). Bentham or Aristotle in the Development Process? An Empirical Investigation of Capabilities and Subjective Well-Being Around the World. *World Development*, vol. 68, no. 1, pp. 163–179.

Greenberg, J., Koole, S., and Pyszczynski, T. (eds.) (2004). *Handbook of Experimental Existential Psychology*. New York, NY: Guilford.

Greene, J. (2014). *Moral Tribes: Emotion, Reason and the Gap Between Us and Them*. London, UK: Atlantic Books.

Gregory, A. (2015). Hedonism. In G. Fletcher (ed.), *Routledge Handbook of Philosophy of Well-Being*, pp. 113–123. London, UK: Routledge.

Guinote, A. (2017). How Power Affects People: Activating, Wanting, and Goal Seeking. *Annual Review of Psychology*, vol. 68, no. 1, pp. 353–381.

Guinote, A., and Vescio, T. (2010). *The Social Psychology of Power*. New York, NY: Guilford.

Haidt, J. (2001). The Emotional Dog and Its Rational Tail. *Psychological Review*, vol. 108, no. 4, pp. 814–834.

Haidt, J. (2012). *The Righteous Mind: Why Good People Are Divided by Politics and Religion*. New York, NY: Penguin.

Haidt, J., and Algoe, S. (2004). Moral Amplification and the Emotions That Attach Us to Saints and Demons. In J. Greenberg, S. Koole, and T. Pyszczynski (eds.), *Handbook of Existential Psychology*, pp. 322–335. New York, NY: Guilford.

Haley-Jones, K., and Fessler, D. (2005). Nobody's Watching? Subtle Cues Affect Generosity in an Anonymous Economic Game. *Evolution and Human Behaviour*, vol. 26, no. 3, pp. 245–256.

Hanson, R. (2013). *Hardwiring Happiness: How to Reshape Your Brain and Your Life*. London, UK: Ryder.

Hanushek, E. (1986). The Economics of Schooling: Production and Efficiency in Public Schools. *Journal of Economic Literature*, vol. 24, no. 3, pp. 1141–1177.

Harari, Y. (2011). *Sapiens: A Brief History of Humankind*. New York, NY: Harper.

Harsanyi, J. (1981). Morality and the Theory of Rational Behaviour. In A. Sen and B. Williams (eds.), *Utilitarianism and Beyond*. Cambridgeshire, UK: Cambridge University Press, pp. 39–62.

Harter, S. (1999). *The Construction of the Self*, second edition. New York, NY: Guilford.

Harter, S. (2012). Emerging Self-Processes During Childhood and Adolescence. In M. Leary and J. Tangney (eds.), *Handbook of Self and Identity: Second Edition*, pp. 680–715. New York, NY: Guilford.

Harter, S., Bresnick, S., Bouchey, H., and Whitesell, N. (1997). The Development of Multiple Role-Related Selves During Adolescence. *Development and Psychopathology*, vol. 9, no. 4, pp. 835–854.

Hausman, D. (2015). *Valuing Health: Well-Being, Freedom, and Suffering*. New York, NY: Oxford University Press.

Haybron, D. (2001). Happiness and Pleasure. *Philosophy and Phenomenological Research*, vol. 62, no. 3, pp. 501–528.

Haybron, D. (2008). *The Pursuit of Unhappiness: The Elusive Psychology of Well-Being*. Oxford, UK: Oxford University Press.

Haybron, D., and Tiberius, V. (2015). Well-Being Policy: What Standard of Well-Being? *Journal of the American Philosophical Association*, vol. 1, no. 4, pp. 712–733.

Heady, B. (2010). The Set-Point Theory of Well-Being Has Serious Flaws: On the Eve of a Scientific Revolution? *Social Indicators Research*, vol. 97, no. 1, pp. 7–21.

Heady, B., Muffels, R., and Wagner, G. (2014). National Panel Studies Show Substantial Minorities Recording Long-Term Change in Life Satisfaction: Implications for Set Point Theory. In K. Sheldon and R. Lucas (eds.), *Stability of Happiness: Theories and Evidence on Whether Happiness Can Change*, pp. 101–121. New York, NY: Academic Press.

Heathwood, C. (2015). Desire Fulfilment Theory. In G. Fletcher (ed.), *Routledge Handbook of Philosophy of Well-Being*, pp. 135–147. London, UK: Routledge.

Heidegger, M. ([1927] 1962). *Being and Time*. Trans. J. Macquarie and E. Robinson. Malden: MA: Blackwell.

Heintzelman, S., and King, L. (2014). Life Is Pretty Meaningful. *American Psychologist*, vol. 69, no. 6, pp. 561–574.

Heintzelman, S., Kushlev, K., Lutz, L., Wirtz, D., Kanippayoor, J., Leitner, D., et al. (2020). ENHANCE: Evidence for the Efficacy of a Comprehensive Intervention Program to Promote Durable Changes in Subjective Well-Being. *Journal of Experimental Psychology: Applied*, vol. 26, no. 2, pp. 360–383.

Hektner, J., Schmidt, J., and Csikszentmihalyi, M. (2007). *Experience Sampling Method: Measuring the Quality of Everyday Life*. Newbury Park, CA: Sage.

Helliwell, J. (2020). Three Questions About Happiness. *Behavioural Public Policy*, vol. 4, no. 2, pp. 177–187.

Heppen, J., and Ogilvie, D. (2003). Predicting Affect from Global Self-Discrepancies: The Dual Role of the Undesired Self. *Journal of Social and Clinical Psychology*, vol. 22, no. 4, pp. 347–368.

Hertwig, R., and Grüne-Yanoff, T. (2017). Nudging and Boosting: Steering or Empowering Good Decisions. *Perspectives on Psychological Science*, vol. 12, no. 6, pp. 973–986.

Higgins, T. (1987). Self-Discrepancy Theory: A Theory Relating Self and Affect. *Psychological Review*, vol. 94 no. 3 pp. 319–340.

Higgins, T. (1991). Development of Self-Regulatory and Self-Evaluative Processes: Costs, Benefits and Tradeoffs. In M. Gunnar and A. Sroufe (eds.), *Self-Processes and Development: The Minnesota Symposium on Child Development*, vol. 23. pp. 125–166. Hillsdale, NJ: Erlbaum.

Hill, C., Kline, K., Miller, M., Marks, E., Pinto-Coelho, K., and Zetzer, H. (2019). Development of the Meaning in Life Measure. *Counselling Psychology Quarterly*, vol. 32, no. 2, pp. 205–226.

Hindriks, F., and Douven, I. (2018). Nozick's Experience Machine: An Empirical Study. *Philosophical Psychology*, vol. 31, no. 2, pp. 278–298.

Hirai, T. (2017). *The Creation of the Human Development Approach*. Basingstoke, UK: Palgrave Macmillan.

Hixon, J., and Swann, W. (1993). When Does Introspection Bear Fruit? Self-Reflection, Self-Insight and Interpersonal Choices. *Journal of Personality and Social Psychology*, vol. 64, no. 1, pp. 34–43.

Hochschild, A. (2016). *Strangers in Their Own Land: Anger and Mourning on the American Right*. New York, NY: The New Press.

Howard, G., and Dailey, P. (1979). Response-Shift Bias: A Source of Contamination of Self-Report Measures. *Journal of Applied Psychology*, vol. 66, no. 2, pp. 144–150.

Howell, R., Chenot, D., Hill, G., and Howell, C. (2011). Momentary Happiness: The Role of Psychological Need Satisfaction. *Journal of Happiness Studies*, vol. 12, no. 1, pp. 1–15.

Human Rights Watch (2018). *China: Events of 2018*. https://www.hrw.org/world-report/2019/country-chapters/china-and-tibet.

Huppert, F. A., and So, T. T. C. (2013). Flourishing Across Europe: Application of a New Conceptual Framework for Defining Well-Being. *Social Indicators Research*, vol. 110, no. 3, pp. 837–861.

Hursthouse, R. (1999). *On Virtue Ethics*. Oxford, UK: Oxford University Press.

Husser, J., and Fernandez, K. (2018). We Are Happier than We Realize: Underestimation and Conflation in Measuring Happiness. *Journal of Happiness Studies*, vol. 19, no. 2, pp. 587–606.

Hutz, C., Midgett, A., Pacico, J., Bastianello, M., and Zanon, C. (2014). The Relationship of Hope, Optimism, Self-Esteem, Subjective Well-Being, and Personality in Brazilians and Americans. *Psychology*, vol. 5, no. 6, pp. 514–522.

Ilardi, B., Leone, D., Kasser, T., and Ryan, R. (1993). Employee and Supervisor Ratings of Motivation: Main Effects and Discrepancies Associated with Job Satisfaction and Adjustment in a Factory Setting. *Journal of Applied Social Psychology*, vol. 23, no. 21, pp. 1789–1805.

Iyengar, S., and Lepper, M. (1999). Rethinking the Value of Choice: A Cultural Perspective on Intrinsic Motivation. *Journal of Personality and Social Psychology*, vol. 76 no. 3 pp. 349–366.

Jacobs-Bao, K., and Lyubomirsky, S. (2013). The Rewards of Happiness. In I. Boniwell, S. David and C. Ayers (eds.), *Oxford Handbook of Happiness*, pp. 119–133. Oxford, UK: University Press.

James, W. (1890). *Principles of Psychology*. Chicago. MI: Encyclopaedia Britannica.

Jang, H., Kim, E., and Reeve, J. (2012). Longitudinal Test of Self-Determination Theory's Motivation Mediation Model in a Naturally Occurring Classroom Context. *Journal of Educational Psychology*, vol. 104, no. 4, pp. 1175–1188.

Jang, H., Reeve, J., Ryan, R., and Kim, A. (2009). Can Self-Determination Theory Explain What Underlies the Productive, Satisfying Learning Experiences of Collectivistically Oriented Korean Students? *Journal of Educational Psychology*, vol. 101, no. 3, pp. 644–661.

Jang, H., Reeve, J., and Deci, E. (2010). Engaging Students in Learning Activities: It Is Not Autonomy Support or Structure, but Autonomy Support and Structure. *Journal of Educational Psychology*, vol. 102, no. 3, pp. 588–600.

Jazaieri, H., Jinpa, G., McGonigal, K., Rosenberg, E., Finkelstein, J., Simon-Thomas, E., Cullen, M., Doty, J., Gross, J., and Goldin, P. (2013). Enhancing Compassion:

A Randomised Controlled Trial of a Compassion Cultivation Program. *Journal of Happiness Studies*, vol. 14, no. 4, pp. 1113–1126.

Jevons, W. (1871). *The Theory of Political Economy*. New York, NY: Macmillan and Co.

Johnson, E., Vincent, N., and Ross, L. (1997). Self-Deception Versus Self-Esteem in Buffering the Negative Effects of Failure. *Journal of Research in Personality*, vol. 31, no. 3, pp. 385–405.

Jung, C. ([1928] 2017). The Spiritual Problem of Modern Man. In W. Dell and C. Baynes (trans.), *Modern Man in Search of a Soul*, pp. 226–254. Eastford, CT: Martino Fine Books.

Jupp, E., Pykett, J., and Smith, F. (eds.), (2016). *Emotional States: Sites and Spaces of Affective Governance*. London, UK: Routledge.

Kabat-Zinn, J. (2003). Mindfulness-Based Interventions in Context: Past, Present and Future. *Clinical Psychology: Science and Practice*, vol. 10, no. 2, pp. 144–156.

Kagan, S. (1984). Me and My Life. *Proceedings of the Aristotelian Society*, vol. 94, pp. 309–324.

Kahneman, D. (1999). Objective Happiness. In D. Kahneman, E. Diener, and N. Schwartz (eds.), *Wellbeing: The Foundations of Hedonic Psychology*, pp. 3–25. New York, NY: Russell Sage Foundation.

Kahneman, D. (2011). *Thinking, Fast and Slow*. New York, NY: Penguin.

Kahneman, D., and Deaton, A. (2010). High Income Improves Evaluation of Life but Not Emotional Well-Being. *Proceedings of the National Academies of Sciences USA*, vol. 107, no. 38, pp. 16489–16493.

Kahneman, D., Diener, E., and Schwarz, N. (1999). *Wellbeing: The Foundations of Hedonic Psychology*. New York, NY: Russell Sage Foundation.

Kahneman, D., Frederickson, B., Schreiber, C., and Redelmeier, D. (1993). When More Pain Is Preferred to Less: Adding a Better End. *Psychological Science*, vol. 4, no. 6, pp. 401–405.

Kahneman, D., and Krueger, A. (2006). Developments in the Measurement of Subjective Well-Being. *Journal of Economic Perspectives*, vol. 20, no. 1, pp. 3–24.

Kahneman, D., Krueger, A. B., Schkade, D. A., Schwarz, N., and Stone, A. (2004a). A Survey Method for Characterising Daily Life Experiences: The Day Reconstruction Method. *Science*, vol. 306, no. 5702, pp. 1776–1780.

Kahneman, D., Krueger, A., Schkade, D., Schwarz, N., and Stone, A. (2004b). Toward National Well-Being Accounts. *American Economic Review*, vol. 94, pp. 429–434.

Kahneman, D., Krueger, A., Schkade, D., Schwarz, N., and Stone, A. (2006). Would You Be Happier if You Were Richer? A Focusing Illusion. *Science*, vol. 30, no. 5782, pp. 1908–1910.

Kahneman, D., and Tversky, A. (1979). Prospect Theory: An Analysis of Decision Under Risk. *Econometrica*, vol. 47, no. 2, pp. 263–291.

Kaiser, C. (2021). Using Memories to Assess the Intrapersonal Comparability of Wellbeing Reports. *Journal of Economic Behaviour and Organisation*, vol. 193, no. 1, pp. 410–442.

Kapteyn, A., Smith, J., and Van Soest, A. (2013). Are Americans Really Less Happy with Their Incomes? *Review of Income and Wealth*, vol. 59, no. 1, pp. 44–65.

Kashdan, T. B., Biswas-Diener, R., and King, L. A. (2008). Reconsidering Happiness: The Costs of Distinguishing Between Hedonics and Eudaimonia. *The Journal of Positive Psychology*, vol. 3, no. 4, pp. 219–233.

Kasser, T. (2003). *The High Price of Materialism*. Cambridge, MA: MIT Press.

Kasser, T., and Ahuvia, A. (2002). Materialistic Values and Well-Being in Business Students. *European Journal of Social Psychology,* vol. 32, no. 1, pp. 137–146.

Kasser, T., and Ryan, R. (1993). A Dark Side of the American Dream: Correlates of Financial Success as a Central Life Aspiration. *Journal of Personality and Social Psychology,* vol. 65, no. 2, pp. 410–422.

Kasser, T., and Ryan, R. (1996). Further Examining the American Dream: Differential Correlates of Intrinsic and Extrinsic Goals. *Personality and Social Psychology Bulletin,* vol. 22, no. 3, pp. 280–287.

Kasser, T., and Ryan, R. (2001). Be Careful What You Wish For: Optimal Functioning and the Relative Attainment of Intrinsic and Extrinsic Goals. In P. Schmuck and K. Sheldon (eds.), *Life Goals and Well-Being: Towards a Positive Psychology of Human Striving,* pp. 116–131. Ashland, OH: Hogrefe and Huber.

Kaufman, S., Yaden, D., Hyde, E., and Tsukayama, E. (2019). The Light Triad Versus Dark Triad of Personality: Contrasting Two Very Different Profiles of Human Nature. *Frontiers in Psychology,* vol. 10, no. 1, pp. 1–26.

Keng, S., Smoski, M., and Robbins, C. (2011). Effects of Mindfulness on Psychological Health: A Review of Empirical Studies. *Clinical Psychology Review,* vol. 31, no. 6, pp. 1041–1056.

Keyes, C., Schmotkin, D., and Ryff, C. (2002). Optimizing Well-Being: The Empirical Encounter of Two Traditions. *Journal of Personality and Social Psychology,* vol. 82, no. 6, pp. 179–196.

Kierkegaard, S. ([1843] 2005). *Fear and Trembling.* Trans. A. Hannay. London, UK: Penguin.

Kierkegaard, S. ([1849] 2008). *The Sickness unto Death.* Trans. A. Hannay. London, UK: Penguin.

King, L., and Hicks, J. (2012). Positive Affect and Meaning in Life: The Intersection of Hedonism and Eudaimonia. In P. Wong (ed.), *The Human Quest for Meaning: Theories, Research and Applications,* second edition, pp. 125–142. London, UK: Routledge.

King, L., and Hicks, J. (2020). The Science of Meaning in Life. *Annual Review of Psychology,* vol. 72, no. 7, pp. 1–24.

King, L., Hicks, J., Krull, J., and Del Gaiso, A. (2006). Positive Affect and the Experience of Meaning in Life. *Journal of Personality and Social Psychology,* vol. 90, no. 1, pp. 179–196.

Knabe, A., and Rätzel, S. (2011). Scarring or Scaring? The Psychological Impact of Past Unemployment and Future Employment Risk. *Economica,* vol. 78, no. 31, pp. 283–293.

Knight, J., and Gunatilaka, R. (2014). Subjective Well-Being and Social Evaluation: A Case Study of China. In A. Clark and C. Senik (eds.), *Happiness and Economic Growth,* pp. 179–215. Oxford, UK: Oxford University Press.

Kolb, D. (2009). Too Bad for Women or Does It Have to Be? Gender and Negotiation Research over the Past Twenty-Five Years. *Negotiation Journal,* vol. 25, no. 4, pp. 515–531.

Köke, S., and Perino, G. (2017). For "Better" or "Worse": A Direct Approach to Elicit Preference Rankings from Life Satisfaction Data. **WiSo-HH Working Paper No. 2017/43.**

Kraut, R. (1989). *Aristotle on the Human Good.* Princeton, NJ: Princeton University Press.

Kraut, R. (2009). *What Is Good and Why? The Ethics of Well-Being.* Cambridge, MA: Harvard University Press.

Krekel, C., Ward, G., and De Neve, J. (2019). Employee Well-Being, Productivity, and Firm Performance. Saïd Business School Working Paper 2019-04.

Kring, A. (2008). Emotion Disturbances as Transdiagnostic Processes in Psychopathology. In M. Lewis, J. Haviland-Jones, and L. Feldman-Barrett (eds.), *Handbook of Emotions*, third edition, pp. 691–708. New York, NY: Guilford.

Krueger, A., and Schkade, D. (2008). The Reliability of Subjective Well-Being Measures. *Journal of Public Economics*, vol. 92, no. 8–9, pp. 1833–1845.

Kruger, J., and Dunning, D. (1999). Unskilled and Unaware of It: How Difficulties in Recognising One's Own Incompetence Lead to Inflated Self-Assessment. *Journal of Personality and Social Psychology*, vol. 77, no. 6, pp. 1121–1134.

Kruse, E., Chancellor, J., Ruberton, P., and Lyubomirsky, S. (2014). An Upward Spiral Between Gratitude and Humility. *Social Psychological and Personality Science*, vol. 5, no. 7, pp. 805–814.

Kuhl, J., and Koole, S. (2004). Workings of the Will: A Functional Approach. In J. Greenberg, S. Koole, and T. Pyszczynski (eds.), *Handbook of Experimental Existential Psychology*, pp. 431–448. New York, NY: Guilford.

Kuppens, P., Realo, A., and Diener, E. (2008). The Role of Positive and Negative Emotions in Life Satisfaction Judgements across Nations. *Journal of Personality and Social Psychology*, vol. 95, no. 1, pp. 66–75.

Lacey, H., Loewenstein, G., Riis, J., Fagerlin, A., Smith, D., and Ubel, P. (2008). Are They Really That Happy? Exploring Scale Norming in Estimates of Well-Being. *Health Psychology*, vol. 27, no. 6, pp. 669–675.

Lafont, C. (2015). Deliberation, Participation, and Democratic Legitimacy: Should Deliberative Mini Publics Shape Public Policy? *The Journal of Political Philosophy*, vol. 23, no. 1, pp. 40–63.

La Guardia, J., Ryan, R., Couchman, C., and Deci, E. (2000). Within-Person Variation in Security of Attachment: A Self-Determination Theory Perspective on Attachment, Need Fulfilment and Well-Being. *Journal of Personality and Social Psychology*, vol. 79, no. 3, pp. 367–384.

Laurin, J., Joussemet, M., Tremblay, R., and Boivin, M. (2015). Early Forms of Controlling Parenting and the Development of Childhood Anxiety. *Journal of Child and Family Studies*, vol. 24, no. 11, pp. 3279–3292.

Layard, R. (2005). *Happiness: Lessons from a New Science*. New York, NY: Penguin.

Layard, R., Clark, D., Knapp, M., and Mayraz, G. (2007). Cost-Benefit Analysis of Psychological Therapy. *National Institute Economic Review*, no. 202, pp. 90–98.

Layard, R., and Ward, G. (2020). *Can We Be Happier? Evidence and Ethics*. London, UK: Pelican Books.

Leary, M. (2012). Sociometer Theory. In P. Van Lange, A. Kruglanski, and E. Higgins (eds.), *Handbook of Theories of Social Psychology*, pp. 151–159. Thousand Oaks, CA: Sage Publications Ltd.

Leary, M., and Baumeister, R. (2000). The Nature and Function of Self-Esteem: Sociometer Theory. *Advances in Experimental Social Psychology*, vol. 32, no. 1, pp. 1–62.

LeBar, M. (2013). *The Value of Living Well*. Oxford, UK: Oxford University Press.

Lerner, J., and Tetlock, P. (2003). Bridging Individual, Interpersonal and Institutional Approaches to Judgement and Decision Making: The Impact of Accountability on Cognitive Bias. In S. Schneider and J. Shanteau (eds.), *Emerging Perspectives on Judgement and Decision Research*, pp. 431–457. Cambridge, UK: Cambridge University Press.

Lewis, M. (2008). Self-Conscious Emotions: Embarrassment, Pride, Shame and Guilt. In M. Lewis, J. Haviland-Jones, and L. Feldman-Barrett (eds.), *Handbook of Emotions: Third Edition*, pp. 742–756. New York, NY: Guilford.

Lim, C., and Putnam, R. (2010). Religion, Social Networks and Life Satisfaction. *American Sociological Review*, vol. 75, no. 6, pp. 914–933.

Lindqvist, E., Östling, R., and Cesarini, D. (2008). Long Run Effects of Lottery Wealth on Psychological Well-Being. *The Review of Economic Studies*, vol. 87, no. 6, pp. 2703–2726.

Linville, P. (1987). Self-Complexity as a Cognitive Buffer Against Stress-Related Illness and Depression. *Journal of Personality and Social Psychology*, vol. 52, no. 4, pp. 663–676.

Little, B. (2006). Personality Science and Self-Regulation: Personal Projects as Integrative Units. *Applied Psychology: International Review*, vol. 55, no. 3, pp. 419–427.

Little, B. (2015). The Integrative Challenge in Personality Science: Personal Projects as Units of Analysis. *Journal of Research in Personality*, vol. 56, no. 1, pp. 93–101.

Locke, E., and Latham, G. (1990). *A Theory of Goal-Setting and Task Performance*. Englewood Cliffs, NJ: Prentice-Hall.

Loewenstein, G., and Ubel, P. (2008). Hedonic Adaptation and the Role of Decision and Experience Utility in Public Policy. *Journal of Public Economics*, vol. 92, no. 8–9, pp. 1795–1810.

Lordan, G., and McGuire, A. (2018). *Healthy Minds Interim Paper*. London, UK: Education Endowment Foundation.

Lucas, R. (2007). Long-Term Disability Is Associated with Lasting Changes in Subjective Well-Being: Evidence from two Nationally Representative Longitudinal Studies. *Journal of Personality and Social Psychology*, vol. 92, no. 4, pp. 717–730.

Lucas, R., Clark, A. E., Georgellis, Y., and Diener, E. (2003). Re-Examining Adaptation and the Set Point Model of Happiness: Reactions to Changes in Marital Status. *Journal of Personality and Social Psychology*, vol. 84, pp. 527–539.

Lucas, R., Clark, A. E., Georgellis, Y., and Diener, E. (2004). Unemployment Alters the Set Point for Life Satisfaction. *Psychological Science*, vol. 15, no. 1, pp. 8–13.

Lucas, R., and Diener, E. (2009). Personality and Subjective Wellbeing. In E. Diener (ed.) *The Collected Works of Ed Diener*. Dordrecht, NL: Springer Science, Social Indicators Research Series 37, pp. 75–102.

Lucas, R., Diener, E., and Suh, E. (1996). Discriminant Validity of Well-Being Measures. *Journal of Social and Personality Psychology*, vol. 71, no. 3, pp. 616–628.

Lucas, R., and Donnellan, M. (2007). How Stable Is Happiness? Using the STARTS Model to Estimate the Stability of Life Satisfaction. *Journal of Research in Personality*, vol. 41, no. 5, pp. 1091–1098.

Luhmann, M., Hoffman, W., Eid, M., and Lucas, R. (2012). Subjective Well-Being and Adaptation to Life Events: A Meta-Analysis. *Journal of Personality and Social Psychology*, vol. 102, no. 3, pp. 592–615.

Lykken, D. (1999). *Happiness: What Studies in Twins Show Us About Nature, Nurture and the Happiness Set-Point*. New York, NY: Golden Books.

Lykken, D., and Tellegen, A. (1996). Happiness Is a Stochastic Phenomenon. *Psychological Science*, vol. 7, no. 3, pp. 186–189.

Lynch, M., La Guardia, J., and Ryan, R. (2009). On Being Yourself in Different Cultures: Ideal and Actual Self-Concept, Autonomy Support, and Well-Being in China, Russia, and the United States. *Journal of Positive Psychology*, vol. 4, no. 4, pp. 290–304.

Lyubomirsky, S., Boehm, J., Kasri, F., and Zehm, K. (2011). The Cognitive and Hedonic Costs of Dwelling on Achievement-Related Negative Experiences: Implications for Enduring Happiness and Unhappiness. *Emotion*, vol. 11, no. 5, pp. 1152–1167.

Lyubomirsky, S., and Ross, L. (1999). Changes in Attractiveness of Elected, Rejected and Precluded Alternatives: A Comparison of Happy and Unhappy Individuals. *Journal of Personality and Social Psychology*, vol. 73, pp. 1141–1157.

Lyubomirsky, S., Sousa, L., and Dickerhoof, R. (2006). The Costs and Benefits of Writing, Talking and Thinking About Life's Triumphs and Defeats. *Journal of Personality and Psychology*, vol. 90, no. 4, pp. 692–708.

MacDonald, G., and Leary, M. (2012). Individual Differences in Self-Esteem. In M. Leary and J. Tangney (eds.), *Handbook of Self and Identity: Second Edition*, pp. 354–378. New York, NY: Guilford.

Marcus, G. (2004). *The Birth of the Mind: How a Tiny Number of Genes Create the Complexity of Human Thought*. New York, NY: Basic Books.

Markus, H., and Kitayama, S. (2003). Models of Agency: Sociocultural Diversity in the Construction of Action. In V. Murphy-Berman and J. Berman (eds.), *Nebraska Symposium on Motivation*, vol. 49, pp. 1–57. Lincoln, NE: University of Nebraska Press.

Marsh, H., Huppert, F., Donald, J., Horwood, M., and Sahdra, B. (2020). The Well-Being Profile (WB-Pro): Creating a Theoretically Based Multidimensional Measure of Well-Being to Advance Theory, Research, Policy, and Practice. *Psychological Assessment*, vol. 32, no. 3, pp. 294–313.

Martela, F., and Ryan, R. (2016). The Benefits of Benevolence: Basic Psychological Needs, Beneficence, and the Enhancement of Well-Being. *Journal of Personality*, vol. 84, no. 6, pp. 750–764.

Martela, F., and Sheldon, K. (2019). Clarifying the Concept of Well-Being: Psychological Need Satisfaction as the Common Core Connecting Eudaimonic and Subjective Well-Being. *Review of General Psychology*, vol. 23, no. 4, pp. 458–474.

Martin, L. Campbell, W., and Henry, C. (2004). The Roar of Awakening: Mortality Acknowledgement as a Call to Authentic Living. In J. Greenberg, S. Koole, and T. Pyszczynski (eds.), *Handbook of Existential Psychology*, pp. 431–448. New York, NY: Guilford.

Matthews, G. (2008). Finding and Keeping Purpose in Life: Wellbeing and Ikigai in Japan and Elsewhere. In G. Matthews and C. Izquierdo (eds.), *Pursuits of Happiness: Well-being in Anthropological Perspective*. New York, NY: Berghahn Books, pp. 167–185.

McAdams, D. (1993). *The Stories We Live By: Personal Myths and the Making of the Self*. New York, NY: William Morrow & Co.

McAdams, D., and Janis, L. (2004). Narrative Identity and Narrative Therapy. In L. Angus and J. McLeod, *The Handbook of Narrative and Psychotherapy*, pp. 158–171, Thousand Oaks, CA: Sage.

McAdams, D., and McLean, K. (2013). Narrative Identity. *Current Directions in Psychological Science*, vol. 22, no. 3, pp. 233–238.

McClelland, T. (2013). *Nothin' but Blue Skies: The Heyday, Hard Times, and Hopes of America's Industrial Heartland*. New York, NY: Bloomsbury Press.

McClimans, L., Bickenbach, J., Westerman, M., and Schwartz, C. (2013). Philosophical Perspectives on Response Shift. *Quality of Life Research*, vol. 22, no. 7, pp. 1871–1878.

McConnell, A., Strain, L., Brown, C., and Rydell, J. (2009). The Simple Life: On the Benefits of Low Self-Complexity. *Personality Psychology Bulletin*, vol. 35, no. 7, pp. 823–835.

McCullough, M., Emmons, R., and Tsang, J. (2002). The Grateful Disposition: A Conceptual and Empirical Topography. *Journal of Personality and Social Psychology*, vol. 82, no. 1, pp. 112–127.

McCullough, M., Kimeldorf, M., and Cohen, A. (2008). An Adaptation for Altruism? The Social Causes, Social Effects and Social Evolution of Gratitude. *Current Directions in Psychological Science*, vol. 17, no. 4, pp. 281–285.

McGregor, D., Morelli, P., Matsuoko, J., Rodenhurst, R., Konh, N., and Spencer, M. (2003). An Ecological Model of Native Hawaiian Well-Being. *Pacific Health Dialogue*, vol. 10, no. 1, pp. 106–128.

McGregor, I. (2003). Defensive Zeal: Compensatory Conviction About Attitudes, Values, Goals, Groups and Self-Definition in the Face of Personal Uncertainty. In S. Spencer, S. Fein, M. Zanna, and J. Olson (eds.), *Motivated Social Perception: The Ontario Symposium*, vol. 9, pp. 73–92. Mahwah, NJ: Erlbaum.

McGregor, I. (2004). Zeal, Identity and Meaning: Going to Extremes to Be One Self. In J. Greenberg, S. Koole, and T. Pyszczynski (eds.), *Handbook of Existential Psychology*, pp. 182–199. New York, NY: Guilford.

McGregor, I. (2009). Offensive Defensiveness: Toward an Integrative Neuroscience of Compensatory Zeal After Mortality Salience, Personal Uncertainty and Other Poignant Self-Threats. *Psychological Inquiry*, vol. 17, no. 4, pp. 299–308.

McGregor, I., and Holmes, J. (1999). How Storytelling Shapes Memory and Impressions of Relationship Events over Time. *Journal of Personality and Social Psychology*, vol. 76, no. 3, pp. 403–419.

McGregor, I., and Marigold, D. (2003). Defensive Zeal and the Uncertain Self: What Makes You So Sure? *Journal of Personality and Social Psychology*, vol. 85, no. 5, pp. 838–852.

McGregor, I., Prentice, M., and Nash, K. (2009). Personal Uncertainty Management by Reactive Approach Motivation. *Psychological Inquiry*, vol. 20, no. 4, pp. 225–229.

McGregor, I., Zanna, M., Holmes, J., and Spencer, S. (2001). Compensatory Conviction in the Face of Personal Uncertainty: Going to Extremes to Be Oneself. *Journal of Personality and Social Psychology*, vol. 80, no. 3, pp. 838–852.

Meiklejohn, J., Phillips, C., Freedman, M., Griffin, M., Biegel, G., Roach, A., et al. (2012). Integrating Mindfulness Training into K–12 Education: Fostering the Resilience of Teachers and Students. *Mindfulness*, vol. 3, no. 1, pp. 291–307.

Mill, J. S. (1863). *Utilitarianism*. London, UK: Fields, Osgood & Company. Accessed on 12/08/2017 from: https://www.utilitarianism.com/mill1.htm.

Moore, M., and Fresco, D. (2012). Depressive Realism: A Meta-Analytic Review. *Clinical Psychology Review*, vol. 32, no. 6, pp. 496–509.

Morf, C., and Mischel, W. (2012). The Self as a Psycho-Social Dynamic Processing System: Towards a Converging Science of Selfhood. In M. Leary and J. Tangney (eds.), *Handbook of Self and Identity: Second Edition*, pp. 21–49. New York, NY: Guilford.

Morgan, J., and Farsides, T. (2009). Measuring Meaning in Life. *Journal of Happiness Studies*, vol. 10, no. 1, pp. 197–214.

Morisano, D., Hirsh, J., Peterson, J., Pihl, R., and Shore, B. (2010). Setting, Elaborating, and Reflecting on Personal Goals Improves Academic Performance. *Journal of Applied Psychology*, vol. 95, no. 2, pp. 255–264.

Munger, M. (2013). Recycling: Can It Be Wrong, When It Feels So Right? *Cato Unbound*, June 2013. https://www.cato-unbound.org/2013/06/03/michael-c-munger/recycling-can-it-be-wrong-when-it-feels-so-right/

Muriwai, E., Houkamau, C., and Sibley, C. (2015). Culture as Cure? The Protective Function of Maori Cultural Efficacy on Psychological Distress. *New Zealand Journal of Psychology*, vol. 44, no. 2, pp. 14–24.

Mutz, D. (2018). Status Threat, Not Economic Hardship, Explains the 2016 Presidential Vote. *PNAS*, vol. 115, no. 19, pp. E4330–E4339.

Neff, K., and Vonk, R. (2009). Self-Compassion Versus Global Self-Esteem: Two Different Ways of Relating to Oneself. *Journal of Personality*, vol. 77, no. 1, pp. 23–50.

Nehamas, A. (1985). *Nietzsche: Life as Literature*. Cambridge, MA: Harvard University Press.

Nelson, K. (2003). Narrative and Self, Myth and Memory: Emergence of the Cultural Self. In R. Fivush, and C. Haden (eds.), *Autobiographical Memory and the Construction of a Narrative Self*, pp. 3–28. Mahwah, NJ: Erlbaum.

Nelson, K., and Lyubomirsky, S. (2012). Finding Happiness: Tailoring Positive Activities for Optimal Well-Being Benefits. In M. Tugade, M. Shiota, and L. Kirby (eds.), *Handbook of Positive Emotions*, pp. 275–293. New York, NY: Guilford.

Nelson, K., and Lyubomirsky, S. (2016). Gratitude. In S. Friedman, (ed.), *Encyclopedia of Mental Health*, second edition, vol. 2, pp. 277–280. Waltham, MA: Academic Press.

Nettle, D., Harper, Z., Kidson, A., Stone, R., Penton-Voak, I., and Bateson, M. (2013). The Watching Eyes Effect in the Dictator Game: It's Not How Much You Give, It's Being Seen to Give Something. *Evolution and Human Behaviour*, vol. 34, no. 1, pp. 35–40.

Newcomb, M., and Harlow, L. (1986). Life Events and Substance Use Among Adolescents: Mediating Effects of Perceived Loss of Control and Meaninglessness in Life. *Journal of Personality and Social Psychology*, vol. 51, no. 3, pp. 564–577.

Ng, W., and Diener, E. (2014). What Matters to the Rich and the Poor? Subjective Well-Being, Financial Satisfaction, and Postmaterialist Needs Across the World. *Journal of Personality and Social Psychology*, vol. 107, no. 2, pp. 326–338.

Nietzsche, F. ([1881] 1996). *Daybreak*. Trans. R. Hollingdale. Cambridge, UK: Cambridge University Press.

Nietzsche, F. ([1891] 1978). *Thus Spoke Zarathustra: A Book for None and All*. New York, NY: Penguin.

Nietzsche, F. ([1885] 1990). *The Antichrist*. Trans. R. J. Hollingdale. New York, NY: Penguin.

Nietzsche, F. ([1886] 2000). *Beyond Good and Evil: Prelude to a Philosophy of the Future*. Trans. W. Kaufmann. New York, NY: Modern Library.

Nietzsche, F. ([1887] 1974). *The Gay Science*, second edition. Trans. W. Kaufmann. New York, NY: Vintage Books.

Nietzsche, F. ([1888] 2000). *The Genealogy of Morals: A Polemic*. Trans. W. Kaufmann. New York, NY: Modern Library.

Nietzsche, F. ([1889] 1990). *The Twilight of the Idols: Or How to Philosophise with a Hammer*. Trans. R. Hollingdale. New York, NY: Penguin.

Nolen-Hoeksema, S., Wisco, B., and Lyubomirsky, S. (2008). Rethinking Rumination. *Perspectives on Psychological Science*, vol. 3, no. 5, pp. 400–424.

Nolte, S., Elseworth, G., Sinclair, A., and Osborne, R. (2009). A Test of Measurement Invariance Fails to Support the Application of Then-Test Questions as a Remedy to Response Shift Bias. *Journal of Clinical Epidemiology*, vol. 62, no. 11, pp. 1173–1180.

Norman, G. (2003). Hi! How Are You? Response Shift, Implicit Theories and Differing Epistemologies. *Quality of Life Research*, vol. 12, no. 3, pp. 239–249.

Norton, D. (1976). *Personal Destinies: A Philosophy of Ethical Individualism*. Princeton, NJ: Princeton University Press.

Nowlis, V. (1965). Research with Mood Adjective Checklist. In S. Thompkins and C. Isard (eds.), *Affect, Cognition and Personality*. New York, NY: Springer, pp. 171–183.

Nozick, R. (1974). *Anarchy, State and Utopia*. New York, NY: Basic Books.

Nunnally, J., and Bernstein, I. (1994). *Psychometric Theory*. New York, NY: McGraw-Hill.

Nussbaum, M. (2000). *Women and Human Development: The Capabilities Approach*. Cambridge, UK: Cambridge University Press.

Oakley, B. (2008). *Evil Genes: Why Rome Fell, Hitler Rose, Enron Failed, and My Sister Stole My Mother's Boyfriend*. Amherst, MI: Prometheus Books.

Oakley, B., Knafo, A., Madhavan, G., and Wilson, D. (2012). *Pathological Altruism*. New York, NY: Oxford University Press.

Odermatt, R., and Stutzer, A. (2019). (Mis-)Predicted Subjective Well-Being Following Life Events. *Journal of the European Economic Association*, vol. 17, no. 1, pp. 245–283.

OECD. (2013). *Guidelines for Measuring Subjective Well-being*. Paris, FR: Organisation for Economic Cooperation and Development.

Oishi, S., Kushlev, K., and Schimmack, U. (2018). Progressive Taxation, Income Inequality, and Happiness. *American Psychologist*, vol. 73, no. 2, pp. 157–168.

Okulicz-Kozaryn, A. (2015). *Happiness and Place: Why Life Is Better Outside the City*. Basingstoke, UK: Palgrave Macmillan.

Okulicz-Kozaryn, A. (2019). Are We Happier Among Our Own Race? *Economics and Sociology*, vol. 12, no. 2, pp. 11–35.

Oswald, A. (2008). On the Curvature of the Reporting Function from Objective Reality to Subjective Feelings. *Economics Letters*, vol. 100, pp. 369–372.

Oswald, A., and Powdthavee, N. (2008). Does Happiness Adapt? A Longitudinal Study of Disability with Implications for Economists and Judges. *Journal of Public Economics*, vol. 92, no. 5–6, pp. 1061–1077.

Oxford University Archives (2007). First Woman Graduate of the University. Bodleian Libraries. https://www.bodleian.ox.ac.uk/oua/enquiries/first-woman-graduate.

Oyserman, D., Elmore, K., and Smith, G. (2012). Self, Self-Concept and Identity. In M. Leary and J. Tangney (eds.), *Handbook of Self and Identity: Second Edition*, pp. 21–49. New York, NY: Guilford.

Oyserman, D., and Markus, H. (1990). Possible Selves and Delinquency. *Journal of Personality and Social Psychology*, vol. 59, no. 1, pp. 112–125.

Pan, J. (2015). Gender Segregation in Occupations: the Role of Tipping and Social Interactions. *Journal of Labor Economics*, vol. 33, no. 2, pp. 327–371.

Parfit, D. (1984). *Reasons and Persons*. Oxford, UK: Clarendon.

Pavot, W., and Diener, E. (1993). Review of the Satisfaction with Life Scale. *Psychological Assessment*, vol. 5, no. 2, pp. 164–172.

Peterson, C., and Seligman, M. (2004). *Personal Strengths and Virtues: A Handbook and Classification*. New York, NY: Oxford University Press.

Peterson, J. (1999). *Maps of Meaning: The Architecture of Belief*. London, UK: Routledge.

Phillips, A., and Silvia, P. (2010). Individual Differences in Self-Discrepancies and Emotional Experience: Do Distinct Discrepancies Predict Distinct Emotions? *Personality and Individual Differences*, vol. 49, no. 2, pp. 148–151.

Phillips, J., De Freitas, J., Mott, C., Gruber, J., and Knobe, J. (2017). True Happiness: The Role of Morality in the Folk Concept of Happiness. *Journal of Experimental Psychology: General*, vol. 146, no. 2, pp. 165–181.

Piaget, J. (1960). *The Child's Conception of the World*. Bethesda, MD: Littlefield Adams.Pinel, E., Long, A., Landau, M., and Pyszczynski, T. (2004). I-Sharing, the Problem of Existential Isolation, and Their Implications for Interpersonal and Intergroup Phenomena. In J. Greenberg, S. Koole, and T. Pyszczynski (eds.), *Handbook of Experimental Existential Psychology*, pp. 352–368. New York, NY: Guilford.

Pinker, S. 2002. *The Blank Slate: The Modern Denial of Human Nature*. London, UK: Penguin.

Pflug, J. (2009). Folk Theories of Happiness: A Cross-Cultural Comparison of Conceptions of Happiness in Germany and South Africa. *Social Indicators Research*, vol. 92, no. 3, pp. 551–563.

Plant, M. (2020). A Happy Possibility About Happiness (and Other Subjective) Scales: An Investigation and Tentative Defence of the Cardinality Thesis. Happier Lives Institute Working Paper.https://www.happierlivesinstitute.org/uploads/1/0/9/9/109970865/cardinality_nov2020.pdf

Polderman, T., Benyamin, B., de Leeuw, C., Sullivan, P., van Bochoven, A., Visscher, P., and Posthuma, D. (2015). Meta-Analysis of the Heritability of Human Traits Based on Fifty Years of Twin Studies. *Nature Genetics*, vol. 47, no. 7, pp. 702–709.

Popper, K. ([1934] 1959). *The Logic of Scientific Discovery*. London, UK: Routledge.

Powdthavee, N. (2008). Putting a Price Tag on Friends, Relatives and Neighbours: Using Surveys of Life Satisfaction to Value Social Relationships. *The Journal of Socio-Economics*, vol. 37, no. 4, pp. 1459–1480.

Powdthave, N. (2009). What Happens to People Before and After Disability? Focusing Effects, Lead Effects and Adaptation in Different Areas of Life. *Social Science and Medicine*, vol. 69, no. 12, pp. 1834–1844.

Powdthavee, N. (2012). Jobless, Friendless, and Broke: What Happens to Different Areas of Life Before and After Unemployment? *Economica*, vol. 79, no. 315, pp. 557–575.

Powdthavee, N., and Stutzer, A. (2014). Economic Approaches to Understanding Change in Happiness. In K. Sheldon and R. Lucas (eds.), *Stability of Happiness: Theories and Evidence on Whether Happiness can Change*, pp. 219–245. New York, NY: Academic Press.

PRC (2018). *Progress in Human Rights over the 40 Years of Reform and Opening Up in China*. Beijing, CN: State Council Information Office of the People's Republic of China.

Prinzing, M. (2021). Positive Psychology Is Value-Laden: It's Time to Embrace It. *Journal of Positive Psychology*, vol. 16, no. 3, pp. 289–297.

Putnam, R. (2001). *Bowling Alone: The Collapse and Revival of American Community*. New York, NY: Simon and Schuster.

Putnam, R., and Romney Garrett, S. (2020). *The Upswing: How We Came Together a Century Ago and How We Can Do It Again*. New York, NY: Swift Press.

Pyszczynski, T., Greengerg, J., and Arendt, J. (2012). Freedom Versus Fear Revisited: An Integrative Analysis of the Dynamics of the Defense and Growth of Self. In M. Leary and J. Tangney (eds.), *Handbook of Self and Identity: Second Edition*, pp. 378–404. New York, NY: Guilford.

Rapkin, B., and Schwarz, C. (2004). Toward a Theoretical Model of Quality of Life Appraisal: Implications of Findings from Studies of Response Shift. *Health and Quality of Life Outcomes*, vol. 2, no. 14, pp. 1–12.

Rauch, J. (2018). *The Happiness Curve: Why Life Gets Better After 50*. New York, NY: Thomas Dunne Books.

Rawls, J. (1971). *A Theory of Justice*. Cambridge, MA: Harvard University Press.

Reginster, B. (2006). *The Affirmation of Life: Nietzsche on Overcoming Nihilism*. Cambridge, MA: Harvard University Press.

Reginster, B. (2009). *The Affirmation of Life: Nietzsche on Overcoming Nihilism*. Cambridge, MA: Harvard University Press.

Reis, H., Sheldon, K., Gable, S., Roscoe, J., and Ryan, R. (2000). Daily Well-Being: The Role of Autonomy, Competence and Relatedness. *Personality and Social Psychology Bulletin*, vol. 26, no. 4, pp. 419–435.

Reker, G., and Peacock, E. (1981). The Life Attitude Profile (LAP): A Multidimensional Instrument for Assessing Attitudes Towards Life. *Canadian Journal of Behavioural Science*, vol. 13, no. 3, pp. 264–273.

Ricard, M. (2003). *Happiness: A Guide to Developing Life's Most Important Skill*. London, UK: Atlantic Books.

Ricard, M. (2014). A Buddhist View of Happiness. *Journal of Law and Religion*, vol. 29, no. 1, pp. 14–29.

Robbins, L. (1934). *An Essay on the Nature and Significance of Economic Science*. London, UK: Macmillan and Co.

Robeyns, I. (2017). *Wellbeing, Freedom, and Justice: The Capability Approach Re-examined*. Cambridge, UK: Open Book Publishers.

Rochat, P. (2003). Five Levels of Self-Awareness as They Unfold in Early Life. *Consciousness and Cognition: An International Journal*, vol. 12, no. 4, pp. 717–731.

Roemer, L., Lee, J., Salters-Pedneault, K., Erisman, S., Orsillo, S., and Mennin, D. (2009). Mindfulness and Emotion Regulation Difficulties in Generalized Anxiety Disorder: Preliminary Evidence for Independent and Overlapping Contributions. *Behavioural Theory*, vol. 40, no. 2, pp. 142–154.

Ross, M. (1989). Relation of Implicit Theories to the Construction of Personal Histories. *Psychological Review*, vol. 96, no. 2, pp. 341–357.

Roth, G., Shahar, B., Zohar-Shefer, Y., Benita, M., Moed, A., Bibi, U., Kanat-Maymon, Y., and Ryan, R. (2017). Benefits of Emotional Integration and Costs of Emotional Distancing. *Journal of Personality*, vol. 86, no. 6, pp. 919–934, doi: 10.1111/jopy.12366.

Routledge, C., and Arndt, J. (2009). Creative Terror Management: Creativity as a Facilitator of Cultural Exploration After Mortality Salience. *Personality and Social Psychology Bulletin*, vol. 35, no. 4, pp. 493–505.

Røysamb, E., Bang Nes, R., and Vittersø, J. (2014). Well-Being: Heritable and Changeable. In K. Sheldon and R. Lucas (eds.), *Stability of Happiness: Theories and Evidence on Whether Happiness can Change*, pp. 9–36. New York, NY: Academic Press.

Ruberton, P. M., Kruse, E., and Lyubomirsky, S. (2016). Boosting State Humility via Gratitude, Self-Affirmation and Awe: Theoretical and Empirical Perspectives. In E. Worthington, D. Davis, and J. Hook (eds.), *Handbook of Humility*. London, UK: Routledge, pp. 260–273.

Ruttenberg, T. (2013). Wellbeing Economics and Buen Vivir: Development Alternatives for Inclusive Human Security. *The Fletcher Journal of Human Security*, vol. 33, no. 1, pp. 68–93.

Ruiz-Mirazo, K., Etxeberria, A., Moreno, A., and Ibàñez, J. (2000). Organisms and Their Place in Biology. *Theory in Biosciences*, vol. 119, no. 3–4, pp. 209–233.

Russell, B. (1930). *The Conquest of Happiness*. London, UK: Routledge.

Russell, D. (2012). *Happiness for Humans*. Oxford, UK: Oxford University Press.

Ryan, R. (1993). Agency and Organization: Intrinsic Motivation, Autonomy and the Self in Psychological Development. In J. Jacobs (ed.), *Nebraska Symposium on Motivation*, vol. 40, pp. 1–56. Lincoln, NE: University of Nebraska Press.

Ryan, R., and Deci, E. (2000). Self-Determination Theory and the Facilitation of Intrinsic Motivation, Social Development and Well-Being. *American Psychologist*, vol. 55, pp. 68–78.

Ryan, R., and Deci, E. (2004). Autonomy Is No Illusion: Self-Determination Theory and the Empirical Study of Authenticity, Awareness and Will. In J. Greenberg, S. Koole, and T. Pyszczynski (eds.), *Handbook of Experimental Existential Psychology*, pp. 431–448. New York, NY: Guilford.

Ryan, R., and Deci, E. (2017). *Self-Determination Theory: Basic Psychological Needs in Motivation, Development, and Wellness*. New York, NY: Guilford.

Ryan, R., Deci, E., and Huta, V. (2008). Living Well: A Self-Determination Theory Perspective on Eudaimonia. *Journal of Happiness Studies*, vol. 9, no. 1, pp. 139–170.

Ryan, R., Deci, E., and Vansteenkiste, M. (2016). Autonomy and Autonomy Disturbances in Self-Development and Psychopathology: Research on Motivation, Attachment, and Clinical Process. In D. Cichetti (ed.), *Developmental Psychopathology*, vol. 1, pp. 385–438. Hoboken, NJ: John Wiley and Sons Inc.

Ryan, R., and Huta, V. (2009). Happiness as Healthy Functioning or Happiness as Wellbeing: The Importance of Eudaimonic Thinking (Response to the Kashdan et al., and Waterman Discussion). *The Journal of Positive Psychology*, vol. 4, no. 3, pp. 202–204.

Ryff, C. (1989a). Beyond Ponce de Leon and Life Satisfaction: New Directions in Quest of Successful Aging. *International Journal of Behavioural Development*, vol. 12, no. 1, pp. 35–55.

Ryff, C. (1989b). Happiness Is Everything, or Is It? Explorations on the Meaning of Psychological Well-Being. *Journal of Personality and Social Psychology*, vol. 57, no. 6, pp. 1069–1081.

Ryff, C. (2012). Existential Well-Being and Health. In P. Wong (ed.), *The Human Quest for Meaning: Theories, Research and Applications*, second edition, pp. 233–248. London, UK: Routledge.

Ryff, C., and Singer, B. (2008). Know Thyself and Become What You Are: A Eudaimonic Approach to Psychological Well-Being. *Journal of Happiness Studies*, vol. 9, no. 1, pp. 13–39.

Sacks, D., Stevenson, B., and Wolfers, J. (2010). Subjective Well-Being, Income, Economic Development and Growth. *NBER Working Paper 16441*.

Salzman, M., and Halloran, M. (2004). Cultural Trauma and Recovery: Cultural Meaning, Self-Esteem, and the Reconstruction of the Cultural Anxiety Buffer. In J. Greenberg, S. Koole, and T. Pyszczynski (eds.), *Handbook of Experimental Existential Psychology*, pp. 231–246. New York, NY: Guilford.

Samuelson, P. (1938). A Note on the Pure Theory of Consumers' Behaviour. *Economica*, vol. 5, no. 17, pp. 61–71.

Samuelson, P. (1948). Consumption Theory in Terms of Revealed Preference. *Economica: New Series*, vol. 15, no. 60, pp. 243–245.

Santelices, B. (1999). How Many Kinds of Individuals Are There? *Trends in Ecology and Evolution*, vol. 14, no. 4, pp. 918–931.

Sartre, J. ([1938] 2000). *Nausea*. Trans. R. Baldick. New York, NY: Penguin.

Sartre, J. ([1943] 2005). *Being and Nothingness*. Trans. H. Barnes. London, UK: Routledge.

Sartre, J., and Beauvoir, S. de. (1946). *Existentialism Is a Humanism*. Trans. P. Mairet. https://www.marxists.org/reference/archive/sartre/works/exist/sartre.htm.

Schacter, S., and Singer, J. (1962). Cognitive, Social and Physiological Determinants of Emotional State. *Psychological Review*, vol. 69, no. 5, pp. 379–399.

Schartz, B., Ward, A., Lyubomirsky, S., Monterosso, J., White, K., and Lehman, D. (2002). Maximizing Versus Satisficing: Happiness Is a Matter of Choice. *Journal of Personality and Social Psychology*, vol. 83, no. 5, pp. 1178–1197.

Schkade, D., and Kahneman, D. (1998). Does Living in California Make People Happy? A Focussing Illusion in Judgements of Life Satisfaction. *Psychological Science*, vol. 9, no. 5, pp. 340–346.

Schmidt-Traub, G., Kroll, C., Teksoz, K., Durand-Delacre, D., and Sachs, J. (2017). National Baselines for the Sustainable Development Goals Assessed in the SDG Index and Dashboard. *Nature Geoscience*, vol. 10, no. 8, pp. 547–555.

Schreiber, C., and Kahneman, D. (2000). Determinants of the Remembered Utility of Aversive Sounds. *Journal of Experimental Psychology*, vol. 129, no. 1, pp. 27–42.

Schutte, L., Negri, L., Delle Fave, A., and Wissing, M. (2019). Rasch Analysis of the Satisfaction with Life Scale Across Countries: Findings from South Africa and Italy. Online first at *Current Psychology*, vol. 40, pp. 4908–4917.

Schwartz, C., Bode, R., Repucci, N., Becker, J., Sprangers, M., and Fayers, P. (2006). The Clinical Significance of Adaptation to Changing Health: A Meta-Analysis of Response Shift. *Quality of Life Research*, vol. 15, no. 9, pp. 1533–1550.

Schwartz, C., and Sprangers, M. (2010). Guidelines for Improving the Stringency of Response Shift Research Using the ThenTest. *Quality of Life Research*, vol. 19, no. 2, pp. 455–464.

Schwartz, C., Sprangers, M., Carey, M., and Reed, G. (2004). Exploring Response Shift in Longitudinal Data. *Psychology and Health*, vol. 19, no. 1, pp. 51–69.

Schwartz, C., Stucky, B., Rivers, C., Noonan, V., Finkelstein, J., and RHSCIR Network (2018). Quality of Life and Adaptation in People with Spinal Cord Injuries: Response Shift Effects from 1 to 5 Years Postinjury. *Archives of Physical Medicine and Rehabilitation*, vol. 99, no. 8, pp. 1599–1608.

Schwarz, N., and Clore, G. (1983). Mood, Misattribution, and Judgements of Well-Being: Informative and Directive Functions of Affective States. *Journal of Personality and Social Psychology*, vol. 45, no. 3, pp. 513–523.

Schwarz, N., Strack, F., and Mai, H. (1991). Assimilation and Contrast Effects in Part-Whole Question Sequences: A Conversational Logic Analysis. *Public Opinion Quarterly*, vol. 55, no. 1, pp. 3–23.

Sedikides, C., Gaertner, L., and Vevea, J. (2005). Pancultural Self-Enhancement Reloaded: A Meta-Analytic Reply to Heine (2005). *Journal of Personality and Social Psychology*, vol. 89, no. 4, pp. 539–551.

Seligman, M. (1992). *Helplessness: On Depression, Development and Death*. New York, NY: Freeman.

Seligman, M. (2011). *Flourish: A Visionary New Understanding of Happiness and Well-Being*. New York, NY: Free Press.

Seligman, M. (2012). *Flourish: A Visionary New Understanding of Happiness and Well-Being*. Melbourne, AU: William Heineman Australia.

Seligman, M., Ernest, R., Gillham, J., Reivich, K., and Linkins, M. (2009). Positive Education: Positive Psychology and Classroom Interventions. *Oxford Review of Education*, vol. 35, no. 3, pp. 293–311.

Selman, R. (2003). *The Promotion of Social Awareness*. New York, NY: Russell Sage.

Sen, A. (1999a). *Development as Freedom*. Oxford, UK: Oxford University Press.

Sen, A. (1999b). *Commodities and Capabilities*. Oxford, UK: Oxford University Press.

Shapiro, D. (1981). *Autonomy and Rigid Character*. New York, NY: Basic Books.

Shapiro, S., Carlson, L., Astin, J., and Freedman, B. (2006). Mechanisms of Mindfulness. *Journal of Clinical Psychology*, vol. 62, no. 3, pp. 373–386.

Sheldon, K. (2002). The Self-Concordance Model of Healthy Goal Striving: When Personal Goals Correctly Represent the Person. In E. Deci and R. Ryan (eds.), *Handbook of Self-Determination Research*, pp. 65–86. Rochester, NY: Rochester University Press.

Sheldon, K. (2013). Individual Daimon, Universal Needs, and Subjective Well-Being: Happiness as the Natural Consequence of a Life Well-Lived. In A. Waterman (ed.), *The Best Within Us: Positive Psychological Perspectives on Eudaimonia*, Washington, DC: American Psychological Association, pp. 207–226.

Sheldon, K., Abad, N., Ferguson, Y., Gunz, A., Houser-Marko, L. Nichols, C., Lyubomirsky, S. (2009). Persistent Pursuit of Need-Satisfying Goals Leads to Increased Happiness: A 6-Month Experimental Longitudinal Study. *Motivation and Emotions*, vol. 34, no. 1, pp. 39–48.

Sheldon, K. M., Boehm, J., and Lyubomirsky, S. (2013). Variety Is the Spice of Life: The Hedonic Adaptation Prevention Model. In I. Boniwell, S. David, and A. Conley Ayers (eds.), *The Oxford Handbook of Wellbeing*, pp. 901–914. Oxford, UK: Oxford University Press.

Sheldon, K., and Cooper, M. (2008). Goal Striving Within Agentic and Communal Roles: Functionally Independent Pathways to Enhanced Well-Being. *Journal of Personality*, vol. 76, no. 3, pp. 415–448.

Sheldon, K., and Elliot, A. (1998). Not All Personal Goals Are Personal: Comparing Autonomous and Controlled Reasons for Goals and Predictors of Effort and Attainment. *Personality and Social Psychology Bulletin*, vol. 24, no. 5, pp. 546–557.

Sheldon, K., and Elliot, A. (1999). Goal Striving, Need Satisfaction, and Longitudinal Well-Being: The Self-Concordance Model. *Journal of Personality and Social Psychology*, vol. 76, no. 3, pp. 482–497.

Sheldon, K., Elliot, A., Ryan, R., Chirkov, V., Kim, Y., Wu, C., Demir, M., and Sun, Z. (2004). Self-Concordance and Subjective Well-Being in Four Cultures. *Journal of Cross Cultural Psychology*, vol. 35, no. 2, pp. 209–223.

Sheldon, K., and Houser-Marko, L. (2001). Self-Concordance, Goal Attainment, and the Pursuit of Happiness: Can There Be an Upward Spiral? *Journal of Personality and Social Psychology*, vol. 80, no. 1, pp. 152–165.

Sheldon, K., and Kasser, T. (1995). Coherence and Congruence: Two Aspects of Personality Integration. *Journal of Personality and Social Psychology*, vol. 68, no. 3, pp. 531–543.

Sheldon, K., and Krieger, L. (2014). Service Job Lawyers Are Happier than Money Job Lawyers, Despite Their Lower Income. *Journal of Positive Psychology*, vol. 90, no. 3, pp. 219–226.

Sheldon, K. M., and Lucas, R. E. (2014). *Stability of Happiness: Theories and Evidence on Whether Happiness Can Change*. London, UK: Academic Press.

Sheldon, K., and Lyubomirsky, S. (2012).The Challenge of Staying Happier: Testing the Hedonic Adaptation Prevention Model. *Personality and Social Psychology Bulletin*, vol. 38, no. 5, pp. 670–680.

Sheldon, K., Ryan, R., Deci, E., and Kasser, T. (2004). The Independent Effects of Goal Contents and Motives on Well-Being: It's Both What You Pursue and Why You Pursue It. *Personality and Social Psychology Bulletin*, vol. 30, no. 4, pp. 475–486.

Sheldon, K., Ryan, R., and Reis, H. (1996). What Makes for a Good Day? Competence and Autonomy in the Day and in the Person. *Personality and Social Psychology Bulletin*, vol. 22, no. 12, pp. 1270–1279.

Sheldon, K., and Schuler, J. (2011). Needing, Wanting, and Having: Integrating Motive Disposition Theory and Self-Determination Theory. *Journal of Personality and Social Psychology*, vol. 101, no. 5, pp. 1106–1123.

Sheldon, K., and Vansteenkiste, M. (2005). Personal Goals and Time Travel: How Are Future Places Visited, and Is It Worth It? In A. Strathman and J. Joireman (eds.), *Understanding Behaviour in the Context of Time: Theory, Research and Application*, pp. 143–163. Mahwah, NJ: Erlbaum.

Shin, L., and Lyubomirsky, S. (2014). Positive Activity Interventions for Mental Health Conditions: Basic Research and Clinical Applications. In J. Johnson and A. Wood (eds.), *The Handbook of Positive Clinical Psychology*, pp. 349–363. New York, NY: Wiley.

Showers, C. (1992a). Compartmentalization of Positive and Negative Self-Knowledge: Keeping Bad Apples out of the Bunch. *Journal of Personality and Social Psychology*, vol. 62, no. 6, pp. 1036–1049.

Showers, C. (1992b). Evaluatively Integrative Thinking About Characteristics of the Self. *Personality and Social Psychology Bulletin*, vol. 18, no. 6, pp. 719–729.

Showers, C. (2002). Integration and Compartmentalization: A Model of Self-Structure and Self-Change. In D. Cervone and W. Mishcel (eds.), *Advances in Personality Science*, pp. 271–291. New York, NY: Guilford.

Showers, C., and Zeigler-Hill, V. (2012). Organisation of Self-Knowledge: Features, Functions and Flexibility. In M. Leary and J. Tangney (eds.), *Handbook of Self and Identity: Second Edition*, pp. 105–123. New York, NY: Guilford.

Sides, J., Tesler, M., and Vavreck, L. (2018). *Identity Crisis: The 2016 Presidential Campaign and the Battle for the Meaning of America*. Princeton, NJ: Princeton University Press.

Silvia, P., and Eddington, K. (2012). Self and Emotion. In M. Leary and J. Tangney (eds.), *Handbook of Self and Identity: Second Edition*, pp. 425–445. New York, NY: Guilford.

Simmel, G. ([1903] 1950). *The Metropolis and Mental Life*. Trans. K. Wolff. New York, NY: Free Press.

Simon, L., Arendt, J., Greenberg, J., Pyszczynski, T. amd Solomon, S. (1998). Terror-Management and Meaning: Evidence That the Opportunity to Defend the Worldview in Response to Mortality Salience Increases the Meaningfulness of Life in the Mildly Depressed. *Journal of Personality*, vol. 66, no. 3, pp. 359–382.

Simon, M. (2017). Want a Robot to Walk Like You Do? Don't Expect It to Look Human. *Wired*. https://www.wired.com/story/want-a-robot-to-walk-like-you-dont-expect-it-to-look-human/

Sin, N., and Lyubomirsky, S. (2009). Enhancing Well-Being and Alleviating Depressive Symptoms with Positive Psychology Interventions: A Practice-Friendly Meta-Analysis. *Journal of Clinical Psychology*, vol. 65, no. 5, pp. 467–487.

Singer, J. (2004). Narrative Identity and Meaning Making Across the Adult Lifespan: An Introduction. *Journal of Personality*, vol. 72, no. 3, pp. 437–460.

Singh, R. and Alexandrova, A. (2020). Happiness Economics as Technocracy. *Behavioural Public Policy*, vol. 4, no. 2, pp. 236–244.

Slattery, J., and Park, C. (2012). Clinical Approaches to Discrepancies in Meaning: Conceptualization, Assessment and Treatment. In P. Wong (ed.), *The Human Quest for Meaning: Theories, Research and Applications*, second edition, pp. 497 – 520. London, UK: Routledge.

Slavin, M., and Kreigman, D. (1992). *The Adaptive Design of the Human Psyche: Psychoanalysis, Evolutionary Biology, and the Therapeutic Process*. New York, NY: Guilford.

Smith, A. (1759). *The Theory of Moral Sentiments*. Edinburgh, SCT: Kincaid.

Smith, D., Schwarz, N., Robert, T., and Ubel, P. (2006). Why Are You Calling Me? How Study Introductions Change Response Patterns. *Quality of Life Research*, vol. 15, no. 4, pp. 621–630.

Smyth, J., True, N., and Souto, J. (2001). Effects of Writing About Traumatic Experiences: The Necessity for Narrative Structuring. *Journal of Social and Clinical Psychology*, vol. 20, no. 2, pp. 161–172.

Solomon, S. (2012). The Social Psychology of Meaning, Mortality and Choice: An Integrative Perspective on Existential Concerns. In P. Shaver and M. Mikulincer (eds.), *Meaning, Mortality and Choice: The Social Psychology of Existential Concerns*, pp. 401–418. Washington, DC: American Psychological Association.

Sorrentino, R., and Roney, C. (2000). *The Uncertain Mind: Individual Differences in Facing the Unknown*. Philadelphia, PA: Psychology Press.

Sorrentino, R., Yang, Y., and Szeto, A. (2009). Uncertainty Management: To Fear or Not to Fear? *Psychological Inquiry*, vol. 20, no. 4, pp. 240–244.

Specht, J., Egloff, B., and Schmukle, S. (2011). The Benefits of Believing in Chance or Fate: External Locus of Control as a Protective Factor for Coping with the Death of a Spouse. *Social Psychological and Personality Science*, vol. 2, no. 2, pp. 132–137.

Sprangers, M., Van Dam, A., Broersen, J., Lodder, L., Wever, L., Visser, M., et al. (1999). Revealing Response Shift in Longitudinal Research on Fatigue—The Use of the ThenTest Approach. *Acta Oncologia*, vol. 38, no. 6, pp. 709–718.

Springer, K., and Hauser, R. (2006). An Assessment of the Construct Validity of Ryff's Scale of Psychological Well-Being: Method, Mode, and Measurement Effects. *Social Science Research*, vol. 35, no. 4, pp. 1080–1102.

Springer, K., Hauser, R., and Freese, J. (2006). Bad News Indeed for Ryff's Six-Factor Model of Well-Being. *Social Science Research*, vol. 35, no. 4, pp. 1120–1131.

Stevenson, B., and Wolfers, J. (2013). Subjective Well-Being and Income: Is There Any Evidence of Satiation? *American Economic Review*, vol. 103, no. 3, pp. 598–604.

Steel, P., Schmidt, J., and Shultz, J. (2008). Refining the Relationship Between Personality and Subjective Well-Being. *Psychology Bulletin*, vol. 134, no. 1, pp. 138–161.

Steele, C., Spencer, S., and Lynch, M. (1993). Self-Image Resilience and Dissonance: The Role of Affirmational Resources. *Journal of Personality and Social Psychology*, vol. 64, no. 6, pp. 885–896.

Steger, M. (2006). An Illustration of Issues in Factor Extraction and Identification of Dimensionality in Psychological Assessment Data. *Journal of Personality Assessment*, vol. 86, no. 3, pp. 263–272.

Steger, M. (2010). Experiencing Meaning in Life: Optimal Functioning at the Nexus of Well-Being, Psychopathology, and Spirituality. In V. Wong (ed.), *The Human Quest for Meaning: Theories, Research and Applications*, pp. 165–184. London, UK: Routledge.

Steger, M., and Frazier, P. (2005). Meaning in Life: One Link in the Chain from Religion to Well-Being. *Journal of Counselling Psychology*, vol. 52, no. 4, pp. 574–582.

Steger, M., Frazier, P., Oishi, S., and Kaler, M. (2006). The Meaning in Life Questionnaire: Assessing the Presence of and Search for Meaning in Life. *Journal of Counseling Psychology*, vol. 53, no. 1, pp. 80–93.

Steger, M., Kashdan, T., and Oishi, S. (2008). Being Good by Doing Good: Eudaimonic Activity and Daily Well-Being Correlates, Mediators and Temporal Relations. *Journal of Research in Personality*, vol. 42, no. 1, pp. 22–42.

Steger, M., Kashdan, T., Sullivan, B., and Lorentz, D. (2008). Understanding the Search for Meaning in Life: Personality, Cognitive Style, and the Dynamic Between Seeking and Experiencing Meaning. *Journal of Personality*, vol. 76, no. 2, pp. 199–228.

Stevens, S. (1946). On the Theory of Scales of Measurement. *Science*, vol. 103, pp. 677–680.

Stevenson, B., and Wolfers, J. (2009). The Paradox of Declining Female Happiness. *American Economic Journal: Economic Policy*, vol. 1, no. 2, pp. 190–225.

Stevenson, B., and Wolfers, J. (2013). Subjective Well-Being and Income: Is There Any Evidence of Satiation? *American Economic Review*, vol. 103, no. 3, pp. 598–604.

Stewart, M., and Whiteford, P. (2018). Balancing Efficiency and Equity in the Tax and Transfer System. In M. Fabian and R. Breunig (eds.), *Hybrid Public Policy Innovations: Contemporary Policy Beyond Ideology*, pp. 204–232. London, UK: Routledge.

Stiglitz, J., Sen, A., and Fitoussi, J. (2009). *Report by the Commission on the Measurement of Economic Performance and Social Progress*. Paris, FR: Commission on the Measurement of Economic Performance and Social Progress.

Stillman, S., Gibson, J., McKenzie, D., and Rohorua, H. (2015). Miserable Migrants? Natural Experiment Evidence on International Migration and Objective and Subjective Well-Being. *World Development* vol. 65, issue C pp. 79–93.

Stone, A., and Mackie, C. (eds.) (2013). *Subjective Well-Being: Measuring Wellbeing, Suffering and Other Dimensions of Experience*. National Research Council Report. Washington, DC: National Academies Press.

Stone, A., Shiffman, S., and DeVries, M. (1999). Ecological Momentary Assessment. In D. Kahneman, E. Diener, and N. Schwarz (eds.), *Well-Being: The Foundations of Hedonic Psychology*, pp. 26–39. New York, NY: Russell Sage.

Strack, L., Martin, N., and Schwarz, N. (1988). Priming and Communication: Social Determinants of Information Use in Judgements of Life Satisfaction. *European Journal of Social Psychology*, vol. 18, no. 5, pp. 429–442.

Strauss, C., Lever Taylor, B., Gu, J., Kuyken, W., Baer, R., Jones, F., and Cavanagh, K. (2016). What Is Compassion and How Can We Measure It? A Review of Definitions and Measures. *Clinical Psychology Review*, vol. 47, no. 1, pp. 15–27.

Stronge, S., Sengupta, N., Barlow, F., Osborne, D., Houkamau, C., and Sibley, C. (2016). Perceived Discrimination Predicts Increased Support for Political Rights and Life Satisfaction Mediated by Ethnic Identity: A Longitudinal Analysis. *Cultural Diversity and Ethnic Minority Psychology*, vol. 22, no. 3, pp. 359–368.

Stutzer, A., and Frey, B. (2006). Does Marriage Make People Happy, or Do Happy People Get Married? *Journal of Socio-Economics*, vol. 35, no. 2, pp. 326–347.

Sugden, R. (2018). *The Community of Advantage: A Behavioural Economist's Defence of the Market*. Oxford, UK: Oxford University Press.

Summerfield, P. (2012). *Women Workers in the Second World War: Production and Patriarchy in Conflict*. London, UK: Routledge.

Sumner, L. (1996). *Welfare, Happiness and Ethics*. Oxford, UK: Oxford University Press.

Sumner, R., Burrow, A., and Hill, P. (2014). Identity and Purpose as Predictors of Subjective Well-Being in Emerging Adulthood. *Emerging Adulthood*, vol. 3, no. 1, pp. 46–54.

Swann, W. (2011). Self-Verification Theory. In P. Van Lange, A. Kruglanski, and E. Tory-Higgins (eds.), *Handbook of Theories of Social Psychology*, vol. 2, pp. 23–42. Thousand Oaks, CA: Sage.

Swann, W., and Buhrmester, M. (2012). Self-Verification: The Search for Coherence. In M. Leary and J. Tangney (eds.), *Handbook of Self and Identity*, second edition, pp. 405–424. New York, NY: Guilford.

Tangney, J., Niedenthal, P., Covert, M., and Barlow, D. (1998). Are Shame and Guilt Related to Distinct Self-Discrepancies? A Test of Higgins' 1987 Hypothesis. *Journal of Personality and Social Psychology*, vol. 75, no. 1, pp. 256–268.

Tangney, J., and Tracy, J. (2012). Self-Conscious Emotions. In M. Leary and J. Tangney (eds.), *Handbook of Self and Identity*, second edition, pp. 446–478.

Tesser, A. (2000). On the Confluence of Self-Esteem Maintenance Mechanisms. *Personality and Social Psychology Review*, vol. 4, no. 4, pp. 290–299.

Thirlwall, A., and Pacheco-López, P. (2017). *Economics of Development: Theory and Evidence*, tenth edition. London UK: Macmillan International.

Thompson, R. (2006). The Development of the Person: Social Understanding, Relationships, Conscience, Self. In N. Eisenberg, W. Damon, and R. Lerner (eds.), *Handbook of Child Psychology—Volume 3: Social, Emotional and Personality Development*, sixth edition, pp. 24–98. New York, NY: Wiley.

Tiberius, V. (2008). *The Reflective Life: Living Wisely Within Our Limits*. Oxford, UK: Oxford University Press.

Tiberius, V. (2018). *Well-Being as Value Fulfillment: How We Can Help Each Other to Live Well*. New York, NY: Oxford University Press.

Tiberius, V., and Hall, A. (2010). Normative Theory and Psychological Research: Hedonism, Eudaimonism, and Why It Matters. *Journal of Positive Psychology*, vol. 5, no. 3, pp. 212–225.

To, S., and Sung, W. (2017). Presence of Meaning, Sources of Meaning, and Subjective Well-Being in Emerging Adulthood: A Sample of Hong Kong Community College Students. *Emerging Adulthood*, vol. 5, no. 1, pp. 69–74.

Tomasello, M., Carpenter, M., Call, J., Behne, T., and Moll, H. (2005). Understanding and Shared Intentions: Origins of Cultural Cognition. *Behavioural and Brain Sciences*, vol. 28, no. 5, pp. 675–691.

Tryon, W., and Radzin, A. (1972). Purpose in Life as a Function of Ego-Resiliency, Dogmatism and Biographical Variables. *Journal of Clinical Psychology*, vol. 28, no. 4, pp. 544–545.

Tugade, M., and Fredrickson, B. (2004). Resilient Individuals Use Positive Emotions to Bounce Back from Negative Emotional Experiences. *Journal of Personality and Social Psychology*, vol. 86, no. 2, pp. 320–333.

Tversky, A., and Kahneman, D. (1986). Rational Choice and the Framing of Decisions. *The Journal of Business*, vol. 59, no. 4, Part 2, pp. S251–S278.

Ubel, P., Jankovic, A., Smith, D., Langa, K., and Fagerlin, A. (2005). What Is Perfect Health to an 85 Year-Old? Evidence for Scale Norming in Subjective Health Ratings. *Medical Care*, vol. 43, no. 10, pp. 1054–1057.

Ubel, P., Peeters, Y., and Smith, D. (2010). Abandoning the Language of "Response Shift": A Plea for Conceptual Clarity in Distinguishing Scale Norming from True Changes in Quality of Life. *Quality of Life Research*, vol. 19, no. 4, pp. 465–471.

United Nations (2015a). *The Millennium Development Goals Report 2015*. New York, NY: United Nations.

United Nations (2015b). *Transforming Our World: The 2030 Agenda for Sustainable Development*. New York, NY: United Nations.

Van Boven, L., and Gilovich, T. (2003). To Do or to Have? That Is the Question. *Journal of Social and Personality Psychology*, vol. 85, no. 6, pp. 1193–1202.

Van den Bos, K. (2009). Making Sense of Life: The Existential Self Trying to Deal with Personal Uncertainty. *Psychological Inquiry*, vol. 20, no. 4, pp. 197–217.

Van den Bos, K. (2009). On the Psychology of the Uncertain Self and the Integration of the Worldview Defense Zoo. *Psychological Inquiry*, vol. 20, no. 4, pp. 252–261.

Van Dierendonck, D. (2004). The Construct Validity of Ryff's Scales of Psychological Well-Being and Its Extension with Spiritual Well-Being. *Personality and Individual Differences*, vol. 36, no. 3, pp. 629–643.

van Leeuwen, C., Post, M., van der Woude, L., de Groot, S., Smit, C., van Kuppevelt, D., and Lindeman, E. (2012). Changes in Life Satisfaction in Persons with Spinal Injury

During and After Inpatient Rehabilitation: Adaptation or Measurement Bias? *Quality of Life Research*, vol. 21, no. 9, pp. 1499–1508.

Van Praag, B., and Frijters, P. (1999). The Measurement of Welfare and Wellbeing: The Leyden Approach. In E. Diener, D. Kahneman, and N. Schwartz (eds.), *Wellbeing: The Foundations of Hedonic Psychology*, pp. 413–433. New York, NY: Russell Sage Foundation.

Van Praag, B., and Ferrer-i-Carbonell, A. (2004). *Happiness Quantified: A Social Calculus Approach*. Oxford, UK: Oxford University Press.

Vansteenkiste, M., Duriez, B., Simons, J., and Soenens, B. (2006). Materialistic Values and Well-Being Among Business Students: Further Evidence of Their Detrimental Effects. *Journal of Applied Social Psychology*, vol. 36, no. 12, pp. 2892–2908.

Veblen, T. (1899). *The Theory of the Leisure Class*. http://moglen.law.columbia.edu/LCS/theoryleisureclass.pdf.

Veenhoven, R. (1995). World Database of Happiness. *Social Indicators Research*, vol. 34, no. 3, pp. 299–313.

Veenhoven, R., and Hagerty, M. (2006). Rising Happiness in Nations 1946–2004: A Reply to Easterlin. *Social Indicators Research*, vol. 79, no. 3, pp. 421–436.

Vess, M., Arndt, J., and Schlegel, R. (2011). Abstract Construal Levels Attenuate State Self-Esteem Reactivity. *Journal of Experimental Social Psychology*, vol. 47, no. 4, pp. 861–864.

Vittersø, J. (2013). Feelings, Meanings, and Optimal Functioning: Some Distinctions Between Hedonic and Eudaimonic Well-Being. In A. Waterman (ed.), *The Best Within Us: Positive Psychology Perspectives on Eudaimonia*, pp. 39–56. Washington, DC: American Psychological Association.

Vittersø, J. (2014). Functional Well-Being: Happiness as Feelings, Evaluations and Functioning. In I. Boniwell and S. David (eds.), *The Oxford Handbook of Happiness*, pp. 227–244. Oxford, UK: Oxford University Press.

Vittersø, J., Biswas-Diener, R., and Diener, E. (2005). The Divergent Meanings of Life Satisfaction: Item Response Modelling of the Satisfaction with Life Scale in Greenland and Norway. *Social Indicators Research*, vol. 74, no. 2, pp. 327–348.

Vittersø, J., Oelmann, H., and Wang, A. (2009). Life Satisfaction Is Not a Balanced Estimator of the Good Life: Evidence from Reaction Time Measures and Self-Reported Emotions. *Journal of Happiness Studies*, vol. 10, no. 1, pp. 1–17.

Vittersø, J., Søholt, Y., Hetland, A., Thorsen, I., and Røysamb, E. (2010). Was Hercules Happy? Some Answers from a Functional Model of Human Well-Being. *Social Indicators Research*, vol. 95, no. 1, pp. 1–18.

Vitrano, C. (2013). *The Nature and Value of Happiness*. Boulder, CO: Westview Press.

Waldfogel, J., Craigie, T., and Brooks-Gunn, J. (2010). Fragile Families and Child Well-Being. *Future Child*, vol. 20, no. 2, pp. 87–112.

Wallace, H., and Tice, D. (2012). Reflect Appraisal Through a 21st-Century Looking Glass. In M. Leary and J. Tangney (eds.), *Handbook of Self and Identity: Second Edition*, pp. 124–140. New York, NY: Guilford.

Waterman, A. (1990). Personal Expressiveness: Philosophical and Psychological Foundations. *Journal of Mind and Behaviour*, vol. 11, no. 1, pp. 47–74.

Waterman, A. (1992). Identity as an Aspect of Optimal Psychological Functioning. In T. Gullota and R. Montemajor (eds.), *Identity Formation During Adolescence: Advances in Adolescent Development*. Newbury Park, CA: Sage, vol. 4, pp. 50–72.

Waterman, A. (1993). Two Conceptions of Happiness: Contrasts of Personal Expressiveness (Eudaimonia) and Hedonic Enjoyment. *Journal of Personality and Social Psychology*, vol. 64, no. 4, pp. 678–691.

Waterman, A. (2007a). Doing Well: The Relationship of Identity Status to Three Conceptions of Well-Being. *Identity: An International Journal of Theory and Research*, vol. 7, no. 4, pp. 289–307.

Waterman, A. (2007b). On the Importance of Distinguishing Hedonia and Eudaimonia when Considering the Hedonic Treadmill. *American Psychologist*, vol. 62, no. 6, pp. 612–613.

Waterman, A. (2008). Reconsidering Happiness: A Eudaimonist's Persective. *The Journal of Positive Psychology*, vol. 3, no. 4, pp. 234–252.

Waterman, A. (ed.) (2013). *The Best Within Us: Positive Psychology Perspectives on Eudaimonia*. Washington, DC: American Psychological Association.

Weijers, D. (2014). Nozick's Experience Machine Is Dead, Long Live the Experience Machine! *Philosophical Psychology*, vol. 27, no. 4, pp. 513–535.

Weimann, J., Knabe, A., and Schöb, R. (2015). *Measuring Happiness: The Economics of Well-Being*. Cambridge, MA: MIT Press.

Weinstein, N., and Ryan, R. (2011). A Self-Determination Theory Approach to Understanding Stress Incursion and Responses. *Stress and Health*, vol. 27, no. 1, pp. 4–17.

Weinstein, N., Ryan, R., and Deci, E. (2010). Motivation, Meaning, and Wellness: A Self-Determination Perspective on the Creation and Internationalization of Personal Meanings and Life Goals. In P. Wong (ed.), *The Human Quest for Meaning: Theories, Research and Applications*, second edition, pp. 81–106. London, UK: Routledge.

Whillans, A. (2020). *Time Smart: How to Reclaim Your Time and Live a Happier Life*. Cambridge, MA: Harvard Business Review Press.

White, M., and Dolan, P. (2009). Accounting for the Richness of Daily Activities. *Psychological Science*, vol. 20, no. 8, pp. 1000–1008.

Wilding, C. (2015). *Cognitive Behavioural Therapy: Evidence-Based, Goal-Oriented Self-Help Techniques*. Boston, MA: Teach Yourself.

Wilson, D. (2002). *Darwin's Cathedral: Evolution, Religion, and the Nature of Society*. Chicago, IL: University of Chicago Press.

Wilson, D. (2015). *Does Altruism Exist? Culture, Genes, and the Welfare of Others*. New Haven, CT: Yale University Press.

Winkelmann, L., and Winkelmann, R. (1998). Why Are the Unemployed So Unhappy: Evidence from Panel Data. *Economica*, vol. 65, no. 257, pp. 1–15.

Witter, R., Stock, W., Okun, M., and Haring, M. (1985). Religion and Subjective Well-Being: A Quantitative Synthesis. *Review of Religious Studies*, vol. 26, no. 4, pp. 332–342.

Wood, A., Froh, J., and Geraghty, W. (2010). Gratitude and Well-Being: A Review and Theoretical Integration. *Clinical Psychology Review*, vol. 30, no. 7, pp. 890–905.

Woodard, C. (2012). Classifying Theories of Welfare. *Philosophical Studies*, vol. 165, no. 3, pp. 787–803.

Woodard, C. (2015). Hybrid Theories. In G. Fletcher (ed.), *Routledge Handbook of Philosophy of Wellbeing*, pp. 161–175. London, UK: Routledge.

Woodman, T., and Hemmings, S. (2008). Body Image Self-Discrepancies and Affect: Exploring the Feared Body Self. *Self and Identity*, vol. 7, no. 4, pp. 413–429.

Wong, V. (ed.), (2010). *The Human Quest for Meaning: Theories, Research and Applications*. London, UK: Routledge.

Yap, M., and Yu, E. (2016). Operationalising the Capability Approach: Developing Culturally Relevant Indicators of Indigenous Well-Being—An Australian Example. *Oxford Development Studies*, vol. 44, no. 3, pp. 315–331.

Yalçin, I., and Malkoç, A. (2015). The Relationship Between Meaning in Life and Subjective Well-Being: Forgiveness and Hope as Mediators. *Journal of Happiness Studies*, vol. 16, no. 4, pp. 915–929.

Zelmer, J. (2003). Linear Public Goods Experiments: A Meta-Analysis. *Experimental Economics*, vol. 6, no. 1, pp. 299–310.

Index

For the benefit of digital users, indexed terms that span two pages (e.g., 52–53) may, on occasion, appear on only one of those pages.